"Bailey's book is a double anatomy—one of a city, the other of its filmic depictions. His astonishing talents as a researcher yield historical ore that his astonishing critical acumen turns into film-lover gold. Even when you disagree with his conclusions, the connections he makes will send your own thinking into heretofore unconsidered dimensions."
—Glenn Kenny, author of *Made Men: The Story of Goodfellas*

"*Fun City Cinema* is a beautifully exhaustive, insightful, and engrossing study of New York City and the movies that reflected its political, economic, and cultural shifts over a century. Bailey writes eloquently not just about the importance and artistry of these films, but also how they helped shape our sense of the city in which they were set. This is a marvelous history of the Big Apple seen through the eyes of an incisive film critic who serves as a knowledgeable, ingratiating tour guide."
—Tim Grierson, author of *This Is How You Make a Movie*

"*Fun City* is an astonishing history of NYC told through the films that shot on the streets and the politics that shaped each era. From the glamor of early talkies to the grit of film noir to the dirty old New York of the 1970s. Page after page of fascinating behind the scenes tales of classics like *Sweet Smell of Success*, *Midnight Cowboy*, *Taxi Driver*, and *Uncut Gems*. It's a book full of insightful prose and great photos that I found impossible to put down.
—Larry Karaszewski, cowriter of *Ed Wood*, *The People vs. Larry Flint*, and *Dolemite Is My Name*

"*Fun City Cinema* is my favorite sort of film book. Jason Bailey takes us on a tour through not just New York cinema, but the city that gave birth to it and the fantastic, absurd, glorious ways in which New York's history is, all on its own, stranger than fiction. New York owes much to the cinema, and the cinema owes much back, and *Fun City Cinema* is a wild and gorgeous ride through that brilliant relationship."
—Alissa Wilkinson, film critic for *Vox*

"An un-put-downable work of political, cultural, and cinema history. You'll walk away from it knowing so much more about New York, about America, and about how some of the greatest films ever made came to be. You'll also have a mountain of new movie recommendations to start making your way through."
—Bilge Ebiri, film critic for *New York* magazine/*Vulture*

"*Fun City Cinema* is an express train that makes local stops at long-for-gotten stations, pausing long enough to conjure the ghosts out of their hiding places and up onto the streets where they stalk, strut, and drift through a city that is, on the surface always changing. Jason Bailey's accomplishment is that he sees and feels his way through those changes to the city's tough irreducible core. He could have called this book *The Lights Above, the Grit Below*. He's in touch with both."
—Charles Taylor, author of *Opening Wednesday at a Theater or Drive-In Near You: The Shadow Cinema of the American '70s*

To Lucille and Alice—
my two favorite New
York productions,

Abrams,
New York

New
York City
and the
Movies
That
Made It

Jason
Bailey

Foreword by
Matt Zoller Seitz

FUN CITY CINEMA

**FOREWORD**                                             **8**
by Matt Zoller Seitz

**INTRODUCTION**                                         **12**

**1920–1929:**                                           **20**
The Gaudy Spree,
Mass Media, and
*The Jazz Singer*

**1929–1939:**                                           **44**
The Crash,
the Depression,
and *King Kong*

**1940–1949:**                                           **86**
The War, the Boom,
and *The Naked City*

**1950–1959:**                                           **98**
The Power Brokers and
*Sweet Smell of Success*

**1960–1969:**                                           **122**
Fun City, John Lindsay,
and *Midnight Cowboy*

**1970–1979:**                                           **160**
Fear City, Blackouts,
and *Taxi Driver*

**1980–1989:**                                           **216**
Two Cities, Ed Koch,
and *Wall Street*

**1990–2000:**                                           **258**
City in Transition,
the Indie Movie Boom,
and *Kids*

**2001–2010:**                                           **284**
9/11, Recovery,
and *25th Hour*

**2011–2020:**                                           **316**
Wealth, Bohemia,
and *Frances Ha*

**EPILOGUE**                                             **346**

**SELECTED BIBLIOGRAPHY**                               **350**

**ACKNOWLEDGMENTS**                                     **351**

**IMAGE CREDITS**                                       **352**

# FOREWORD

## By Matt Zoller Seitz

I'm sitting here beside you on a southbound B train, going from Columbus Circle to Atlantic Avenue, reading Jason Bailey's *Fun City Cinema*. It's a lavishly illustrated coffee-table book—what *Vanity Fair* writer James Wolcott memorably termed "a lap-crusher"—and thus not the kind of thing you'd normally see a person reading on the train. You ask me why I brought it. Or maybe I just imagine that you asked me. This is New York, and in New York, people start talking to you on trains for no reason. This is what I tell you:

New York is not just a city. It's The City.

Los Angeles is the city of angels and the city of dreams, but it will never be The City.

New York knows it. Los Angeles knows it. And the entertainment industry knows it.

That's why movies and TV shows are shot in New York despite the expense and hassle, or shot someplace else (Toronto, Cincinnati, Yonkers, downtown Los Angeles, a backlot in Culver City) and ask us to pretend they're in New York. *Whaddayagonnado*, change the setting to Cleveland?* Moviemaking as an industry began on the East Coast of the United States but migrated to Southern California, where the weather was nicer, the real estate cheaper, and where producers could re-create almost any environment. But mentally, spiritually, and often geographically, moviemaking always tends to drift back east, because New York City was always the greatest standing film set of them all—because it was real. You could feel it, hear it, smell it . . . even when it was filmed to evoke dreams or nightmares. When the Avengers assembled, they didn't do it in Los Angeles. When Godzilla finally surfaced in the US, he didn't descend upon Houston. Like Holly Golightly and the Corleones, they went to New York.

How many cities have this many nicknames and fictional alter egos? New York is the Big Apple. But it's also Metropolis: Fritz Lang's and Superman's. And it's Gotham City, even though Chicago keeps trying to muscle in and claim the name (*Fughedaboudit*, Chicago). New York is the place Snake Plissken escaped from. Eighteen years later, Snake escaped from LA and nobody gave a shit.

Every fictional city since the origin of mass-produced pictorial art starts to sketch its vision of urban density, glamour, and scale with New York as its muse, then adds or subtracts details. New York is realer than real, hard as hell, and it's an Emerald City calling seven generations of Dorothys. It's the city of mean streets and the sweet smell of success, the place where gutters ran red in the summer of Sam, just five years after the real-life dog day afternoon. See the midnight cowboy and the taxi driver, the working girl and Tootsie, the Joker and the King of Comedy and the Black private dick who's the sex machine to all the chicks, all moving among the masses in Times Square. See the pickup on South Street and the verdict of 12 angry men and the torment of the 25th hour. See the sun rise over Brooklyn Heights as Loretta Castorini, buzzed on love and dressed to the nines, kicks a can down the street.

**FOLLOWING SPREAD**
Still image from *Claudine* (1974), directed by John Berry, photographed by Gayne Rescher

* New Yorkers can always tell when filmmakers are faking New York, by the way. The streets are too clean and depopulated, and the blues and grays aren't right.

Foreword

You can't ask for a better book about this setting than *Fun City Cinema: New York and the Movies that Made It*.

And you couldn't ask for a better guide than my friend Jason Bailey, who wrote this book.

▬

The first thing you should know about Jason is that he's a self-identifying rather than native-born New Yorker—part of a group that E. B. White identified as a "person who was born somewhere else and came to New York in quest of something." Speaking for myself, as a similarly naturalized New Yorker who left his hometown of Dallas in 1995 and never looked back, this detail enhances rather than diminishes Jason's credentials, because New York is a lot—seriously, goddamn it, for real now, a *lot*—to take if you weren't raised there. Learning to live in New York is like learning to live in the ocean if you spent your whole life on land. You don't just have to acclimate, you have to evolve. That's never gonna happen unless, like Jason, you were secretly a New Yorker all along.

I'd had many online interactions with Jason since he moved to New York in 2006, but I didn't meet him in person until a cold night in November 2013 when we ended up sitting next to each other at a film screening. Jason had arrived a few minutes before me. He had not yet removed his topcoat and porkpie hat. He seemed lost not merely lost in thought, but in misery, shoehorned into the theater's too-narrow seats, half hunched over the row in front of him, chin on the chair-back, staring at the blank screen as if it might suddenly light up and show him the answers to whatever conundrum had put him in a funk.

Once I got to know Jason, I understood it wasn't any one thing that put him in that zone. It's his default vibe. Jason has that irascible/romantic "I fume because I care" energy that radiates off the sorts of New Yorkers who are described by neighbors as "The Mayor of the Block." He has the thoughtful/edgy face of a character actor who would've acted in ten New York flicks a year back in the '70s, most likely playing the chain-smoking detective who makes horrifying jokes at crime scenes or the henchman who delivers a message to a state's witness in a racketeering case while they're taking their kids to the zoo.

His favorite curse words are motherfucker, asshole, and shit. His favorite insults are dispshit, dumbfuck, and dumb asshole. His favorite New York bridge is the George Washington, because it's the one that he could see from his apartment window while he was writing this book. His favorite subway lines are the A, because of Duke Ellington, and the 6, because it's the one in *The Taking of Pelham One Two Three*. I'll always associate that last movie with Jason because every time I rave about a film that he thinks is garbage, he looks at me like Walter Matthau right after he hears Martin Balsam sneeze.

Jason is almost six-foot-four, by the way. I didn't realize this until after the screening, when he stood up. It was like watching a Swiss Army knife unfold. When we walk side by side down New York streets, we look like Joe and Ratso.

One time I ate dinner at an Upper West Side diner with Jason. He griped about the coffee for two hours while ordering refills.

That's what it means to love New York.

Jason loves New York.

▬

This book loves New York. It loves movies set in New York. More than anything else, it identifies and savors the New Yorkness of New York.

"Fun City" is right. You can inflect it all sorts of ways. You can hear Audrey Hepburn pealing it while skipping down Fifth Avenue. You can hear Mickey Rourke whispering it while bleeding out in a Bowery gutter, refusing to die till he's finished his last smoke.

As the title confirms, this is not just a catalog of movies that happen to be set in New York. It's *about* New York City as a birthplace to, and a dream-prompt for, films that described New York and sold New York, exposed New York and lied about New York, praised New York and buried New York. Some were shot elsewhere (like *King Kong*, all versions of which end at the base of a Manhattan skyscraper). But the overwhelming majority were filmed in the city.

The waxing and waning attraction between Hollywood talent and New York production deals (and soundstages) forms a major part of Jason's epic. He plays keen attention to how different mayors (movie stars in their own rights: heroes, antiheroes, clowns, thugs) shaped the temperament and worldview of films shot while they held office. We understand that *Midnight Cowboy*, *Shaft*, *Joe*, and *The French Connection* were as much about the wannabe-Bobby-Kennedy, patchwork-quilt liberalism of John Lindsay as they were about their characters. Ditto the Ed Koch-era's *Cruising*, *After Hours*, *Wall Street*, *Working Girl*, *Fatal Attraction*, and *Fort Apache, The Bronx*, which in retrospect feel like surly hangovers from New York's "Fear City" period, asking how things could be better and concluding that the answer was "yuppies buying lofts."

Because there are thousands of films that are wholly or partly set in or concerned with New York, the book is necessarily selective, but the author has thought through his rationales for including and excluding titles to the point where you can appreciate his logic even when it results in a favorite being omitted or de-centered. When Jason first told me he was doing this book, and that it would be segmented into decades, each focusing on a defining film, I argued with him over the wisdom of putting Oliver Stone's *Wall Street* at the center of the '80s chapter instead of Spike Lee's *Do the Right Thing*. He insisted that it made more sense to give Lee the spotlight—or the Towers of Light—in the '00s chapter, which is built around the *25th Hour*, and sure enough, when you arrive at the latter chapter after digesting the ones about the '80s and '90s, the book's internal logic is impeccable: an economic-sociological through line connects the neo-noir seediness of *Taxi Driver*, the brylcreemed-and-suspendered finance-bro machismo of *Wall Street*, and the broken lostness of Lee's post-9/11 eulogy for an already-dying New York—the Scorsese/Lumet New York—that was euthanized under the rubble. The eight million stories of the naked city are—

This is my stop! Talk to you later.

—Brooklyn, March 2021

# INTRODUCTION

On the afternoon of May 11, 1896, a young man named William Heise hailed a horse-drawn carriage outside the West 28th Street workshop of his boss, Thomas Edison. He carried with him Edison's latest marvel, a motion picture camera, which the carriage helped him schlep five blocks to the three-way intersection of Broadway, Sixth Avenue, and 34th Street, better known as Herald Square. Heise set up the camera in a window at the south end of the busy interchange, pointed it toward the action, and began to crank. The images he recorded—of passing streetcars, top-hatted pedestrians, beat cops, and a passing elevated train—ran barely a minute. But that film (titled, in the matter-of-fact custom of the period, *Herald Square*) was, legend has it, the first motion picture ever shot on the streets of New York.

*Herald Square* would premiere the following week, just shy of the one-year anniversary of the first public screening in the city—and the world. Motion pictures had previously been seen by one viewer at a time, on the tiny screens of devices like the Kinetoscope, but on May 20, 1895, the Latham company opened the doors of their theater at 156 Broadway to present their four-minute film of the May 4 fight between boxers Young Griffo and Charles Barnett, shot on the roof of Madison Square Garden. "The opening," wrote Terry Ramsaye in *A Million and One Nights: A History of the Motion Picture*, one of the first film history texts, "ill-advised and imperfect as it was, was the first public showing of motion pictures on a screen in all the world. The pictures flickered and danced and glimmered. It was only a ghost of a show, but it was the first."

Reporting on the screening for the *New York World*, Howard B. Hackett wrote:

> *Life-size presentations they are and will be, and you won't have to squint into a little hole to see them. You'll sit comfortably and see fighters hammering each other, circuses, suicides, hangings, electrocutions, shipwrecks, scenes on the exchanges, street scenes, horse-races, football games . . . just as if you were on the spot during the actual events . . . You will see actual people and things as they are.*

When *Herald Square* unspooled in May, Edison and his team discovered there were few things as thrilling to audiences as "actual things" and "people as they are"—and from their home base in Manhattan, they had a seemingly limitless supply of

both. The films they made of the city were called "actualities," and they didn't have characters or plots; they were, in a sense, mini-documentaries, capturing a minute or two of a specific place or event, which was often contained in their titles: *Panorama from the Tower of the Brooklyn Bridge* (1899); *Skyscrapers of New York City from the North River* (1903); *Interior*

ill image from *Herald Square* (1896). Directed by James H. White, photographed by William Heise.

*N.Y. Subway, 14th St. to 42nd St.* (1905). New Yorkers loved seeing these images projected on the theater screen, their daily lives as entertainment, right alongside the jugglers, singers, and comedians. Audiences elsewhere thrilled at these glimpses of a world so far removed from their own, via filmstrips that captured ot only the sights of the original American metropolis but also for the first time) those images in motion—and at top speed.

"It is difficult to overstate the impact of these primitive ilms," James Sanders writes, in his invaluable history *Celluloid Skyline*. "They haunt us with the knowledge that what they show s not a stage but an actual place; that the people in them are not actors, but real New Yorkers; that they offer no invented storyline, but ordinary, everyday life." It was a lucky accident, hen, that the nascent film industry was located in a city bursting with dramatic activities—but then again, perhaps it wasn't, as New York was about the only place the film industry *could've* been born. It was the center of the universe, not just in terms of entertainment (home of both the burgeoning Broadway theater scene and the administrative offices for the nationwide vaudeville and burlesque circuits), but invention, industry, and finance as well.

As the nineteenth century bled into the twentieth, the actuality (and actuality-inspired experimental films) gave way to the story-driven short. Films like *The Life of an American Policeman*

and *What Happened on Twenty-Third Street, New York City* would use the city as a living film set, a background against which to set chases and comic set pieces. As the century's first decade continued, the form evolved further, with city scenes and establishing shots used to supplement dramatic stories primarily shot in film studios—initially a loosely defined term, as the first film stocks were so fast, and thus required so much light to register an image, movies could be shot only in direct sunlight. So Edison and his competitors initially

constructed their "sets" on the roof-tops of the buildings that housed their workshops and production facilities.

Eventually both film stock and artificial lighting improved, and film-makers were able to build proper studios for indoor shooting. But then, as now, Manhattan real estate was a costly proposition, particularly for the kind of space Edison, Biograph, Vitagraph, and the rest needed to house not only settings and costumes but supplies. They found some relief in the boroughs of Brooklyn, Queens, and the Bronx, where studios were built and put to rapid use in the years that followed, as well as across the Hudson in towns like Fort Lee, New Jersey, which offered not only expansive and inexpensive real estate, but also a variety of non-urban backgrounds.

But by the 1910s, California was calling. The next gener-ation of moviemakers, many of them New Yorkers, was driven out of the city and across the country not only by the West Coast's surplus of cheap land and labor, but also by its perpetual mild weather (making outdoor shooting possible year-round). "Weather in New York is extremely unreliable and unpredict-able, and I'm sure once they got a dose of that Los Angeles climate, it was hard to resist," explains film historian Leonard Maltin. And there were other advantages to shooting in what was, quite literally, the Wild West. "Within an hour you could be in the mountains, you could be in the desert, you could be at the beach," says Maltin. "It was sparsely populated, and there were very few restrictions, if any, on where they could shoot

CLOCKWISE FROM TOP LEFT
Still images from: *Skyscrapers of New York City, from the North River* (1903), photographed by G. B. Smith; *Interior N.Y. Subway, 14th St. to 42nd St.* (1905), photographed by G. W. "Billy" Bitzer; *Lower Broadway* (1902), photographed by Robert K. Bonine; *Panorama from the Tower of the Brooklyn Bridge* (1899), photo-graphed by G. W. "Billy" Bitzer.

All those wonderful stories about Mack Sennett just going to a park and inventing a movie on the spot—that kind of thing was not exaggeration."

Most of all, on the West Coast, producers and directors were free from the threats of Edison and the other New York studios, which had joined forces and pooled their technological patents to create a prohibitory trust aimed at squeezing out the newbies. Their efforts would have the opposite effect; those independent exiles included Adolph Zukor, Samuel Goldwyn, Louis B. Mayer, and William Fox, moguls who would reign over Hollywood for decades to come.

There were still occasional bursts of activity out east; for example, when motion pictures began to talk (see chapter one), and suddenly needed actors who could do so, the Biograph Studios in the Bronx and (especially) the Kaufman Astoria Studios in Queens accommodated Broadway stars making extra money shooting talking pictures during the day and working onstage at night. But for the most part, pictures set in New York were shot in Hollywood studios, with their casts and crews (and sometimes just the latter) shooting exteriors in NYC, or more often using Gotham-inspired street sets constructed on their California backlots. The issues of geographic proximity and inflated cost simply made on-location shooting impossible for most New York stories.

So it's worth examining both why storytellers continued to set their films there, when they could present only a rough facsimile of that distinctive locale, and why the films that *did go* to the trouble to shoot in

Still image from *Twenty-Four Dollar Island* (1927), directed and photographed by Robert J. Flaherty.

so. Much of the explanation is tied up in mere identification. Westerns have no precise locality, beyond the vast area west of the Mississippi, and so great Westerns have been set everywhere from Kansas to Wyoming to Arizona. Stories of rural living and small-town life are equally nebulous. But when a film is set in The City, that city is usually New York.

—

Yet, because New York is a real city, with its own history, spirit, and soul, what we're witnessing in the films made there is a conversation of connections and reflections between the fictional lives in their foregrounds and the real lives happening behind them. And in the great New York films, those elements elevate each other. *The Jazz Singer* may be a semi-schmaltzy (and unquestionably racist) showbiz chestnut, but it's one informed not only by the explosion of mass culture in New York City in the 1920s (an environment in which it felt like anyone could reasonably become a star), but also by the questions of assimilation and tradition that loomed over its vast immigrant population. *King Kong* is one of the great urban monster movies, but the existential threat of its title character is not unconnected to the Depression that roared at New Yorkers throughout the 1930s—for good measure, from atop a new skyscraper that seemed, for a time, to represent a glamour and prosperity that was no longer in the city's grasp.

And when the difficulties of shooting in New York decreased, the dialogue between real New York and reel New York somehow grew, by sheer coincidence of timing, more

Still image from *What Happened on Twenty-Third Street, New York City* (1901), directed by George S. Fleming and Edwin S. Porter, photographed by Porter.

tense and contentious. One of Mayor John V. Lindsay's campaign promises, and first executive actions, was the formation of the Mayor's Office of Film, Theatre & Broadcasting—a one-stop shop intended to eliminate the red tape and copious permits of NY filmmaking. It did so, perhaps too well. The explosion of production that followed its establishment in the mid-1960s coincided directly with the most troubled period of the city's history, a quarter-century beset by rising crime, increasing debt, decreases in public service and servants, and general urban anarchy. And that period was captured over the course of the next two decades, vividly, in the likes of *Midnight Cowboy*; *The French Connection*; *Death Wish*; *Dog Day Afternoon*; *Taxi Driver*; *The Warriors*; *Fort Apache, The Bronx*; *Do the Right Thing*; and *After Hours*—portraits of a city's decay and downfall, and ones that (ironically enough) might not have existed at all were it not for the incentives provided by the city itself.

Viewed now, from the safe distance of a Disneyfied and gentrified Manhattan, these films provide us with a window into a past that's been razed and replaced by a safer present. They're fascinating artifacts of cinematic archaeology, and not just for the purposes of then-and-now comparing and contrasting—the porno house where Travis took Betsy for their only date in *Taxi Driver* is now showing the *Harry Potter* stage extravaganza; the corner where the police cruiser carrying the ransom money flips and crashes in *The Taking of Pelham One Two Three* now houses, of course, a Starbucks.

As New York enters its second Roaring Twenties, it seems less spirited and perhaps less itself. 9/11 took a toll; so did the rise of income inequality, rendering the city, more than ever, a place solely by and for the rich. That shift, and the rapid suburbanization that accompanied it, has left New York nearly indistinguishable from other large American cities. And thus the movies become a valuable reminder of what once was. Of those earliest actualities, Sanders writes, "They are, in the end, not *about* the city: they *are* the city—one or two minutes of it transposed precisely, second by second, from then to now." The New York movies that would follow weren't actualities; they had characters and plots and staged action, and run a good deal longer than one or two minutes. But when their characters take to the streets of The City, those actualities are still happening in the background, and in their own unique ways, each of them—from *The Crowd* and *Breakfast at Tiffany's* to *Saturday Night Fever* and *25th Hour* and everything in between—is an accidental documentary of what The City was at the precise point of its production, and not a moment longer. All of those movies, taken together, tell their own version of the history of New York

# 1920

# The Gaudy Spree, Mass

The story of the movie that would both alter the course of film history and further alienate New York City from that industry began, humbly enough, on a stage in Champaign, Illinois. It was April 1917, the show was *Robinson Crusoe, Jr.*, and the star was Al Jolson, whose performance hit a young undergraduate in the audience like a thunderbolt. "I shall never forget the first five minutes of Jolson," Samson Raphaelson later recalled, "his velocity, the amazing fluidity. . . . When he finished, I turned to the girl beside me, dazed with memories of my childhood on the East Side." The words he claimed to have spoken to her would form the basis of his short story "The Day of Atonement," published five years later: "My God, this isn't a jazz singer. This is a cantor!"

The story Raphaelson would write took its inspiration from the old Jewish folktale about a cantor who yearns to sing opera—a story particularly poignant to Rabbi Moses Yoelson, who led prayers and sang Jewish hymns in a tiny synagogue in Srednicke, a small village in Russian Lithuania. But Moses put such thoughts out of his head; he had a family to raise, four children in all (another died in infancy). The youngest was a little boy, Asa.

Asa was still small when his family emigrated to the United States. Moses went first, in 1891, to establish residency, find work, and make enough money to send for his wife and children, but Russian Jews were not permitted to travel freely. A family friend helped smuggle the rabbi out of Russia on a raft, among the workmen of his wood business. To blend in among the workers, Moses Yoelson—the father of the boy who would later rename himself Al Jolson— blackened his face.

Moses would eventually find work as a cantor at the Talmud Torah Congregation in Washington D.C., sending for his family four years later. But wife Naomi would die the following year, and Moses had difficulty with the children—particularly Asa, whose grief over his mother's death manifested itself in disciplinary problems that eventually prompted Moses to turn his son over to a Catholic home for boys. The young man eventually found an outlet for his considerable energy: He was drawn to show business, working in circuses, burlesque houses, and vaudeville theaters, in both Washington D.C. and New York City, where he would occasionally escape to sing, shine shoes, and sell newspapers before being dragged back to the nation's capital by his father.

Over the course of those early years, Asa changed his first name to Al and then simplified his last name to Jolson. Like many of his contemporaries, he began to perform in blackface, which he claimed was suggested by an African American dresser; it soon became his trademark. "It was as though he had a mask, behind which he could shelter and hide his problems," explained biographer Michael Freedland. "It also seemed to make him twice the personality he had been before."

Moses and Naomi Yoelson.

The Gaudy Spree, Mass Media, and *The Jazz Singer*

Jolson ascended to stardom quickly, thanks to his electrifying stage presence and knack for self-promotion (he famously placed an ad in *Variety*, promising, "Watch me—I'm a wow"). On a visit to San Francisco in 1906, that self-confidence manifested itself in a catchphrase; facing a tough crowd of blue-collar theatergoers in a makeshift theater, the singer announced, "All right, all right, folks—you ain't heard nothing yet," and he would deliver that same promise at every performance for the next forty-four years.

Jolson was a Broadway star by the time he made his first motion picture ten years later. Intended only for screening at a fund-raiser for the Traffic Police's Benefit Fund, the Vitagraph short didn't impress Jolson at all. "I'm no good if I can't sing," he said with a shrug, and figured that was the end of his experiment in pictures.

——

Meanwhile, the film industry was also second-guessing itself. As surely as the business had settled in California, it began, piecemeal, to tiptoe back. "Two years ago the City of Our Lady the Queen of the Angels was gloating over the threatened annihilation of New York as a rival in the field of picture production," according to the *Times* in November 1920, doing a bit of gloating itself in noting that filmmakers working out of Los Angeles, "a city only about a tenth as large as New York," were having trouble finding acceptable actors, costumes, and other "articles essential to 'truly artistic' productions."

And thus, in late 1919, D. W. Griffith returned to the East Coast, purchasing a twenty-eight-acre estate in Mamaroneck, New York, about an hour by train from Grand Central, which he used as his base of

Aerial view of D. W. Griffith's Mamaroneck Studios and estate.

production for the next four years. "In the future, I can't see any other centre possible for the picture producer who seeks the best of everything," he told the *Times*. From the beginning, one of his aims was to coax Al Jolson up to Mamaroneck and make a proper picture, but the singer—who was by now the king of Broadway, taking up permanent residence in a series of shows at the Winter Garden Theatre—resisted. "I'm no actor," he told the director, but Griffith wouldn't take no for an answer, and he finally wore his star down. Griffith developed a vehicle for Jolson called *Mammy's Boy*, and took out a full-page ad in *Movie Weekly*, announcing, "Famous Black Face Comedian Becomes Griffith Star."

The shoot was a disaster. Jolson felt off-balance from the start, unable to adjust to playing to the camera after years of laughter and cheers from packed houses. Certain that he wasn't coming across, he asked to see the rushes and was so unhappy with what he saw, he told Griffith he wasn't finishing the picture. He walked out of the screening room and sailed off to Europe. Griffith, who had already spent $71,000 and shot six reels of film, sued the actor for breach of contract. The suit dragged on for three years; in 1926, Griffith finally won the case, though Jolson was ordered to pay only $2,627 of the $500,000 Griffith was demanding.

By then, Griffith's Mamaroneck experiment was long over. Things were equally touch-and-go in the city through the twenties. The biggest investment was made by Paramount—then still known as Famous Players–Lasky—which took advantage of the recent subway accessibility to Queens by building a $2.5 million production facility in the borough's Astoria neighborhood, which opened in October 1920.

The honeymoon period was brief. By the time the Astoria studio opened, the industry was buckling under a postwar economic depression, and the studio ceased operation a mere nine months later. "The Famous Players Studio in Long Island is done, gone and forgotten," cackled the Hollywood trade paper *Camera!* "They have started shipping lights to the West Coast, stripping the studio clean." But the wake was also short-lived. Within a year, with the recession over and California studios back to capacity, Paramount began shipping its productions cross-country again.

The Astoria studio was soon operating at full steam, cranking out 103 features (about 40 percent of the studio's output) over the next five years. It became the preferred home for Hollywood-soured stars like Gloria Swanson and Louise Brooks. "The place was full of free spirits, defectors, refugees, who were all trying to get away from Hollywood and its restrictions," Swanson wrote in her autobiography, *Swanson on Swanson*. "There was a wonderful sense of revolution and innovation in the studio in Queens." Brooks, as was her style, was more blunt. "To love books was a big laugh," she recalled of working out west. "There was no theater, no opera, no concerts—just those god-damned movies."

——

There was, to put it mildly, more than those god-damned movies in New York. When the city closed the book on the Great War with a giant victory parade up Fifth Avenue in September 1919, it was ready to let its hair down, to let go of the bloodshed and fear, to roar into the twenties with reckless abandon, embracing social fads, new music and dances, galvanizing sports figures, and a general affinity for what was not yet dubbed "pop culture." Columnist Westbrook Pegler dubbed it "the Era of Wonderful Nonsense," and its inhabitants wanted to dance, and they wanted to cheer, and they wanted to have a good time.

The Gaudy Spree, Mass Media, and *The Jazz Singer*

Mayor Jimmy Walker rides
in a parade with Charles
Lindbergh, 1927.

Most of all, they wanted to drink. In theory, the adoption of the Eighteenth Amendment (aka the Volstead Act, aka Prohibition) should have curbed that. But a *New York World* poll, taken not long after the ban took effect at midnight on January 16, 1920, found "an overwhelming opposition to Prohibition by the man in the street." The bars closed, but more than twice as many illegal drinking establishments replaced them—up from fifteen thousand before Prohibition to at least thirty-two thousand after, most of them controlled by the mob. All the law did, New Yorkers grumbled, was remove the democratization of drinking; the neighborhood saloons frequented by the working class disappeared, but the affluent could still imbibe freely at private clubs and speakeasies. When the mayor of Berlin visited the city in 1929, he asked Mayor Jimmy Walker, "When does the Prohibition law go into effect?"

Mayor Walker was not the man to ask. A notorious party animal, he spent his evenings zipping from one party to the next in his chauffeur-driven Duesenberg, nattily dressed in tailored suits—there were seventy of them, it was said, and he had a dressing room installed under his City Hall office so that he could more easily change clothes up to three times a day. Walker's supporters and the New York press (and there were plenty who qualified as both) would affectionately dub him "the nightclub mayor." With all the partying and changing, he tended not to make it to bed until rather late, and that tardiness would extend to the following workday. He took seven vacations, totaling 143 days, in his first two years in office; by the end of his first term, he was basically a part-time employee of the city.

Few objected, at least not loudly; Walker was put up for the job, and zealously protected in it, by the city's Tammany Hall political machine. His constituents looked past his flaws, and perhaps even embraced them, because somewhere deep inside the man, they saw themselves. "The reason for his vast popularity," wrote columnist Ed Sullivan, "was that Jimmy Walker somehow or other seemed to be New York brought to life in one person." Journalist Henry F. Pringle put it another way: "The jazz age is in office in New York."

Pringle was correct, in more ways than one. Like a flapper partying deep into the night without care for the consequences, Walker's New York was living perilously in the moment, increasing its municipal debt by nearly $100,000 a day to bankroll an ambitious program of infrastructure, municipal improvements, parks, and schools.

The city's fiscal health was precariously tethered to that of the real estate and stock markets. Those members of the "new money" class joined the city's Gilded Age tycoons of banking, oil, steel, and rail, and by 1927, three thousand of the country's fifteen thousand millionaires lived in New York City. (Simultaneously, in what would become a familiar refrain, a third of the city's families lived well below the poverty line.) The booming private sector would keep the city afloat, Walker insisted, and for a while, he was right.

In the meantime, the city seemed to run off of a pool of creative energy and shared vitality. Midtown Manhattan was the center of that pool, with a cornucopia of nightclubs, booking agencies, recording and radio studios, music publishers, and Broadway and vaudeville stages within walking distance. At the clubs, writers traded witticisms while society

The Gaudy Spree, Mass Media, and *The Jazz Singer*

The Aristocrat of Harlem

The Famous Cotton Club

average of 225 new Broadway shows opened per year, at more than seventy active theaters. (Twenty-six new stages opened between 1924 and 1929 alone.)

One of those shows was *The Jazz Singer*. Samson Raphaelson had taken the kernel of an idea that formed after seeing Jolson perform, and turned it into a story full of connections to Jolson's biography. The protagonist of Raphaelson's short story "The Day of Atonement" was Jakie Rabinowitz, who, like Jolson, was a rabbi's son who breaks with his family to become a secular singer. Like Jolson, Jakie shortened and Anglicized his name to "Jack Robin"; both the performer and the character further alienated their fathers by marrying a Gentile.

Raphaelson had the opportunity to thank Jolson personally for his inspiration when they met in 1924, as the writer was adapting the story into the play. Jolson expressed an interest in starring, but felt it should be a full-scale Jolson musical revue; the author envisioned something smaller and simpler, a drama with a song or two for effect. The two parted as friends, and when *The Jazz Singer* made its Broadway debut in September of the following year, Jolson's vaudeville contemporary George Jessel took on the role of Jakie Rabinowitz. Jessel figured the show would be his meal ticket; he could tour it for years, make it his signature role.

■

Broadway was cresting, but vaudeville was over. As the decade turned, those variety venues were gradually converted into movie palaces, and no city in the world had more of them than New York. They needed product to put on their screens—more than even the prolific studios were providing. And thus the studio facilities in New York and New Jersey that had been abandoned in the westward migration were taken over by independent producers, for whom nationwide circulation was now an option, thanks to the recent creation of non-studio distribution entities like First National and United Artists.

Joseph Schenck produced pictures for his wife Norma Talmadge and sister-in-law Constance on East 48th Street, in what was dubbed "The Talmadge Studio"; Norma's costume dramas were shot on the ground level, while Constance's sophisticated comedies were made on the second floor, and (for a time) Fatty Arbuckle's knockabout shorts were produced on the third. David O. Selznick worked out of studios in the Bronx and Fort Lee, New Jersey (and, occasionally, in the city itself), before taking over the Talmadge studio. And William Randolph Hearst built the extravagant Cosmopolitan-International studio in East Harlem, for the twin (but often overlapping) purposes of producing adaptations of popular plays, and vehicles for his mistress Marion Davies.

The inexpensive studio rentals would also attract producers of "race movies," created specifically for exhibition in segregated theaters; chief among them was Oscar Micheaux, the entrepreneur, author, and publisher, who arrived in New York in 1920 and produced a series of low-budget films by, for, and about African Americans.

This mad dash of production and distribution was all of a piece with the general acceleration of culture in the postwar era. As historian Ann Douglas explains, "The war revved up the dizzying pace of change and reinforced acceleration itself, the trademark of American life, as the most valuable asset any society could possess, at least in modern times." It was a time of advancements grand and everyday: airplanes, skyscrapers, chain stores, phonographs, radios, radio networks, tabloid journalism, popular songs, jazz music, musical comedy, spectator

gals danced with mobsters and chorus girls chatted up tycoons. When those venues wound down for the night, revelers would jump in their taxis and cars and head uptown to Harlem to catch the floor show at the Cotton Club or Connie's Inn; when those venues closed their doors, there would be food and music at "rent parties" that lasted until dawn.

The effects of this casual cross-cultural pollination reverberated through the artistic landscape. The era's revolution in popular songwriting came from artists like Rodgers and Hammerstein, George and Ira Gershwin, and Cole Porter, who were directly inspired by black culture; Gershwin expressed an explicit desire to "catch the rhythm of these interfusing peoples—to show them clashing and blending." High and low culture mixed in similar style on the stage and in silent cinema. Downtown and uptown, from burlesque to Broadway, in Tin Pan Alley and around the Algonquin Round Table, the city was creating its own new language and ethos—crafting an ultramodern idea of what it meant to be an American, and dramatizing it in film, song, and stage.

From their brownstone on West 48th Street, Boni & Liveright published works by Ernest Hemingway, William Faulkner, T. S. Eliot, Eugene O'Neill, Ezra Pound, and e e cummings. There were new magazines, *Time* and *Vanity Fair* and, most of all, the *New Yorker*. There were newspapers galore, including the new *Daily News*, which grew its circulation to twice that of the staid *Times* in four years by capturing the vernacular and energy of the era and packaging it in a slick tabloid style, complemented by its snappy photographs, a popular selection of comics, and the increasingly vital sports pages, which captured the exploits of Babe Ruth, Lou Gehrig, and Jack Dempsey.

The city became the center of production for both radio equipment and radio programs; the first commercial broadcast station went on the air in 1920, and by the end of the decade, more than six hundred stations were sending their signals into more than twelve million homes. Broadway was booming as well—over the course of the twenties, an

sports, advertising, bestsellers, literary magazines—"the first age," Douglas writes, "of mass media." And seemingly all of it emanated from one place: The City on the East Coast. "The whole world revolves around New York," Duke Ellington wrote in his autobiography. "Very little happens anywhere unless someone in New York presses a button."

With that centralization in mind, it shouldn't come as a surprise that the development, and much of the initial production, of the talking picture was centered in Gotham. The experiments in technology, recording, and broadcasting that made synchronous sound possible were there; so were the musicians, singers, and stage stars that made such attractive subjects. The first attempts at talkies were made in New York, from the rudimentary (a Clinton Street theater in which actors stood behind the screen, improvising dialogue to accompany silent films) to the embryonic.

In the early 1910s, Thomas Edison patented a talking picture exhibition device called the Kinetophone, and used his Bronx studio to produce more than 250 short subjects to show it off. They were distributed via the Keith-Albee vaudeville circuit to fifty theaters across North America equipped for the process, which connected a film projector in the back of a theater to a phonograph near the screen, using a cord or belt running over pulleys. When it worked, it was grand; the *Times* reported a fifteen-minute ovation following one New York screening. But the success of the exhibition was entirely in the hands of the projectionist (literally—the sync depended on the consistency of his hand-cranking), and there were reports of out-of-sync films booed and catcalled in other markets. The Kinetophone sank. Edison himself deemed talking pictures a lost cause: "Americans require a restful quiet in the moving picture theater. . . . The stage is the place for the spoken word."

But by the early twenties, several scientists—independent researchers, as well as groups at Western Electric and General Electric—were developing at least five potential sound systems for film. The most advanced was the Phonofilm system, which used electrical impulses to print voice vibrations alongside the images on a filmstrip; a series of short films utilized the process, featuring stage stars like Eddie Cantor and George Jessel. They were seen, by audiences and the industry, the same way the successful Kinetophone shorts were—as a novelty, a diversion, one more act on the bill, but certainly not a replacement for silent films. "Talking pictures are perfected," remarked *Photoplay.* "So is castor oil." It was a non-starter.

It would ultimately take the flop sweat of a minor studio, desperate to set itself apart, to push the talking picture to center stage. The Warner brothers—Jack, Sam, Harry, and Abe—were New Yorkers who entered the motion picture business by operating a chain of nickelodeons. They then formed one of the first film exchanges, in which exhibitors pooled resources and shared prints rather than building individual libraries; they used the profits from that enterprise to start a studio of their own in 1912.

Thirteen years later, struggling against the competition and resources of MGM and Paramount, Harry Warner spearheaded a Hail Mary. The company purchased the Vitagraph Company, which had developed a complicated system of synchronous sound on 16-inch wax discs that ran, at 33 1/3 rotations per minute, for roughly ten minutes—the length of a reel of film. The projectionist would thread up the film in the projector to sync with the first groove of the corresponding record, and as long as that job was done correctly, as long as they were properly

synced, the system's motorized driveshaft would ensure both ran at the same speed. "A new era in motion picture presentation has arrived," the company promised its exhibitors, in a July newsletter. "The marvelous Vitaphone process, which will have its first public presentation at the Warner Theater on August 6, will revolutionize the industry."

For once, it wasn't just hype. The program of Vitaphone shorts and the feature film *Don Juan* (the first Vitaphone feature, though it used the process only for synchronized music and sound effects) opened at the Warner on August 6, 1926, and stayed there until April of the following year. In a rave review, the *Times* insisted Vitaphone was "not to be put with the labor-saving devices of this machine age but rather with the inventions that minister to the enlightenment or entertainment of the world." The program made its way to Grauman's Egyptian Theatre in Los Angeles at the end of October, and the reception was nearly as rapturous. "The house applauded, cheered and stamped with its feet," reported *Variety*.

Warner Bros. immediately decreed that music be added to all of the features on its forthcoming slate, and ramped up production on the Vitaphone shorts. Fox, meanwhile, hurried its Movietone system—an optical method, in the spirit of Photofilm—into the marketplace. But the other studios hedged their bets. In February 1927, the remaining studios and distributors signed a mutual agreement to spend the next year selecting an industry standard between the two incompatible competitors; it also gave them some time to wait for the sound fad to fade, and they were certain it would. But before that year had passed, the Warners would shake up the industry anew.

━━

The stage version of *The Jazz Singer* ran a robust thirty-eight weeks in New York; it might have run longer if Jessel hadn't bowed out due to a film commitment in California. The day before the star's departure in June 1926, Raphaelson sold the film rights to Warner Bros. The studio already had Jessel under a three-year contract, so his casting seemed a foregone conclusion; its agreement with the author indicated that the film couldn't be released until at least May 1927, to avoid competition with the touring company production of the play, so Jessel could front that tour and still star in the movie. Ernst Lubitsch was floated as director.

But while Jessel was on tour, the stakes changed. Following the *Don Juan* debut, Warner Bros. decided *The Jazz Singer* was going to be a Vitaphone production—not just with a musical score, but also with synchronized songs. By then, Lubitsch's contract with Warners had ended, and he had moved to Paramount; WB turned the picture over to *Don Juan* director Alan Crosland.

Jolson, meanwhile, had been paid a whopping $25,000 to star in a Vitaphone short that ran ahead of the second Vitaphone feature, Syd Chaplin's *The Better 'Ole*. "The Vitaphone has given me the biggest thrill I've ever had, and after this year I'm going to play with it," he told a newspaper columnist after the shoot; and *A Plantation Act*, in which he sang three songs in blackface and assured his audience, "You ain't heard nothin' yet, folks," became the breakout hit Warners had paid so handsomely for.

Maybe it was the rhapsodic reception to that short (and the muted response to Jessel's screen appearances to date) that landed Jolson in *The Jazz Singer*. Maybe it was a matter of money; one story went that Jessel asked for a bump when it became a sound film, which he felt

The Gaudy Spree, Mass Media, and *The Jazz Singer*

would kill the golden goose of future stage productions, and producer Darryl F. Zanuck reportedly half-joked, "Jesus, for the sort of money Jessel wants we can get Jolson," which sounded less like a joke the more they thought about it. Jessel offered the least believable explanation: that he walked off the production because the studio wouldn't meet his demands for a Jewish director and Jewish actors to play his parents. (Had that change not been made, Leonard Maltin says, we might not be talking about *The Jazz Singer* today, "because Jessel, though talented, was no Jolson. And he was reminded of it the rest of his life!")

Whatever the reason, Jolson signed a contract to star in *The Jazz Singer*, and perform six songs as part of that commitment, on May 26, 1927. Zanuck and company talked Jolson into taking part of his salary in Warner Bros. stock, which appealed to his love of a gamble—and his willingness to bet on himself. His eight weeks on the film would begin on July 11, after completing a nightclub engagement; in the interim, the ending of the story was rewritten, so that the protagonist returned to the stage after singing in the synagogue for his dying father. Even on film, it was presumed, audiences would simply not accept the idea of Al Jolson leaving showbiz.

*The Jazz Singer* began production in New York, mostly for location shots. Crosland and his crew took exteriors of the Winter Garden Theatre at 49th and Broadway, which had opened back in 1911 with a production of *La Belle Paree* that was Jolson's first major Broadway success (he would subsequently star in several productions there, including *Vera Violetta*, *The Honeymoon Express*, and the previously mentioned *Robinson Crusoe, Jr.*); the original plan was to take photographs of the theater's interior and re-create it on a soundstage, but Jolson knew he'd feel more at home on the real thing, and suggested shooting there instead.

The Warners took the opportunity to drum up a bit of advance publicity and a free crowd. They threw a tarp over the marquee, putting up a makeshift sign over the covering as they shot inside (WARNER BROTHERS PICTURES, INC. WILL SHOOT SCENES TODAY OF THE NEW YORK WINTER GARDEN FOR THEIR FORTHCOMING PRODUCTION, AL JOLSON IN *THE JAZZ SINGER*). Once that sign had drawn a proper crowd, the tarp was removed to reveal the signage needed for the film (WINTER GARDEN—JACK ROBIN—THE JAZZ SINGER), and the cameras rolled. Jolson eventually came out to greet the onlookers turned extras, and treated them to an impromptu street performance. "You know, I could go on like this for hours," Jolson announced at its conclusion, "but we all had a hard day. Besides, we're tying up traffic. Suppose we call it a night, and you all come back in a few months to see yourself in the picture!"

The crew also took exterior shots of the Rabinowitz's neighborhood on the Lower East Side. Crosland snuck the Orchard Street wide shots from the second-floor window of a restaurant across the street and put the camera under a burlap drop in the back of a moving truck to get the tracking shot of Yudelson (Otto Lederer) walking among the pushcarts and kibitzers, and the brief scene of Jack/Jolson returning to his boyhood home. Once those scenes were in the can, the production packed up and headed back to California to shoot the interiors—and the sound sequences.

Legends persist that the decision to record not only synchronous songs but also dialogue was some sort of impulsive, "Let's catch this lightning in a bottle" moment, brought on by Jolson's appealing on-set ad-libs. But the call had already been made and announced before cameras rolled; on July 8, while Crosland was working in New York and Jolson was finishing his nightclub gig, an item in *Motion Picture News* noted that Warner Bros. was "planning to use dialogue in certain scenes of this production—dialogue with musical accompaniment."

There would ultimately be only two of those scenes: his patter before singing "Toot, Toot, Tootsie, Goodbye," including Jolson's catchphrase "You ain't heard nothin' yet," a particularly appropriate choice for the first words of on-screen dialogue in motion picture history; and a seemingly ad-libbed monologue from Jolson to his mother (Eugenie Besserer) about their rosy future, done as he vamps an instrumental break to the song "Blue Skies." The latter was shot (and simultaneously

**LEFT**
Still image of Al Jolson in *A Plantation Act* (1926), directed by Philip Roscoe.

**OPPOSITE**
Still images from *The Jazz Singer* (1927), directed by Alan Crosland, photographed by Hal Mohr.

recorded) on the afternoon of August 30, 1927, at the tail end of a series of days in which the company's sole objective was shooting the sound numbers. (They were shot one per day, each like a separate short film, by the Vitaphone unit.) The "Blue Skies" sequence was the final piece of the production; two weeks later, the score for the silent scenes was in the can, and the premiere was set for October 6 at the Warners' Theatre in New York—shortly after the end of Yom Kippur, the High Holiday at the center of the picture's climax.

Had *The Jazz Singer* been, as intended, just another stage play adapted to the silent screen (as *Variety* accurately described it, "a pleasant enough sentimental orgy dealing with a struggle between religion and art"), it would have most likely disappeared into the dustbin of history. It is remembered, almost entirely, because it sings and (briefly) talks; as such, it foreshadows both the stage-bound family melodramas and backstage musicals that would dominate the early years of talking picture production. But there are some noteworthy bits of subtext. As film historian Scott Eyman notes in his essential *The Speed of Sound*, "it marks one of the few times Hollywood Jews allowed themselves to contemplate their own central cultural myth, and the conundrums that go with it. *The Jazz Singer* implicitly celebrates the ambition and drive needed to escape the shtetls of Europe and the ghettos of New York, and the attendant hunger for recognition."

Those questions of assimilation are present in Raphaelson's original story, which describes Jakie thus: "He lived in New York, and his slender, well-set-up figure was draped in perfectly fitting suits of Anglo-Saxon severity, and his dark hair was crisply trimmed and parted after the fashion of young America." The cantor father complains, "It's too good here in America—too much money—too much telephones and trains and 'ragtime,'" while his mother insists, "But he's an American boy. And he's a good boy." That Americanization runs through the film as well ("*Jack Robin* is my name now," he reminds his mother, in his letters home), which lends a bizarre, unspoken dimension to Jolson's casual application of blackface makeup before going onstage for his big

The Gaudy Spree, Mass Media, and *The Jazz Singer*

The original theatrical
poster for *The Jazz Singer*
(1927).

**ABOVE**
Still image from *The Jazz Singer* (1927), directed by Alan Crosland, photographed by Hal Mohr.

**BELOW**
Original program for *The Jazz Singer*'s 1927 debut at the Warners' Theater in New York.

musical number (complete with "nappy" wig and a big, toothy smile)—a sequence that has rendered the film all but impossible to screen or celebrate in recent years, and rightfully so. Blackface, as both a cultural and historical signifier of white supremacy, carries a heavier burden than this lightweight musical drama can shoulder, no matter how innovative it proved to be. Yet it's telling that Jakie finds the application of the artificial and offensive mask of minstrelsy most helpful to better hide his true, Jewish self.

Not that the reviews were focusing on such concerns. "To a first night Broadway mob," reported *Variety*, "that ["Mammy"] finale was a whale and resulted in a tumultuous ovation. Jolson personally has never been more warmly greeted than at this premiere." The trade paper's subsequent review put it more succinctly: "an impressive triumph of both Mr. Jolson and the Vitaphone over the formerly silent drama." The whiplash from sync songs and effects to title-card dialogue (cards even appear during songs) is, indeed, jarring; as Eyman writes, "This sudden reversion to an abruptly passé convention is far more damaging to the traditions and values of silent cinema than any all-talkie could have been."

*The Jazz Singer* was not quite as warmly received when it premiered at the Warners' Theatre's Hollywood Boulevard counterpart at the end of the year, but there was probably some self-interest at stake in that house. Frances Goldwyn, wife of independent producer Samuel, recalled gazing over the crowd and seeing "terror on all their faces, as they realized the game they had been playing for years was finally over." They drove home in silence, in a car shared with MGM's Irving Thalberg and his wife, actress Norma Shearer. All four would survive the transition to talkies. Others were not so lucky.

Jolson, however, did just fine. His next picture, *The Singing Fool*, was an even bigger hit than *The Jazz Singer*, bringing in $5.5 million and becoming the highest-grossing movie of all time, a title it held until *Gone with the Wind*'s release eleven years later. Like *The Jazz Singer*, it was only a partial "talkie," intermingling songs and dialogue with silent sequences. In between the two Jolson vehicles, Warners released the first "all-talking" Vitaphone feature, a quickie expansion of a two-reel comedy, produced for the bargain-basement price of $23,000; it quickly grossed a jaw-dropping $1.2 million. It was called *The Lights of New York*. It was shot entirely on the Warner Bros. lot in Burbank.

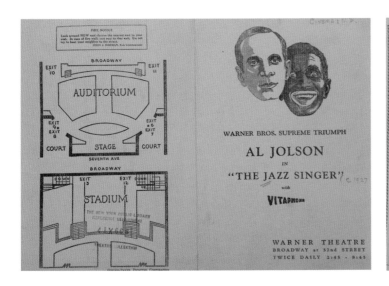

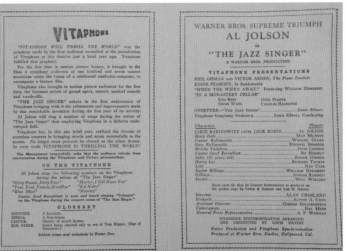

NOW SHOWING

MANHATTA

SKYSCRAPER SYMPHONY

SPEEDY

THE CROWD

# MANHATTA

## 1920

### Directors: Charles Sheeler and Paul Strand

# SKYSCRAPER SYMPHONY

## 1929

### Director: Robert Florey

Dubbed "the first consciously-produced avant-garde U.S. film" by historian Jan-Christopher Horak, *Manhatta* was originally released as an extended actuality (or "scenic"). But, from our perspective, it plays more like the coda to that movement, a culmination of twenty-plus years of such films, less defined by observation than the idea that the city is telling a story—millions of them, in fact, every day.

It begins with an entrance, as men pour into the city off the ferry (a few making suspicious eye contact with the camera), but that opening is a fake-out; photographers Charles Sheeler and Paul Strand are less interested in the journeys of the city's citizens than with the majesty of its structures. And thus they capture its skyscrapers and steamships, its cemeteries and bridges, its sidewalks and streets. But for once, these images aren't random; they're organized by visual motifs (like the ways in which smoke fills the sky), building to an ornate crescendo.

Strand was a New Yorker and Sheeler hailed from Philadelphia; *Skyscraper Symphony* director Robert Florey (who helmed the short film the same year he co-directed the Marx Brothers' first feature, *The Cocoanuts*) hailed from France, and the shift in perspective, from natives to outsider, is pronounced. Florey shoots the imposing structures from low (and slightly tilted) angles, seemingly intimidated by their height and scope; after these initial, locked-down compositions, the camera goes handheld, and increasingly herky-jerky, as though the city is bearing down on the cameraman (and, by extension, the viewer), followed by a series of dancing double exposures and tilted Dutch angles.

*Skyscraper Symphony* is, essentially, the story of the civilian in the city, overwhelmed by its increasingly ubiquitous behemoths—terrified of them, in stark contrast to *Manhatta*, which seems to find them thrilling. That such a shift could occur in the space of time between 1920 and 1929 tells us quite a bit about that decade, and the mental state of city dwellers at its conclusion.

**RIGHT**
Still image from *Manhatta* (1921), directed by Charles Sheeler and Paul Strand.

**BELOW**
Still image from *Skyscraper Symphony* (1929), directed by Robert Florey.

# SPEEDY

## 1928

### Director: Ted Wilde

Harold Lloyd's final silent film offers up some of the most expansive views of twenties-era New York in a narrative feature, thanks to the actor/producer's decision to supplement the footage shot at his California studio (where he built an expansive replica of the Sheridan Square neighborhood in the West Village) with several weeks of location shooting, beginning in mid-August 1927. The baked-in themes of speed and movement—the first title card describes New York as a city "where everybody is in such a hurry that they take Saturday's bath on Friday so they can do Monday's washing on Sunday"—allowed the company to cover quite a bit of ground: In addition to several chase scenes, director Wilde staged scenes through Midtown, under the 59th Street Bridge, in front of the Plaza Hotel, on Wall Street, on Coney Island, and at Yankee Stadium (where Lloyd drops off a late-for-the-game Babe Ruth, in an enjoyable cameo).

The extended location shoot—reportedly planned for four weeks but stretching to at least eight—inched the picture's budget up to the then-astronomical $1 million, but it paid off. The climactic chase sequence through Lower Manhattan is a marvel, an urban counterpart to *The General*, in which our hero *must* keep New York's last horse car in motion (even when it's missing a horse); it plays now like a dry run for *The French Connection*, complete with hairy close calls incorporated into the final cut. And while the mirthful trip to Coney Island became a bit of a cliché in this era (similar scenes appear in *The Crowd, The Cameraman, It!*, and others), Lloyd spends more than a reel there, building several ingenious comic bits.

Like Buster Keaton, who had to shoot New York exteriors for that year's *The Cameraman* at the break of dawn on a Sunday to avoid being mobbed by fans, a star like Lloyd was going to draw crowds. To place his star in city scenes inconspicuously, Wilde used similar tricks as *The Crowd*'s King Vidor and *The Jazz Singer*'s Alan Crosland, hiding his camera under the cover of laundry wagons and the like. But traffic snags ensued when the production closed off streets for the closing chase, a problem further exacerbated by crowds that had turned up for a peek at Lloyd. (They were disappointed; he was shooting at Coney Island while the second-unit crew handled the first section of the chase, and out sick for the latter stretch.)

The film's extended stay in New York seems to have allowed the spirit of the city to seep in, in a way it often didn't in films that mixed quickie Gotham exteriors and establishing shots with California studio photography. It is, in many ways, the prototypical big-city comedy: brash, fast-paced, and smart.

Still image from *Speedy* (1928), directed by Ted Wilde, photographed by Walter Lundgrin.

# THE CROWD

## 1928

## Director: King Vidor

Still image from *The Crowd* (1928), directed by King Vidor, photographed by Henry Sharp.

John Sims is the all-American boy—born on the Fourth of July, even. From that day forth, he's told that he's special, destined to be "somebody big," and he leaves his small town at twenty-one to become "one of the seven million that believe New York depends on them." Stories of small-town kids who take on, and take over, the big city were commonplace in the teens and twenties; in *The Crowd*, director King Vidor instead dramatizes how this vast, overpopulated metropolis grinds dreams and individuality into dust.

"Making your own world is a big responsibility," Vidor explained. "A lot of people try it, but fail. Most people just go along with it." If he was going to tell a story that ran so contrary to norms, the director realized, he couldn't tell it in the customary manner. So he plucked his leading actor from a group of extras on the MGM lot ("I thought that if I put a star into that part, [the audience] would never believe that he was the common, unknown man who was losing his identity in the crowd"), and complemented the Culver City studio shoot with five weeks of exterior location photography in New York City.

"For scenes of the sidewalks of New York, we designed a pushcart perambulator carrying what appeared to be inoffensive packing boxes," he recalled. "Inside the hollowed-out boxes there was room for one small-sized cameraman and one silent camera. We pushed this contraption from the Bowery to Times Square and no one ever detected our subterfuge." The director would hang out next to the pushcart, leaning nonchalantly and discussing the shots with his cameraman; pedestrians, who didn't recognize the lightly made-up figures nearby as actors, were none the wiser.

In his establishing shots of the bustling city, Vidor called on the tools of actualities, newsreel photography, and stylized experimentation of *Manhatta* and *Skyscraper Symphony*. But his portraiture of domestic misery and pre-Depression poverty—in which our John and his long-suffering wife Mary find themselves out of work, out of money, and out of sorts—is closer to the neorealist movement of the 1940s than the silent melodrama of *The Crowd*'s day. Audiences were unsurprisingly resistant to this unapologetically downbeat picture, but it stands as one of the first films to fully capture (without romanticizing) the unsparing toughness of city life.

# 1929

# The Crash, the Depression, and *King Kong*

# 1939

**"Say, is this the moving picture ship?"** asks Charles Weston, the casting agent, and a night watchman confirms it is; the ship is named *The Venture*, and it's about to embark on a "crazy voyage" with a destination seemingly known only by the picture's director, Carl Denham. These are the opening lines of Merian C. Cooper and Ernest B. Schoedsack's *King Kong* (1933), establishing it immediately as not just a monster movie, but a movie about movies—with opening scenes set, and initial conflicts created, not by a giant gorilla but by the monster problems of casting, press manipulation, and box office.

The Marx Brothers in a still image from *The Cocoanuts* (1929), directed by Robert Florey and Joseph Santley, photographed by George Folsey.

These were subjects close to its creators. A journalist, pilot, and explorer, Cooper had fought in the Great War, where he met cinematographer Schoedsack—then working as a newsreel combat photographer, though he had learned his craft shooting knockabout comedies for Mack Sennett. They reconnected after the war, when Cooper suggested Schoedsack film an around-the-world expedition Cooper was covering, and that collaboration led them to develop a new kind of silent picture: the "natural drama," in which they would shape documentary footage of distant lands and people into a narrative adventure.

"There was what one distributor, Milestone Films, called the Age of Exploration," explains Leonard Maltin, "and audiences were well conditioned to documentary films—starting with *Nanook of the North*, and going on through with *With Byrd at the South Pole* and a whole bunch of such films, that depicted the exploits of both explorers and what we call adventurers."

The first two such features Cooper and Schoedsack directed, *Grass* (1925) and *Chang* (1927), were modest financial successes for Paramount, though their exhibitors insisted the films could have done bigger business if they had included a love story. Their next collaboration, an adaptation of A. E. W. Mason's *The Four Feathers* (1929), jettisoned the documentary angle altogether and did, in fact, include a love story, featuring a young starlet named Fay Wray. But Paramount's meddling frustrated Cooper, so when Pan Am Airways and Western Air Express offered him a desk job in New York in 1929, he took it. As far as he was concerned, he was done making movies.

Not that there was much work for him on the East Coast anyway. If *King Kong*'s opening scenes strike a false note, it's when Weston insists he can't provide an actress for so dangerous a job; in fact, no casting agent would turn away New York film work, for any reason. The Gotham-based studios, particularly Paramount's facility in Astoria, had seen a brief uptick in activity in the first flush of talkie production, as the studio—"just a stone's throw from Broadway," as its publicity materials noted—was an ideal base of production of two-reel comedies and musical programmers. *The Letter*, New York's first all-talking movie, was shot in Astoria in late 1928; over the following year, Paramount produced four dozen shorts and ten features there. Warners/Vitaphone, RKO, MGM, and Pathé also set up shop on the East Coast and increased productivity, also with an emphasis on musical and comedy shorts, which were filling the pre-feature spots previously taken by live entertainment in modern movie houses.

The features typically fell into two categories: musical extravaganzas, ideal for showing off the "all singing, all dancing, all talking" directive of the moment (typically in the form of "backstagers," in which sudden bursts of song and dance were not only narratively sound, but necessary as well); and film adaptations of stage successes, with the camera sitting in for the theatergoer. Stage stars like the Marx Brothers valued these gigs because they were "sunlighting," shooting the film version of their last hit, *The Cocoanuts*, in Astoria during the day, then heading into the city for that evening's performance of their new play, *Animal Crackers*.

But the boom was short-lived. Within the next year, Hollywood studios were wired for sound, and the creaky old studios back east—many of them dating back to the earliest days of the form, haphazardly retrofitted for talkie production—were showing their age. The studios had completed their raids of the Broadway and vaudeville boards, and of the New York literary scene, and had determined whom to poach.

And then, following the catastrophic events of the fall of 1929, they couldn't afford to maintain two production centers anyway.

———

There had been stock market troubles before: the Panic of 1873 (triggering a six-year depression), the 1920 bombing of Wall Street, a brief depression after World War I. But by the late 1920s, the stock market had become what historian Edward Robb Ellis dubbed "one vast permanent floating crap game," with at least one million participants, from titans of industry to grocers and chauffeurs. One hundred seventy-three million shares were traded on the floor of the New York Stock Exchange in 1920; by 1928, that number was up to 920 million. Secretary of Commerce Herbert Hoover predicted that "with the policies of the last eight years we shall soon, with the help of God, be in sight of the day when poverty will be banished from this nation"; he used that confidence (summarized in the campaign slogan "Four More Years of Prosperity") to crush New York governor Al Smith in the 1928 presidential election.

But late in the summer of 1929, a few Cassandras (like Andrew Mellon of the Federal Reserve, financial advisor Robert Babson, banker Paul Warburg, and *New York Times* financial editor Alexander Noyes) attempted to sound the alarm. They were dismissed, even chastised for causing temporary ruptures on the Street. But the market was climbing to untenable levels, and they knew it. That fall, it fell.

The reckoning finally came on October 24, 1929: "Black Thursday." Early in the day, brokers began trying to sell margin accounts, and found no buyers. By late morning, the floor was in panic mode, and up in the high-rises of the city, executive ticker tapes were running up to thirty minutes behind. A group of high-powered bankers met at noon, formed a plan to put money back onto the floor, and managed to rally the market, somewhat, that day and Friday. But on Monday, October 28, it fell again, and there was no saving it this time. "It was a country-wide collapse of open-market security values," reported the *Times*, "in which the declines established and the actual losses taken in dollars and cents were probably the most disastrous and far-reaching in the history of the Stock Exchange." On Tuesday the 29th, it all crashed.

The crash wiped out nine million savings accounts. Five thousand banks failed. Eighty-five thousand businesses went down. The national income was chopped in half. The city didn't register the effects right away; local bankers and businessmen insisted this was a temporary financial rupture, and Jimmy Walker was reelected two weeks later, handily defeating a plucky challenger named Fiorello La Guardia, in a race that never delved into questions of the economy.

Then people began losing their homes. Unemployment skyrocketed. The city budget's precarious dependence on property tax fell to pieces, and the city had to borrow on anticipated future revenues, racking up millions in debt.

Within a year of the crash, construction in the city was down 50 percent. Ambitious skyscrapers were scrapped or modified: a 110-story tower on 42nd Street was cancelled, the City Bankers Trust building at 20 Exchange Place was scaled down from 75 to 54 floors, and the hundred-story Metropolitan Life tower on Madison Avenue was stopped at its 33rd floor "base." But two skyscrapers, racing for the title of the tallest building in the world, had gone too far to come up short. And another, against all logic, would soon join them.

A crowd gathers outside the New York Stock Exchange after the crash.

**49**

Why were so many wealthy men so anxious to put their imprint on the Manhattan skyline? "It was part advertising, part proof of their company's success, and part economics in deriving the most office space from the narrow plot of land," surmises Neal Bascomb, in his riveting history *Higher*—but there was more to it than that. Perhaps the movies could explain it better. In the 1932 drama *Skyscraper Souls*, Warren William plays David Dwight, a wealthy industrialist and the mastermind of a hundred-story office building in Manhattan. Near the film's conclusion, he lays it all out. "I've achieved something big!" he exclaims. "A million men sweated to build it: mines, quarries, factories, forests. Men gave their *lives* to it! I hate to tell you how many men dropped off these girders while they were going up. But it was worth it—nothing's created without pain and suffering! A child is born, a cause is won, a building is built!"

It took the construction crew of the Chrysler Building at 42nd and Lexington Avenue ninety minutes to install the vertex that would top their structure, its point glistening at 1,046 feet above the city, quietly making it the tallest building in the world. They did it without fanfare, so as not to tip off their downtown rivals, who were putting up the Manhattan Company Building at 40 Wall Street. No one noticed it that day, because they added it so quickly and efficiently. And then no one noticed it the next day, because the stock market crashed.

By the end of 1930, all illusions were gone: The country had plunged into economic disaster. It hit the heartland before it reached New York City, but soon nightclubs were closing, Broadway houses were empty, and only pawnshops and churches were reporting an uptick in business. In 1931, ninety-five starvation deaths were reported. Groucho Marx, who lost everything in the Crash, quipped that he knew things were bad when "the pigeons started feeding the people in Central Park."

Government officials and wealthy industrialists attempted to project a spirit of willful optimism; after all, New Yorkers were tough, and they weren't going to go down without a fight. Financier John Jakob Raskob insisted, against the advice of several friends, that he was going forward with his ambitious plan for another skyscraper on the former site of the Waldorf-Astoria Hotel, Crash and Depression notwithstanding—despite genuine concerns that even once it was built, he wouldn't be able to fill it. None of that mattered to Raskob. He was building, he insisted, "a monument to the future." He wasn't going to be terrified by the present.

And another New Yorker was looking toward the future as well. In the May 30, 1931 issue of the *New Yorker*, Gilbert Seldes profiled Merian C. Cooper, the filmmaker turned airline executive. But that turn, Seldes reported, wasn't complete. "He is very likely to make another picture soon," Seldes wrote. "He has a place in mind, he has an idea, but he is a little secretive."

The place and idea came to Merian C. Cooper one afternoon in February 1930. He was leaving his office in Midtown when he saw an airplane buzzing the New York Life Insurance Building, then one of the tallest in Manhattan. "Without any conscious effort of thought," he recalled, "I immediately saw in my mind's eye a giant gorilla on top of the building."

This oft-told tale may have been simplified for easy promotional and historical consumption; he was also inspired by a book about the dragon lizards of Komodo, envisioning a story in which his giant ape battled the escaped Komodo dragons. He wrote up a treatment and pitched it to his old Paramount boss, Jesse L. Lasky, but Lasky thought

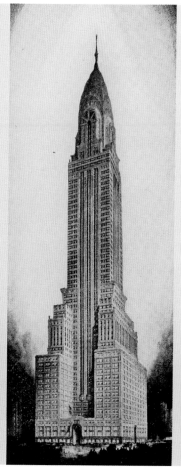

The evolving design of the
Chrysler Building.

it sounded too expensive. Cooper next went to David O. Selznick, who said he'd have trouble putting the financing together. However, Selznick reconnected with Cooper in 1931; the independent producer had taken a job as vice president in charge of production at the struggling RKO Radio Pictures. He wanted Cooper to come work for him in the production office, and promised him the opportunity to produce films of his own. Cooper's foray into the airplane business came to an end.

Cooper put Schoedsack on the payroll right away, hiring his old pal and collaborator to direct an adaptation of Richard Connell's 1930 short story "The Most Dangerous Game," for which RKO built an elaborate jungle set on its Culver City lot. Cooper then went to work reviewing the studio's current slate. One of the shakier prospects was an in-production feature called *Creation*, in which a luxury yacht crashes onto a forgotten island inhabited by dinosaurs. About twenty minutes of footage had been completed, but the budget was spiraling out of control and Selznick was contemplating cutting their losses. Cooper agreed; the footage, he felt, was lacking in drama and action.

But there was something in it he liked. The island's prehistoric creatures were eerily convincing, thanks to the stop-motion animation work of an effects artist named Willis O'Brien. Cooper savvily saw that putting the kibosh on *Creation* could also help his percolating gorilla movie: He could not only hire O'Brien but also repurpose the work he'd already done on *Creation*. What would have been an expense for his movie would instead be a loss on someone else's. Extending this philosophy of frugality, he realized that, since the studio had already built a jungle set for *The Most Dangerous Game*, he could recycle that for his movie as well. These creative solutions in hand, he pitched the project to his boss anew.

**RIGHT**
Empire State at about
3/4 completion.

**RIGHT**
Empire State at about
3/4 completion.

**FAR RIGHT**
The Empire State Building,
photographed May 18,
1931, less than one month
after its official opening.

**BELOW**
Empire State construction
workers guiding hoisting
cable.

Selznick liked it. The RKO board was less enthusiastic, concerned that even with Cooper's corner-cutting, the budget would be far too high for such a strange-sounding picture (and from a struggling studio). Selznick suggested a compromise: If Cooper put together a test presentation, showing the board exactly what he and O'Brien could do, maybe that would coax them into a green light.

Cooper swung into action. He hired the bestselling novelist Edgar Wallace to pen a screenplay, not only for his skill but also for his speed (he banged out his draft in about four days) and versatility, figuring he'd also have Wallace pen a tie-in novel. Sadly, barely a month after Wallace completed his script for what was then called *The Beast*, he died. Cooper passed the script to *The Most Dangerous Game* screenwriter James A. Creelman, who did another pass and retitled it *The Eighth Wonder*. But his services were required to rewrite *The Most Dangerous Game*, so Cooper hired Ruth Rose to do the final draft, female screenwriters not yet being the endangered species they would become in the industry.

Rose had worked with Cooper and Schoedsack on some of their "natural dramas," falling in love with (and eventually marrying) the latter; her draft streamlined the story, added several of its best-remembered lines, and revised the characters of Carl Denham and Jack Driscoll to more closely resemble Cooper and her husband (complete with their distaste for unnecessary romantic subplots). And she fine-tuned the picture's climax, in which, Cooper had decided, the giant primate, running amok in The City, should climb to the top of its tallest building. By then, in early 1932, there was a new holder of that title.

———

The rapid-fire construction of what had been dubbed the Empire State Building—scheduled to open in May 1931—required the place-ment of ten million bricks and sixty thousand tons of steel in roughly six months. Five hundred loads of materials and machinery came onto the job site every day—an average of one truck per minute per eight-hour day—handled by a crew of more than 3,400 men. Materials were distributed through the building by a miniature railway system. "So great is the concentration of work," reported the *Times* that summer of 1930, "that many of the men do not even descend to the street for their midday meals." Instead, temporary lunch counters were strategi-cally placed throughout the building-in-progress.

Amid this excitement, the openings of the Chrysler and Manhattan Company Buildings—within a day of each other in late May 1930—couldn't help but feel anticlimactic. A controversy had raged over which was truly the taller building, with H. Craig Severance and company insisting the Manhattan Company Building was taller because it had the highest inhabitable space (as opposed to the Chrysler's vertex). But it only mattered in the short term. The Chrysler Building was, as the *New York World* put it, "the king for a day," with all eyes already glancing toward the rising building at 34th and Fifth.

In the meantime, the city fell deeper into the dregs of the Depression. There were runs on banks, hunger riots, employment implosions (the financial, garment, and construction industries all took massive hits), and widespread evictions, leading thousands of citizens to take shelter in "Hoovervilles"—named after the wildly ineffective president—in Central Park and along the East and Hudson Rivers. Destitute men gathered around bonfires on the Bowery. Every morning, around two thousand people lined up in that mile-long street's breadlines. Harlem was hit especially hard; unemployed white workers were taking the menial jobs that they'd long ago cast off to African Americans, and as a result, the *New York Herald Tribune* estimated Harlem's unemployment rate was five times higher than that of the rest of the city.

"The sky or whatever it was seemed to be shutting the people down in the streets so that they crawled along them more dismally, dumbly, ignobly than ever," writer Edmund Wilson noted in a 1931 journal entry. "The life, the excitement had partly gone out of the city—the heart had been taken out of it."

On the morning of May 1, 1931, President Hoover powered up the Empire State Building from a remote button in the White House. The two hundred engraved invitations to its opening were the hottest ticket in town, but there was no question this building's beginning was also the end of an era. It was "a new record in building height which is likely to stand for many years," reported the *Times*. "Realty men agree that the office skyscrapers of today have approached the limit of economic practicability in height."

That was putting it mildly. The timing of the three giant new skyscrapers couldn't have been worse; they had offices to rent, at exactly the moment when businesses across the country were dying. Opening last,

Unemployed workers in front of a shack with Christmas tree, East 12th Street.

**53**

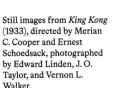

Still images from *King Kong* (1933), directed by Merian C. Cooper and Ernest Schoedsack, photographed by Edward Linden, J. O. Taylor, and Vernon L. Walker.

Empire got the worst of it; for years, it was barely a quarter full. Raskob told the cleaning crew to leave the lights on when they cleaned the building at night, to make it look less deserted. It earned a quirky but cruel nickname: "Empty State Building."

It would, however, have one major occupant soon enough.

In late May and early June of 1932, Cooper shot the live-action scenes for his test reel, using the jungle set for the still-shooting *Most Dangerous Game*—and some of its cast, most notably supporting player Robert Armstrong and ingénue Fay Wray (whom Cooper famously pitched with the promise "You will have the tallest, darkest leading man in Hollywood"). The *Game* set would be struck once that picture was complete, so Cooper seized on its availability and shot all of the jungle scenes he could, whether they were planned for the test reel or not, and in spite of the fact that the script was still in flux; the actors used the Creelman draft, or improvised. Cooper directed these scenes at night while Schoedsack used the sets and actors during the day, though the *Game* director became increasingly irritated by Cooper's takeover of his film.

O'Brien worked up the miniatures and effects (or, as they were called at the time, "technical scenes"), and contributed a completed sequence from the abandoned *Creation*. Cooper presented the test reel to the RKO board in late June, and though there were still some holdouts, enough of the execs were on board to approve the picture for an August shoot.

In the meantime, Schoedsack (whom Cooper had asked to co-direct), cinematographer Edwin Linden, and their second unit crew flew to New York City to pick up the handful of exteriors they'd need for the opening and closing sequences: establishing shots (night and morning) of the New York Harbor and Hoboken docks, fighter planes taking off and flying in formation to face Kong, and wide shots of the skyline, Empire State, and the street below. (Schoedsack also acquired blueprints of the mooring mast atop the building so that they could faithfully reproduce it, in miniature, back in California.)

This was, by this time, standard operating procedure for the many, many motion pictures set in New York: principal photography on interior and constructed backlot sets in California, supplemented by a handful of

rear-projection or establishing shots (or, for lower-budget pictures, scene-setting images from existing stock footage) of the city. The *Times* explained this process with the breathlessness of an exposé in a 1933 article about the making of Frank Borzage's *Man's Castle*, headlined "Artful Camera Illusions": "The camera crew which went to New York had no idea of the picture they were helping to make. They had definite instructions. They were to 'shoot' certain windows and obtain certain long 'shots.' . . . Less than 6,000 out of a total of 180,000 feet photographed for the picture were taken in New York City. It is this 6,000 feet, later cut and recut until only 450 feet remained, which created the illusion that the whole film was photographed in its authentic locale, New York City."

And there were more and more scribes in California who knew what they were writing about. Studios had attempted to lure New York literary types out to work in the movies during the twenties (Herman Mankiewicz famously telegraphed Ben Hecht, MILLIONS ARE TO BE GRABBED AROUND HERE AND YOUR ONLY COMPETITION IS IDIOTS STOP DON'T LET THIS GET AROUND), but most had demurred, preferring the jazzy New York scene. After losing their shirts in the Crash, and watching the Depression slow Broadway production to a crawl, they reconsidered and went to where the money was.

Yet New York was still in their hearts, so the version of the city they created in their scripts was outsized, tinged with nostalgia—faster and snappier than the hobbled metropolis it had become. "It was a feeling that started with the most common of emotions, homesickness," writes James Sanders in *Celluloid Skyline*, "for the way of life the writers had left behind, and for the city that had made it possible. It was burnished by the effect that distance so often has on an absent love—as flaws are forgotten and desire enhanced." Art directors, many of whom had cut their teeth on the Broadway stage, rebuilt the city through similarly rose-colored glasses, creating nightclubs and penthouses that sparkled like the Roaring Twenties, rather than the Bowery Breadline Thirties.

So the studios—themselves founded almost entirely by New Yorkers, and often still run from home offices back east—constructed cinematic versions of "New York" on their backlots: street facades with tenement buildings and shops, subway entrances, Automats, and theaters. "Even as a young person, we understood that there was a code or codification in images," recalls Martin Scorsese. "There were streets that we kind of

sensed were not real, but we accepted, we *wanted* them to be real." New York–style lampposts, fire hydrants, and stoops signified the city enough that, when coupled with wide shots of recognizable landmarks like Yankee Stadium and Times Square, viewers would go along. Never mind that the geography was often hilariously mismatched; the climactic car chase of Borzage's 1937 Spencer Tracy picture *Big City* begins at Jack Dempsey's restaurant at 8th Avenue and 50th Street, proceeds down Broadway and through Times Square . . . and then jumps 2,800 miles to the corner of Hollywood Boulevard and Cosmo Street in Los Angeles, where audiences presumably wouldn't notice that the world-famous Schwab's Pharmacy has somehow relocated to the heart of Gotham.

But that was about all the use the studios had for New York City production anymore, and by the time cameras rolled on *King Kong* in 1932, the fate of Paramount's Queens facility made its way into the dialogue. "I used to do extra work now and then over on Long Island," Ann tells director Denham. "The studio's closed now." The film's fruit stand, women's shelter exterior, and Automat scenes were played on sets constructed in Culver City, as well as the scenes atop the Empire State Building, which were shot at the end of principal photography in late October. O'Brien crafted the stop-motion animation sequences, and Linwood G. Dunn and William Ulm created the optical effects. (Dunn was at the beginning of a long career in the field; forty-plus years later, he would supervise the color saturation for the climactic scene of Martin Scorsese's *Taxi Driver*.)

RKO was already banging the drum. A small notice appeared in the *Los Angeles Times* on January 9, 1933, promising, "The imaginative standard-bearer may turn out to be this *King Kong*. . . . This sort of picture is one of the rarest sort to find its way to the screen." The *New York Times* followed suit a few days later: "Executives who have viewed the film in its present form are emphatic in their declaration that it will out-thrill any similar effort on the screen." *King Kong* opened on March 2 at Radio City Music Hall, the city's biggest movie theater—and across the street, in the second-biggest, the RKO Roxy. Over the first four days of its run, it sold out all ten shows per day.

In his review in *The Nation*, William Troy noted the irony of "an audience enjoying all the sensations of primitive terror and fascination within the scientifically air-cooled temple of baroque modernism that is Mr. Rockefeller's contribution to contemporary culture," but there

The Crash, the Depression, and *King Kong*

above
Leading lady Fay Wray
with co-director Merian C.
Cooper.

below
Still image from *42nd Street*
(1933), directed by Lloyd
Bacon, photographed by
Sol Polito.

was plenty of terror waiting for them out on Sixth Avenue. This was the bleakest moment of the Depression; Franklin Delano Roosevelt was inaugurated two days after *Kong* premiered, giving his "We have nothing to fear but fear itself" address, and the following Monday, he had to declare a nationwide financial holiday to prevent a run on the banks.

Some audiences couldn't leave their troubles at the door. The *New Yorker* reported "an elderly Jewish gentleman" responding to Kong's rampage through the city with a firm "Tchk, tchk, tchk, vorse den Hitler!" Or maybe it was less direct. The early years of the Depression had uncovered what social workers called the "new poor": first able-bodied manual laborers, then white-collar workers, who always considered themselves safely middle-class and now found themselves seemingly unemployable. "As the months passed, and particularly as people who had achieved a measure of economic security lost their jobs, the recession became a psychological event as well as a social and economic one," writes historian Mason B. Williams. "Many of those who lost their jobs struggled with these emotions as well as with the immediate challenges of getting bills paid and groceries purchased." It was a city paralyzed by fear and hopelessness; the giant gorilla, roaring from his perch atop the city, couldn't have been a more apt metaphor.

▬

*King Kong* would gross approximately $2 million in its initial theatrical run, playing successful engagements throughout 1933, a year of great upheaval in the city and the country. Citizens had finally turned on Mayor Walker, who first denied the charges of bribes, payoffs, and secret slush funds leveled by Samuel Seabury, a special investigator appointed by Governor Franklin Delano Roosevelt. But Walker would ultimately resign; John O'Brien, another Tammany man, took over the office in a 1932 special election. In the next regularly scheduled mayoral election the following year, O'Brien lost badly to the Republican candidate: Fiorello La Guardia, mounting a spectacular comeback from his overwhelming defeat four years earlier.

Gone too was the Prohibition of alcohol that Walker so openly flouted, repealed on December 5 with Utah's ratification of the Twenty-First Amendment, the thirty-sixth state to do so. (Organized crime in the city moved to gambling, protection, prostitution, and drugs to cover the loss of this cash cow.) When La Guardia—nicknamed "Little Flower," the translation of his Italian first name—was inaugurated in January 1934, the half-Jewish, half-Italian first-generation New Yorker faced a greater challenge than any of the ninety-eight mayors who preceded him. There was a $31 million budget deficit and $82 million in debt obligations. Infrastructure was crumbling. Tens of thousands of New Yorkers were homeless. The national jobless rate was at an all-time high of 23.6 percent, with half the men in the state of New York either unemployed or working only part-time, and more than a million-and-a-half New Yorkers on emergency relief. Desperate to support their families, many took to the streets to sell apples.

La Guardia swung into action, with a flurry of activity meant to put New Yorkers to work and get the city's financial house in order. Though a Republican, he believed in a program of unemployment insurance, progressive taxation, and government-funded work programs, and in those ideas, he found an unlikely but invaluable ally: Democratic President Roosevelt, with whom he worked in tandem throughout the decade to secure funding for city works projects and huge pieces of federal projects like the Civil Works Administration (CWA), Public Works Administration (PWA), and Works Progress Administration (WPA),

This illustration from the French periodical *L'Illustration* details how models, mattes, and monkey suits were used to create the climax of the film. (Everett Collection)

The Crash, the Depression, and *King Kong*

creating jobs for New Yorkers and building infrastructure and resources for the city.

Such tireless work helped La Guardia win the mayoral election of 1937 handily, though the WPA began to struggle shortly thereafter. A double-dip recession that year had called the effectiveness of the New Deal into question, and propelled a new class of anti-spending Republicans into Congress in the 1938 midterms. And some controversies swirled around the politics of the WPA's "Federal One" arts, music, and theater projects, which funded public art and education, as well as theatrical and music performances, around the city.

One struggling area of the New York art scene that saw no assistance from the WPA was film production. Moviegoing was at an all-time high during the Depression—the quarter-dollar cinema ticket was the most affordable form of entertainment, and 65 percent of the population attended the movies regularly—but there were few attempts to create more work on the East Coast. Newspapermen turned scribes Ben Hecht and Charles MacArthur, disillusioned with the Hollywood machine, made a much-publicized return to New York in 1934 to oversee the production of four features at the Astoria studios; the *Times*'s Andre Sennwald accurately described them as "the white hopes of the independent film," but their efforts were indifferently received (and, according to some reports, indifferently made).

The trouble with New York–based independent production, Sennwald wrote, was that East Coast facilities simply couldn't provide filmmakers with the proper sheen of professionalism. "One of the inescapable facts about the motion picture is that the technical costs of good production are too excessive to be shouldered with the enthusiasm which, in the theatre, is capable of producing such important groups as the Theatre Union or the Provincetown Players," he wrote. "Most of our finest cinema artists are shackled to the Hollywood system by the circumstance that they need a staggering sum of money with which to imprison their dreams on celluloid."

It would take decades for affordable equipment (and adjustments of audience expectation) to close that gap. In the meantime, production in New York was confined primarily to the niches. Industrials, "race" films, and exploitation pictures took advantage of a talent pool that would work cheap. The major newsreel companies were all headquartered in the city. Max Fleischer's Popeye cartoons were produced in Midtown, and Walt Disney recorded the music and effects tracks for the first Mickey Mouse cartoons in New York. There were short films by Broadway headliners, comedy stars on their way up (like Bob Hope, the Ritz Brothers, and Danny Kaye) and down (Buster Keaton and Fatty Arbuckle), and three-minute musical shorts produced for the Mills Novelty Company's "musical juke boxes"—an early precursor to the music video.

But high-profile production remained elusive. The new technology of television rattled around through the decade, but even after its public debut at the World's Fair of 1939—held in Queens's Flushing Meadows, funded partially by the WPA—it remained out of grasp. La Guardia had managed to stem the tide of Depression and put New Yorkers back to work, but even he couldn't convince Hollywood's power brokers to return to the city. "I can't see why the motion picture producers don't make pictures here," he said in October 1939. "The rents are high and the wages are high, but you would get your money's worth." He spent that fall working diligently on a plan to create a production center, a "Cinema City" counterpart to Radio City. "We are going to make motion pictures in New York," he stated confidently, studiously ignoring that the Biograph Studios in the Bronx, one of the oldest and most reliable in the city, had closed its doors just that September.

In a November editorial, *Times* film critic Bosley Crowther predicted skepticism from "the gentlemen of Hollywood," whom he felt "do not believe that an industry which has invested $112,000,000 in studios and other equipment in one section of the country should scrap those properties and move elsewhere at great expense." A few weeks later, MGM and Lowe's president Nicholas Schenck told La Guardia as much. (Talking to reporters after, Schenck claimed he was merely there to invite the mayor to the premiere of his new movie, "which he first inadvertently called *Going with the Wind*.")

La Guardia did his best to save face by announcing, according to a January 1940 update in the *Times*, "a number of independent motion picture producers had agreed to make movies in New York City," and that "several major producers had expressed general agreement with his plan to transfer the cinema industry from Hollywood to New York." But very little came of the public campaign. *King Kong* had pushed moviemaking forward technologically, but the real-world versions of Carl Denham and Ann Darrow would still have to go west to find work. When East Coast film production finally increased in the 1940s, it wasn't because of Cooper and Schoedsack's behind-the-camera portraiture, nor due to the mayor's crusade. It was because the world was at war.

# NOW SHOWING

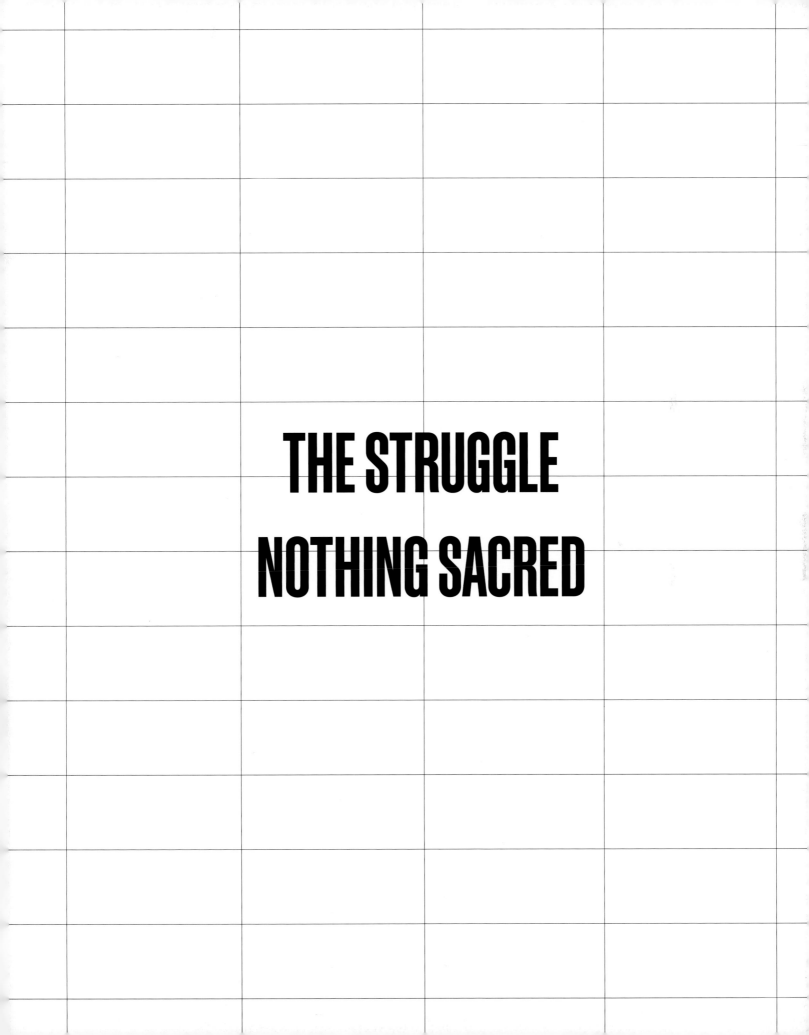

# THE STRUGGLE

# NOTHING SACRED

# THE STRUGGLE

## 1931
## Director: D. W. Griffith

Though a pioneer of cinema, David Wark Griffith never felt entirely comfortable in Hollywood. He started his career in New York and returned there in 1919 (to Mamaroneck, to be precise) in an ultimately unsuccessful attempt to set up an ongoing East Coast operation. He returned to Hollywood when it failed, but in a bit of circularity that wouldn't have been out of place in a Griffith film, he subsequently finished his career in New York.

The 1920s had not been kind to the filmmaker. His last genuine commercial success was *Orphans of the Storm* (1921), and he'd struggled to connect with audiences the rest of the decade, which made his transition to talkies even rougher than his peers'. His first talking picture was a dry, poorly received biopic of Abraham Lincoln; his second (and last) was another passion project, inspired by his own struggles with alcoholism, which he partially financed himself.

As storytelling, *The Struggle* is no great shakes—it's a draggily paced and often preachy kitchen-sink melodrama by way of temperance play. But viewed as something of a prototype for the neorealist movement, it's fascinating. This rare Depression-era picture genuinely depicts (and grapples with) the circumstances of poverty, and Griffith had initially planned to shoot in Astoria. But it was unavailable, so he ended up using Audio-Cinema's Bronx facility; perhaps due to the age of the facility or his limited budget, the apartment set of the struggling family is appropriately lived-in and run-down.

What's more, rather than constructing sets for his exteriors, Griffith shot on the streets and sidewalks of the Bronx near the studio. There's an electricity to these real locations—a jolt of grit that sets them apart from the patently artificial "New York streets" on the studio backlots—and a verisimilitude that boosts authenticity to the performances and scenarios, particularly when he shoots dialogue scenes on real street corners (an elevated subway train passes in the reflection of a saloon window).

Alas, audiences were not yet prepared for this level of realism, and the film opened and closed in December 1931. His experimentation was not applauded; it was not even understood. In her 1969 autobiography, his former leading lady Lillian Gish expressed pity that poor Mr. Griffith had been "forced to shoot some scenes outdoors."

**LEFT**
Still image from *The Struggle* (1931), directed by D. W. Griffith, photographed by Joseph Ruttenberg.

# NOTHING SACRED

## 1937
## Director: William A. Wellman

Still image from *Nothing Sacred* (1937), directed by William A. Wellman, photographed by W. Howard Greene.

Hyperbolic, scene-setting, on-screen text is one of the most durable devices of the New York movie, but the prologue for *Nothing Sacred*, penned by the great Ben Hecht, is an all-timer. "This is New York," it announces, "skyscraper champion of the world, where the Slickers and Know-It-Alls peddle gold bricks to each other, and where Truth, crushed to Earth, rises again more phony than a glass eye."

Right away, a tone of big-city cynicism is established, and the story that follows only bolsters that jaded perspective. Fredric March is Wallace Cook, star reporter for the *New York Morning Star*, whose increasingly lazy reporting ends up perpetrating the "hoax of the century," in which a simple bootblack, claiming to be a Sultan, insisted he was funding a massive complex with "27 halls of learning and culture" and "27 arenas of art." (The film was released during the ongoing construction and opening of Rockefeller Center.)

Busted down to the obits, city slicker Cook heads to the sticks. "I'll dig up a story that'll make this town swoon!" he vows, and travels to Warsaw, Vermont, to find Hazel Flagg (Carole Lombard), a brave girl with radium poisoning. It turns out she was misdiagnosed, but she's not going to let that stop her from taking a trip to New York City on the newspaper's dime. "Listen, we'll show you the town," he promises her. "We'll take you everywhere. You'll have more fun than if you lived a hundred years in this moth-eaten yep-and-nope village." She does indeed—DOOMED GIRL HAILED BELLE OF NEW YORK CITY blasts the *Morning Star*'s headline, before Hecht (a recovering newspaperman) dramatizes that old chestnut: yesterday's paper wrapping today's fresh fish.

But there's an undercurrent of quiet melancholy to the picture's screwball frivolity. When Hazel heads out to nightclubs and wrestling matches, her presence, and sad story, puts a damper on everyone's good time; announcements are made, moments of silence are observed, and tears are shed.

Conventional wisdom holds that 1930s audiences loved light entertainment, like the glamorous Fred Astaire–Ginger Rogers musicals and the wild Marx Brothers comedies, because they offered pure escape from their everyday woes—and, indeed, the films that dealt with the troubles of the moment (like Dudley Murphy's ... *One Third of a Nation* ...) were not rousing successes. But a few screwball comedies managed to incorporate elements of social commentary without breaking the spell; Gregory La Cava's *My Man Godfrey* concerns a daft socialite (also Lombard) whose life is changed by a "forgotten man" (William Powell) she finds in the New York City dump during a scavenger hunt, while La Cava's *Fifth Avenue Girl*, released three years later, is a kind of reverse *Godfrey* wherein a wealthy industrialist (Walter Connolly) meets a poor but engaging young woman (Ginger Rogers) in Central Park and invites her to come disrupt his Fifth Avenue home.

# 1940

# The War, the Boom, and *The Naked City*

# 1949

**PREVIOUS SPREAD**
Behind-the-scenes still
from *The Naked City*.

**ABOVE**
Mark Hellinger, as seen in
the trailer for *The Roaring
Twenties* (1939).

Mark Hellinger wasn't just a quintessential New Yorker; he had the kind of origin story that could've happened only in the city, of an eager young newspaperman who slowly turned into the kind of colorful character he'd made a career covering. A native of the Yorkville section of Manhattan, Hellinger got his first taste of the world of entertainment at the tender age of eighteen, working as a waiter in the Greenwich Village nightclub the Redhead; he began to pursue his interest in writing on the side, first penning copy for Lane Bryant department stores, then for the theatrical weekly *Zit's*. In 1923, he joined the staff of the *New York Daily News*, at the height of its dominance, as the city's first reporter/columnist assigned specifically to the Broadway beat. He was all of twenty years old.

Seven years later, following a salary dispute with the *News*, Hellinger moved to the *New York Daily Mirror*. His widely syndicated column evolved into a complete Sunday page, which would often include reporting, jokes, mini-reviews, sports predictions, political opinions, and the most popular feature: his short stories, "swift, sobby little tales" spun "out of the raw material to be found on the Broadway beat," according to a *Collier's* profile. At the height of its success, Hellinger's Sunday page claimed a readership of eighteen million people. And because the Broadway world was an insular (some might say incestuous) one, other columnists began writing about Hellinger, and legends grew around him too. He was the fastest one-finger typist in town, they said. He never took a free meal. He shaved twice a day and owned two hundred shirts, none of them white. He carried all his money in loose ten-dollar bills, which he distributed freely to maître d's and chorus girls for column tips. He called everybody "Baby."

That kind of success and notoriety would've been enough for a lot of men, but Hellinger got itchy easily. He started writing and producing for the New York stage—an easy transition, since he knew everybody there—and the boys out west bought the rights to make a couple of those plays into films. There were offers then, as early as 1933, to go out to Hollywood and work as a writer, but Hellinger held out; he wanted to wait for a better gig, a supervisory position where he wasn't just another scribe working for somebody else, and in 1937, he got it.

The Warner Bros. deal that finally tore Mark Hellinger away from the city he loved was, according to a *PM New York* profile, "a 'learn-the-business' kind of contract," in which he would start as a screenwriter and then move into producing. He hit a home run the first time out, with the 1939 Jimmy Cagney picture *The Roaring Twenties*; the "ace columnist and author" was prominently featured in its trailer, tapping away at his typewriter under the banner "I COVERED THE ROARING TWENTIES." Hellinger would reteam with its director, Raoul Walsh, to produce the Bogart hits *They Drive by Night* (1940) and *High Sierra* (1941). It seemed like nothing could slow him down.

———

The audience at Radio City Music Hall had barely settled in to their Sunday matinee of *Suspicion*, the new Alfred Hitchcock picture starring Cary Grant and Joan Fontaine, when the lights snapped on and a man strode to the center of the stage. Marilyn Tako was only five years old that December day, but her memory of what he said (relayed in a 2007 TV special) was clear as a bell: "'Pearl Harbor has been bombed by the Japanese. Everyone is to report to their units.' People were crying. I didn't know exactly what a war was or what was happening, but I knew that everyone was upset, so I was upset."

Radio listeners were receiving the news around the same time. WABC's broadcast of the New York Philharmonic started late because John Charles Daly's 2:30 p.m. newscast went over. "The attack also was made on all military and naval activities on the principal island of Oahu," the newsman told them. Those who were tuned in to WOR's broadcast of the Sunday game between the New York Giants and the Brooklyn Dodgers (then also the name of an NFL franchise) heard the flash at 2:25: "Japanese bombs have fallen on Hawaii and the Philippine Islands. Keep tuned to this station for further details. We now return you to the Polo Grounds." In his Fifth Avenue apartment, Mayor Fiorello La Guardia heard those first bulletins and raced to City Hall. He may have thought, along the way, about how he'd seen it coming.

The country's economic woes had mostly drowned it out, but the drumbeat of war had been beating steadily since Adolf Hitler was

Eleanor Roosevelt and Mayor La Guardia in the latter's office in Washington, as the First Lady is sworn in as Mayor La Guardia's assistant in the Office of Civilian Defense.

appointed chancellor of Germany in January 1933. Within a month, the Reichstag fire had provided Hitler with the cover to suspend civil liberties and begin his campaign of terror; he was burning books by May. Within days, one hundred thousand New Yorkers participated in an anti-Hitler March from Madison Square to the Bowery. In a moment of (to put it mildly) fiscal belt-tightening, the city pledged a million dollars to help Jews escape Germany—and many of them did, writers and artists and scientists, who found in the city safety and security but not necessarily opportunity. Jobs were scarce, even for intellectuals, especially for new immigrants who didn't speak English. Soon many of them were joining the breadlines.

Mayor La Guardia served, at the urging of Roosevelt himself, as the head of the Office of Civilian Defense, which FDR established in May 1941 to create protocols and coordination between state, federal, and local agencies to prepare for (and react to) attacks on their soil. This was a particular fear for La Guardia, and not unfounded: Hermann Goering spent years pushing for the Luftwaffe, Germany's aerial warfare branch, to bomb New York (and indeed, after the war, Allied forces discovered German maps targeting several points in Lower and Midtown Manhattan). At the opening of the Harlem Center for Active Service Men, he called for the involvement and support of the city. "Our country is faced with real danger at this very moment," he warned. "There is no telling what may happen in a few days in the Far East."

The date was November 29, 1941.

▬

By 4 p.m. on the afternoon of December 7, crowds of thousands were gathered in Times Square. The scrolling news ticker—the "zipper," as it was colloquially known—on the *New York Times* building was one of the few sources for immediate news; all the Sunday papers had gone to press Saturday night save for the *New York Enquirer*, which dominated the newsstands with its JAPS ATTACK PEARL HARBOR headlines. La Guardia went over the airwaves at WNYC at 5:15 p.m., warning listeners that "we are not out of the danger zone by any means," and that all New Yorkers should be on alert for "murder by surprise."

The city was on edge. The German enclave of Yorktown, where nationalist spirit ran so high that one notorious store sold swastika banners and distributed anti-Semitic literature, changed almost overnight. Signs in German were replaced, sauerkraut was taken off menus and replaced with "liberty cabbage," and the Garden Theatre on 86th Street hastily removed the title of its current German film offering from the marquee and its posters from the display.

Foreign imports weren't the only films that would take a hit. Now, La Guardia clearly had greater concerns than bringing film production back to New York, and the rationing and regulations—specifically of lumber, metal, and film stock—that helped solidify the shutdown of the East Coast studios during World War I would return.

Which is not to say films weren't being made in New York; in fact, the Astoria facility became the most prolific movie studio in the world. But the general public didn't see most of its product. On January 27, 1942, the US Army Signal Corps acquired the Astoria studio, and it became

Fiorello La Guardia speaks at a Madison Square D-Day rally, 1944.

70

The War, the Boom, and *The Naked City*

the Signal Corps Photographic Center (SCPC for short), dedicated solely to the production of training films.

And produce them it did. More than two thousand men and women, working three shifts throughout the day and night, filled the studio's stages, screening rooms, and editing suites. The output was staggering: 813 (mostly two-reel) films by year two, 1,016 by year three. The movies were what they were, instructional and educational films, primarily produced for Army personnel. But the sheer volume of the work, and the manpower required to make it, did something the impatient studios and ambitious independents had failed to do in the twenties and thirties: They built an East Coast filmmaking infrastructure, in which technicians, directors, actors, and writers could make a living and practice their craft. And when the war ended, a new medium was ready to welcome them.

■

The wartime years were lean ones in Gotham, with rations on metal, gas, rubber, food, and even light, with frequent air raid drills giving way to all-out lights-out orders that switched off the skyscrapers, the neons of Times Square, and the *Times* zipper. But employment was finally rising. New York didn't see the swift uptick in war production jobs other major metropolises were seeing—the kind of industrial manufacturing required for the military wasn't centered in the city, and its dockworkers took a hit when shipping was diverted to other ports thanks to the German U-boats that were sinking ships in the Lower New York Bay—but the ripple effects would make their way to the city soon enough.

Chief among them was the boost to the entertainment economy. Soldiers and sailors streamed through the city on twenty-four-hour leaves and weekend passes, and locals, slowly but surely, found themselves with disposable income and the desire for diversion. Suddenly restaurants, nightclubs, Broadway theaters, concerts, and museums were packed again. Servicemen made a beeline to the Stage Door Canteen, underneath the West 44th Street Theatre, where they could enjoy free sandwiches and soft drinks and the main attraction: dances and attention from starlets and hostesses. (In the 1945 film *The Clock*, Robert Walker is a soldier on a two-day pass in the city. It was shot entirely on the MGM lot and included a giant replica of Penn Station.)

And servicemen filled the movie theaters. They were routinely given free passes and, as the war crept on, were more likely to see movies reflecting the conflict in general or their experience in particular: Humphrey Bogart in (of course) *Casablanca,* or infiltrating a group of New York Nazis in *All Through The Night*; *Buck Privates, In the Navy*, and *Keep 'Em Flying*, the trio of service comedies from the hot new comedy team of Abbott and Costello; or Ronald Reagan in the screen version of Irving Berlin's hit *This Is the Army*. On their way through the lobby, civilians could show their support by buying war bonds, an investment encouraged by bumpers before and after the feature picture; some theaters gave away tickets as an incentive for war bond purchases.

The movies Mark Hellinger was making in this period, in his lucrative tenures at Warners and 20th Century Fox, weren't quite so connected to the war effort, but the writer/producer offered himself up for service as well. In 1944, he took a one-year hiatus from producing to cover the war for the Hearst newspapers, and when he returned to Hollywood, he

struck out on his own. Mark Hellinger Productions made a splashy debut with the first film adaptation of Ernest Hemingway's *The Killers* (1946); the company also produced the drama *Swell Guy* (1946), the Bogart/Barbara Stanwyk picture *The Two Mrs. Carrolls* (1947), and the prison movie *Brute Force* (1947). The latter teamed Hellinger, for the first time, with the Harlem- and Bronx-raised director Jules Dassin.

■

Roosevelt won an unprecedented fourth term in the fall of 1944, promising to win the war, continue the recovery from the Depression, and lead the postwar world. But he would not see it through; FDR died on April 12, 1945, of a massive brain hemorrhage. The news hit New York that afternoon, prompting an outpouring of grief that culminated in a remarkable tribute: At 3:55 on the afternoon of April 14, as a light rain fell and Roosevelt's funeral service began in Washington D.C., the city of New York came to a standstill for its fallen president. Planes were grounded. Trolley cars and subway trains stopped in their tracks; traffic officers halted all cars. Telephone service was paused. The Stock Exchange, department stores, and most offices were closed for the day. The movie theaters didn't open until six p.m.

Two weeks later, another death was met mostly with indifference. The headline came across the zipper around five p.m. on May 1: HITLER IS DEAD. A beat cop's first reaction, quoted by the *Times*, captured the mood of the city: "So, the bum's dead, eh? What difference does it make now?"

On the morning of May 8, the city (and the country, and the world) got the news they'd been waiting for: President Truman announced the surrender of Germany to Allied forces. There was celebration in the streets; crowds packed into Times Square, where, when night fell, the neon lights were finally switched back on. Those crowds gathered again (two million of them, at their height) at the end of the summer. On August 6, Truman issued a statement announcing the bombing of Hiroshima—the result of the Manhattan Project, named for its research and development on the campus of Columbia University—and one week later, the bulletin finally rolled across the zipper: "OFFICIAL— TRUMAN ANNOUNCES JAPANESE SURRENDER." A twenty-minute roar filled Times Square. It was a celebration, but also a commemoration, of the nearly nine hundred thousand New Yorkers who had served and the more than sixteen thousand who had died in the conflict.

Everything was ending, or beginning again. The Stage Door Canteen served its last serviceman on November 1; later that month, after a war-long hiatus, the Macy's Thanksgiving Day Parade returned. La Guardia had announced, less than a month after Roosevelt's death, that he would not seek a fourth term as mayor. By the time he left the office, La Guardia was a Republican in name only, and unsurprisingly, his successor was a Democrat: King County district attorney William O'Dwyer, who more than doubled the votes of Republican Jonah J. Goldstein (himself barely besting Newbold Morris, candidate for the "No Deal" party). La Guardia would live less than two years after leaving his post, succumbing to pancreatic cancer on September 20, 1947. "A city of which he was as much a part as any of its public buildings awoke to find the little firebrand dead," went the *Times* obituary. "Its people had laughed with him and at him, they had been entertained by his antics and they had been sobered by his warnings, and they found it difficult to believe that the voice he had raised on their behalf in the legislative halls of city and nation, on street corners and over the radio, was stilled forever."

President Franklin Delano
Roosevelt.

The war years may have been bad for New York narrative filmmaking, but the postwar years were a boom—and the spark that lit the fuse was an incident from the war itself. The storefront at 309 East 92nd Street in Yorktown wasn't just a distribution point for Nazi paraphernalia in the days before Pearl Harbor; its back room was a headquarters for would-be Nazi spies. As the war wound to a conclusion, a 20th Century Fox producer named Louis de Rochemont pitched the brass on a dramatization of how the FBI took the spy ring out. But de Rochemont's background wasn't in genre movies; he had produced *March of Time* newsreels and suggested an approach that fused drama and documentary. They would shoot on the real locations where the story occurred: Columbus Circle, the Federal Courthouse, and Bowling Green, though *not* the storefront itself, which their story transformed into a town house (and the film's shooting location was around the block on 93rd).

The kind of newsreels de Rochemont produced didn't just offer practical experience for the producer, who was used to making the kind of on-the-fly adjustments for weather and crowds that scared mainstream moviemakers off of shooting in the city. They had also conditioned the audience to their aesthetics. In those pre-television days, the newsreels were how people "saw" the news, and during the war, they were hungry for it. Images that jettisoned the slick polish of studio production felt less like manufactured drama and more like real life.

*The House on 92nd Street* (1945) capitalized on that perception. "This story is adapted from cases in the espionage files of the Federal Bureau of Investigation," went the opening on-screen text. "The scenes in this picture were photographed in the localities of the incidents depicted, Washington, New York, and their vicinities; wherever possible, in the actual place the original incident occurred." The picture even went so far as to include actual surveillance films, taken by the FBI during the investigation, of activities outside the German embassy.

The film itself is a mixed bag, a rather dry celebration of federal authorities, mixing chases and shoot-outs with flag-waving and back-patting. But it established a style for many of the New York movies that followed: a step-by-step law enforcement procedural, shot on location, emphasizing verisimilitude over melodrama. Filmmakers embraced this new leeway, perhaps also due to the war; Leonard Maltin theorizes, "It may be that so many filmmakers had gone off to war overseas, and they rejected the artifice of making everything in Hollywood on a back lot or a soundstage."

In light of *The House on 92nd Street*'s success, its studio, 20th Century Fox, would continue to invest in the expense of New York units, grabbing establishing scenes for Elia Kazan's *Gentleman's Agreement* and footage of the Macy's Thanksgiving Day Parade for *Miracle on 34th Street* (both 1947). And *House*'s director, Henry Hathaway, so enjoyed the process that he shot portions of several subsequent films in the city, including *The Dark Corner* (1946), *Kiss of Death* (1947; see sidebar on page 86), and *Fourteen Hours* (1951). For *Kiss of Death*, he even included an opening text that mirrored *The House on 92nd Street*'s: "All scenes in this motion picture, both exterior and interior, were photographed in the State of New York on the actual locale associated with the story." The last three words are telling. *Story.* The hunger for documentary realism was now extending into the realm of fiction.

Those films—along with Abraham Polonsky's *Force of Evil* (1948; see sidebar on page 86), Robert Siodmak's *Cry of the City* (1948), and Anthony Mann's *Side Street* (1950)—came to be regarded as classic

**OPPOSITE**
Crowds pack into Times
Square to celebrate the
Japanese surrender on
V-J Day, 1945.

*films noir*, where the grittiness of the authentic urban location under-scored the darkness at the center of their stories, and often of their protagonists. That perception fell in line with a subtle undertone in Hollywood-made New York films of the era. In 1940, the *New York World-Telegram* published an investigation of "the sly Hollywood campaign to disparage New York on screen," which it attributed, not unconvincingly, to Mayor La Guardia's attempts to "muscle in on the film-production racket." With dialogue like "That dump is too big and noisy for me" and "Maine isn't far enough away from this miserable, dirty, foul city," as well as images of congestion, cruelty, and disorder, the contrast between the dream city of the 1930s movies and the dirty metropolis of the 1940s couldn't have been more striking.

"The city has never been so uncomfortable, so crowded, so tense," E. B. White wrote, in his seminal 1949 essay turned book *Here Is New York*. "Money has been plentiful and New York has responded." The sense of community was disappearing, he noted: "Police now ride in radio prowl cars instead of gumshoeing around the block swinging their sticks." Neighborhoods no longer felt like villages, enclaves that connected their inhabitants to the old country; now it was a scrambled, international city, symbolized by the United Nations Headquarters, which began construction in 1947. "What we are going to build will be vital to the continuance of the largest and most dynamic city in the world," La Guardia announced. He was right. And there was a cost.

Whatever was happening to the city, it was happening to the entire country. America, writes the historian John Strausbaugh, "was suffering a kind of collective post-traumatic stress disorder. Following a decade of the Depression, the war had ripped an entire generation of Americans from family farms, small towns, and big-city neighborhoods and hurled them out to the wide world where they witnessed and often participated in the most shocking savagery and depravity humanity can dis-play. . . . Now that the war was over, millions of GI Joes and Rosie the Riveters were expected—and often wanted—to settle back into 'normal' lives." But what was normal now?

▬

The precise story of how Mark Hellinger came to produce *The Naked City* varies. In *The Mark Hellinger Story: A Biography of Broadway and Hollywood*, Jim Bishop contends that the producer pitched the film's innovative concept to its original writer, Malvin Wald: "Hellinger said that he wanted to do a film about his hometown, New York. He had seen a lot of films about the metropolis, but all of them showed the flashing signs of Times Square and then faded to an interior set which could have been anywhere. He wanted this film to reek of authenticity. It had to be so New Yorkish that it would look like a documentary."

But this was a glowing official biography, written by a friend and published four years after the death of its subject. Contemporary accounts, including Wald's, posit the more likely scenario that Wald pitched the idea of shooting a full feature on the streets of New York to Hellinger, who responded as any sensible producer would: How on earth do we do *that*? But Wald had answers. He was one of a generation of filmmakers who learned their craft working in the armed forces' motion picture units during the war (many of them studied under masters like John Ford, Howard Hawks, and John Huston, who'd volunteered for service). Wald, who'd written documentary scripts for the First Motion Picture Unit of the Army Air Force, told Hellinger that the run-and-gun techniques they'd used overseas could work to make a quick, dirty, and immediate feature picture.

There was another movement, happening on the other side of the war, that came into play as well. Italy's biggest studio, Cinecittà, was controlled by Mussolini, which rendered it unavailable to anyone to his left (in other words, most filmmakers); after the war, Allied bombings had rendered it unusable to anyone at all. Out of necessity, Italian directors like Roberto Rossellini and Vittorio De Sica shot out in the city streets, crafting masterpieces like *Bicycle Thieves, Germany Year Zero, Shoeshine*, and *Rome: Open City* that captured the struggles of postwar Europe, free of the fakery of the studio. Those films weren't just popular in Italy; urban, intellectual American audiences were drawn to their directness and power. Before the war, explained *noir* cinematographer John Alton, "Hollywood was addicted to the candied . . . type of sweet unreal photography." But the films audiences saw during the war "were starkly real. Explosions rocked the camera, but they also rocked the

world, and with it rocked Hollywood out of its old-fashioned ideas about photography."

According to Wald, Hellinger was skeptical, so the writer begged him to go to Jules Dassin for a second opinion. Hellinger's *Brute Force* director not only felt this could be "an important breakthrough film," but also wanted to helm it himself, "and was prepared to face any challenges arising from the unique semi-documentary approach." Satisfied, Hellinger sent the writer to New York for a week of intensive research. While there, he shadowed cops, hung out in forensic labs, and sat in on lineups. "The point I made, as a result of my research," he recalled, "was that crimes are solved by hard work, by many people, not just a Sherlock Holmes."

The screenwriter dug through police files, eventually landing on the case that would form the basis of his screenplay: the unsolved 1923 death of model Dorothy "Dot" King, the "Broadway Butterfly" whose rich suitors were suspected but never charged with her murder. He turned that case into the story of Jean Dexter, an ex-model whose murder is investigated by NYPD homicide detective Lt. Dan Muldoon (Barry Fitzgerald), a wise old Irish cop, and his younger partner, Jimmy Halloran (Don Taylor). Their expansive investigation takes them all over Manhattan and the inner boroughs, with plenty of opportunities to pause for local color along the way.

Wald titled his screenplay *Homicide*, which didn't exactly set Hellinger's heart racing. So Wald brought him *The Naked City*, a recently published collection by Arthur Fellig, better known by the *nom de plume* Weegee.

**PREVIOUS SPREAD**
Behind-the-scenes still from *The Naked City*.

**LEFT**
Still image from *The House on 92nd Street* (1945). Directed by Henry Hathaway, photographed by Norbert Brodine.

**CLOCKWISE FROM TOP RIGHT**
Still images from *Force of Evil* (1948), directed by Abraham Polonsky, photographed by George Barnes; *The Dark Corner* (1946), directed by Henry Hathaway, photographed by Joseph MacDonald; *Kiss of Death* (1947), directed by Henry Hathaway, photographed by Norbert Brodine; *The Tattooed Stranger* (1950), directed by Edward Montagne, photographed by William O. Steiner.

The War, the Boom, and *The Naked City*

**ABOVE**
Jules Dassin (on ladder),
producer Mark Hellinger
(in white tie), and crew,
shooting *The Naked City*
under the Williamsburg
Bridge.

**BELOW**
Lt. Dan Muldoon (Barry
Fitzgerald) arrives at the
scene of the crime; a
behind-the-scenes still on
the apartment location.

Described by an editor as "a rather portly, cigar-smoking, irregularly shaven man who has seen and recorded a great deal of ugliness and disaster," Weegee was a freelance newspaper photographer who prowled the streets of Gotham by night, tuned in to a police radio, showing up at crime scenes and capturing stark, hard images of the city's underbelly. "To me a photograph is a page from life," he wrote in the book, "and that being the case, it must be real."

Hellinger paid Weegee $3,500 for the rights to his title, plus some money on the side to take photos during the shoot. But his title wasn't all the film borrowed; cinematographer William Daniels worked in a similarly crisp and simplified style, using new, faster film stocks, sharper lenses, and more efficient lighting kits. True to his word, Dassin came on as director; he would later deem Hellinger "a nice man, and a producer who took care of the director." Dassin brought in his go-to writer, Albert Maltz (later one of the Hollywood Ten) to brush up the dialogue, and got to work casting, filling many of the roles with New York stage and radio actors unknown to moviegoers (and thus more credible as cops, suspects, and witnesses). The exception to the rule was star Fitzgerald, a recent Oscar winner for *Going My Way*, whom Wald said resisted the role of Muldoon "because he didn't see himself as a detective"—in other words, a Bogart, running and shooting. The screenwriter assured the actor that the detectives he'd observed didn't run and shoot, but sat, thought, strategized, and interrogated. Fitzgerald took the role (and ended up running and shooting, too).

The production team got to work on the backbreaking logistics of the shoot, which would ultimately take the unit to 107 locations over 84 days in the summer of 1947, schlepping from the Upper West to the Lower East Side, from Times Square to Bellevue, and from Brooklyn Heights to Astoria, Queens. (As critic Amy Taubin noted, "They weren't shooting icons—they weren't shooting the Statue of Liberty, they weren't shooting the Empire State Building.") The New York office of Universal Pictures, which co-produced the film with Hellinger's company, sent him grim missives of their progress: "An application is required for each location and must be filed at least twenty-four hours in advance. Quite often we shoot three or four locations a day. . . . It is obvious that this form of application has been improvised for picture taking, because of a lack of any definite procedure for this type of work. This permit certainly creates a hardship for us." Hellinger reached out to Mayor O'Dwyer, whom he'd known since his newspaper days, to help

**ABOVE**
Jules Dassin directs.

**RIGHT**
A crowd gathers to watch
Jules Dassin shoot a scene
from *The Naked City*.

The War, the Boom, and *The Naked City*

smooth out the process. As a result, the Department of Commerce and Public Events established, per the *Times*, a small division to "advise cinema producers on the processing of applications within the police, the Borough Presidents, and other departments for location permits in filmmaking."

Paperwork was one problem; crowds were another. New Yorkers treated the shoot like the big deal it was, following actors from hotels to locations, creating massive crowds that slowed down the production and created headaches for Dassin and his crew. "We had all kinds of tricks to hide the camera," Dassin recalled, including portable news-stands and floral delivery trucks. "But my favorite . . . I had one guy with me for most of the film, he was great, I would put him up on the ladder about 200 yards away, with an American flag. And he would be ranting about the society in our time, and people would rush to him, and I'd get my shot."

"The police weren't as cooperative as they could've been," Wald explained, "so the film ran into great difficulties." Crowds got out of control; a July 1947 set report from the *New York World-Telegram* captures a shoot disrupted by the students from nearby P.S. 160, out for their lunch break, who "swarmed over the sound mixer, shouted mocking answers to Mr. Taylor's spoken lines, wormed through the

1940–1949

crowd, and clambered up Bill Daniels's platform." City officials held up production until the big shots from Hollywood greased their palms, an actor was briefly pulled away from a scene by riding off on the wrong train, and Dassin stepped on a rusty nail in an empty lot and was rushed to the hospital. The film went about a half-million dollars over budget.

But Hellinger was pleased with the results—so much so, he decided to narrate the picture himself, using his hard-boiled newspaperman's tones to not only explain the police procedures and bridge the gaps in the narrative, but also to break the fourth wall and articulate the importance of the film itself. Over an opening helicopter shot of the city—without the customary title card or credits—Hellinger tells his audience, "I may as well tell you frankly that it's a bit different from most films you've ever seen. . . . The actors played out their roles on the streets, in the apartment houses, in the skyscrapers of New York itself. And along with them, a great many thousand New Yorkers played out their roles also."

Hellinger oversaw the film's editing through the fall of 1947, fine-tuning his narration, fretting over the music, and finally turning his attention to other projects—including the Edward G. Robinson vehicle *Harness Ball*, described by *Pic* magazine as "another Manhattan coppers yarn," presumably replicating *Naked City*'s location shooting. And then that December, about a week after the first *Naked City* preview, Hellinger died of heart failure (coronary thrombosis, to be precise). He was only forty-four.

▬

Universal chose to keep Hellinger's narration intact—though there was some discussion and concern that it would give the unintended effect of the producer haunting the film from beyond—and when it was released in March 1948, the press hung on the twin hooks of the location photography and Hellinger's passing. "Mark Hellinger's Own Epitaph: A Film That Stars the City He Loved," went the headline in *Mirror* magazine, explaining that "the star of the film is New York, Hellinger's birthplace, the city of which he wrote long and lovingly."

The reviews were enthusiastic. "These on-the-spot touches, together with the film's thrilling melodrama, superb direction and unequaled performances, raise *Naked City* to rank as one of the finest pictures of the year," raved *Cue*. *Look* called it "a thrilling whodunit," while *Variety* granted, "New York has been made a pretty exciting place by Mark Hellinger. *Naked City* can stand as a fitting memorial." But the *Herald Tribune*'s Howard Barnes contended that beyond the "authority of on the spot photography in New York," the picture was "little more than a carefully contrived screen thriller," and the *Times*'s Bosley Crowther concurred: "Thanks to the actuality filming of much of its action in New York . . . the seams in a none-too-good whodunit are rather cleverly concealed."

But New York audiences were electrified, after years of fakery, by the sight of their familiar haunts on-screen. "If you're in the theater on Second Avenue and Sixth Street," explains Martin Scorsese, "if you saw something come up like *Naked City*, you could hear the kids saying, 'Hey, that's where I live. Hey, look, that's my neighborhood.' People were cheering."

And few contemporary critics seemed to grasp the subtlety of what Dassin and his screenwriters were attempting to convey about the city and its inhabitants. The locations weren't just showing off the city; they were conveying its vastness. "In studio-built New York," James

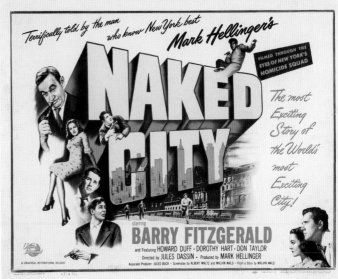

**OPPOSITE ABOVE**
Dassin and his crew squeeze in to a tenement staircase.

**OPPOSITE BELOW**
Shooting the climax on the Williamsburg Bridge.

**ABOVE**
The opening shot of *The Naked City*. Directed by Jules Dassin, photographed by William Daniels.

**BELOW**
The original theatrical poster.

**THIS SPREAD**
The city as captured in *The Naked City* (1948). Directed by Jules Dassin, photographed by William Daniels.

Sanders writes in *Celluloid Skyline*, "detectives often walked the streets, searched for clues, and, with any luck, apprehended their suspect. But given the confines of the backlot 'city,' their enterprise usually had a circumscribed, anecdotal quality, a search not through a whole metropolis but a few streets or, at most, a single district. And the pursuit of the criminal—even if enlivened by a chase—could only turn so many corners before returning to familiar ground."

But there was no familiar ground in *The Naked City*, which spends much of its running time on the shoe-leather work of chasing down leads and asking questions, to the taunting of everyone from the criminal ("Try and find me. This is a great, big beautiful city. Just try and find me") to the film's own producer/narrator ("How are your feet holding out, Hal?"). The shot-on-location procedural imitators that would follow *The Naked City*, like *The Sleeping City*, *The Killer That Stalked New York*, and *The Tattooed Stranger* (all 1950), took this notion and ran with it; the latter includes the line "I'll find that grass if I have to graze every vacant lot in the Bronx," followed by a montage cutting between a city map and a series of park locations, where a police detective and a pretty young botanist shake their heads and toss notebooks.

More importantly, *The Naked City* takes pains not just to capture authentic locations and the closely observed particulars of police work, but also the rhythms of everyday life for average, working-class, commuting New Yorkers, a far cry from the kind of sparkling penthouse dwellers that New York movies typically had at their centers. This focus is apparent from the film's opening scenes, snapshots of city life that include thought-bubble voice-overs of night workers and early risers, the last of whom is Fitzgerald's Lt. Muldoon. "We show life in the city, people go about their work," explains Wald on the film's audio commentary, and "not until later will we find out he's a detective."

Thus, the groundwork is laid from the beginning for the film's famous closing line: "There are eight million stories in the naked city. This . . . has been one of them." (The picture's final image is less remembered, but perhaps just as potent: a newspaper, with this murder above the fold, swept up and thrown into the trash.) Historian Dana Polan flags a side effect of these pointedly fly-on-the-wall pictures: "a kind of voyeurism," in which we're allowed to observe, without guilt, the lives—and often, the crimes—of those eight million inhabitants. A number of these films go so far as to frame those observations through windows, as though we're literal passersby peeking in on those we share sidewalk and subway space with. *The Naked City*'s opening murder is viewed through an open window; so is the crime at the center of *The Window* (shot at the Pathé studios and on the Upper East Side not long after *The Naked City*, in November 1947), witnessed by a tenement kid sleeping on a fire escape during a summer heat wave, and the assault witnessed by the protagonist of Stanley Kubrick's *Killer's Kiss* (1955). Windows play prominent roles in Alfred Hitchcock's *Rope* (1948) and, of course, *Rear Window* (1954), both set in New York but shot on California sets. And Hitch's most famous through-the-window shot, the opening of *Psycho*, was preceded by the skyline pan to an apartment window that opens Billy Wilder's Gotham-set *The Lost Weekend* (1945). (Its closing lines play like an early draft for those of *The Naked City*, released three years later: "Out there in that great big concrete jungle, I wonder how many others there are like me?")

To some extent, this democratizing of the city's inhabitants is all of a piece with the politics of the film's creative team—two writers and a director who would all be blacklisted by the House Un-American Activities Committee scare of the following decade—and indeed Dassin later said of the final cut, "There's much that was taken out, because I

87

87 87

87

The War, the Boom, and *The Naked City*

**RIGHT AND BELOW**
New York City in the 1940s, as captured in *The Naked City* (1948). Directed by Jules Dassin, photographed by William Daniels.

**OPPOSITE**
*Killer's Kiss* director Stanley Kubrick, on the set of *The Naked City* as a still photographer.

shot it to contrast, in the big city, the different lives in big cities. . . . Many cuts were made, and I'm sure to this day that they were not made with Mark's knowledge. I think they got their hands on it after Mark died."

On the other hand, it's a film very much on the side of law, order, and authority. As Sanders notes, *The Naked City* assures its audience (in the city and elsewhere) that while the crime is sensational, it "goes out of its way to explain to you that this is really an anomaly," and that "the life of New York is an orderly one. The city, as a whole, is a healthy place." This stands in stark contrast to later city portraiture, like *The French Connection* and *Death Wish*, where the city has gone topsy-turvy, and the police are essentially toothless and powerless.

But the city was mostly crime-free and still community-minded when *The Naked City* was made—the last gasp of an era based on street life and neighborhoods, before the ubiquity of television pulled its inhabitants indoors. "They caught it in the last moments," according to Sanders. The reach of *The Naked City* would extend into the new medium, where the picture's wise old cop/green, bookish rookie dynamic would become a standby, and where the police procedural boilerplate would eventually extend to *Dragnet*, *Miami Vice*, *NYPD Blue*, and *Law & Order*.

Not to mention *Naked City*, which would itself become a popular television series in the late fifties and early sixties, providing early opportunities for an array of New York actors. Burgeoning Gotham filmmakers also found it useful, though not in terms of conventional employment. Recalling his film school days, Martin Scorsese said, "When we would go to shoot those films in '63 to '65, New York was not at all used to films being shot on the street. So the easiest answer we gave to everybody asking, 'What are you shooting, what are you doing' was *Naked City*, because that was the only thing people were used to. They'd say, 'Absolutely,' and leave us alone."

By that time, however, film crews on the streets of New York were no longer an anomaly. Mark Hellinger took a risk, surmounting considerable logistical and financial barriers to better capture the city he loved. And thanks to that risk, filmmaking in the city would never be the same.

# NOW SHOWING

ON THE TOWN

THE LOST WEEKEND

KISS OF DEATH

FORCE OF EVIL

# ON THE TOWN

## 1942

## Director:
## Stanley Donen, Gene Kelly

When the crew of sailors come tumbling out of their ship onto the docks of New York at 6 a.m. sharp—a timestamp that rolls across the bottom of the screen in the font and style of the Times Square news ticker—and the focal trio (Gene Kelly, Frank Sinatra, and Jules Munshin) announces their plan to see everything in "New York, New York / a wonderful town," the dock foreman is skeptical. "What can happen to ya in one day?" he asks. "What do you think you're gonna do?"

The short answer: everything, in the breakneck five-minute "New York, New York" montage, which takes them from the Statue of Liberty to Grant's Tomb, and several points in between. ("Gee, it's 9:30 already!" notes Sinatra's Chip, at the number's conclusion.) Directors Donen and Kelly originally proposed, in essence, the movie musical version of *The Naked City*: shooting the entire picture on location. "The studio executives all said, 'Singing and dancing, coming down the streets of New York? You're crazy,'" Kelly said. The "New York, New York" number was the compromise: the studio granted the filmmakers nine days of location shooting for that opening sequence, with the understanding that they'd shoot the rest on the Metro lot with the customary assistance of rear projections, second unit establishing shots, and stock footage.

If anything, the tricky shoot that May of 1949 confirmed the execs' worst fears about production in Gotham. The entire sequence is set outdoors, so of course several days were lost to bad weather. Crowds gawked at the stars wherever they went. And Sinatra, the bobby-soxer's favorite, was particularly hard to shoot—especially when word leaked that he was on the streets of Little Italy, where the company was mobbed by screaming fans.

But the city couldn't have asked for a better advertisement: it's a romantic toe-tapper, to be sure, but also an NYC travelogue, with stops at the Museum of Natural History, Chinatown, Rockefeller Center, Coney Island, and (of course) the top of the Empire State Building. For moviegoers at the time, *On the Town* was revelatory. "It wasn't a matte shot, it wasn't a fake Brooklyn Bridge," film critic Amy Taubin recalled of the opening sequence. "And if you lived in New York all your life, you could tell the difference."

Still image from *On the Town* (1949), directed by Gene Kelly and Stanley Donen, photographed by Harold Rosson.

92

# THE LOST WEEKEND

## 1945

## Director: Billy Wilder

"Mr. Burnham, there are a lot of bars on Third Avenue," growls the barkeep. "Do me a favor, will ya? Get out of here and buy it somewhere else." But Don Burnham doesn't—he's a creature of habit, in thrall to his alcoholism, and Billy Wilder's *The Lost Weekend* is in many ways the template for the contemporary addiction drama, jettisoning the hysterics of *Reefer Madness* and *Cocaine Fiends* for sensitive character exploration and psychological insight.

The story of an alcoholic writer (Ray Milland) and his long weekend of bottoming out while left alone in the city, *The Lost Weekend*, true to the period, shoots most of its New York interiors—particularly his Upper East Side apartment and P.J. Clarke's Saloon, Don's preferred drinking spot—on California soundstages. But Wilder was able to persuade his bosses at Paramount to permit a brief location shoot, where scenes were taken at the drying-out ward of Bellevue Hospital (a first), as well as several, mostly wordless exterior street scenes.

The most memorable finds Don dragging his typewriter up Third Avenue, from 55th to 110th Street, desperately searching for a pawnshop so that he can hawk the machine for drinking money. But the shutters are all shut—it's Yom Kippur. Wilder shot the sequence in a single Sunday, when the shops were indeed closed, and chose not to close off the street; instead, in the style of *The Crowd* and *The Jazz Singer*, he stashed the cameras in bakery trucks and atop buildings, to mix his actor into the natural location. The choice works, giving the sequence a harrowing realism that grounds the melodrama surrounding it.

**OPPOSITE**
Still image from *The Lost Weekend* (1945). Directed by Billy Wilder, photographed by John F. Seitz.

# KISS OF DEATH

## 1947

### Director: Henry Hathaway

# FORCE OF EVIL

## 1949

### Director: Abraham Polonsky

20th Century Fox's original theatrical trailer for Henry Hathaway's *Kiss of Death* was constructed not as the then-standard assemblage of dialogue, images, cast introductions, and unattributed praise. Instead, it was presented as "A Report from Walter Winchell," the world-famous, hard-boiled New York gossip columnist, seen at a desk behind a microphone as though delivering one of his radio reports. The subject? He'd just come from a screening room on the Fox lot, where he'd viewed "a picture of my town, New York, and my time, now." He praised *Kiss of Death* by comparing it to two other shot-on-location films: "Like *Boomerang* and *The House on 92nd Street*, it has *authenticity* written all over it."

The fact that Fox made that idea the explicit hook of the picture's advertising campaign goes a long way toward explaining why these two classic *films noir* were shot, the former in full and the latter in part, in New York City. Because on reflection, neither of them necessarily *had* to take place there; though steeped in the worlds of organized crime, they could've easily been set in Los Angeles, or set in New York but shot on the backlot.

But these tightly wound thrillers, which get darker and sweatier the deeper their protagonists go into the muck, benefit from their low-to-the-ground look; even the simplest of neighborhood walk-and-talk scenes have an indefinable but undeniable naturalism. In comparison, the "New York street" scenes of something like *East Side, West Side* or *Gentleman's Agreement* feel patently false.

And that authenticity rang especially true for locals. "I love *Force of Evil* so much; it made such a major impact on my life," said Martin Scorsese. "And one of the key things in watching that film was identifying the places where it was shot, those five or six location scenes. How can I put it? When we saw those locations, that made it ours, it happened to *us*, and it happened right here. And there's the proof."

**OPPOSITE RIGHT**
Still image from *Force of Evil* (1948). Directed by Abraham Polonsky, photographed by George Barnes.

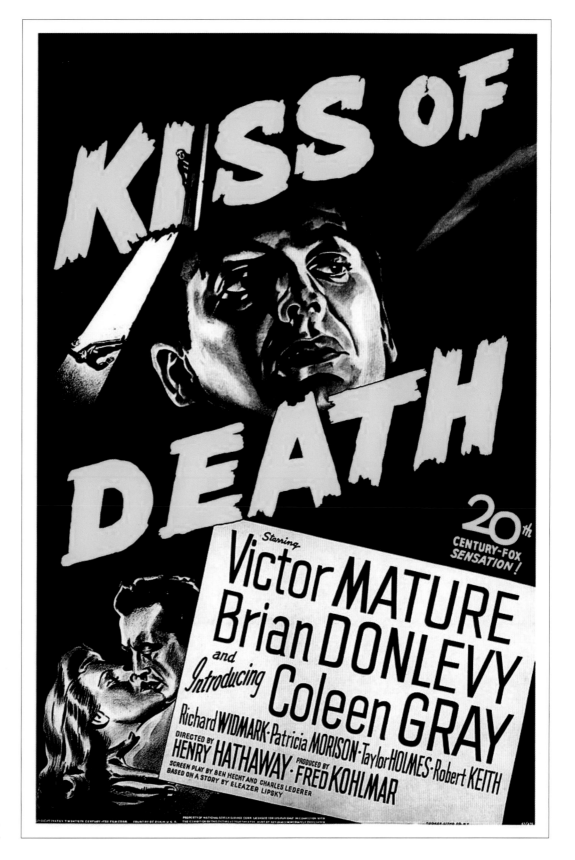

# 1950

# The Power Brokers and *Sweet Smell of Success*

# 1959

When Mark Hellinger died on December 21, 1947—less than three months before *The Naked City*'s release in March 1948—one of the most heartfelt tributes came from the typewriter of Walter Winchell. According to Hellinger's biographer, Jim Bishop, the two columnists had spent many a long night together in the 1920s and 1930s, moving between the city's restaurants, bars, and nightclubs. "No matter where they set out to go," Bishop wrote, "Hellinger, with black slick hair, snap-brim hat and twinkling blue eyes, always murmured, 'Adventure, Walter, adventure.'" When Hellinger died, Winchell wrote, "People who hardly knew him liked him, and those who knew him loved him." He ended the column as his departed friend would have: "Adventure, Mark. Adventure."

By 1937, Hellinger was hired by Jack Warner and continued the adventure in Hollywood, but Winchell stayed behind and became one of the most influential figures in entertainment, journalism, and New York City. By 1940, Winchell's column in the *New York Daily Mirror*—a heady mixture of gossip, conjecture, endorsements, and smears—was running in a thousand papers across the country. His Sunday-night radio program, in which he rattled off his best items in a breakneck monologue (beginning, traditionally, with the greeting "Good evening, Mr. and Mrs. North America, and all the ships at sea, let's go to press"), was a regular entry in the top ten of the Hooper ratings, and occasionally topped it, outperforming the entertainment programs of Jack Benny, Fred Allen, and Bob Hope. Between the two mediums, Winchell reached something like fifty million Americans every week.

"People like to tell tales," Winchell liked to say. "If I take the rap for what they tell me, they'll tell a lot." A vaudeville failure uniquely suited to his particular era—defined by Prohibition, the rise of the tabloid, and a general, slangy cynicism—Winchell was notorious for his lasting grudges, his toxic relationships with stringers and press agents, and his monstrous ego. Fellow newspaperman Ernest Cuneo, in a moment of exasperation, once asked Winchell, "Don't you ever talk about anything but yourself?"

"Name a more interesting subject," Winchell snapped back.

Before long, Winchell began popping up in the very plays and movies he was reporting on. He co-starred in two short films, *The Bard of Broadway* (1930) and *Beauty on Broadway* (1933); he also appeared in *Broadway Through a Keyhole* (1933), a thinly veiled account of Al Jolson's marriage to Ruby Keeler, for which Winchell received a "story by" credit. He would make brief appearances, always as himself and usually uncredited (no credit was necessary), in films like *Daisy Kenyon* (1947) and *A Face in the Crowd* (1957), and he narrated *Beau James* (1957), a biopic with Bob Hope as Mayor Jimmy Walker. His name is dropped in Budd Schulberg's notorious Hollywood novel *What Makes Sammy Run?* and in George Cukor's 1954 New York comedy *It Should Happen to You*, in which would-be celebrity Gladys Glover (Judy Holliday) announces, "Look! Walter Winchell! That makes the seventh big name I've seen tonight!"

Winchell's most noteworthy film appearance, however, did not mention his name. But everyone knew it was him.

■

"I knew Winchell," Ernest Lehman recalled in 2010. "I was the guy on the other end of the phone. He'd go into a thirty-minute tirade about Ed Sullivan, then he'd say, 'Who is this?'" Lehman worked for Irving Hoffman, one of the many press agents and writers who circled Winchell, trying desperately to get their clients' names into his column. "We were a frightened bunch of people," he explained. "We knew [our] lives were in the hands of a small group of columnists. It's hard to believe the columns were that important in those days." Hoffman—who also penned a *Hollywood Reporter* column under the title "Tales of Hoffman"—was one of the few press agents (or people in general) whom Winchell considered a friend, and was thus one of the best in the business, boasting an enviable client list and a busy office equipped with an adjoining bedroom.

But Lehman was not cut out for this racket. A Long Island kid with a nervous stomach, he went into PR because it offered more financial security than fiction writing, his first love. He first fused these worlds in

1946 when he began a novel titled *You Scratch My Back . . .*; he never finished it, but out of its wreckage came two short stories, "Hunsecker Against the World" and "It's the Little Things That Count," both of which featured a Winchell-esque entertainment columnist named Harvey Hunsecker. A couple of years later, unable to continue bending himself into the moral pretzels required by the job, he quit and went back to writing about Hunsecker—this time through the lens of Sidney Wallace, a low-level press agent trying desperately to stay in Hunsecker's good graces. He saw this as his chance to atone for "having done some pretty terrible things as a press agent." Lehman showed the resultant novella, *Sweet Smell of Success*, to Hoffman. His old boss hit the roof.

"Ernie," he asked, "how can you do this to me? Everybody's going to think I'm Sidney! Everybody's going to think Hunsecker is Winchell! You have things in here that only somebody who's close to Winchell would know!" Lehman changed a few of the more obvious details, but to no avail: Hoffman didn't talk to Lehman for more than a year.

Luckily, others did. The novella was first published in *Cosmopolitan* under the title "Tell Me About It Tomorrow"; the reason, Lehman wrote in 1981, was that "the then editor, Herbert R. Mayes, didn't want the word 'smell' in his magazine." But the piece was well received, and Winchell reportedly tried saving face by ringing up rival Louis Sobel and cackling, "Hey, did you read that story Ernie wrote about you?!"

But nobody was buying that—and nobody wanted to wander into Winchell's sights by adapting it into a movie. In 1949, Lehman's Los Angeles agent, George Willner, wrote to his client with an update: "The big problem still remains the resemblance to Winchell. . . . I went to all places where I thought it would do some good, but I still ran up against the same problem. . . . I'll say one thing for your story—it set this town on its ear, and Ernest Lehman's name is probably as well-known out here now as any of the top ten or twelve writers." Lehman didn't have to be told twice. He headed to Hollywood.

In 1950, that exodus remained a necessity—there was still no mainstream filmmaking presence in New York City to speak of. But as the decade continued, the introduction of new technological advances made the possibility of location shooting cheaper and more feasible. A key innovation was Eastman Kodak's 1954 introduction of Double-X film stock, which boasted a light sensitivity more than twice that of its predecessors, thus enabling the shooting of nighttime exteriors. Later in the decade, 16mm cameras were introduced with synchronous sound capabilities; the lightweight camera eliminated the need for extra audio recording equipment, allowing directors and cinematographers to shoot fast and dirty, on the streets rather than the backlot.

But studios looked down at the grainier 16mm image, and it was mostly consigned to underground filmmakers like Kenneth Anger and Robert Frank, and documentarians like the Maysles brothers and D. A. Pennebaker—people who make movies "about real things, people, places," as explained by Pete Sheppard (Jack Lemmon), who's making a documentary about Central Park in *It Should Happen to You*.

The majors mostly continued to use the city as they had for decades. Three years after shooting the *Naked City*–style police procedural *The Wrong Man* (1956) entirely on location in Queens and Manhattan side streets, Alfred Hitchcock returned to the city to shoot a few scenes for *North by Northwest* (1959), but confined himself to the likes of Grand Central Terminal and the Plaza Hotel. Billy Wilder drew more than a

**ABOVE**
Ernest Lehman.

**OPPOSITE**
Billy Wilder directs Marilyn Monroe during the New York street shooting of the subway grate scene in *The Seven Year Itch*.

thousand onlookers on the night of September 15, 1954, shooting a scene for *The Seven Year Itch* in which Marilyn Monroe's skirt is blown up by a subway passing under the grating at 52nd Street and Lexington Avenue. The image made newspapers around the world, but that's not the version of the scene in the movie; it was reshot on the Fox lot, ostensibly due to issues with the location sound, though some whispered the entire New York shoot was a (successful) publicity stunt.

Yet, slowly but surely, as the decade continued, filmmakers with less on the line began taking more chances. Anthony Mann's *Side Street* (1950) points to an evolution; it begins as a crime picture in the *Naked City* mold, with an opening voice-over that mirrors *City*'s iconic closer, and a story that similarly concerns the media-friendly murder of a pretty girl. But then Mann veers, digging into the psychology of a semi-criminal who gets in over his head, adopting a dynamic, energetic approach that showcases the everyday beauty of the city without seeming a mere travelogue. Andrew L. Stone's lurid thriller *Cry Terror!* (1958) has a dose of the newfangled forensic investigation stuff from the late-forties procedurals, but its highlight is a riveting race-against-the-clock sequence in which a desperate mother (Inger Stevens) attempts to navigate the city's streets, highways, and traffic to save her daughter and husband. (It also features, in its subway-track climax, one of the first instances of that NYC standby, the "Death by Third Rail.") Henry Hathaway returned to the city to shoot exteriors for *Fourteen Hours* (1951), a would-be ledge jumper and workaday cop story most notable as a proto–*Dog Day Afternoon*; much attention is paid to the gathering crowd, gawking and jeering and kibitzing, as well as the impatient crowd-control cops, the story-chasing reporters and photographers, and the scrum of cabbies, sending out for coffee and sandwiches while betting on when the poor sap will jump.

For his low-budget, independently-produced sophomore effort *Killer's Kiss* (1955), New York photographer Stanley Kubrick used borrowed equipment and shot guerilla-style in Penn Station and Times Square, capturing the latter's increasingly gaudy world of neon lights and flashy storefronts (as well as the reactions of confused passersby to the events staged for Kubrick's frequently hidden cameras). And Martin Ritt's *Edge of the City* (1957) dived into the neighborhoods, showcasing the lesser-seen and lived-in but no less impressive environs of Harlem and the Upper West Side.

In its narrative of longshoremen and union rot, *Edge* was reminiscent of another fifties groundbreaker. Shot over the bitter-cold winter of 1953–54, Elia Kazan's *On the Waterfront* (1954) used real dock locations and real dockworkers—under the watchful eye of real union reps—to tell its story of corruption and danger in the harbors on either side of the Hudson.

The directors who chose to shoot in New York found themselves working under primitive conditions, at least compared to their facilities out west. Directors like Kazan, Hitchcock, and newcomer Sidney Lumet had to make due with studio facilities like the 54th Street Fox Studio, Brooklyn's Flatbush Vitagraph Studios, and the Bronx's Gold Medal Studio, all of which dated back to the silent era. Luckily, the network of technicians that had spent the past decade making government and industrial films in Astoria were amenable to improvisation—as were the city's new generation of storytellers. The rival technology of television was still based primarily out of New York City, and the medium's "golden age" live dramas, dialogue- and character-driven teleplays for anthology series like *Studio One* and *Playhouse 90*, became a training ground for gifted scripters (Paddy Chayefsky, Rod Serling, Horton

**ABOVE**
Robert Moses at work.

**BELOW**
Mayor Robert F. Wagner speaks at the dedication of the New York Library for the Blind, 1953.

The Power Brokers and *Sweet Smell of Success*

Foote, Gore Vidal), directors (Lumet, John Frankenheimer, Arthur Penn), editors (Dede Allen, Ralph Rosenblum), and other craftspeople, who would help change the way movies were made and viewed in the years to come. They would also lay the groundwork for a "New York style" of filmmaking and storytelling, which moved at a faster pace, focused on working-class and/or ethnic characters, and eschewed Hollywood glamour.

Television even ended up creating a pipeline for feature-film material. Lumet's feature debut, *12 Angry Men* (1957), was first performed on *Studio One* (directed by Franklin J. Schaffner), and Reginald Rose's teleplay was virtually untouched for the film adaptation. It was nominated for three Oscars; two years earlier, the film version of the *Philco Television Playhouse* production *Marty* (which retained both director Delbert Mann and screenwriter Chayefsky) would win the Oscar for Best Picture, Best Screenplay, and Best Actor Ernest Borgnine, as well as the Palme d'Or at the Cannes Film Festival. Aside from ensuring Mann and Chayefsky's bankability—they would reteam for the New York–set (and shot) *The Bachelor Party* (1957) and *Middle of the Night* (1959)—*Marty*'s critical reception and copious awards made it a commercial success for distributor United Artists and the picture's independent producers, actor Burt Lancaster and business partner Harold Hecht.

New production entities like Hecht-Lancaster Productions weren't as tied to the traditional mode of backlot-centered production; if they'd have to pay to rent stages and sets anyway, the logic went, why not spend that money to just shoot on location? The studio system itself was beginning to collapse, thanks to the increasing popularity and ubiquity of television, as well as the 1948 Supreme Court *United States v. Paramount Pictures* decision, which effectively broke up the monopolies by which the seven major studios had dominated film production and distribution. Contract stars were now free agents, and several took the opportunity not only to negotiate higher fees for their services, but also to establish production companies to generate their own projects.

Among the majors, United Artists proved the most amenable to making deals with these star-driven entities; that had been the company's M.O. since it was established in 1919 by Charles Chaplin, D. W. Griffith, Mary Pickford, and Douglas Fairbanks. And they made a deal with Hecht-Lancaster, which gave them hits in not only *Marty* but also the Lancaster vehicles *The Crimson Pirate* (1952), *Vera Cruz* (1954), and *Trapeze* (1956). The latter paired him with Tony Curtis; both that film and *Vera Cruz* were co-produced by writer turned producer James Hill, who was brought on as a partner to the newly christened Hecht-Hill-Lancaster productions in early 1957. Among their ambitious slate of projects for that year was a feature-film adaptation of Ernest Lehman's *Sweet Smell of Success*.

▬

The decade had barely begun when Mayor William O'Dwyer's reign came to an unceremonious end, done in by a bookmaking and police corruption scandal that would end with the resignation of more than one hundred cops, police commissioner William O'Brien, two of his top aides, and Mayor O'Dwyer himself. Into the office, via the laws of succession, stepped City Council president Vincent Impellitteri, a former legal secretary who had ascended to the council presidency, as legend had it, simply by virtue of his indisputably Italian name and Manhattan residency, a bit of ethnic and geographic balance deemed necessary by Democratic Party bosses for the ticket of Brooklyn Irish

Mayor Robert Wagner (right) joined by Robert Moses (left) and Federal Housing Authority representative Frank Meistrell (center) on a housing project tour.

mayor O'Dwyer and Jewish Brooklyn comptroller Lazarus Joseph. He was spectacularly ill-suited for the job and was roundly defeated in the 1953 primary by Robert F. Wagner. Jr.

But neither O'Dwyer nor Impellitteri nor Wagner really ran the city in this period anyway. The man who held the most power was Robert Moses, who had entered government in 1924, ascended it within a decade, and seized it with a death grip. He would hold multiple supervisory positions at once (he once held twelve simultaneously), his reach extending from parks to bridges to tunnels to highways to public housing, controlling large pockets of city, state, and federal funds. "Other men hold real power—shaping power, executive authority—for four years, or eight, or twelve," wrote Robert Caro in his essential biography *The Power Broker.* "Robert Moses held shaping power over the New York metropolitan region for forty-four years." In that time, he treated the city like "a giant *Monopoly* board, shuffling properties as casually as if [he] were playing cards."

Moses built a kingdom for himself within the city, funded by millions of dollars in nickel-and-dime toll fees generated by taxpayer-funded bridges and tunnels, which he could spend at his sole discretion and with no oversight, creating a system wherein, according to historian Craig Steven Wilder, "the voice of the people hardly mattered at all." He surrounded himself with sycophants, and treated politicians and reporters to lavish parties and private events, racking up favors that he could cash in later. O'Dwyer and Impellitteri basically gave him free rein; Moses took such advantage of the latter's lack of experience that Comptroller Lazarus would write in his diary, "There's no important act Impellitteri takes or does that he doesn't consult Mr. Moses."

Wagner, elected on a platform of reform, attempted to diminish Moses's influence and was steamrolled immediately. Moses wasn't letting go without a fight; as Caro explains, he had by then perfected a system to "replace graft with benefits that could be derived with legality from a public works project." But he wasn't just interested in lining his pockets. "More and more," Caro wrote, "the criterion by which Moses selected which city-shaping public works would be built came to be not the needs of the city's people, but the increment of power a project could give him. Increasingly, the projects became not ends but means—the means of obtaining more and more power."

He wasn't the only one. His system of "honest graft" was exploited by other men in power, or seeking it—borough presidents, bankers, Tammany men, union leaders—to trade various "fees" and "commissions" for opportunities and influence. Moses manipulated it all, from the twenties through the fifties, until he finally met his match in the person of Governor Nelson Rockefeller. "His arrogance was easy, charming, gracious—the arrogance of a man handed at birth the power to enforce his will," Caro wrote. "It was not the hard, glittering, abrasive arrogance of a Robert Moses who had had to fight and scheme for that power. But it was equally unshatterable."

Ernest Lehman had done quite well in Hollywood, penning the screenplays to *Executive Suite* and *Sabrina* (both 1954), as well as *Somebody Up There Likes Me* and *The King and I* (both 1956). But a *Sweet Smell* film remained a non-starter. "The film could only have been made by Hecht-Hill-Lancaster," Lehman said in 2000. "They dug it. Nobody else did, really." The company only felt ready to make the deal in 1955 because times were changing. The era of Joseph McCarthy, whom Winchell had enthusiastically supported, was finally coming to an

**ABOVE**
Still images from *A Face in the Crowd* (1957, directed by Elia Kazan, photographed by Gayne Rescher) and *It Should Happen to You* (1954, directed by George Cukor, photographed by Charles Lang).

**BELOW**
Clifford Odets in his 1930s glory days.

The Power Brokers and *Sweet Smell of Success*

**ABOVE**
Tony Curtis in a still image
from *Sweet Smell of Success*
(1957), directed by
Alexander Mackendrick,
photographed by James
Wong Howe.

**OPPOSITE**
Burt Lancaster in a still
image from *Sweet Smell of
Success* (1957), directed by
Alexander Mackendrick,
photographed by James
Wong Howe.

end, and the blacklist he'd prompted was dying off; Lancaster, who some accused of communist sympathies, and who had hired the blacklisted Waldo Salt to co-write *The Crimson Pirate*, undoubtedly took some pleasure in its demise.

And Winchell himself was in decline. His conservatism, and its accordant mean-spiritedness, was beginning to alienate readers and listeners. He was accused of giving a softball interview to mob boss (and friend) Frank Costello, and was embroiled in an embarrassingly petty smear campaign against entertainer Josephine Baker. The *New York Post* (then a liberal publication) ran a series of articles attacking Winchell, who predictably responded by calling managing editor James Wechsler a communist. (To get out of a million-dollar libel suit, Winchell's paper and network forced him to publicly retract his statements.)

More importantly, Winchell lost his audience. His high-strung presence translated poorly to television, where he first simulcast his radio show and then, in 1956, attempted a variety program that was cancelled after thirteen weeks due to low ratings. (To add insult to injury, his old newspaper rival Ed Sullivan flourished in the same format.) By this time, his syndication had dwindled from one thousand newspapers to a mere hundred and fifty. (The *Mirror* itself would close up shop in 1963.)

This curdling of a one-man institution no doubt contributed to an atmosphere in which the cynical but ultimately upbeat newspaper pictures of the thirties and forties gave way to a more acidic view of media. Billy Wilder began the decade with his poison-penned *Ace in the Hole* (1951); the time wasn't quite right for it, and audiences stayed away. But in 1954, Cukor's *It Should Happen to You* focused on the vapidity of celebrity and the gullibility of a media that makes people famous simply,

it seems, for the act of being famous. ("What's the good of trying to be above the crowd all the time?" its heroine finally decides, subtly invoking King Vidor's classic. "What's the matter with just being part of the crowd?") In 1956, José Ferrer directed and starred in *The Great Man*, a kind of proto–*Sweet Smell* crossed with *Citizen Kane*, as a gossip reporter tasked with assembling a radio obit for a fabulously famous yet universally despised media figure (it was said to be inspired by TV and radio host Arthur Godfrey). While *Sweet Smell* was in production, Kazan and *On the Waterfront* writer Budd Schulberg were reteaming for *A Face in the Crowd*, in which a seemingly rube-ish, folksy Southerner (Andy Griffith) becomes a deceitful demagogue with the help of the radio microphone and television camera. And in 1959, Daniel Mann's *The Last Angry Man* featured headline-hunting print and TV journalists distorting the story of a noble neighborhood doctor.

All were set, at least in part, in New York City. This made sense; feature filmmaking aside, it was still the country's media capital. And it was also, even more than Washington D.C., still where the most influential figures wielded and abused their power.

━━━

Burt Lancaster was cut from a similar cloth. "Burt had the power," Ernest Lehman recalled. "He was the famous movie star. He had the money, which Harold Hecht didn't have. . . . In terms of publicity and power, Burt Lancaster had both. Hecht was the nobody." Lancaster wielded that power at every opportunity, frequently cutting his partner with his words, once even picking Hecht up and threatening to toss him from a window.

Considering Lancaster's psychological similarity to J. J. Hunsecker, and the eerie parallels between his relationship with Hecht and Hunsecker's

with Sidney, it's somewhat surprising to learn that he initially planned only to produce *Sweet Smell of Success*. In that position, he heard the desperate pleas of his old co-star Tony Curtis to play Sidney (rechristened Sidney Falco for the film). "All they had to tell me was New York," he later said. "I was raised in that city. I should have done it as the first movie I ever made." That desperation is palpable in the performance, sweetened by the subtext of the younger actor—widely dismissed, at that point, as a lightweight, pretty-boy teen idol—working up a sweat to earn the respect of his more esteemed co-star. "The best thing in it is Curtis," proclaims filmmaker Oliver Stone, who crafted a similar central relationship for his 1987 film, *Wall Street*. "Curtis is unbelievable. It's a hallmark for him."

Lehman's original agreement with Hecht-Hill-Lancaster was to both write the screenplay adaptation and (for the first time) direct. For Hunsecker, Lehman wanted to cast Orson Welles, but the more Lancaster worked with Lehman on the script, the more he started to imagine himself in the role. "He was fascinated," Lehman recalled. "It's like he smelled that this could be a different role for him—no hero." Lancaster expanded on that idea in the original press notes: "The hero is a man with a mission, with everything else expendable, and he can be extremely exasperating. But take the villain—he has awareness of the human values, plays off them, takes advantage of them, laughs at them. The villain, in other words, toys with life. He has, for all his evil, a sense of humor. He's got the color. He's got my vote."

Once Lancaster had cast that vote, the project changed. "That's when it became a bigger venture," Lehman explained, "more important." Lancaster's name above the title meant United Artists was willing to finance it; it also meant they weren't going to hand it over to a first-time director, if Hecht-Hill-Lancaster ever intended to in the first place. "They [promised him] that, I feel, because they wanted to get the property," Curtis surmised in 2000. Hill confirmed, but with a caveat: "Ernie didn't want to work on the picture at all, or he wouldn't have made a demand like that." Lehman had a nervous stomach and didn't handle stress well. Orson Welles might have eaten him alive on a set; Lancaster definitely would.

To replace the writer who'd literally lived the story, the producers took an unexpected turn. Alexander Mackendrick was best known for *The Ladykillers* and *The Man in the White Suit*, snappy British comedies from the legendary Ealing Studios; "What would he know about the world of Broadway and New York nightlife?" asked the screenwriter, not unreasonably. But Hecht-Hill-Lancaster had Mackendrick under contract, and the project he'd been working on was falling apart, so that was that. And he was up for the challenge. "I'd always hankered to make a melodrama," he wrote, "and felt this was a chance to get out of a reputation for cute British comedies."

His concerns were with the screenplay: "Just about every scene consisted of an exchange between two people sitting at a table in a restaurant, at a bar, or in a nightclub. The screenplay was nothing but talk." He anticipated working with Lehman to open up the script, but Lehman's stomach had other ideas. After a bout of blackout-level pain

sent him to the hospital, the screenwriter's doctors ordered him to Hawaii to recover. That was September 1956; shooting was scheduled to begin in New York that December. Mackendrick needed a script doctor, and fast.

Luckily for him, Clifford Odets was also under contract with Hecht-Hill-Lancaster. Once the most celebrated progressive playwright in the country, with five plays running simultaneously in 1935 (when he was all of twenty-nine years old), Odets had left New York shortly thereafter for Hollywood money, and had wrestled with guilt over "selling out" ever since. But he still had his chops, and he was an ideal replacement for Lehman, thanks to his knowledge of the Broadway scene—and personal interactions with Winchell himself, whom he described in his diaries as "a vortex of vanity." He was hired for three weeks of polishing and handed in his rewrite on October 9.

But that wasn't the end of his work; over the fall, he pounded out eleven more drafts of the script and more revisions of individual scenes. "What Clifford did," Mackendrick wrote, "was to dismantle the structure of every single sequence in order to rebuild situations and relationships into scenes that had much greater tension and dramatic energy." He tightened and squeezed Lehman's tale, set over a couple of locomotive-paced New York days and nights, in which the desperate Sidney

**LEFT**
Original theatrical poster for *Sweet Smell of Success*.

**OPPOSITE**
Still images from *Sweet Smell of Success* (1957), directed by Alexander Mackendrick, photographed by James Wong Howe.

reluctantly helps J. J. break up a romance between a jazz musician and J. J.'s sister Susan (Susan Harrison). Sidney envisions a strengthening of the bond between the two men—and, of course, more items in J. J.'s column—but the scheme backfires, on both of them.

Odets's work pointedly dodges the idealism of the leftist, proletarian drama on which he made his name. In an earlier, arguably simpler era, Sidney Falco would've been a conventionally heroic protagonist whose well-honed sense of right and wrong would have offered the viewer an easy entry point, and whose journey would have culminated in toppling J. J. Hunsecker and everything he stands for. By the 1950s, such optimism was unthinkable; our "hero" hopes not to make the world a better place, or make himself a better person, but merely to leech off of J. J.'s celebrity and power, to partake of his corruption himself. It was a jaundiced, jaded worldview that was increasingly how business was done, and not only New York.

When the company headed out east to start shooting, Odets was brought along to do another draft on the train and keep reworking the script as they shot. He was initially stashed in the Essex Hotel, but Mackendrick quickly found he needed the writer in closer proximity. "It was about three or four in the morning," Curtis recalled, "and it was cold, bitter, and miserable. Between shots, I was strolling around, and I heard this *tik-tik-tik* coming from inside the prop truck. So I go in, and there's Clifford Odets, sitting in an overcoat, huddled over his typewriter."

Working in this kind of hand-to-mouth fashion, however, did not make for an easy shoot. "One of the most frightening experiences of my life was to start shooting in the middle of Times Square at rush hour with an incomplete script," Mackendrick later said. Of course, if he'd made *Sweet Smell* as a backlot job, none of that would have mattered; they could've gone to other sets while scenes were rewritten or reshot them in the blink of an eye. But Mackendrick knew that for the heightened, theatrical dialogue and melodramatic situations to play, they had to feel authentic. And to get that authenticity, he had to immerse his characters (and his actors) in the fast-paced desperation of New York at night.

To accomplish this, he hired the great cinematographer James Wong Howe, equally brilliant as an artist and a technician; in the latter capacity, he was up on the latest advances in film stock and lenses that would allow them to shoot on the streets of New York after dark. As a result, Leonard Maltin says, Howe was able "to really give you a sense of what it was like at dusk, at dawn, in the wee hours of the morning. . . . The look of it has that sometimes intangible *feel* of New York City. Hard to put into words."

The company shot scenes outside the Ziegfeld and Palace Theaters (Odets and producer James Hill can be seen at the latter), in Times Square and Duffy Square, at the Brill Building, and outside the 21 Club and Toots Shor's. While scouting locations in the city before production, art director Edward Carrere and a crew of still photographers spent days taking hundreds of still photographs of 21 and Shor's; production manager Richard McWhorter and set dresser Edward Boyle spent time at the establishments as well. Back in Hollywood, McWhorter and Boyle went to work crafting exact replicas of the interiors, which were waiting for the company when they returned from the East Coast; in these settings, Howe could move the walls for his cameras (and spare the producers the expense of shutting down the restaurants). He was able to make additional visual modifications for the sake of style, building

Still images from
*Sweet Smell of Success*
(1957), directed by
Alexander Mackendrick,
photographed by
James Wong Howe.

the nightclub sets two feet off the ground in order to place smoke pots underneath, creating a gleaming effect by smearing the walls with oil. That gleaming, present throughout the picture, couples with the deep, inky blacks of Howe's cinematography to give the picture a gorgeous richness, almost a shimmer. It makes the film sparkle like a diamond, which creates a fascinating tension; under the diamond are the same bugs that crawl under any common rock.

Howe was also responsible for the key physical modification to Lancaster's imposing presence: his horn-rimmed glasses. Lancaster wore spectacles off-screen and initially refused Mackendrick's request to don them for the role. But he relented, and Howe used hard, top lighting to create shadows with the rims, falling over his cheekbones and particularly his eyes. "The shadows cast by the glasses onto Lancaster's face give him the skeletal look of a walking corpse," writes Sam Kashner, in *Vanity Fair*'s account of the production. "It's as though Hunsecker were already a dead man, his soul long since squeezed out of him by the machinery of power."

Not that Lancaster needed help to be imposing on set. "Burt was really scary," composer Elmer Bernstein said. "He was a dangerous guy. He had a short fuse. He was very physical. You thought you might get punched out. . . . It was a miracle that [Sandy] finished that film. In fact, I think that film is what finished Sandy." Mackendrick certainly felt finished when it began screening for preview audiences and he realized "the fans were not only going to dislike it, they were going to *resent* it." The main challenge, it seemed, was its smartest bit of casting: "What you had was an audience that liked Tony Curtis and thought he was a nice, open-faced kid on the make. And when it slowly dawned on them that he was the shit of all time, the result was physical. You could see them curling up, crossing their arms and legs, recoiling from the screen in disgust." Lancaster certainly offered no relief. The most succinct audience reaction card read, "Don't touch a foot of this film. Just burn the whole thing."

Critics were generally more appreciative. *Time* and the *New York Herald Tribune* both put it on their year-end top-ten list, though the *New Yorker*'s John McCarten dismissed it as "melodramatic razzle-dazzle," and the *Nation*'s Manny Farber compared it to "a high-powered salesman using empty tricks and skills." General audiences rejected it outright—it was Hecht-Hill-Lancaster's first box-office flop, losing a half-million dollars. No one was more delighted by its commercial failure than Walter Winchell, who refused to see it and didn't comment on it in his column ("I don't fool with the Lehmans of the world," he allegedly said), except a brief notice six months after its release, reporting on its losses.

But as the years passed, it became clear that *Sweet Smell of Success* was simply ahead of its time. Fifties audiences went to the movies for Technicolor melodramas and widescreen epics, stories with exactly the kind of easily delineated heroes and villains Lancaster wrote of wanting to complicate; this was a movie where everyone lies, cheats, and/or leers. Even Sidney, our ostensible protagonist, is a sleaze, an unapologetic and admitted social climber ("Hunsecker's the golden ladder to the places I want to get . . . way up high, where it's always balmy") who uses as much as he's used, who'll sell out anyone and anything to get ahead.

It would take the artistic evolutions of the 1960s and 1970s for bummer endings, challenging antiheroes, and psychological warfare to enter the moviemaking mainstream, for the picture to find its audience. Critics began to write essays deconstructing its style and analyzing its themes. Martin Scorsese sung its praises ("one of the most daring, startling, savage [pictures] ever made about show business and power in this country"), as did Oliver Stone ("The snap and crackle and pop of Odets and Lehman, it works, it just *works*"). A gender-swapped remake was announced in 1981, with Faye Dunaway playing the Lancaster role, and, as he did, producing, though it was never made. In 2002, *Sweet Smell* returned to its original home: It was adapted into a Broadway musical.

By then, the city had mainlined the movie, and vice versa. *Sweet Smell* is one of the first films that really seems to live in New York City, and to understand its distinctive landscape: the nightclubs, the restaurants, the open-air newsstands and hot dog joints, the wet streets. And the soundtrack matches it: a messy montage of honking horns, police radios, passerby chatter, and Bernstein's big, brassy score, heavy on the hi-hat. This would become the visual and aural palate of NYC cinema.

And the cinema was, finally, coming back to New York. In April 1959, the *Times* reported on the fruits of "a two-year campaign by the city to bring a substantial amount of moving-picture-making back to New York," estimating that a total of one hundred million dollars had been spent "for production, creative and performing talents, and laboratory processing and distribution" of features, documentaries, training films, and television commercials. In that period, shooting permits had ticked up from 168 in 1956 to 340 in 1957 to 638 in 1958.

Those permits were handled by a division of the city's Department of Commerce and Public Events, first established around the time of *The Naked City*'s production. But in that decade, it had proven a bit of a boondoggle—a "complicated, vexatious, and time-consuming" process, by the city's own (later) admission. If the city was going to get serious about film production, it was going to have to streamline that process.

And in the next decade, by some miracle, it did.

NOW SHOWING

# LITTLE FUGITIVE

# ON THE BOWERY

# SHADOWS

# LITTLE FUGITIVE

## 1953

## Directors: Ray Ashley, Morris Engel, Ruth Orkin

The narrative/documentary hybrid style that dominates 1950s New York City moviemaking, and pointed the way toward the gritty realism conjured up by the phrase "New York movie," owes no small debt to this 1953 independent film from the team of Ashley, Engel, and Orkin. Shot in Brooklyn with a cast of first-time actors, it concerns a neighborhood kid named Joey Norton (Richie Andrusco) who is convinced by his pranking playmates that he killed his older brother. Terrified, the little boy runs away to Coney Island, where he spends an eventful day playing, working, and trying to make his own way—a Brooklyn riff on *Rome, Open City*.

The filmmakers knew they could never make the movie in the intimate style they hoped via conventional methods (particularly since the low-budget production was shooting at Coney Island without permission). Instead, Engel, a former Navy combat photographer, reached out to Charlie Woodruff, a fellow combat photog and amateur inventor. Woodruff developed a lightweight, silent 35mm camera, which Engel could either hold in his hands or mount on a lightweight rig attached to his chest—an early prototype for the Steadicam setup.

The direct line from *Little Fugitive* to *On the Bowery* to *Shadows* is sharp and inarguable, each film immersing itself in its locations but moving a step further from documentary and into narrative, dialogue, and characterization. The intimate, handheld photography would become a defining feature of not only early New York cinema, but also the French New Wave that would begin at the decade's conclusion. And its practitioners weren't just influenced by its style, but by the film's top-to-bottom, independent production and self-distributed release. "Our New Wave would never have come into being," François Truffaut admitted, "if it hadn't been for Morris Engel, who showed us the way to independent production with *Little Fugitive*."

Still image from *On the Bowery* (1956), directed by Lionel Rogosin, photographed by Richard Bagley.

# ON THE BOWERY

## 1956

## Directors: Lionel Rogosin

Still image from *On the Bowery* (1956), directed by Lionel Rogosin, photographed by Richard Bagley.

Director Rogosin, a World War II vet, took in the influence of wartime documentary and European neorealism to craft this portrait of life on the Bowery, the downtown neighborhood populated by the city's homeless, castoffs, and alcoholics. Rogosin embedded himself on the Bowery, living with his subjects, working with them to create his story and tell it correctly, and casting non-actors to play slightly fictionalized versions of themselves.

The opening frames, under the credits and past them, are documentary images, setting the scene but also establishing a tone of close-to-the-ground realism. Buildings are busted out. Trash lines the streets, one pile directly in front of a NO DUMPING sign. Destitute men sleep on the sidewalk. And because it had been discontinued but not yet demolished, the elevated tracks of the Third Avenue line sit empty, a potent metaphor for this abandoned stretch of the city.

So immediate are these images that when the semiscripted scenes begin, they feel captured rather than staged. Much of the picture centers on the rough characters at the Bowery Bar, populated by the kind of faces that you just didn't see in movies then—and rarely do now. These are faces that have seen things, conveying a history beyond what an actor can typically convey. Into this unforgiving world wanders Ray Slayer (all of the "actors" keep their own names), who just finished a stretch working for the railroad over in New Jersey; he has a suitcase of clothes and a few dollars in his pocket. He quickly meets a Bowery regular, Gorman Hendricks, who will help relieve him of both.

In the Ray/Gorman relationship, we see an embryonic version of the tricky bond between *Midnight Cowboy*'s Joe Buck and Ratso Rizzo—the naïve newcomer and the guy who knows the score, who both takes the new guy under his wing and takes advantage. But *On the Bowery* isn't much driven by plot; Rogosin's documentary instincts make him more interested in the day-to-day goings-on of a street where every day blurs with the next. His characters drink, black out, do odd jobs, drink more, and occasionally get robbed and/or beaten. All that they do, be it work or panhandle or steal, is to get enough money for a little more booze; the film's constant refrain is "How 'bout a drink," the all-purpose solution for pain, boredom, anger, whatever.

Rogosin's time with his subjects pays off not only in the performances—the dialogue scenes are a tad stiff, but nonetheless convincing—but also in the story's inside-out telling, walking their streets, speaking their language. Most of all, it knows what they know: The only way out of this life is to leave this block. "Get off this Bowery and stay off this place," Gorman advises Ray, giving him a few bucks. But one of the other bar fellows is more skeptical: "Let me tell you something: He'll be back"; and while Rogosin's haunting final scene doesn't definitively answer that question one way or another, it's not hard to guess.

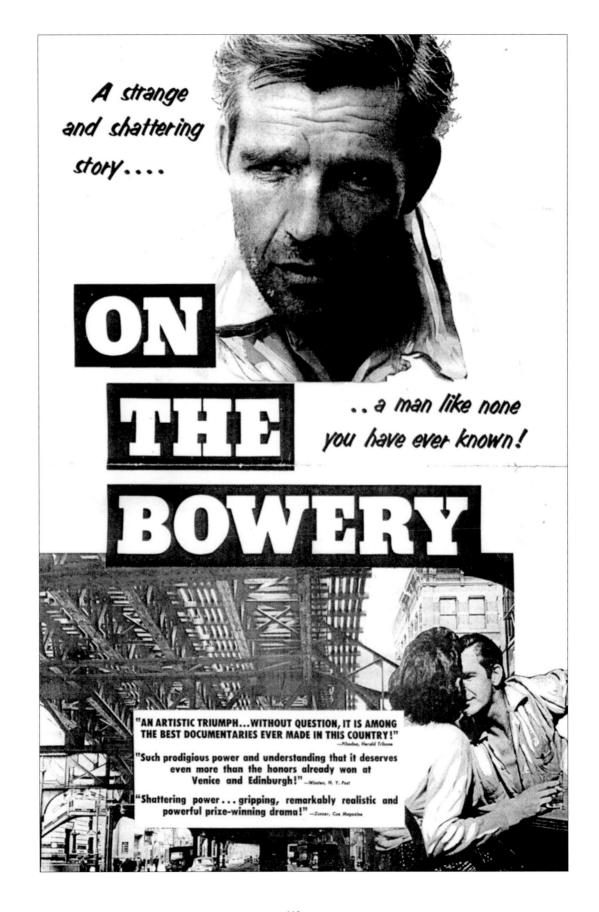

# SHADOWS

## 1959

## Directors: John Cassavetes

"Actor John Cassavetes can be seen roaming the Broadway area these nights," reported the *New York World-Telegram and Sun* in February 1957, "trailing a camera and an entourage of young actors, writers, friends and cautious policeman." Cassavetes was, at that time, a rising young television and film actor, firmly New York based; as such, he also hustled up a bit of extra scratch teaching acting classes and workshops. Out of those workshops, he began to explore the possibilities opened up by improvisations, finding that scenes would go in more interesting (and genuine) directions when he instructed his actors to dispense with the scripts but stay in character. And he began to wonder if that specific kind of electricity could be captured by a motion picture camera.

The actors had no script (an end credit announces, proudly, THE FILM YOU HAVE JUST SEEN WAS AN IMPROVISATION), working only from a typewritten synopsis the director wrote and circulated, with characters based on themselves. "*Shadows* is the story of people in a city," he wrote in the *Observer Weekend Review*, "not ten million, but just a few, a specific group, a picture of a family that lives just out of the bright lights of Broadway." In interviews, Cassavetes called *Shadows* "an off-Broadway movie," and orchestrated it in that off-the-grid spirit; equipment was borrowed from friends, power was politely siphoned from neighbors, street scenes were shot without permits, and taxis idled off-camera in several such scenes, ready to spirit away the cast and crew if the cops started sniffing around.

**OPPOSITE**
Still image from *Shadows* (1959), directed by John Cassavetes, photographed by Erich Kollman.

# 1960

# Fun City, John Lindsay, and *Midnight Cowboy*

In retrospect, perhaps John Lindsay was the only mayor who could've brought moviemaking back to New York City—not because he was a savvier politician than La Guardia or Wagner or any of his predecessors, but because he was the only one who was a frustrated actor. In his 1965 campaign, he appeared alongside the likes of Sammy Davis Jr. and Liza Minnelli; shortly into his term, the *Village Voice*'s Jack Newfield referenced his "younger-than-44-years Hollywood face" and called him "Robert Stack–handsome." Less than two months after taking office, he appeared as himself on a Gene Kelly television special, and the next year he fronted a onetime Broadway benefit performance of *Mister Mayor*, a musical extravaganza created for His Honor by *Cabaret*'s John Kander and Fred Ebb. Years earlier, while serving in Congress, Lindsay moonlighted as the narrator of an off-Broadway revival of *John Brown's Body*, telling the *New York Times*, "I am the greatest ham in the world. . . . If the voters throw me out in November, I know where I'm going—on stage."

It was the kind of thing most politicians said as a joke, but John Lindsay wasn't joking. He considered pursuing acting as a younger man before deciding to play it safe and first enter law, then politics. His parents had climbed their way up from working-class backgrounds and instilled in him the notion that money was not to be taken for granted; John Vliet Lindsay and his twin brother, David, were born in 1921, and growing up in the midst of the Great Depression no doubt swung him to fiscal responsibility as well. A graduate of the Yale School of Law, he worked as a trial lawyer for five years, spending his days at a respected New York firm and his nights at the city's Young Republican Club. His work on the 1952 Eisenhower campaign led to a job in that administration, serving under Attorney General Herbert Brownell and working on, among other issues, civil rights and immigration.

In April 1958, he returned to New York to run for Congress in Manhattan's Seventeenth District—the Silk Stocking District, as it was called, as it included the high-dollar digs of Fifth and Park Avenue. He won his primary by barely two thousand votes and squeaked out an eight-thousand-vote victory in the general, but his margins got wider each cycle; by 1962, he beat his Democratic opponent by more than two to one. The *Times* called him "one of the bright hopes of the Republican Party."

It needed one. By 1964, the party was in disarray, with frothing presidential candidate Barry Goldwater trounced in that year's election by Lyndon B. Johnson. Lindsay boosted his profile by attending the party's national convention and pleading for a more liberal platform, and then, worried by the rhetoric of Goldwater's campaign, choosing not to support his party's candidate that fall. He came out looking like a genius and seized on the moment to declare the current iteration of the Republican Party "a pile of rubble." It was time to rethink the party's approach to social issues, civil rights, and spending. He could best boost that approach, he reasoned, from Manhattan's City Hall. And from that office, he would create the agency that got movie cameras cranking in New York City again.

▬

As always, there had been glimmers of hope that mostly faded to dust. A March 1963 article in the *New York Times* trumpeted the imminent construction of the Michael Myerberg Studios at Roosevelt Field on Long Island, with Bosley Crowther noting that while studios had loosened their insistence on studio-lot photography, "New York must have some new film studios if it is to capture any of the production that is running away from Hollywood—or running back in that direction." The complex was built, but it didn't cause the turnaround Crowther hoped for; it, like most of the New York spaces, was predominantly used for TV production and B movies like *Santa Claus Conquers the Martians* (1964).

Occasional features—usually the work of directors willing to throw their weight around and demand verisimilitude—managed to make their way to the city for, at the very least, a few days of *On the Town*–style location shooting. Billy Wilder's *The Apartment* (1960), a sparkling rom-com with the sleaze and desperation of *Sweet Smell* right under the surface, and Blake Edwards's *Breakfast at Tiffany's* (1961; see sidebar on page 154) constructed its New York apartment and office sets on California soundstages, but brought out its casts and crews to shoot exteriors. Edward Dmytryk's amnesia thriller *Mirage* (1965) was shot entirely in New York, to its benefit; the authentic locations contribute to the protagonist's sense of displacement and confusion, and help convey the sense of feeling unknown and alone in this giant, anonymous city.

Meanwhile, independent filmmakers bucked convention and made their New York movies on the sly. Jack Garfein's *Something Wild* (1961), shot over seven weeks in the fall of 1960 on a budget of less than a million dollars, opens with a Saul Bass–designed credit sequence that frames the denizens of the city at extreme low and high angles, in giant wide or suffocatingly close compositions; everyone and everything is oppressive and overwhelming. Our heroine (Carroll Baker, then Garfein's wife) is literally skipping home from her subway stop when she's pulled into the bushes in a public park and raped. Garfein's direction and Eugene Shuftan's cinematography put us through the ordeal and its aftermath with her, dramatizing how her trauma exacerbates the stresses of the city (packed subway, dirty streets, noisy neighbors)—and vice versa.

Other Gotham moviemakers eschewed the conventions of Hollywood altogether. Taking advantage of technical advances in mobile cinematography and sound, as well as relaxing regulation of adult subject matter, filmmakers like Jack Smith, Jonas Mekas, Stan Brakhage, Shirley Clarke, and (most notoriously) Andy Warhol used tiny budgets and local talent to create a robust New York underground film scene. "They seemed to be less polished, which gave it a special sort of special resonance to us," recalls Martin Scorsese, then a student filmmaker at NYU. "And if it was less polished, that changed what one thought about what a film should look like, what it should be. . . . That made you realize that cinema, it could be *anything*."

Those directors didn't just find artistic fulfillment; films like Smith's *Flaming Creatures*, Warhol's *Chelsea Girls*, and Clarke's *The Cool World* were financially lucrative as well, discovering an audience exhausted by the bloated, lumbering musical extravaganzas of mainstream studios and receptive to new ideas, new forms, and taboo destruction.

"The smart people of Hollywood who unfortunately wish to preserve the *status quo* at any price very well might be worried about what's going on in New York," British film critic Russell Robbins told *Carnival* magazine. "The answer to the question of what's wrong with Hollywood is on the verge of being demonstrated by the Eastern *avant garde*, [with] such emphasis and clarity that it is only a matter of time before the cliché masters on the West Coast lose their audiences forever."

But the stark contrast between their modes of working—between the guerilla-style, run-and-gun production of the independents and the by-the-book, big-footprint methodology of their high-budget counterparts—continued to make New York City production all but impossible for the studios. The paperwork was overwhelming. City agencies often made permits contingent on script approval. And the police payoffs were pricey. ("In fact we used to budget for it," Sidney Lumet recalled. "You'd start shooting at seven-thirty in the morning and have to take care of all three shifts.")

"I don't think you will find an average of more than two or three top pictures a year turned out here," producer Max Youngstein predicted in 1964, around the time he shot scenes from *Fail Safe* at the Myerberg Studios. "New York City has had a great opportunity in recent years to become the center of the entire motion picture industry, but our city administration has done nothing to encourage it, and has done a great deal to hinder it. The situation is nothing short of stupid. [In Los Angeles], motion picture companies get immediate cooperation from the city government. Here they get nothing but talk."

▬

But the city was changing. Greenwich Village was becoming a center of culture, not only thanks to the burgeoning folk music revival, but also the "beatnik" scene surrounding it. Civil rights demonstrations became a near-daily occurrence. Tenants protested the slum-like conditions their inattentive landlords refused to address. There were six days of riots in Harlem and Brooklyn in July 1964 following the police shooting of a fifteen-year-old black youth. (The officer responsible, Lt. Thomas Gilligan, was cleared by a grand jury and allowed to rejoin the force.) Tensions increased. The middle class fled to the suburbs, and major companies (and contributors to the tax base) fled the area altogether. The 1960 census registered a decrease in New York City's population, for the first time ever. Standard & Poor's lowered the city's credit rating. Unemployment, poverty, and crime rates rose, and a climate of fear followed and eventually eclipsed them. A 1964 *New York Times* article reported a "paralyzing and constant fear for personal safety" among citizens of the Upper West Side, where "apprehension over frequent muggings, thefts, robberies and other forms of violence cause many

**OPPOSITE**
Still image from *The Apartment* (1960), directed by Billy Wilder, photographed by Joseph LaShelle

**ABOVE**
Still image from *Breakfast at Tiffany's* (1961), directed by Blake Edwards, photographed by Franz F. Planer.

**BELOW LEFT**
Still image from *Mirage* (1965), directed by Edward Dmytryk, photographed by Joseph MacDonald.

**BELOW RIGHT**
Still image from *Something Wild* (1961), directed by Jack Garfein, photographed by Eugen Schüfftan.

residents to 'seal themselves in at night' and not venture outdoors after dark."

That combination of fear and apathy found an avatar in Kitty Genovese, who (the legend went) was stalked, stabbed for more than half an hour, and ultimately killed late one night outside a subway station in Kew Gardens, Queens, while nearly forty neighbors in a nearby apartment building didn't help or even call the police. (The real story turned out to be quite a bit more complicated, but tales of big-city selfishness aren't known for their nuances.)

New York was caught in a bind, from a public relations perspective, because it was a major media center—and thus there was no shortage of breathlessly apocalyptic stories about the decline of the city. A 1965 *Time* magazine article called the city's current iteration "a cruel parody of its legend." That same year, *Look* magazine characterized the city as "dirty, thirsty, tired, scared, old, worn, fouled and poor"; *Fortune*'s missive characterized it as "a city destroying itself." *U.S. News & World Report* argued that daily life for New Yorkers "had tended to become more and more unsettled, uncomfortable and downright dangerous, less and less pleasant."

But the most thorough accounting of the city's shortcomings came from its own *Herald Tribune*. In the January 25, 1965, edition (under the memorable front-page headline "New York, Greatest City of the World—and Everything Is Wrong with It"), the daily paper kicked off an ongoing series titled "New York City in Crisis." "In the complex years since the end of World War II, the creative channels have clogged up," went the editorial. "The city's simple problems require complex answers. And the complex problems seem to have no solutions at all."

And one of those complex problems, everyone seemed to agree, was Times Square.

■

"Forty-second Street between Seventh and Eighth Avenues is an enigma to New Yorkers concerned with the deterioration of the midway of Manhattan," wrote Milton Bracker on the front page of the March 14, 1960, *Times*. "Virtually everyone interested in the face the city turns to hundreds and thousands of tourists annually is uneasy about the situation." The problems, as detailed by Bracker: the ten all-night movie houses, or "grind joints"; their street displays, emphasizing "sex and violence," that "attract undesirables, especially in the late hours"; the arcades and dirty bookstores; the transients loitering on the sidewalks, at the bus station, and in the all-night cafeterias. And that wasn't all.

Fun City, John Lindsay, and *Midnight Cowboy*

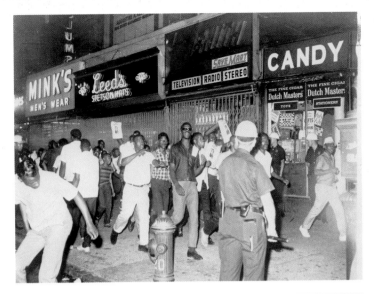

"Homosexuality," Bracker all but whispered, "is an obvious problem on Forty-Second Street."

It's important to note that the seediness of Times Square was not, at that writing, a recent phenomenon. At the turn of the century, 42nd Street was an extension of the tawdry Tenderloin district, full of dance halls, boardinghouses, and brothels; it only became a city center when the new subway station, converging several lines, opened there in 1904. (Around the same time, one of the first cinematic depictions of the area was recorded: *Panorama from the Times Building* (1902), a two-minute actuality film that pans across the emerging Midtown theater district, past the giant Hippodrome, and lands at one of the most frequently filmed images in the world, the three-way intersection of Broadway, Seventh Avenue, and 47th Street, "the center of the world.")

Even then, the blossoming Broadway scene was supplemented by bawdier entertainments, from the leering girlie shows of Florenz Ziegfeld to the booze-fueled pleasures of cabarets, lobster restaurants, nightclubs, saloons, and speakeasies. In the 1920s and 1930s, even as the area's legitimate theaters took flight, the storefronts were inhabited, according to historian Herbert Asbury, by "a raucous jungle of chop-suey restaurants, hot-dog and hamburger shops . . . radio and phonograph stores equipped with blaring loud-speakers, cheap haberdasheries, fruit juice stands, dime museums, candy and drug stores . . . flea circuses, penny arcades, and lunch counters which advertised EATS!"

Such pleasures made Times Square a desirable destination for visiting sailors and soldiers during World War II and, later, the beatniks and hipsters of the 1950s and early 1960s. Jack Kerouac's 1950 novel, *The Town and the City*, includes scenes at the Nickel-O, a stand-in for the Pokerino, a pinball arcade on 42nd where Kerouac hung out with his Beat brethren (and a whole lot of speed freaks); even the bourgeois *Breakfast at Tiffany's* includes a scene of Holly and Fred blowing off steam by scoping out the burlesque shows.

But Times Square always, always stood for sex. According to James Traub's history *The Devil's Playground*, "in 1901, vice investigators identified 132 sites where prostitutes plied their trade in the area bounded by Sixth and Eighth Avenues and 37th and 47th Streets. . . . Forty-third Street between Broadway and Eighth, where the *New York Times* was to move its office, was known as Soubrette Row, for most of the brownstones on the block functioned as brothels." Nothing—not Prohibition nor wars nor police profiling—slowed down the Times Square sex trade, and in 1950, the opening of the Port Authority Bus Terminal exponentially increased the supply of fresh-off-the-bus recruits . . . of both sexes.

The area had long been gay-friendly, thanks to both its anything-goes atmosphere and the proximity to the theater district. Male "hustlers" had plied their wares alongside their female counterparts for decades; historian Timothy Gilfoyle found an early-thirties tabloid paper claiming, "The latest gag about 2 A.M. is to have your picture taken with one or two pansies on Times Square." Two important novels captured what this world had become by the early 1960s. John Rechy's *City of Night*, published in 1963, concerns a young hustler working his way across the country ("I would think of America as one vast City of Night stretching from Times Square to Hollywood Boulevard. . . . One-night stands and cigarette smoke and rooms squashed in loneliness"). And in 1965 came James Leo Herlihy's story of Joe Buck, a handsome fellah from Texas who boards a bus for The City. "What to do when he got to New York?"

**RIGHT**
Times Square, circa 1961.

**COUNTERCLOCK-
WISE FROM BELOW**
Cinematic impressions of
Times Square, from
*Panorama from Times
Building, New York* (1905,
photographed by Wallace
McCutcheon), *Speedy* (1928,
directed by Ted Wilde, pho-
tographed by Walter
Lundgrin), *Kiss of Death*
(1947, directed by Henry
Hathaway, photographed by
Norbert Brodine), and
*Killer's Kiss* (1955, directed
and photographed by
Stanley Kubrick).

Fun City, John Lindsay, and *Midnight Cowboy*

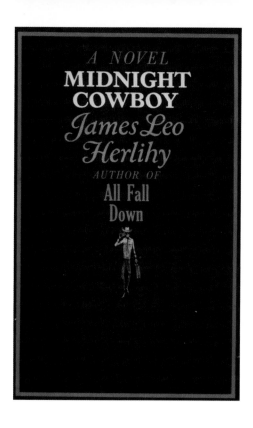

Herlihy wrote. "Shee-it, what could be simpler? Head for Times Square and follow his nose. Suddenly up ahead was the Manhattan skyline, buildings like markers in a crowded graveyard. Joe's hand moved to his crotch, and under his breath he said, 'I'm gonna take hold o' this thing and I'm gonna swing it like a lasso and I'm gonna rope in this whole fuckin' island.'" Herlihy gave his book a title that conjured up both desperation and tradition, neon and Americana. He called it *Midnight Cowboy*.

While *Midnight Cowboy* was hitting shelves, John Lindsay was hitting the streets. He announced his candidacy on May 13 (partially compelled, he admitted, by the *Herald Tribune*'s "New York City in Crisis" series, which quoted him as slagging Mayor Wagner and predicting, "If we don't get going again soon, New York will become a second-class city"), and Mayor Wagner announced less than a month later that he would not seek a third term. Not that Lindsay was by any means a shoo-in; since the incorporation of Greater New York City in 1898, the city had elected exactly two Republican mayors—John Purroy Mitchel and La Guardia—and neither toed anything resembling the party line.

But Lindsay had a few strokes of luck. Conservative commentator William F. Buckley entered the race as a third-party candidate, and what could have been a spoiler instead allowed Lindsay to more clearly define himself as a liberal Republican, as opposed to the Goldwater strain of the party represented by Buckley. Their Democratic opponent was comptroller Abraham Beame, a fifty-nine-year-old establishment candidate whom Lindsay easily framed as another Wagner. His admirers in mass media helped; in the *World-Telegram*, Murray Kempton wrote, "He is fresh, and everyone else is tired," a turn of phrase so succinct that the candidate's advisors appropriated it as a campaign slogan.

It underscored the fortuitous timing of Lindsay's emergence as a post-Kennedy candidate who, Republican or no, called to mind many of the late president's key qualities: youth, good looks, optimism, enthusiasm. Piecing together a coalition of young voters, Jewish voters, frustrated Republicans, and minorities, Lindsay eked out a victory: 43.3 percent to Beame's 39.5, with Buckley siphoning off 12.9 percent.

And with that, he got to work. John V. Lindsay was sworn in as mayor of New York City on New Year's Eve of 1965; when he and his team arrived at City Hall, they discovered Wagner's people had left them, according to the *Times*, "no paper clips, no mimeograph or carbon paper, no scissors, all the things necessary to run a City Hall." Wagner himself had skipped out on the swearing-in, heading to Mexico on a family vacation that afternoon and telling reporters, "This is Lindsay's show now."

It wasn't hard to guess what he was running from. The Transport Workers Union contract was set to expire at five a.m. on New Year's Day, Lindsay's first day on the job, with the looming threat of a shutdown that would affect the combined six million New Yorkers who relied on subway or bus service daily. The timing was awkward—Lindsay didn't want to step on the toes of the still-serving mayor, while Wagner felt no obligation to include in negotiations the candidate who'd spent months bashing him or to fix a crisis that would fall on his successor's watch. Lindsay didn't meet with the union until December 27, and it didn't go well; the respective parties dug in, and on New Year's morning, the trains and busses ground to a halt. They stayed that way for nearly two weeks.

**ABOVE**
The original cover of Leo Herlihy's novel *Midnight Cowboy*.

**OPPOSITE LEFT**
Lindsay on the campaign trail, 1965.

**OPPOSITE RIGHT**
Mayor Lindsay at the first public hearing on proposed executive capital budget.

That first morning, Lindsay walked the three and a half miles to work, pleading with fellow citizens not to drive into Manhattan if they could help it and closing the schools for the following day. Asked by the press to give a message to New Yorkers, the mayor replied, "Thanks for the cooperation and for toughness, for good spirit and good cheer. This is a fun and exciting city even when it's a struck city." A few days later, the *New York World Journal Tribune*'s Dick Schaap picked up on the phrase and made it the centerpiece of his column. "Not long after the transit strike began the other day," Schaap wrote, "Mayor John Lindsay went on radio and television to announce that New York is a fun city. He certainly has a wonderful sense of humor. A little while later, Lindsay cheerfully walked four miles from his hotel room to City Hall, a gesture which proved that the fun city had a fun Mayor."

The nickname "Fun City" stuck—initially aspirational, as Lindsay found "in those two words the essence of what he'd hoped to do with New York," according to Sean Deveney, who took the phrase as the title for his book on the Lindsay years. But as the sixties continued, it was more often deployed as Schaap had intended: ironically, in sharp contrast to the increasingly dysfunctional metropolis New York City had become.

▬

John Schlesinger wasn't looking for a new project when a friend recommended *Midnight Cowboy*; he'd decided to follow up his international critical and commercial sensations *Billy Liar* and *Darling* with a big-budget adaptation of *Far from the Madding Crowd*. But he was taken by the possibilities of James Leo Herlihy's novel. "I felt it was a subject to which I could tune in," he said upon the film's release, "even though it wasn't my own experience and I haven't the same sort of fantasies and illusions as Joe Buck. What I could do was sympathize with the character. I understand what it's like to be lonely, and to be a

failure. . . . *Midnight Cowboy* is about loneliness and delusion; it is also about the emergence of some sort of human dignity from degradation, and the need to feel for another human being."

His regular producer passed, telling the not-yet-out-as-gay Schlesinger, "This is faggot stuff. This will destroy your career." So Schlesinger rang up producer Jerome Hellman, with whom he'd almost collaborated a few years earlier, asking if he could send the book over. "I thought that the relationship between the two guys was something that would work," Hellman recalled. "But that if there was any hint of homosexuality it would be a catastrophe. I was a little embarrassed to say that, because when I met John he was still carrying on this charade of being a straight man. . . . I said, 'Okay, look, it'll be very hard to get money for it—we'll have to work for nothing—but I'd love to try to do it with you.'"

After flirting with hiring Gore Vidal—who instead proposed Schlesinger turn his novel *The City and the Pillar* into a film—the pair commissioned playwright Jack Gelber (who'd written the play that became Shirley Clarke's *The Connection*) to adapt the screenplay. Schlesinger went away to shoot *Far from the Madding Crowd*, and Gelber wrote two drafts of the script. But neither the director nor his producer was satisfied with Gelber's work, so they parted company with the playwright. Improbably enough, they landed on Waldo Salt.

Salt was an up-and-coming screenwriter when his refusal to name names in front of the HUAC got him blacklisted. He wiled away the 1950s writing for television (under his wife's name) before the crumbling of the blacklist in the early sixties put him back to work. His agent, George Litto, heard about the *Midnight Cowboy* job and sent Hellman a Salt script called *The Artful Dodger*, which had what Hellman called "that totally fragmented feeling that we'd been searching for"; he took

Fun City, John Lindsay, and *Midnight Cowboy*

Peter Falk, Jack Lemmon,
and Mayor Lindsay on the
Williamsburg Bridge during
the filming of *Luv* (1967).

a meeting with Salt, who dazzled him with both his ideas and his preparation. "He had analyzed the book and he'd analyzed the characters and he had a memo for me, outlining his approach to the film. I sent it off to John, who was shooting *Far from the Madding Crowd*, and with it a note of my own, saying that I thought this guy might be the answer to our prayers. I got a wire back saying, 'Just hire him immediately, and start work.' So I did."

With a screenwriter locked in, Hellman felt confident enough to take the project to United Artists, where he'd just made (in New York) *The World of Henry Orient*. He had an ally in David Picker, the hip young head of production (and nephew of co–studio head Arnold Picker) responsible for several of the studio's sixties successes, including the *Pink Panther* and James Bond franchises. Picker liked the book and wanted to work with Schlesinger, but warned Hellman, "My partners here, the older men in the company, aren't going to understand it. So it's got to be [no more than] $1 million, all-in!"

Hellman knew it wouldn't be enough, but decided they'd rather take the green light now and worry about the budget later. The deal was announced in the June 12, 1966, *New York Times*, which noted that Schlesinger "has joined forces with producer Jerome Hellman to make his first film here in its entirety." And just a few days earlier, the proposition of shooting a feature film in its entirety in New York had become much, much simpler.

In a May 11 report on the commencement of principal photography for Warner Bros.' *Any Wednesday*, the *Times*'s Vincent Canby noted that five more features would be shot, in whole or in part, in the city that summer. "While New York film people, particularly union representatives, are happy about the spurt in local activity," Canby wrote, "they regard these six features as 'about par for the season' and not indicative of a new trend."

What neither Canby nor those "New York film people" knew was that Mayor Lindsay had pinpointed the encouragement of local film production as a boost not only to the economy, but also to the city's image. He pledged to fix the city's filmmaking problem during the campaign; shortly after his inauguration, he appointed a former newspaperman named Barry Gottehrer to devise a package of suggestions. Gottehrer spent the spring interviewing studio reps and producers, and quickly put together a report focusing on three key proposals: the establishment of a one-stop shop, issuing a single permit (and requiring only a single signature) for production in the city; the creation of a unit of the NYPD to assist film crews undertaking those productions; and the appointment of a special liaison to the mayor, who would facilitate cooperation between that office and any producers who might need their assistance.

Gottehrer's proposals formed the backbone of Executive Order Number 10, which Mayor Lindsay signed on May 31, 1966. In that memorandum lay the establishment of the Mayor's Office of Film, Theatre & Broadcasting, following all of the Gottehrer plan's proposals, and one more besides. "Scripts should not be examined for the purpose of editorial censorship," Lindsay said. "There are adequate laws to safeguard the public interest in this area without resorting to municipal censorship."

Local media coverage was rhapsodic. "In an executive order dated May 31, the mayor drastically simplified the almost Kafkaesque procedures

Fun City, John Lindsay, and *Midnight Cowboy*

**ABOVE**
Still images from *You're a
Big Boy Now* (1966),
directed by Francis Ford
Coppola, photographed by
Andrew Laszlo

**BELOW LEFT
TO RIGHT**
Still images from *The World
of Henry Orient* (1964),
directed by George Roy
Hill, photographed by Boris
Kaufman and Arthur J.
Ortnitz; *Greetings* (1968),
directed by Brian De Palma,
cinematography by Robert
Fiore; *Barefoot in the Park*
(1967), directed by Gene
Saks, photographed by
Joseph LaShelle; *You're a
Big Boy Now* (1966),
directed by Francis Ford
Coppola, photographed by
Andrew Laszlo.

that producers had previously had to go through to get permission to shoot on location here," reported the *New Yorker*, in an item optimistically titled "A Beginning." The *Times*'s Canby noted that "18 features will have been in work here during the first nine months of the year. Last year, only 13 films came to town, and in 1964, nine." And they weren't just boosting the city's profile; "they are pouring hundreds of thousands of dollars into the city's economy."

To keep that positive coverage of the initiative (and the mayor) in the papers, Joy Manhoff Flink—the newly appointed "Mayor's Executive Coordinator of Film Making in New York"—arranged for Lindsay to make set visits to the first batch of productions. The invited press corps snapped photos of Lindsay posing with *Wait Until Dark*'s Audrey Hepburn and *Up the Down Staircase*'s Sandy Dennis, or clowning around on the Manhattan Bridge with *Luv*'s Jack Lemmon and Peter Falk. It was a win-win arrangement: The city got valuable press for the celebrity mayor and this signature initiative, while the filmmakers got early promotion for their productions.

And sometimes they got more. One of the first high-profile productions that summer was *You're a Big Boy Now*, an adaptation of David Benedictus's novel by a young Francis Ford Coppola. His screenplay adaptation moved the book from London to New York and changed its protagonist's place of employment from a dinky shoe store to the vast, gorgeous main building of the New York Public Library on Fifth Avenue. "He was hooked on those marble stairways and sweeping archways, that immense reading room, those miles and miles of bookshelves," wrote the *New York World Journal Tribune*'s William Peper, but "officials were not anxious to have the library cluttered up with a lot of crazy movie people." Luckily, "he had movie-struck Mayor Lindsay on his side," and Lindsay "asked them to please cooperate." They did, shooting in the building on Sundays, when the library was closed to the public.

Recurring visual motifs abound in that first batch of pictures, which also included *Up the Down Staircase, Barefoot in the Park*, and *The Incident* (all 1967); *Madigan, What's So Bad About Feeling Good?, The Odd Couple*, and *Greetings* (all 1968); and *The April Fools* (1969)—as well as *The World of Henry Orient* (1964) and *A Thousand Clowns* (1965), which preceded Executive Order Number 10. Most feature an opening-credit sequence of hustle-bustle New York photography—skylines and busy sidewalks and congested traffic—less as a commentary on the story than as a nudge in the ribs to the viewer (*See, we really shot it here!*).

Many also incorporate scenes that insert their characters into that hustle-bustle—while still using the tricks of the era of *The Jazz Singer* and *The Crowd*, shooting on the sly from passing cars or with hidden cameras.

And several include sequences of their characters running amok through the city and its landmarks: Bernard chasing his kite through Central Park in *You're a Big Boy Now*; the young girl protagonists following Henry throughout town in *Henry Orient*; the main trio of young men frolicking in Central Park in *Greetings*. These moments are, first and foremost, of their time stylistically, echoing as they do the work of Richard Lester in general and *A Hard Day's Night* in particular, scenes that exist primarily to convey the youth and energy of their characters (and filmmakers). But they're also showing off the new freedom of movement throughout the city allowed by Lindsay's initiative.

Stage adaptations like *Barefoot in the Park*, *Luv*, *The Odd Couple*, and *A Thousand Clowns* used their location photography specifically as a means to "open up" their theatrical settings—to infuse their stories with a refreshing, urban texture in between scenes of people talking in apartments (or, more accurately, sets of apartments). In an essay for the collection *America's Mayor*, James Sanders notes that in the case of *A Thousand Clowns*, its unemployed protagonist (Jason Robards) treats the city as "a kind of spectacular, full-sized stage set, through which he is free to wander joyfully, like an overgrown child, finding delight in its endless surprises and discoveries, its hidden corners and unexpected vistas." Director Fred Coe adopts the same attitude—as does many a New York filmmaker who came after. (As soon as 1968, William Greaves's metatextual, Central Park–shot *Symbiopsychotaxiplasm: Take One* would include, in detail, the woes of its New York production.)

But one aspect of *You're a Big Boy Now* is particularly striking. On Bernard's first night after settling into his new digs—his first solo apartment of his young adult life—his first pilgrimage is to the notorious Times Square. Coppola's camera soaks up the luridness nearly as eagerly as his protagonist: lingerie displays, grindhouse marquees, dirty bookstores, and adult arcades (a world that the director was more than passingly familiar with; his first two credited directorial efforts were so-called nudie cuties). None of this was invented or staged, certainly, and as promised, the Mayor's Office did not interfere. But it's noteworthy that from the very beginning, in one of the first films to benefit not only from Lindsay's initiative but also from his direct

**TOP**
Jon Voight and John Schlesinger.

**ABOVE**
Dustin Hoffman and John Schlesinger.

135

involvement, we're treated to a documentary-style portrait of the city's scuzziest district.

—

Hellman and Schlesinger might not have used Jack Gelber's script, but Gelber made one invaluable contribution to *Midnight Cowboy*. As Hellman remembered, while they were working together, the playwright suggested they take in an off-Broadway play starring an actor he thought might make a good Ratso. "It was a one-character drama, a caretaker in the basement of a factory," the producer recalled. "And the caretaker was Dustin Hoffman. I was bowled over. I went, 'Oh, shit, this guy was born to play Ratso Rizzo.'" And there was a financial incentive: A no-name off-Broadway actor wouldn't break their meager budget. He sent the book to Hoffman, who eagerly took the role.

Of course, a funny thing happened on the way to *Midnight Cowboy*. During its lengthy period of pre-production and fund-raising, Hoffman went off to make *The Graduate* for Mike Nichols, and when that film took the nation by storm in December 1967, it made him a movie star. What could've been a disaster for the filmmakers became a coup; Hoffman still wanted to make the movie, despite the advice of the likes of Nichols, whom Hoffman remembered asking, "I made you a star, and you're going to throw it all away? You're a leading man, and now you're going to play this? *The Graduate* was so clean, and this is so dirty."

Schlesinger, also bothered by the contrast, took some convincing. Hoffman suggested they meet—late one night at an Automat in Times Square, arriving in a dirty raincoat, with his hair slicked back and a bad case of five-o'clock shadow. "And John," Hoffman recalled, "whom I loved from the very beginning, looked at me, and he looked around, and he said, 'I've only seen you in the context of *The Graduate*, but you'll do quite well.'"

But Hoffman was no longer the bargain he had been in his off-Broadway days. Hellman went back to Picker at UA: "Hey, look, this guy is our Ratso Rizzo, we've been on him for years, and now we've gotta sign him. But he's a hot commodity." The $150,000 paycheck Picker authorized was more than the combined salaries of Hellman, Schlesinger, and Salt, but it meant more to them than that. For the first time, the producer recalled, they thought, "Hey, we're going to get to make this fucking movie, because UA's not going to want to blow their $150,000."

Now there was the matter of finding their Joe Buck. They could've gone the movie-star route: Schlesinger's three-time leading lady Julie Christie slid a copy of the script to her boyfriend Warren Beatty, who wanted the role so badly he offered to film a "secret screen test." But Schlesinger thought it would be a stretch to cast Beatty as a failed prostitute: "If he were the male hustler, the lines would be out to Fire Island!" (Some poor executive even suggested cleaning up the script and repurposing it as an Elvis Presley vehicle.) It was Marion Dougherty, the casting director who was shaking up the film industry with her finds from the New York theater scene, who suggested Jon Voight.

Voight made a splash with his turn in Ulu Grosbard's 1965 production of *A View from the Bridge*, opposite Robert Duvall (Hoffman, coinciden-tally enough, had worked as an assistant director and assistant stage manager on the show). Schlesinger was skeptical; he thought the actor was "too butch looking, baby-faced, or whatever." Dougherty pressed the filmmakers to test him. It ultimately came down to Voight and another up-and-comer, Michael Sarrazin. Schlesinger chose the latter.

Unfortunately for Sarrazin, he was under contract to Universal—which tripled the price for the loan-out when they discovered Schlesinger wanted him. The producer and director went back to the screen tests and invited Hoffman, who had read against each of them, to weigh in. "Look, they're both good actors," Hoffman told them. "I will be happy to make the picture with either of them. But I will tell you one thing. When I was watching these tests with Michael, I was looking at myself. When I was watching the test with Jon Voight, I was looking at Jon Voight." Voight got the part—and a paycheck of $17,500.

He went to Texas to work on his accent. Hoffman studied street people in Times Square and on the Bowery, deciding the character's limp would be the result of a gimpy leg. He put a pebble in his shoe to throw off his amble and seized on the unusual shoes costume designer Ann Roth had picked out for him. "They were these cockroach-in-the-corner shoes, *cucaracha* shoes, very pointed toes," Roth said. "He hadn't seen that end of his body in the mirror in his mind. So when they got on him, they threw him into a different posture, and suddenly there was somebody in front of me who was not Dustin Hoffman."

Both actors wanted to do their best for the picture—and for each other. A bit of healthy competition, stemming from their time on the New York stage, kept each on his toes. "It's not that you don't want the other one to be good, you just don't want to look bad," Hoffman explained. So there was some suspicion. It bubbled up early on, with a scene Schlesinger wanted to shoot during pre-production of the characters walking over a bridge. It was a wide shot, no sound, and Hoffman was worried that he didn't have the character's walk or cough yet.

"We were trying to act up a storm, not knowing what the fuck we were doing," Hoffman recalled. "And because I was so nervous that I was going to come across fraudulent and not have the right cough, I tried to do the cough as realistically as I could. Each time, I tried to do it more realistically until, finally, I did it so realistically I threw up all over Jon." The actor, understandably shaken, sought out his director. "Later," Hoffman said, "Schlesinger told me that Jon had gone up to him afterwards and said—he was so happy to have gotten the part, and he knew that I gave him a good word—'You know, Dustin's a great actor and everything, and I'm just asking you because I don't want to tell him how to play his character, but is he going to do that in a lot of scenes?' He thought I'd steal every scene if I threw up on him. He thought that was a choice I made, like the gloves were off."

Lindsay's efforts, meanwhile, were already paying off. In January 1967, he co-hosted the presentation of the New York Film Critics Circle Awards; in March, he received an award for "outstanding service to the motion picture and television industry" from the Film Producers Association. Between those ceremonies, he spearheaded an effort asking Local 52, the studio mechanics union, to match the labor costs of Hollywood productions for any films made entirely—from top to bottom, including post-production—in the city. (Producers contended that labor costs in New York were as much as 25 percent higher than in Los Angeles.) The union ultimately agreed to a one-year matching agreement.

That April, Lindsay and the city's Office of Cultural Affairs sponsored a three-day, free-to-the-public Festival of New York films, including *The Crowd*, *On the Town*, *On the Waterfront*, *On the Bowery*, and the premiere of *You're a Big Boy Now*. "In a brief welcome," the *Times* noted, "the Mayor reported that within the next six weeks nine feature films are scheduled to go into production here, with five to be shot here in their entirety." One of those films was *What's So Bad About Feeling Good?*, which Lindsay granted permission to shoot inside City Hall. (The customary set visit was much easier for His Honor that day: He only had to travel about thirty feet.)

There were some hiccups. While shooting *The President's Analyst* on the streets of Greenwich Village in June 1967, a scene of actor James Coburn being chased by two movie cops was interrupted by a real policeman, who "gave him a couple of lumps on the head when he resisted," according to the *Times*'s Peter Millones. "The Mayor sent him a basket of fruit."

Fun City, John Lindsay, and *Midnight Cowboy*

Still images from *Midnight Cowboy* (1969), directed by John Schlesinger, photographed by Adam Holender.

Voight on "The Deuce."

But overall, the establishment of the Mayor's Office was a smashing success. By the end of the Lindsay administration, 366 films had been shot in the city, and studios and directors weren't the only ones who benefited. New York–based cinematographers (many trained in the live television days) like Gordon Willis, Michael Chapman, and Owen Roizman were redefining the way people looked at and thought about The City. And a host of New York stage actors were suddenly finding lucrative film work—not just leads like Hoffman and Sandy Dennis (whose nervous personality was a particularly good fit for the era), but the kind of character actors Dougherty and her assistant (and soon a casting titan in her own right) Juliet Taylor championed. "It became one of the great resources of shooting a movie in New York," she said, "to have a real interesting, realistic, eccentric, earthy sort of cast." And they had their pick of them; as Jerry Schatzberg, director of *The Panic in Needle Park*, notes, "On stage, many of these people were above the title."

Maybe they didn't have traditional "movie star" looks, but they were undeniably authentic, and that overall shift in expectations for screen acting was key to the effectiveness of these films—and of the "New Hollywood" movement of the following decade. "After *The Pawnbroker* came out," producer Roger Lewis told Vincent Canby, "everyone was congratulating Sidney Lumet on the great performances he had got from all the amateurs. Hell, they weren't amateurs, they were just New York actors who didn't look like actors!"

▬

After one more round of budget battles, Hellman managed to get the numbers down from their post-Hoffman proposal of $3.1 million to a more acceptable $2.3 million. Picker gave them the green light, and *Midnight Cowboy* was a go. Production was set to commence in New York in April 1968; they just needed a cinematographer.

Adam Holender arrived in New York from Poland in 1966—"A Polish boat delivered me to Montreal," he says, "and I came to New York by Greyhound bus from Montreal," an initial impression of the city he would subsequently re-create through Joe Buck's eyes. "Schlesinger came to New York looking for a cinematographer," Holender says, "and he wanted somebody of a younger generation and similar background to his. He came from England, I came from Poland." In other words, like Schlesinger, Holender was an outsider. "I guess if you come from another place," Holender reflects, "you are sensitized to what this place

has to offer—to a much larger extent than somebody who grew up here. For John, New York was also new; I guess both of us were curious."

In what Holender describes as "a very thoughtful and long pre-production period," he and Schlesinger took in their surroundings. "I came from Warsaw. It was a miserable, gray, oppressive Communist place. I came to New York, and it was like an explosion to all of the senses one could have." They noted the wild marquees, the neon and the billboards, the desolation of the diners, and, most of all, the blasé indifference of the city dwellers. "There was always something that seemed more frantic going on just off-camera," Schlesinger explained. During pre-production, he watched in amazement as a man lay on the sidewalk, asleep or comatose or perhaps even dead, in front of the luxury department store Bonwit Teller—unbothered by pedestrians, who simply stepped around him. "People just avoided going anywhere near him, and it both horrified and fascinated me, and I put it in," he said, moving the location to the exterior of the more iconic Tiffany & Co. It got a huge reaction from audiences: "Anything that dealt with the hardness of life there, and the lack of compassion or patience even, the time it would take to help a stranger, people ate that up."

The most disturbing images, of course, were found in Times Square. When Joe Buck arrives in New York, he rents a skeezy room in a dumpy hotel overlooking 42nd, and though we're never told explicitly why he goes there, we have to assume it's the same reason everyone does: because it's the center of everything. And when Joe's plan to collect the riches of unhappy city women proves unsurprisingly flawed, he's reduced to sleeping in grindhouses and cruising under their marquees. Schlesinger was fascinated by the cognitive dissonance between the inhabitants and the visitors, between the people who worked in Midtown and the people who lived there. "I'm fascinated when I see the West Side start to come out of their hutches in the morning," he told a *Look* reporter on a set visit, describing "a mixture of violence, desperation and humor all on one street." That was the mixture he had to capture on celluloid.

Such a stew could only be staged to a point. "I had this idea to put the camera on the sidewalk in Times Square," Holender recalls, "and film what we wanted to film from across the street. I had an idea that I was going to create a Trojan horse, and that was a very substantial wooden box, sort of like for delivery of big furniture. It had, inside, an opening for a lens to be placed." It was the old hidden-camera trickery from the silent era, updated with faster and longer lenses; they also used handheld cameras and faster film stock to grab scenes with minimal setup. (Under Lindsay, crews had that kind of flexibility. "It was a heck of a lot easier, from my perspective, than my two earlier shoots in New York," Hellman said, "where we literally had to pay people off left and right, just to keep shooting.")

Such run-and-gun ingenuity was required to film the movie's most iconic moment. As Hoffman tells it, Holender and his camera were hiding in a van to shoot a scene of Rizzo and Joe walking and talking down a couple of city blocks—which they couldn't afford to close off. "It was a difficult scene logistically because those were real pedestrians and there was real traffic," Hoffman recalled, "and Schlesinger wanted to do it in one shot—he didn't want to cut." Timing their progress to the traffic lights and whims of their fellow pedestrians proved more difficult than they'd imagined. "It was many takes, and then the timing was right. Suddenly we were doing this take and we knew it was going to work. We got to the signal just as it went green, so we could keep walking. But it just happened—there was a real cab trying to beat the signal. Almost hit us."

In that moment, Hoffman did the unthinkable: He broke character. When you watch the scene, you hear his voice change—it drops out of Rizzo's high register into a gruff, lower pitch much closer to Hoffman's own, as the frustrated actor bangs on the hood and shouts at the cabbie: "I'm walkin' here! I'm walkin' here! Up yours, you sonofabitch!" What he meant, he would later explain, was "We're shooting a scene here, and this is the first time we ever got it right, and you have fucked us up." But it also works for the moment, and the character—not just what he's saying, but the way he says it, as if Rizzo is temporarily adopting a tough-guy voice and stance that he's had to learn to survive on these streets.

Schlesinger, for his part, would always claim the line wasn't an improvisation, and recalled setting the taxi and staging the confrontation. (It's also possible that he was simply remembering, as Hoffman would, that he was so delighted with the off-the-cuff moment that he re-staged it for subsequent takes.) But he certainly wasn't closed off to improvisations, on set or especially in rehearsals, where he would let the actors go on tape, have the tapes transcribed, and ask Salt to rework the scene using the best moments and ideas. (Salt also stayed involved by appearing in the film—or, rather, his voice did, on the other end of the phone with Sylvia Miles, bow-wow-wowing at her dog.)

One of the key scenes to benefit from this kind of exploration was the "You're beginning to smell" scene, in which the two men poke, prod, and provoke each other as their living situation becomes more dire. "We had to investigate the nature of two people living together," Schlesinger said, "starting off in a rather hostile fashion—not trusting each other, eventually beginning to break that reserve down, and knowing each other much better, and starting to overtly criticize each other as part of the living-together process."

The scene did all of that, but it was also one of the few to address the homoerotic element of their relationship overtly, albeit via Rizzo's doth-protest-too-much "strictly for fags" diatribe. What's happening in the scene is much trickier—and trickier still was what was happening off-camera. Schlesinger was gay, recently out, and not quite sure how to navigate in the hyper-masculine environment of a New York film set. "The crew were these Irish and Italians from Long Island. They were a terrible old boys' network," said Michael Childers, Schlesinger's

**TOP AND CENTER**
Still images from *Midnight Cowboy* (1969), directed by John Schlesinger, photographed by Adam Holender.

**BOTTOM LEFT**
Still image from *No Way to Treat a Lady* (1968), directed by Jack Smight, photographed by Jack Priestley.

**BOTTOM RIGHT**
Still image from *The Detective* (1968), directed by Gordon Douglas, photographed by Joseph F. Biroc.

Still images from *Flesh* (1968), directed and photographed by Paul Morrissey.

romantic partner and production assistant on the film. "You had to be a son or a nephew to get into the union, which was right-wing and horrible."

"I don't know whether he thought they would beat him up," Hellman said, "but he certainly thought they'd say, 'You fucking faggot, you're not telling me what to do—go fuck yourself.'" Schlesinger himself would only say, in retrospect, "This was not the happiest experience working on this film. I didn't get on well with the crew."

With that kind of intolerance right there in the room, the director had a constant reminder of exactly how implicit his film would have to be. When Hoffman quizzed the director on the exact nature of the central relationship, Schlesinger admonished him: "Oh God! Please! It was hard enough to get the financing. Now all we have to do is tell them that we're making a homosexual film. I was hoping we would get the college crowd. We'll get no one."

Instead, much of the film's queerness, at least in regard to their relationship, is in pauses, subtext, and reactions. The close-ups when Rizzo first asks Joe to stay with him are uncomfortably close and intimate; you can all but touch the sweat on their faces. When Joe fixes himself up in their mirror and compliments himself ("There you are, you handsome devil you!"), there's a quiet longing in Rizzo's concurrence ("Not bad. Not bad. For a cowboy, you're okay"). It's not hard to guess that Joe's inability to perform with Shirley (Brenda Vaccaro) after the party is fueled, aside from any latent tendencies, by the fact that he's worried about Rizzo after his fall down the stairs. (The musical accompaniment as he "shows" her that he's not gay or fey is just mock-heroic enough to puncture his efforts.) And the sadness on Joe's face at the film's end is more than that of someone who has lost a friend; it's tinged with panic, the realization that he's returning to a place of loneliness.

"The story is of this relationship between the two men," Schlesinger would later say, admitting that its celebration of their love "probably was" one of the reasons he was attracted to the story. "It was a theme that had never been really tackled before." It certainly wasn't par for the course in New York cinema in the late 1960s; far more typical was the lurid ugliness of Gordon Douglas's *The Detective* (1968), with Frank Sinatra as an NYPD detective investigating the seamy homosexual underworld, or Jack Smight's *No Way to Treat a Lady* (1968), with Rod Steiger as a serial killer who adopts a variety of showy, wacky disguises, including a kindly Irish priest, a grouchy German building super, and (most unfortunately) a transgender bar dweller and a gay wigmaker. The mincing characterization of the latter is especially cringe-worthy—lisping, swishy, and cheap—but a valuable reminder of exactly how gay men were seen, even in the sophisticated metropolis of Gotham. A month after *Midnight Cowboy*'s release in summer 1969, that tide would finally, slowly start to turn, with the protest and uprising at Greenwich Village's Stonewall Inn.

In the meantime, there were offbeat alternatives. Andy Warhol doesn't appear in *Midnight Cowboy*, but he's inextricably tied to it; he was on the phone with his "Superstar" Viva on June 3, 1968, getting the good news that she'd been cast in a small but important role in *Cowboy*, when Valerie Solanas burst into the office and shot him.

Schlesinger wanted Andy to appear in Viva's scene, a wild "happening" at an industrial/artistic space not unlike Warhol's own Factory (then

**ABOVE AND OPPOSITE**
Still images from *Midnight Cowboy* (1969), directed by John Schlesinger, photographed by Adam Holender.

located at Union Square West and East 16th Street). Warhol had passed—and if he'd had second thoughts, his long recovery from the near-fatal shooting would certainly have prevented it—but had given his blessing to Viva and several other Warhol regulars (including Joe Dallesandro, International Velvet, Taylor Mead, and Ultra Violet) to appear, and for his filmmaking collaborator Paul Morrissey to contribute as well.

The shoot, which Hellman called "a six-day bacchanal" of sex and drugs, was staged at Filmways Studios in Harlem. Holender switches to 16mm film, for reasons both practical (it required less light) and aesthetic—it's as if Joe and Rizzo have wandered into a Warhol movie, rather than the other way around ("We didn't fight it, we just went for it," Holender explains). Viva wandered around with a tape recorder and asked everyone on the set to "say something to Andy, who's in the hospital." Schlesinger was delighted; "He'd say, 'Dahling, they're so wonderfully eccentric,'" said Vaccaro. "He got every wacko in town."

Warhol was initially pleased with the project—and happy to have, at least temporarily, someone else employing his actors. But he would come to see *Midnight Cowboy* as mainstream Hollywood profiting off his scene, and he sought out ways to return the favor. Warhol had an untitled gay cowboy movie in the can that was ready for release; he decided to name it *Lonesome Cowboys* and attract some residual heat. And maybe, since he and Morrissey worked so much quicker and cheaper than the big boys, they could get their own riff on *Midnight Cowboy* into the theaters before the real thing.

Shot in friends' apartments (and surreptitiously on street corners) over six weekends on a budget of three thousand dollars, Morrissey's *Flesh* (1968) feels like exactly what it is: an experimental, low-budget, semi-documentary version of *Midnight Cowboy*, dirtier and seamier and more voyeuristic. It's burdened by the flaws so typical of Warhol and Morrissey's pictures of the period—hard edits, ugly zooms, actors breaking character and fumbling through improvisations—but its self-consciousness somehow translates into grimy authenticity. And the filmmakers, who eagerly courted controversy and censorship, feel none of Schlesinger's hesitancy about the sexual fluidity of their characters; as their lead cheerfully explains, "It's not being straight or not straight, you just do whatever you have to do!"

While Morrissey was making his own *Midnight Cowboy*, the original production had made its way to Miami and then to Texas. The conflicts with the crew only got worse for Schlesinger in the Lone Star State, leading the filmmaker to a full-on anxiety attack on set. Voight discovered his director "red" and "sweating"; "I thought he was having a stroke," the actor said. "And I said, 'John, what's the matter?' He said, 'What're we making here anyway? What will they think of us?' I grabbed him by the shoulders just to shake him out of it, and I said, 'John, we will live the rest of our artistic lives in the shadow of this great masterpiece.'"

As much as Schlesinger dreaded them, the Texas scenes provided a vital contrast to the images of New York—vertical spaces, film historian Stanley Corkin writes, "dwarfing, socially alienating, and indicative of rigid hierarchy." The vision of Texas, on the other hand, is vast, wide, and horizontal; in fact, the opening shot gives us not only the wide, rectangular image of the Southwestern landscape, but also puts another frame (of the drive-in movie screen) inside that frame. It's afternoon, so the screen is blank, but we see and hear children playing

**146**

in front of it—playing, in fact, cowboys and Indians, a form of play-acting equally rooted in their geographic environment as the movie screen inside it.

The Miami sojourn was equally vital. Rizzo sells Joe on the idea of moving to Florida, as New York City seems to be literally collapsing around them; the condemned tenement in which he's squatting will soon be demolished, just like the buildings next door whose rubble they must climb to get "home." But not for long: "You got more ladies in Miami than any given resort area," he promises Joe. And it provides him a mental getaway while he waits for Joe to make their money—a sun-drenched fantasy of their life there, an all-you-can-eat buffet of ease and pleasure. Florida is a dream of freedom, a mental escape from the city's crushing reality. And when the camera catches the reflection of Miami's condos on the windows of the bus, superimposed over Rizzo's fallen visage in the closing scenes, we're reminded of the dream he never saw come true. But the alluring idea of escape would prove a durable one, a distant flight of fancy for the desperate characters of New York movies in the decade to come.

▬

*Midnight Cowboy* wrapped in August 1968. Schlesinger tinkered with the edit as long as United Artists would let him, wondering to the end, per Hellman, if "anyone in their right mind is going to pay money to see this fucking rubbish." But when they finally showed it to the UA brass, including their champion David Picker and his uncle Arnold, the reception was astonishment. "There was dead silence," the younger Picker recalled. "Arnold, who was sitting behind me, leaned forward and said, 'It's a masterpiece.' The room exploded. Everybody was crying."

They loved it so much that they didn't even object when the Motion Picture Association of America, then barely a year old, slapped it with the X rating—not yet a signifier of pornography, but certainly its most restrictive rating. It was the first major studio release to carry the classification. Schlesinger was thrilled. "We felt the X was the correct rating for it," he said. "We had made the film for adults, not children." The studio decided to premiere the film in New York on May 25, 1969, play exclusively in the city for a couple of months, screen at the Berlin Film Festival in July, and let word of mouth build.

It wasn't all positive. Hoffman would remember sitting in the back row at those early screenings and watching people leave in packs when the explicitly homosexual scenes unspooled. James Leo Herlihy also didn't care for some of those scenes—specifically, the ones that didn't appear in his book—and complained to the press at the premiere about the scene of "the deviate act in the balcony of the movie theater." And some of the reviews were mixed. Roger Ebert praised Hoffman and Voight but complained that Schlesinger had "taken these magnificent performances, and his own careful perception of American society, and dropped them into an offensively trendy, gimmick-ridden, tarted-up, vulgar exercise in fashionable cinema." Pauline Kael accused Schlesinger of using "fast cutting and tricky camerawork to provide a satirical background as enrichment to the story, but the satire is offensively inaccurate—it cheapens the story and gives it a veneer of almost hysterical cleverness." Even Rex Reed's positive review concluded, "It all adds up to a collage of screaming, crawling, vomiting humanity which makes *Midnight Cowboy* a nasty but unforgettable screen experience."

But audiences were enraptured. From opening day, lines stretched for blocks, and UA's slow rollout strategy worked. "Popularity of the film hasn't been restricted to N.Y.," *Variety* reported the following April, "but has proven equally a hit in Dallas, Chicago, Detroit, Toronto, Frisco, Milwaukee and Providence, rolling up all-time highs in those cities." It

Voight, Hoffman, and
Schlesinger shoot on the
streets.

would gross $44.8 million in its initial theatrical run—$307 million when adjusted for inflation.

Some of that was the result of a post-Oscars boost. The film got seven nominations: Best Picture, Best Director, Best Adapted Screenplay, Best Actor (both Voight and Hoffman were nominated), Best Supporting Actress (for Sylvia Miles), and Best Editing. The film's team assumed they would lose to *Butch Cassidy and the Sundance Kid*, another buddy movie with bigger box office and a PG rating, so Schlesinger didn't even bother to come (he was already making his next movie, *Sunday Bloody Sunday*, in London), and Hellman got sloshed. But then Salt won, and then Schlesinger, and then Hellman found himself onstage collecting the big prize. It was the first (and last) X-rated movie to win Best Picture.

Voight and Hoffman lost Best Actor, ironically enough, to John Wayne—the subject of a memorable dialogue exchange in their movie ("John Wayne? You wanna tell me *he's* a fag?"). The award felt like one last acknowledgment of the old guard, from the traditional movie stars to serious actors, what Voight dubbed "sons of Brando": "'No, I am who I am, I want to see the warts. When I work, I don't give a damn about having the perfect light and perfect makeup.' We wanted to see it as it was. Tell other stories. *Midnight Cowboy* was a perfect example of that."

∎

By the time Hellman was collecting *Midnight Cowboy*'s Oscars, John Lindsay was fighting for his political life. The establishment of the Mayor's Office of Film, Theatre & Broadcasting and the upswing in film production had been one of the few unqualified successes of his first term. Meanwhile, the crime rate had nearly doubled; taxes had gone up; rents had gone higher; his initiative to create a civilian review board for the NYPD had failed; and six of the major municipal unions had called either work slowdowns or strikes on Lindsay's watch. Murray Kempton, who'd penned the beloved "He is fresh, and everyone else is tired" column back in 1965, now wrote, "Under Lindsay, the air is fouler, the streets dirtier, the bicycle thieves more vigilant, the labor contracts more abandoned in their disregard for the public good . . . than any of these elements ever were under the former mayor, Robert F. Wagner."

State senator John Marchi challenged Lindsay for the 1969 nomination—the city's first mayoral Republican primary in more than a quarter of a century—and then, in an even greater embarrassment, the challenger won. Lindsay was reduced to running as an independent, on the Liberal Party ticket. His advisors realized they couldn't run a conventional campaign and instead cooked up a media strategy centered on a series of TV commercials with the incumbent speaking candidly about his hard-learned lessons and hard-earned wisdom. Cynics dubbed them the "Lindsay eats shit" spots.

But the strategy connected. The combination of his underdog campaign and the shortcomings of his opponents helped the mayor eke out a win with 41 percent of the vote. Lindsay may not have been the savior New Yorkers were hoping for. But for now, it seemed, they were stuck with each other.

And things were going to get worse before they got better. In a February 1969 feature, something of a decade-concluding bookend to their 1960 summary of 42nd Street squalor, the *Times* dubbed Times Square "Cesspool of the World." The complaints were similar: petty crime, juvenile delinquents, prostitution, narcotics, "bookstores that sell magazines of nude women and men in the most specific detail," and "cinematic peep shows that feature preliminaries to love-making."

The city's tourism board could boost its historic sites, its Broadway shows, and its unmatched museums. But this was increasingly what people thought of when they thought of New York, and the films that were being made there—thanks to Lindsay's own initiative—were part of the reason why. "No doubt many of these movies exaggerated New York's problems, but the image of an increasingly dangerous and chaotic city was real enough," writes historian Vincent J. Cannato. "With these portrayals, the image of New York City as a place of danger, decay, and division became solidified in the nation's mind."

When Joe Buck first arrives in New York City, he strides down the packed sidewalks of Fifth Avenue, literally head and shoulders above everyone else; *Midnight Cowboy* is, among other things, the story of how the city cuts him down to size (Ratso Rizzo's size, specifically). Throughout this narrative, the would-be hustler keeps getting hustled: by his first trick, whom *he* ends up paying; by Rizzo, who takes him for an easy ten bucks; by the bespectacled college student, who engages him for sex and then reveals he's broke.

Throughout this adventure, Schlesinger repeatedly contrasts Joe's macho fantasies with his miserable reality. He triumphantly rehearses quitting his dishwashing job, but the execution is mealy-mouthed and half-hearted. He imagines how he'll rough up Rizzo for his con job, but barely touches him when they finally reunite. He rehearses his tough talk in the mirror before confronting his older john, and ends up bullying the poor, pathetic soul. Joe Buck may not be a native New Yorker, but he's a lot like this version of New York: mired in the dissonance between what he fancies himself to be, and what he actually is.

NOW SHOWING

BLAST OF SILENCE

BREAKFAST AT TIFFANY'S

THE PAWNBROKER

ROSEMARY'S BABY

# BLAST OF SILENCE

## 1961

## Director: Allen Baron

When moviegoers began to discover *Blast of Silence* in the 1990s and 2000s, as it popped up at revival houses and finally as part of the Criterion Collection, it seemed an inexplicable anomaly: What *was* this micro-budgeted, pre-indie, pitch-black late *noir*? Where had it come from, and where had it been hiding? Less a crime movie than an existentialist dirge, it tells the story of a hired killer from Ohio who comes to New York City—and finds he's no match for it.

Plot-wise, *Blast of Silence* is unadorned and direct: hitman Frankie Bono (writer and director Allen Baron)

arrives in New York, his train emerging from its tunnel as the narrator recalls the character's painful birth, a broad metaphor that still works. He gets his assignment, arranges for a gun and silencer, waits around for their delivery, does the job, and is then killed himself. The "waiting around" stretch, however, is where the movie gets interesting; our ill-at-ease protagonist runs into an old friend, goes to a party, goes on a date that turns into an attempted rape, and goes to the Village Gate to hear some authentic beatnik bongo music.

Mostly, though, he walks the streets of the city. It's often with a purpose, tracking his mark to plan the execution, or following his drunken gun contact (Larry Tucker, who would go on to co-write several Paul Mazursky pictures) back to his grimy apartment to choke him out. But often he's walking just to walk, wandering the streets of New York on Christmas, past light displays and store windows and the Rockefeller Center Christmas tree, tapping into the strange loneliness and desperation of the holidays in the city.

Baron and cinematographer Merrill Brody captured their time capsule–worthy snapshots of the city—Greenwich Village, Rockefeller Center, the old Penn Station, the marshes that would become Kennedy airport—guerilla-style, shooting without permits on a shoestring budget (reports vary from $50,000 to $65,000). And though it won a critics prize at Locarno and was picked up for release by Universal, the studio buried it on the bottom half of double bills and it remained mostly unknown until its Criterion release in 2008. But lovers of New York cinema already knew its secrets.

Still image from *Blast of Silence* (1961), directed by Allen Baron, photographed by Merrill Brody.

# BREAKFAST AT TIFFANY'S

## 1961
## Director: Blake Edwards

Due to the sheer logistical complexity of making a major motion picture, the first scene of a film is rarely the first scene shot. But the iconic opening sequence of *Breakfast at Tiffany's*, the scene that gives the film its very title, also marked the inauguration of production. Director Blake Edwards was granted one week to shoot on location in New York City, scheduling photography for the exteriors of the New York Public Library, the Women's House of Detention, and Holly and Paul's brownstone on the Upper East Side; the confrontation between Doc and Paul at the Central Park bandshell; a few streetside walk-and-talks; and the elements for the sequence of Holly and Paul doing things they've never done in the city.

But Edwards scheduled the Tiffany's scene first, early in the morning of Sunday, October 2, 1960, figuring that if they were in and out early enough, star Audrey Hepburn might not draw a crowd. He figured wrong; crowds were drawn not by the petite leading lady but by the police cars on the scene, leading passersby to assume the high-end jewelry store had been robbed. Just to be safe, the store had hired twenty extra armed guards for the day, because once that scene was completed, the company moved indoors—the first motion picture ever shot inside Tiffany's, a bargain the retailer was willing to make in exchange for publicity photos of Hepburn sporting their merchandise.

*Tiffany's* also explores notions present in *The Seven Year Itch* (1955): the inherent intimacy of New York apartment neighbors, who spend their days and nights gazing longingly through windows and up fire escapes. (Edwards, a specialist in physical comedy, also marvelously dramatizes the dangers and acrobatics of big cocktail parties in tiny New York apartments.) And in the "tourists in their own town" sequence, Edwards is looking ahead to decades of New York films that would feature city-strolling, lyrical interludes that culminate in a kiss (or more)—the city as aphrodisiac.

*Breakfast at Tiffany's* is one of the final, culture-penetrating portraits of New York City as a glistening, magical fairyland, and it's best approached as such. (Shame about all those Mickey Rooney scenes.)

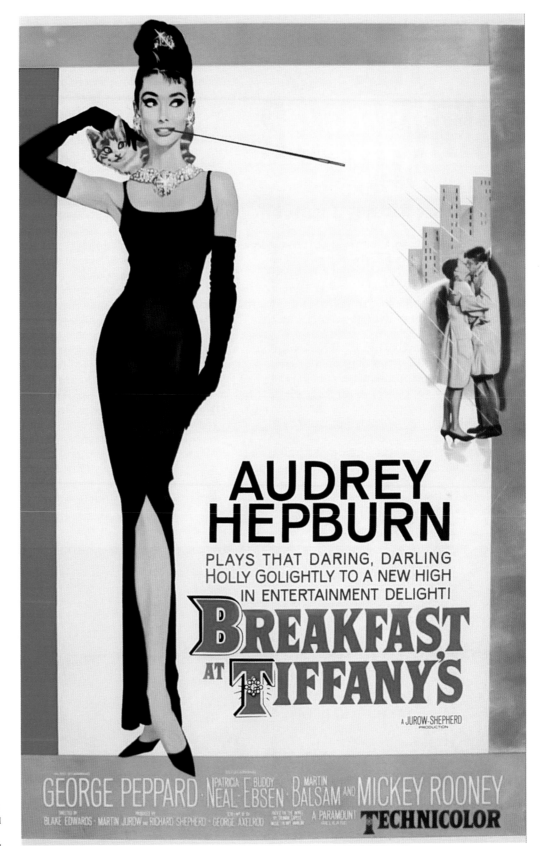

# THE PAWNBROKER

## 1965

## Director: Sidney Lumet

One of the last major New York movies of the pre-Lindsay era, and not only in terms of difficulty of production, Lumet's portrait of a repressed Jewish pawnbroker is, as film historian James Sanders notes, "a period portrait of the kind of ordinary working life that prevailed across much of Manhattan in the first half of the 20th century—the city that remained very much in place through Mayor Wagner's three terms in office." The daily life of Sol Nazerman (Rod Steiger) is a joyless one, a blurring dirge of interactions with a clientele that seems bent on alternately conning and insulting him; some of the richer subtext in the film is found in the tension between Nazerman and his customers (and employee) of color.

Production designer Richard Sylbert built the pawnshop in an existing, empty storefront at Park Avenue and 116th Street, using the space as both the interior and exterior set (allowing a continuity of movement and spatial reality that he and Lumet would return to, a decade later, in *Dog Day Afternoon*). Lumet used hidden cameras to capture the spontaneous reactions of passersby to the violence and panic at the picture's conclusion. Cinematographer Boris Kaufman (*On the Waterfront*, *The World of Henry Orient*) also made use of locations throughout the city for a contemplative sequence of Sol trying to clear his head by, it seems, breaking away from his usual surroundings.

But, for most of the film, he's trapped there; Lumet and editor Ralph Rosenblum underscore his discomfort with the near-subliminal quick-cut flashbacks that quickly became a cliché in late-sixties moviemaking and marketing. But these edits, which connect Nazerman's present to the past horrors of the Nazi concentration camp he survived, are no gimmick, nor are they arbitrary; they're most often triggered by the similarly confining vertical spaces he dwells in: fences, enclosures, the "cage" of his shop counter, and finally (and most hauntingly) the subway car. The subtext is frightening: For Sol Nazerman, the city is as confining and hopeless as a prison camp.

When he finally attempts to verbalize his trauma to a kind neighbor (Geraldine Page), he's still trapped, bound by the fencing around her high-rise balcony. In some compositions, the fading industrial elements of the city—factories and train yards—seem to observe him; in others, he is surrounded by the towers of her adjacent apartment complexes, the city continuing to close in.

Nazerman is a soft-spoken, mildly impatient, but basically emotionless man. He just wants to be left alone, and everyone keeps imposing on his time, because (and this is the inherent conundrum of the antisocial city dweller) you cannot avoid interactions with other people when you live in this kind of proximity, day in and day out. Everything he tries to keep at bay—his neighbors, his past, his very self—will eventually find a way in. It's inevitable. The City always finds a way.

Still image from *The Pawnbroker* (1964), directed by Sidney Lumet, photographed by Boris Kaufman.

The Pawnbroker is "Undoubtedly one of the finest motion pictures in many years…"
—CORONET MAGAZINE

The Pawnbroker is "One of the most remarkably gripping movies of our time!"
—COSMOPOLITAN MAGAZINE

The Pawnbroker is "Full of emotional shocks, it burns into the mind!"
—TIME MAGAZINE

The Pawnbroker is "A shockingly good film… superbly directed… flawlessly acted."
—LIFE MAGAZINE

# ROD STEIGER
# THE PAWNBROKER

ELY LANDAU AND HERBERT R. STEINMANN PRESENT ROD STEIGER IN THE PAWNBROKER CO-STARRING BROCK PETERS WITH JAIME SANCHEZ AND GERALDINE FITZGERALD / DIRECTED BY SIDNEY LUMET / SCREENPLAY BY MORTON FINE AND DAVID FRIEDKIN FROM THE NOVEL BY EDWARD LEWIS WALLANT / MUSIC BY QUINCY JONES / PRODUCED BY ROGER LEWIS AND PHILIP LANGNER / EXECUTIVE PRODUCER WORTHINGTON MINER / DISTRIBUTED BY AMERICAN INTERNATIONAL.    PRINTS BY MOVIELAB

# ROSEMARY'S BABY

## 1968

## Director: Roman Polanski

They call it "The Branford" in the movie, but everybody knows the ornate, Gothic apartment complex that serves as the primary location for Roman Polanski's adaptation of Ira Levin's novel: The Dakota. It's perhaps the most famous apartment building in the city, home (at various points) of Judy Garland, Lauren Bacall, Leonard Bernstein, and John and Yoko, and one of the most enjoyably authentic elements of *Rosemary's Baby* is its understanding of how tall tales and rumors attach themselves to an old property in the city, how a building can acquire a reputation that envelops its appeal as mere real estate. "Awful things happen in every apartment house," Rosemary protests, and she's right. But not like this one.

Director Roman Polanski pushed to shoot on location in New York City, reasoning (correctly) that the story's supernatural elements—it concerns a young woman (Mia Farrow) who is impregnated by the devil himself, to deliver her child to the satanic cult that inhabits their building—would seem both more horrifying and more credible if framed within recognizable scenes of daily city life. (The interiors are shot on soundstages, though production designer Richard Sylbert was friends with Bacall, and modeled the Woodhouse apartment on her residence.)

By shooting in the city, Polanski also underscored the story's specific New York City subtext: the kindness, or at least, tolerance, forced by proximity. At first Rosemary and Guy's neighbors in the Bradford seem, well, neighborly, a point shaded by her response to hearing about the Castevets' charitable actions to young Terry ("It's nice to know there are people like that, when you hear so much about apathy and people who are afraid of getting involved," she says, subtly referencing the hubbub surrounding the murder of Kitty Genovese). But letting these people into your life has a price, as Rosemary discovers when their interference leaves her sickly, pale, and all but broken during pregnancy.

*Rosemary's Baby* was one of Paramount's biggest hits of 1968. It was subsequently re-released as part of what posters dubbed "the greatest double feature of all time" with one of the studio's other 1968 smashes: Gene Saks's film adaptation of Neil Simon's *The Odd Couple*. On one hand, it's a peculiar pairing. On the other, they're both basically movies about discovering how much you'll put up with for a great New York apartment.

**OPPOSITE**
Still image from *Rosemary's Baby* (1968), directed by Roman Polanski, photographed by William A. Fraker.

# 1970

# Fear City, Blackouts, and *Taxi Driver*

# 1979

**PREVIOUS SPREAD**
Robert De Niro and Martin
Scorsese on the set of *Taxi
Driver* (1976).

**ABOVE**
Still image from *Who's That
Knocking at My Door*

Martin Scorsese is arguably the most famous son of Little Italy, so it comes as something of a shock to discover he wasn't even a native of the neighborhood. "I was born in Queens in 1942," he explained in 1992. "We first lived in Corona, near my aunts and uncles. I remember we had a two-family house with a yard in the back that had a tree in it." This picture of semi-suburban bliss doesn't jibe at all with the now-enshrined image of little Marty Scorsese, watching the world from his window. That came later, after the family moved to the Lower East Side following a dispute with the landlord ("I've never found out what it was all about"). They moved into an apartment on Elizabeth Street, third floor front.

By that time, Scorsese had developed health troubles: chronic asthma, complications following a tonsillectomy. "I couldn't run around, so I would see everything from an overhead shot," he explained. "From the third floor, looking down. In my movies, some critics say, 'Oh, he's always doing God's point of view.' No, actually, it's mine. It looks *great* from up there."

When he wasn't watching the wiseguys and neighborhood characters, he was watching television. Movies on television, to be more specific; his first film school was *Million Dollar Movie*, on the local WOR TV 9, which ran one film per week, over and over, twice every day. It was meant to increase access for busy viewers in those pre-VCR, pre-DVR days, but Scorsese would watch all ten showings of the movies he loved, looking for new details and inspirations. He formed ideas for movies of his own, which he would draw out in crude frames—his first storyboards.

But he harbored no real filmmaking aspirations, not yet. His parents, strict Catholics, wanted him to be a priest, and he studied at seminary school in the late 1950s. His grades, however, were dismal, and he was spending more and more time at the local cinema, where he had discovered art-house imports by the likes of Bergman, Truffaut, Antonioni, Godard, and Fellini. His education continued when he entered New York University, studying film under the guidance of Professor Haig Manoogian and making his first short films—comedies, mostly. In 1965, he started a short called *Bring on the Dancing Girls*, a more personal story about listless neighborhood guys like himself. The lead character, J.R., was a thinly veiled avatar for the filmmaker, a lifelong Catholic struggling with questions of temptation and sin in the increasingly permissive 1960s. He cast a young actor named Harvey Keitel in the role. "It was not an accomplished film in any way," he says now. "There were maybe a couple of things in it that I can look at, but that's it."

Scorsese would subsequently expand the film twice: first into a full feature, which screened at the Chicago International Film Festival in 1967 under the title *I Call First* (the *Chicago Sun-Times*'s new film critic, Roger Ebert, gave it a rave review), and then with a distributor-imposed sex sequence the following year, when it was released theatrically under the title *Who's That Knocking at My Door?* The film's opening sequence includes images of religious icons and pasta preparation, accompanied by high-energy rock music. Rarely has a filmmaker's aesthetic been so clearly defined from frame one.

■

"Can New York Survive?" blared the 1969 headline in the *New York Times Magazine*. It was penned by Norman Mailer, part of his sorta-joke campaign for the mayoralty, but the question lingered well into the second term of his opponent, John Lindsay—who had become, by its conclusion (and per the *Village Voice*), "An Exile in His Own City."

That city seemed to be caving in under his feet, sometimes literally; a 1971 Ford Foundation report found "a general deterioration of the city environment, visible and palpable in streets, subways, the air and the water around New York." As employment dropped and quality of life in the city decreased, rents and taxes continued to rise; middle-class residents found more affordable homes and an escape from the stresses of the city in the suburbs of New York State, New Jersey, and Connecticut. This "white flight" had been a steady trickle for years; in the seventies, it became a geyser.

Fear City, Blackouts, and *Taxi Driver*

Scenes from the city's '70 cinema: *Shaft* (1971), directed by Gordon Parks, photographed by Urs Furrer; *Super Fly* (1972), directed by Gordon Parks Jr., photographed by James Signorelli; *Klute* (1971), directed by Alan J. Pakula, photographed by Gordon Willis; *Cops and Robbers* (1973), directed by Aram Avakian, photographed by David L. Quaid.

The solution, some boosters felt, was to replace the missing tax dollars with those of free-spending tourists; the problem, as syndicated columnists Rowland Evans and Robert Novak wrote, was that "Americans do not much like, admire, respect, trust, or believe in New York." In 1971, a consortium of marketing minds, tourism execs, bankers, realtors, and government officials formed the Association for a Better New York (ABNY), a public-private partnership dedicated to putting the city's best face forward for vacationers. New York wasn't "fun city," they insisted—it was the "Big Apple," home of museums, Broadway, restaurants, shopping, the Statue of Liberty.

But the very qualities that were making the city so unattractive to tourists were what drew filmmakers there, to make films that frequently furthered its troublesome cesspool image. "What really pushed New York over the top as Hollywood's location of choice was its image—now being formed in the mind of the national audience—as the capital of urban crisis," writes Miriam Greenberg, in her book *Branding New York: How a City in Crisis Was Sold to the World.* "In general, films about New York in this period were twisting Lindsay's 'Fun City' into a playground of purely sadistic pleasures."

*Times* film critic Vincent Canby was more direct. "Lindsay should never have allowed the filmmakers into the city," he wrote. "It was encouraging the foxes to enter the henhouse."

It was not, to be sure, just the movies' fault. The major television networks, newspapers, and weekly newsmagazines were almost entirely located in New York, and this was the era in which "If it bleeds, it leads" became an all-purpose truism. On light national-news days, a local crime became national news; the kinds of local crimes that were flashy enough were the most violent, and/or class-based, and/or race-based.

That's also the kind of flash filmmakers were creating. "New York City is always New York City," wrote Pauline Kael. "It can't be anything else, and, with practically no studios for fakery, the movie companies use what's really here, so the New York–made movies have been set in Horror City." If the original Fun City films were madcap Gotham-trotting comedies like *You're a Big Boy Now, The World of Henry Orient*, and *A Thousand Clowns*, the Horror City pictures were of the *Midnight Cowboy* mold: gritty dramas of social realism (like the live teleplays that helped create the "New York sensibility" of the 1950s), full of desperate characters trying to stay afloat as the choppy waters of the city rise around them.

In 1971's *Panic in Needle Park* (see sidebar on page 202) and its tragicomic twin *Born to Win*, the heroin addicts of Mid- and uptown hustle, panhandle, prostitute, and do whatever it takes for their daily fix; they live in a world where all the streets are strewn with trash, every buy could be a "hot shot," and every hallway is filled with the sounds of an unattended crying baby. The cops play a little rough, but have some interest in cleaning up the streets and our protagonists; in their blaxploitation cousins, like *Shaft* (1971), *Super Fly* (1972), and *Black Caesar* (1973), the cops are combative at best and corrupt at worst, and our heroes only manage to survive by staying above the fray, remaining their own man. Similar self-interest is found in Bree (Jane Fonda), the cynical call girl of *Klute* (1971) who helps a mild-mannered Pennsylvania detective navigate the New York underworld—for a price.

The fear and despair of these movies—best articulated by *Born to Win*'s antihero J (George Segal) and his cry, "I don't understand it, I keep getting beat! I KEEP GETTING BEAT! I'M SICK OF IT!"—was just a degree or two from comedy, and that pivot was seen in a concurrent movement of farces of urban desperation. A year before *Born to Win*, Segal starred in *Where's Poppa?*, Carl Reiner's pitch-black comedy of senior confusion and social discomfort, in which a major subplot hinges on the presumption that a trip through Central Park after dark will result perhaps in a mugging, or perhaps a rape. (Much to the consternation of the ABNY, the Central Park mugging was a favorite '70s punch line of Johnny Carson, who had moved *The Tonight Show* from New York City to Burbank in 1972.)

Central Park also provides anything but rest and reflection for the Kellermans, George (Jack Lemmon) and Gwen (Sandy Dennis), the Ohio couple at the center of *The Out-of-Towners* (1970). They travel to the city so that George can interview for a possible promotion, and manage to land in the midst of a transit strike, sanitation strike, *and* rainstorm; in the course of their planned weekend of romance and sightseeing, they're mugged, kidnapped, chased by cops, trapped in a protest, and nearly killed.

At the end of the day, however, the Kellermans can flee the hell of the city and return to their suburban comfort. The protagonists of most other contemporary comedies have no such escape route; they're no longer horrified by the trials of New York City living, and simply do their best to hack their way through the day, as those horrors are played for broad laughs. In a documentary film-within-the-film section of Brian De Palma's *Hi, Mom!* (1970), a couple is interviewed on the street while a newspaper vendor is robbed and shot in the background. In Woody Allen's *Bananas* (1971), our protagonist attempts to disappear into his freshly purchased dirty magazine when the elderly woman next to him on the subway is accosted by thugs (including a young Sylvester Stallone); he hurries home to hide behind a total of six door locks (three chains, a dead bolt, a slide, and a metal bar jammed into the floor).

In *The Owl and the Pussycat* (1970), Barbra Streisand rebuffs a group of catcallers, who immediately chase her and George Segal into the subway. In *The Landlord* (1970), rich white kid Elgar Enders (Beau Bridges) has no sooner arrived in front of his new home in Park Slope than he's chased down the block by his new, African American neighbors. Robert Redford is mugged in *The Hot Rock* (1972) while *standing in front of a police station*.

Jules Feiffer's screenplay for *Little Murders* (1971) is the bleakest of all, a nihilistic exaggeration (barely) of the unruliness and disorder of the city. It opens with a woman (Marcia Rodd) awakening to a violent beating outside her apartment window; she calls 911 and gets a busy signal, and is put on indefinite hold when she calls back. So she goes out to rescue the victim (Elliott Gould), who promptly gets up and walks away as the gang turns on his rescuer. Everyone looks out for themselves in this city, plagued with periodic black- and brownouts and random street shootings; its characters finally find happiness by opening up the window and shooting back. Not the subtlest metaphor, but it'll do.

"The city of New York has helped American movies grow up; it has also given movies a new spirit of nervous, anxious hopelessness, which is the true spirit of New York," Kael wrote. "It is literally true that when you live in New York you no longer believe that the garbage will ever be gone from the streets or that life will ever be sane and orderly." That spirit of hopelessness pervades *The Prisoner of Second Avenue* (1975), which reunites *Out-of-Towners* screenwriter Neil Simon with its star Jack Lemmon, and feels like a spiritual sequel to that film: an imagining

Still images from *Where's Poppa?* (1970), directed by Carl Reiner, photographed by Jack Priestley; *The Out of Towners* (1970), directed by Arthur Hiller, photographed by Andrew Laszlo; *Hi, Mom!* (1970), directed by Brian De Palma, photographed by Robert Elfstrom; *Bananas* (1971), directed by Woody Allen, photographed by Andrew M. Costikyan.

of who the Kellermans might have become had they not hightailed it back to Ohio. It traps them in a dumpy fourteenth-floor apartment in the midst of a heat wave and a garbage strike, signs of a city that's irreparably broken; when a radio newsman announces, "City residents were asked to get their shovels in a joint effort to show how New Yorkers can live and work together in a common cause," it's played as the film's final laugh line.

But there's more to *Prisoner* than Simon's usual comedy of neuroticism and inconvenience. "I think I'm losing my mind," Mel (Lemmon) tells his wife, Edna (Anne Bancroft). "I'm unraveling. I'm losing touch. Something is happening to me. I'm losing control. I can't handle anything."

Later, when Mel loses his job and can't find another one, he slips deeper into the darkness; he's unshaven, disheveled, an emasculated mess. When his gainfully employed wife tries to reach out to him, he snaps back, roaring, "DON'T PATRONIZE ME, AND DON'T MOCK ME!" There's real (white male) rage there, in this figure who announces, "I'm gettin' tired of being shoved around!"

It wasn't just the character; there was something in the air. Paul Schrader smelled it, too.

——

The legend of Paul Schrader is nearly as well-cast as that of his frequent collaborator Scorsese: A Michigan native and the child of strict Dutch Calvinists, Schrader didn't see a film until he was eighteen (his family believed them to be evil). He immersed himself in cinema in college and grad school, and flirted with film criticism (he even wrote a heady book of it, *Transcendental Style in Film*), but couldn't make it work. Schrader plunged into a dark period: His wife kicked him out. He lived in his car, drove all night, slept off the day in grimy porno theaters. He developed a bleeding gastric ulcer and checked himself into a hospital.

Somehow, in the midst of that misery and self-destruction, he began to see a character and a story. "The theme," he explained, "was loneliness, or as I realized later, self-imposed loneliness. The metaphor was the taxi, a metal coffin on wheels, the absolute symbol of urban isolation. . . . And I put all that in the pressure cooker of New York City." When he got out of the hospital, he sat down and pounded out a screenplay.

It told the story of Travis Bickle, a restless Vietnam veteran who gets a job as a New York City cabbie, working long nights, priding himself on driving anywhere, even the neighborhoods other drivers dodge. During the day, he drinks, medicates, and goes to porno movies. One day, he spots a vision, Betsy, a beautiful blonde working for a political campaign; they go for coffee, and she's intrigued and attracted enough to grant him a proper date. But Travis blows it, taking her to one of the Times Square theaters where he insists "lots of couples go," and she refuses to speak to him after. Frustrated, Travis instead becomes obsessed with Iris, a pre-teen prostitute whom he thinks he can save, all the while planning to assassinate Senator Charles Palantine, Betsy's employer, in an act of impotent rage. But he loses his nerve and instead murders Iris's pimp Sport, and several other men, in a whorehouse massacre. He attempts to turn his gun on himself but fails; he's out of bullets. Instead, he's hailed as a folk hero.

The story poured out of Schrader like blood, all on the page in ten days. "The script began in the best possible way, which is that it began as self-therapy," he said, forty years later. "There was a person who I was afraid of, who I was afraid I was becoming, and that was this taxi driver.

**OPPOSITE LEFT**
Still images from *The Landlord* (1970), directed by Hal Ashby, photographed by Gordon Willis; *The Hot Rock* (1972), directed by Peter Yates, photographed by Edward R. Brown; *Little Murders* (1971), directed by Alan Arkin, photographed by Gordon Willis; *The Prisoner of Second Avenue* (1975), directed by Melvin Frank, photographed by Philip H. Lathrop.

**OPPOSITE RIGHT**
Director Martin Scorsese, screenwriter Paul Schrader, and producer Michael Phillips on the set of *Taxi Driver*.

And I felt that if I wrote about him, I could just distance him from me."
Once the script was out of his system, he put it aside; he spent six
months away from it, traveling, visiting friends, getting his head
together. His brother Leonard, then stationed in Japan as a missionary,
sent him a letter with an idea for a script, which became *The Yakuza*.
The Schraders sold it to Warner Brothers for $300,000—then the
highest check ever written for a spec screenplay. Bolstered by the big
sale, Schrader felt ready to return to the script about the taxi driver.

It was summer, 1972. Schrader was writing a magazine piece, a profile of
the director Brian De Palma, who would subsequently helm Schrader's
script *Obsession*. But they started out talking about *Taxi Driver*, a script
De Palma liked but recognized he wasn't right for. He passed it to his
next-door neighbor, producer Michael Phillips. "I read it, and I thought I
was looking into a naked soul," Phillips said. "I had never seen anything
like this."

De Palma also passed it to Marty Scorsese. Scorsese had relocated
(albeit temporarily) to the West Coast after *Who's That Knocking*'s
release, using it as a calling card for editing work (including the rock
docs *Woodstock* and *Elvis on Tour*) and to land a gig directing a *Bonnie
and Clyde* rip-off for Roger Corman called *Boxcar Bertha*. "Brian was my
main champion all that time," Scorsese recalls, "from late '60s all the
way through to mid-'70s. And he'd take me to just meet everybody."

"Everybody" was primarily the UCLA and USC crowd, socially awkward
but film-crazy guys like De Palma, John Milius, George Lucas, and the
shyest of them all, Steven Spielberg. They watched each other's rough
cuts and gave each other advice about scripts, or passed them around,
and that's how Scorsese read *Taxi Driver*: "Brian had the script, gave it

to me and said, 'You should do this.'" Scorsese was struck by the script's
simplicity and how it allowed him to interpolate his own ideas. "It's very
spare," he says, "and that cleared away a vision that I had for the
picture. . . . I immediately saw that clearly, how it could be made. How
I should make it, I should say."

The problem was he had to convince Michael Phillips and his wife and
producing partner, Julia. They were casting other names around; maybe
Sydney Pollack, who had directed Schrader's *Yakuza* script, or Milius, or
Irvin Kershner, or maybe Robert Mulligan. Scorsese didn't impress them
much. "Marty slides up to me at parties and tells me in his intense
undertone how much he wants to do this picture," Julia Phillips wrote.
"He is shoulder high, and sometimes I find myself talking out of the side
of my mouth and into the top of his hair. Not a chance. Forget it. Come
back when you've done something besides *Boxcar Bertha*."

By that point, he had—she just hadn't seen it. Scorsese worked with an
NYU classmate, Mardik Martin, on a script they originally called *Season
of the Witch*; it was (the story goes) the result of Scorsese screening
*Boxcar Bertha* for his idol and friend John Cassavetes, who hugged him
afterward and grinned, "Martin, you just spent a year of your life making
a piece of shit!" His assessment was hyperbolic, but the point was clear:
If Scorsese wanted to be a real moviemaker, he couldn't waste his time
on hackwork. He had to do something personal.

*Season of the Witch* was something of a follow-up to *Who's That
Knocking*, again focusing on Harvey Keitel as a guy from the neighborhood torn between his faith and the flesh, between his obligation to his
"business" and his loyalty to his wild, trigger-happy pal Johnny Boy. To
fill that role, Scorsese cast another guy from the neighborhood, whom

OPPOSITE AND
BELOW
Still images from *Mean
Streets* (1973), directed by
Martin Scorsese, photo-
graphed by Kent L.
Wakeford

he'd seen around a lot but never really knew, the son of a painter who'd been making some noise on stage and in his first few film roles. And thus was born the collaboration between Scorsese and Robert De Niro, who would reteam for eight additional films (and counting).

Fund-raising was tough; neither *Who's That Knocking* nor *Boxcar Bertha* had set the box office on fire, and Scorsese was so desperate for financing, he even considered going back to Corman, who agreed to make the movie if Scorsese and Martin rewrote it as a blaxploitation picture. But Scorsese ended up talking Jonathan Taplin, road manager for the music group The Band, into raising the $300,000 budget. That wasn't enough to shoot the New York–set story in the city, but if Scorsese could fake enough of the interiors in LA, he could shoot six days and nights in New York. He and his New York crew (mostly comprising NYU students) shot exteriors, a few key locations, and apartment-building hallways. "You can't fake the hallways," he explained.

The film premiered at the 1973 New York Film Festival under its new title, *Mean Streets*, and was a sensation. Vincent Canby deemed it "an unequivocally first class film"; Pauline Kael called it "a true original of our period, a triumph of personal filmmaking." Warner Brothers picked it up for distribution. Scorsese arranged for Michael and Julia Phillips to screen it privately, and Schrader as well. They were all convinced. And they liked that actor playing Johnny Boy as well.

▬

Lindsay had campaigned in 1965 on the promise of adding civilians to the NYPD's internal review board, but his attempt to implement that promise was met with resistance by representatives of the 27,000-member Patrolmen's Benevolent Association. They turned the proposal into a referendum question and took their case to the people. PBA president John Cassese proclaimed, "I'm sick and tired of giving in to minority groups and their whims and their shouting." The proposal was, per the *Daily News* headline the day after the election, "clobbered."

It would take another panel to alter public opinion. In October 1971, chairman Whitman Knapp commenced hearings of a commission to investigate allegations of corruption in the NYPD; the Knapp Commission report, published in December 1972, found not only multiple instances of "serious misconduct" among the department's rank and file, but evidence of top officials ignoring or even covering up allegations of extortion, bribery, drug trafficking, and worse.

Their star witness was an undercover narcotics cop named Frank Serpico; within a year of the publication of the commission's report, his story had become a feature film. *Serpico* (1973), directed by Sidney Lumet, starred Al Pacino as the whistleblower, first introduced to the trade-offs as "gratuities" as a beat cop on the job ("Charlie's an okay guy, we give him a break on double parking"), then finding himself an object of suspicion when he refuses to partake. "Let's face it," the question goes, "who can trust a cop who don't take the money?" Lumet's evocative direction and Pacino's immersive acting—producer Martin Bregman noted, "There were times when he would walk through the streets in areas where he shouldn't have been walking"—deftly dramatize the hopelessness of the situation, a lack of options that puts Serpico in the sights not of the criminals on the streets, but of his fellow cops.

*Report to the Commissioner* (1975) dipped into similar waters of corruption and cover-up—and pushback (Hector Elizondo's Captain

D'Angelo, implicated in an investigation, warns, "I'll go the mayor, I'll go to the papers, I know where all the bodies are buried"). Michael Moriarty is the picture's idealistic young cop; the corrupt long-timer he's paired with is played by Yaphet Kotto, who had himself played the "good cop" in *Across 110th Street* (1972; see sidebar on page 206). And, as usual, there was a comic riff; in *Cops and Robbers* (1973), two cops who are cheerfully, unapologetically on the take (the title song asks, "They're getting theirs / why don't you get yours?") move from small-time hustles to a daring robbery of a smooth-talking blue-blood banker, just like the ones that were about to take over the city government.

But most New York cop movies of the era were decidedly pro–"law and order," *Dirty Harry*–style narratives that acknowledge and perhaps even (mildly) critique their protagonists' excesses and rule-bending, but ultimately forgive them; after all, what are you gonna do in a place like this? The best of the bunch, William Friedkin's *The French Connection* (1971; see sidebar on page 204), focuses on a cop who is openly racist and unreasonably brutal and frequently endangers his fellow officers, but as his captain notes, "He's a good cop, basically a good cop. He's got good hunches every once in a while." (Friedkin then cuts to the cop in question waking up on a barstool, putting on his hat, and finishing his drink.) In the wake of the film's success, much of its team reunited for *The Seven-Ups*, its title taken from the "good team" of detectives at its center, who do "what a cop is supposed to do."

The most honest cop movie of the era is unquestionably the documentary *The Police Tapes* (1977), assembled from blurry, black-and-white videotapes of the activities of the Bronx's 44th Precinct (home of the highest crime rate in the city) during three months of ride-alongs in 1976. This "candid report" captures grunt work, tense standoffs, welfare complaints, and gallows humor; most of all, it finds plenty of beat cops and higher-ups to share their theories on "the ghetto" and how to better control its residents. Strikingly, they're all Italian and Irish guys.

**ABOVE, CLOCKWISE FROM LEFT**
Still images from *The French Connection* (1971), directed by William Friedkin, photographed by Owen Roizman; *The Seven-Ups* (1973), directed by Philip D'Antoni, photographed by Urs Furrer; *Report to the Commissioner* (1975), directed by Milton Katselas, photographed by Mario Tosi; *Serpico* (1973), directed by Sidney Lumet, photographed by Arthur J. Ornitz.

By that point in the decade, the cop movies had become increasingly hopeless, portraying a force handcuffed by budget cuts, pushy liberals, nosy Internal Affairs investigators, and an unappreciative public, as well as a never-ending supply of amoral suspects. The institution of policing was broken, these movies seemed to suggest, and as one of their protagonists put it, "If the police don't defend us, maybe we oughta do it ourselves." And with that, the Gotham vigilante movie was born.

The embryo came early in the decade. John Avildsen's *Joe* (1970) begins with a setup similar to Milos Forman's gentle, shaggy *Taking Off* the following year: Bill (Dennis Patrick), a concerned, conservative father, journeys into the city to find his wayward, hippie daughter. But instead, he finds an ally: Joe (Peter Boyle), a factory worker who parks on a stool in the "American Bar and Grill" and spouts off such far-right maxims as "All these social workers are nigger lovers!" and "Forty-two percent of all liberals are queer!" and "All I know is these fuckin' kids are gettin' more than we ever did!"

Norman Wexler's complex screenplay grapples with the issues and implications at the story's center, of generational shifts, class divides, and the relationship between violence and virility (or lack thereof). It's a cynical movie, regarding none of its characters with much affection or respect, and by the time Joe and Bill are blasting away at the commune's inhabitants with shotguns, the blunt ugliness of the narrative is overwhelming. *Joe* was an unexpected hit, thanks in no small part to the proximity of its release to the May 8, 1970, "Hard Hat Riot," in which two hundred construction workers attacked a student anti-war protest at Wall Street and Broad Street. When *Joe* hit theaters two months later, its portrait of working-class conservatism struck a nerve, and the $100,000 picture grossed nearly $20 million. (These things go in cycles. Its original poster placed the title character, with a shotgun in one hand and an American flag in the other, under the words KEEP AMERICA BEAUTIFUL.)

But the cycle really kicked into high gear four years later. Michael Winner's *Death Wish* (1974) begins with Paul (Charles Bronson) and Joanna Kersey (Hope Lange) enjoying an island vacation, far from New York; when they return, the city is revealed, behind the opening title, with a ghoulish music sting. Paul returns to work, where he's informed by a co-worker that "there were fifteen murders the first week, and twenty-one the second." His colleague's solution, to "stick 'em in concentration camps," is a bit too much for a "bleeding-heart liberal" like Paul, so he's offered another fix: "Work here and live somewhere else."

**ABOVE**
Still images from *Joe* (1970), directed and photographed by John G. Avildsen; *Law and Disorder* (1974), directed by Ivan Passer, photographed by Arthur J. Ornitz.

**BELOW**
Still images from *Death Wish* (1974), directed by Michael Winner, photographed by Arthur J. Ornitz.

Fear City, Blackouts, and *Taxi Driver*

NYC comptroller turned
Mayor Abraham Beame.

Conveniently enough, just as Paul's co-worker is railing about out-of-control crime and cop shortages, a trio of thugs is following Joanna home from the grocery store. They spray graffiti in the stairway and on the walls of the Kersey's fancy apartment, bringing the dreaded street roughness and squalor into that safe space, the upper-class urban white id dramatized. (As Stanley Corkin notes, their behavior is a *Reefer Madness*–style dramatization of the "Broken Windows" theory that the city would adopt as policy years later—small, quality-of-life crimes, unchecked, lead to larger, more heinous ones.) In a brutal sequence reminiscent of *A Clockwork Orange*, the gang murders Paul's wife and rapes his daughter, and the police tell him there's not much chance of catching the perpetrators—"That's just the way it is." But on a business trip to Arizona, Paul is taken to a gun club, taught that a gun is "just a tool," "like a hammer," and told, "Unlike your city, we can walk our streets and walk through our parks, and feel safe." So he goes back home and goes to work.

*Death Wish* is morally reprehensible but sociologically fascinating. It deploys many of the same tools as *Joe* before it and *Taxi Driver* after, but with none of their philosophical ambiguity; their filmmakers didn't intend audiences to cheer for Joe or Travis Bickle (though some would), but *Death Wish* is pitched squarely as white urban upper-class fantasy, aimed at viewers who will get high on the image of a guy like them taking out a bunch of black, brown, and poor people, just like the ones in *their* cities. With inner-city gentrification on the horizon (starting in the late 1970s and rapidly increasing in the following decades), it's hard not to read films like *Death Wish* or its comic counterpart from the same year, *Law and Disorder*, as the stories of "civilized" white New Yorkers taking their city back—making New York great again, if you will.

In a *New York Post* report on the film's runaway success in Gotham, a sixteen-year-old Bronx High School of Science student deemed *Death Wish* "irresponsible—because it might just be what some unstable person needs to go out on a shooting spree." In one scene from the film, a group of toughs terrorizes the riders of a subway train, and a police officer among them reacts by literally looking the other way. Paul Kersey, on the other hand, hides his gun behind his newspaper, waits for the men to attack, and puts two bullets in each of them. A suspiciously similar scene played out in December 1984, when Bernhard Goetz shot four African American teenagers on the 2 train, claiming the youths were attempting to rob him with screwdrivers. Like Kersey and Bickle, Goetz became a folk hero, with hundreds of New Yorkers calling the police tip line to voice their support. Three years later, Goetz was acquitted of attempted murder.

▬

John Lindsay's improbable second term had gone about as well as his first, which is to say, poorly. Lindsay had always projected the image of the dedicated servant, sleeves rolled up and ready to work; by midway through the second term, his attention was elsewhere, on a disastrous run for the 1972 Democratic presidential nomination. On March 7, 1973, he announced that he would not seek a third term.

His successor couldn't have been a sharper contrast. John Lindsay hailed from the upper middle class and attended Ivy League schools; Abraham Beame grew up in a cold-water flat on the Lower East Side and went to City College. Lindsay moved easily from a congressional seat to City Hall; Beame had been grinding it out in city politics for nearly two decades when he ran for mayor in 1965, losing badly to Lindsay and William F. Buckley. He briefly retired from politics before returning to city government in 1969 as comptroller, a post he'd previously held under Mayor Wagner.

In 1965, Beame looked like a pencil-pusher next to the dashing Lindsay; now Beame looked like the fixer the city so desperately needed. But not everyone was certain. "From the standpoint of setting up the management and control of the city's work, the city is starting all over again," I. D. Robbins wrote in the *Village Voice*. "Because Abe Beame knows the city much better than John Lindsay did, he will probably not make the same mistakes. He will make different ones." He was sworn in on New Year's Day, 1974.

The report landed seven months later. It was created by Fitch Investors Service, a bond-rating agency, and it was bleak news for the city of New York, which had become almost entirely reliant on loans for its fiscal survival. The Fitch report officially downgraded the city's credit rating from A to BB and BBB, for debt maturing, respectively, before and after 1980. The alarm was clear in the accompanying text: "It is true that the

Robert De Niro and Martin Scorsese, embarking on their second collaboration.

Fear City, Blackouts, and *Taxi Driver*

De Niro gets into character.

City has never defaulted on timely payment of debt service when due. It is also true that the City has never faced the financial problems with which it is now confronted."

Beame knew exactly what he was getting into when he took office at the beginning of 1974; after all, he'd been Lindsay's comptroller. By the fall, he'd implemented a freeze on all municipal hiring. It made little difference. The worst was yet to come.

▬

As 1974 drew to a close, Martin Scorsese's *Mean Streets* follow-up, *Alice Doesn't Live Here Anymore*, opened to rave reviews and respectable box office, proving that the young director could deliver on a studio property. The following spring, the film's star, Ellen Burstyn, won the Academy Award for Best Actress; the same night, Robert De Niro won Best Supporting Actor for his work in *The Godfather: Part II*. The Phillipses, who had collected the Best Picture prize the year before for *The Sting*, seized on the opportunity to jump-start *Taxi Driver*.

"It really came together because the talent stuck with the package until it became a bargain," Michael Phillips later explained. "After Bobby had won his Oscar for *The Godfather: Part II*, and Marty was already recognized as a star director, they hung in there at bargain basement prices, and we did this film very cheaply. And David Begelman knew a bargain when he saw it."

Begelman, the talent agent turned head of Columbia Pictures, also offset his distaste for *Taxi Driver* by making the production part of a two-picture deal with the Phillipses. The other half of the transaction was *Watch the Skies*, a UFO script Schrader had written that Begelman thought would be a good fit for his former client Steven Spielberg, then searching for a suitable follow-up to *Jaws*. Spielberg rewrote and retitled the movie, and what would become *Close Encounters of the Third Kind* was such a big production, with such promise for commercial success, that Begelman didn't mind carving out a comparatively minuscule $1.3 million and leaving the Phillipses alone to make their lurid little cabbie movie.

Happy to finally get the green light, the producers and director set about figuring out how to make the movie for so little money (the final cost was $1.9 million). Scorsese, Schrader, and De Niro worked for peanuts, their up-front salaries totaling $130,000, though the director and star also received a small percentage of the profits. Scorsese batted around ideas for cutting costs, even briefly considering shooting the entire film on black-and-white videotape. But one idea he wouldn't entertain was moving the story to a less expensive city. "It wouldn't be the same," he later explained. "It has to be New York, because that's the center for taxi cabs. And like I say, anyone who drives a cab for one night in New York is gonna turn out like Travis."

Instead, Scorsese tightened his belt, planning a quick shoot in the city and maximizing on-set time by storyboarding every shot. "It's all storyboarded completely," he explains, "because in a case like that, when you have very low budget, I prefer designing it way in advance. And during the day, you accomplish as many of those images and editing patterns, shots, camera movements and things like that as you can—always keeping in mind that you *hope* that there's a good accident, or you may have to combine two or three shots into one. It's preparation so you don't go too far over budget, where the studio gets [angry] . . . because we were still working at studios, and that was Columbia and they weren't supportive of the picture at that time."

On the set of *Taxi Driver*.

His team scouted locations, securing shoots in Columbus Circle, in the Garment District, at the Bellmore Cafeteria on 28th and Park Avenue South and Charles' Coffee Shop at 58th and Eighth Avenue, and at two Times Square porno houses: the Lyric Theatre on 42nd and the Show & Tell on Eighth Avenue. By the mid-seventies, following the storefronts and burlesque houses' transformation into porn emporiums, massage parlors, and live sex venues, most of the former movie palaces on "the Deuce" had switched either to seedy exploitation movies or to full-on hardcore pornography, playing continuous programs all night and all day for patrons who alternated shooting up, jerking off, tricking, sleeping, and robbing. "While they remained popular thoroughfares during the daytime," James Traub writes in *The Devil's Playground*, "at night 42nd Street and the Eighth Avenue corridor had descended to an almost feral state."

De Niro, meanwhile, got to work. There had been questions, early on, if he was right for the role; the Phillipses' original co-producer, Tony Bill, envisioned Jeff Bridges or Al Pacino, and Scorsese had originally proposed his then go-to leading man, Harvey Keitel. But it soon became clear that De Niro was the guy for the job. He'd been toying with a script of his own—"basically a guy who was isolated, alone, kind of like the Travis character, which I never really fully realized"—and when he read Schrader's script, "I identified with it, as I think we all did." He talked to Schrader about the autobiographical elements of the character and ended up borrowing the screenwriter's own cowboy boots and army jacket for his costume.

While the film was in pre-production, De Niro was in Italy, shooting *1900* for Bernardo Bertolucci. "When I got to New York, I had like two weeks, I think, to be ready to shoot," he recalled. "And as soon as I got back, I started driving a cab." He worked long shifts, twelve hours, just like Travis, to get comfortable behind the wheel; he also made a little bit of extra money ("around a hundred bucks a week in fares"). *Newsweek* breathlessly reported that in the time he was hacking, he was "propositioned by a homosexual—and handsomely tipped by a prostitute who gave him $5."

A few times, Scorsese rode along. "I sat in the front seat and people got in and [we were] just driving up and down Eighth Avenue. . . . It was a rough area, it still is," he said. "Every fifteen minutes or twenty minutes, you don't know where you're going or what's going to happen to you. You have no control over your life." He would attempt to bring that

**ABOVE, TOP DOWN**
Still images from *Network* (1976), directed by Sidney Lumet, photographed by Owen Roizman; *The Goodbye Girl* (1977), directed by Herbert Ross, photographed by David M. Walsh; *Three Days of the Condor* (1975), directed by Sydney Pollack, photographed by Owen Roizman.

**LEFT**
Still image from *The Eyes of Laura Mars* (1978), directed by Irvin Kershner, photographed by Victor J. Kemper.

uncertainty to life in the film—the feeling that at any second, anyone (including Travis) was capable of anything.

In between fares, the actor and director solidified their bond. "I really felt good about him here," Scorsese recalled. "I felt that we understood each other. It was almost like sign language." Schrader, too, felt that kinship and understanding: "Three people coming together, at a certain point in their lives, all needing to say the same thing. Occasionally, in art, you get lucky, and you're in the right place at the right time with the right people. And I think that was the case with *Taxi Driver*."

▬

*Taxi Driver* was one of forty-six films shot in New York City in 1975. The film industry was bringing somewhere in the neighborhood of forty to fifty million dollars per year into the city, and that wasn't the only benefit for local businesses; in March 1974, the *New York Daily News* reported that restaurants featured in *The French Connection*, *Diary of a Mad Housewife*, and *John and Mary* "reported doing better business in the months after the films were released."

The city wasn't just extending permits. It made the old Court Street station at Boerum Place and Schermerhorn Street in Brooklyn available for films like *Death Wish* and *The Taking of Pelham One Two Three* (see sidebar on page 208), so filmmakers could get their subway scenes without having to shut down active stations. It joined the New York State Council on the Arts to make a sizable investment in renovating and reopening the Astoria studio so that filmmakers would have sound-stages available (it had been all but abandoned in recent years, taken over by looters and squatters).

But the question remains: Why did the city bend over backward to make it easier for filmmakers to shoot in New York, when their product all but universally portrayed the city as a terrible place to live? The answer may be found in the *Daily News*'s anecdote of the making of a scene in *Death Wish*, in which Paul Kersey foils an attempted subway station mugging by shooting the young thug dead. The MTA was understandably reluctant to make Court Street available for the production of such a scene. But, according to the *Daily News*, "Beame got word of the impasse and managed to convince [the Transit Authority] that its image could withstand the films better than it could a veto of the attempts to make them."

As the decade progressed, one can't help but wonder if Beame ever reconsidered this particular cost/benefit analysis. For now, however, the most damaging portrait of the city was presented not in the movie houses, but on the evening news. The mayor's 1974 hiring freeze hadn't moved the fiscal needle one bit, and he was reluctant to make cuts (foreseeing, accurately, the potential political fallout). In 1975, the state took matters into its own hands, with Governor Hugh Carey establishing the Municipal Assistance Corporation (MAC for short) to, in effect, take over the city's finances.

To avoid the city's looming bankruptcy, Beame would have to follow the MAC directives for the upcoming fiscal year, which would begin on July 1. Chief among them were massive layoffs of city workers—including more than five thousand police officers and detectives. With two weeks left in the fiscal year, off-duty cops and firemen began distributing a crude, grisly, four-page pamphlet to tourists arriving at LaGuardia, JFK, Grand Central, and Port Authority. It was titled "Welcome to Fear City—A Survival Guide for Visitors to the City of New York." It advised the reader, perhaps too late, to "stay away from New York City if you possibly can."

Scorsese directs Robert De Niro and Cybill Shepherd.

Scorsese with Harvey
Keitel, his first leading man.

It warned visitors to avoid the streets after six p.m., to avoid public transportation and walking on the streets at all times, and to set not a foot off the island of Manhattan. The front cover was emblazoned with a chilling image of a skull in a black hood; a smaller skull accompanied a smug "Good luck" on the next page. At the bottom of the cover, below the pamphlet's subtitle, was the author byline, just for clarity's sake: "By NYPD, 1975."

The layoffs, many of them announced with mere hours left on June 30, left police stations and libraries all but empty, firehouses padlocked, bridges and tunnels unattended, and daycare centers closed. By July 2, chaos reigned. Ten thousand city sanitation workers had walked off the job, and within days, an estimated fifty-eight thousand tons of garbage sat, uncollected, on the city's fire-hot streets and sidewalks. Citizens were soon setting them on fire—but with fire stations closed (and many of the remaining firefighters calling in sick), most were simply left to burn. The *New York Times* described the scene in East Harlem as a "vast incinerator of flaming garbage," and found a young man who, before tossing a firecracker into a roaring blaze, declared, "If we're going to burn, let the whole city burn."

This was the New York City in which Martin Scorsese and company shot *Taxi Driver*.

▬

"And as far as I was concerned, it was normal," Scorsese laughs. "We were doing [the 2016 TV series] *Vinyl*, and Mick Jagger and I were talking, and he said, 'Marty, didn't you realize that when you were standing on a corner, and behind you there's a wall of trash that hasn't been picked up? That something was amiss?' And I said, 'No, it's just a New York garbage strike.'"

That reality couldn't help but seep into the picture, which seemed timed, purely accidentally, to capture the dark mood of the city that summer. "It was all there," Scorsese says, "and that's what you see in the movie. I mean, you could *taste* it in the air. There was a sense of desperation. There was a sense of violence in the air too. But hot summers—like *Do the Right Thing*, take a look at that—with the heat, everybody's outside, they have no air conditioning, getting on each other's nerves. The whole city was like that."

The mood of the city seemed to synthesize with that of the picture. Crew members scouting locations near Lincoln Center reported seeing a large man, with no provocation, punch an old woman in the mouth. While the crew was in an Upper West Side bodega shooting the scene where Travis (De Niro) kills a stick-up man, a real murder occurred around the corner. "The shoot was hard," Scorsese says, with uncharacteristic understatement. "We shot in places that were very difficult, where we weren't accepted, weren't welcomed, I should say." The City was in a rage that summer—so much so that when a seemingly unwell black man rushes past Iris (Jodie Foster) and her friend, ranting, "I'm going to kill her, I'm going to kill her," some viewers assumed he was not an actor but a real street person Scorsese had captured, like the Times Square drummer. "It's as if the entire city is infected with homicidal rage," writes critic Amy Taubin. "For the girls, however, the black man is just part of the scenery."

But for all Schrader dialogue that reads like newspaper quotes—"Thank God for the rain, which has washed away the garbage and the trash off the sidewalks," "The animals all come out at night," etc.—it's important

**178**

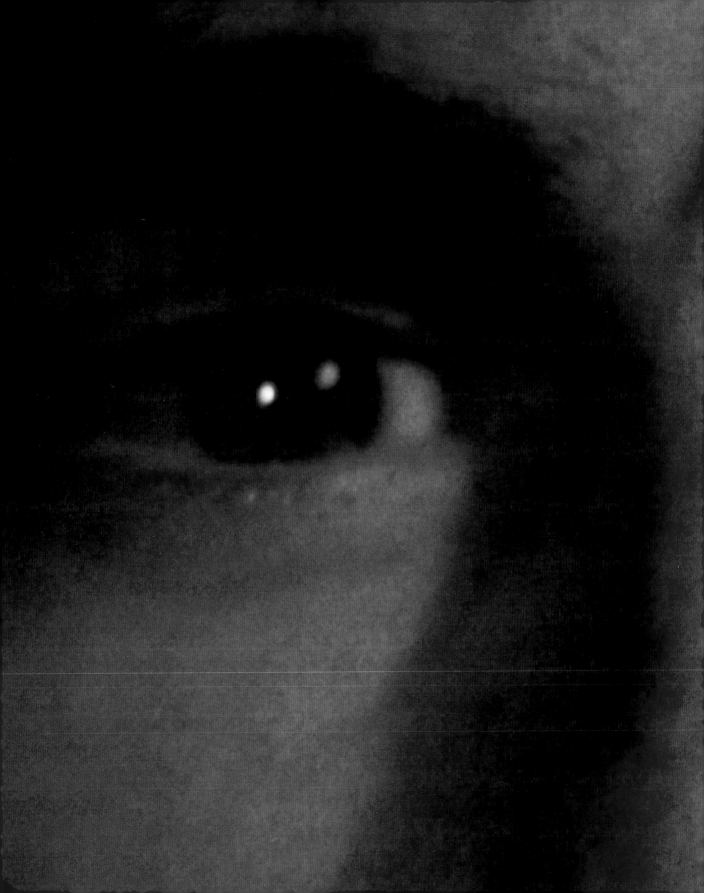

**PREVIOUS SPREAD**
The bulk of *Taxi Driver* is seen from Travis's perspective; it is often seen literally through his eyes. Thus, we often see him looking: through the windshield, into the rear-view mirror, and in this extreme close-up of those eyes, taking in all of the excesses and vice of the city around him.

**THIS SPREAD**
Still images from *Taxi Driver* (1976), directed by Martin Scorsese, photographed by Michael Chapman.

to note that the cumulative effect of *Taxi Driver* is due not to its verisimilitude, but to its stylization. The influence of film noir is omnipresent, from the lonely saxophone of Bernard Herrmann's score to the protagonist's first-person narration to his traumatic background: "Like film noir, *Taxi Driver* is rooted in post-war trauma," Taubin notes. "What World War II was to noir, Vietnam is to the story of Travis Bickle." And if *Taxi Driver* is neo-noir, its specific connection is to the New York *noir* of *Force of Evil*, *Kiss of Death*, and even *The Naked City*. "If someone says it reminded them of 'Mark Hellinger Presents,'" Scorsese shrugged, "I say, why not?"

But the style goes deeper than that. When the film was released, Schrader admitted that although he was happy with Scorsese's direction, "it was not directed the way I would have directed it. I wrote an austere film that was directed in an expressionistic way. I think the two qualities work together. There's a tension in the film that's very interesting."

Travis chooses to drive at night, and in the city's skeeviest locations, all the better to create a nightmare atmosphere. The picture has a bleary-eyed, fever-dream quality, from the opening shot of the taxi emerging from the fog; it drives through symphonies of steam in the street, through the occasional baptism by fire hydrant. "Much of *Taxi Driver* arose from my feeling that movies are really a kind of dream-state, or like taking dope," Scorsese explained. "And the shock of walking out of the theater into broad daylight can be terrifying. I watch movies all the time and I am also very bad at waking up. The film was like that for me—that sense of being almost awake." Producer Julia Phillips, in her memoir *You'll Never Eat Lunch in This Town Again*, chose a blunter phrasing: "*Taxi Driver* is a cokey movie. Big pressure, short scheduled, short money, New York in the summer. Night shooting. I have only visited the set once, and they are all doing blow. I don't see it. I just know it."

Yet it wasn't just the mood of the city that summer that we can now see reflected in *Taxi Driver*. In Charles Palantine (Leonard Harris), the handsome but vapid liberal candidate who insists "We *are* the people" (but never really explains how), it's not hard to see the shadow of John Lindsay. "We can only surmise that the vague liberalism espoused here by the candidate is antithetical to Travis's aggressive, and psychotic, interventionalism," writes Stanley Corkin, who argues that Travis sees, in both Vietnam and Manhattan, "places that need a redeemer who will not allow the conventions of law and custom to stand in the way of resolute actions." It's a thesis that puts little space (aside from some question of endorsement and approval) between Travis Bickle and Paul Kersey.

One can also sense the racial animosity that was brewing in the city at the moment as the white elites of the Municipal Assistance Corporation shifted the expenditures and priorities away from the black and brown underclass while preserving that underclass's position of scorn from white blue-collar workers. "The character is a racist," admitted Schrader, though he pulled his punches a bit by rewriting the original ending, in which Sport and the rest of Travis's victims are black. "We would have fights in the theatre," Schrader explained. "It would have been an incitement to riot." Nevertheless, the character's racism and prejudice remain, between the lines: the suspicion with which he regards the nattily dressed black men in the cafeteria and on the city's sidewalks, how he takes aim at an African American youth on *American Bandstand*, how unblinkingly he offs the black stick-up man in the bodega (the clerk delights in getting in a few retaliatory whacks

Fear City, Blackouts, and *Taxi Driver*

Still images from *Taxi Driver* (1976), directed by Martin Scorsese, photographed by Michael Chapman.

once the robber is down, which seems somehow grislier than the shooting itself).

And then there is Scorsese's own, disturbing appearance. He wasn't originally set to play the role of (per the end credits) "Passenger Watching Silhouette," and had in fact already shot his own Hitchcock-esque cameo as a random man watching Cybill Shepherd walk to work. But when the actor he'd cast (George Memmoli, who played the small but memorable role of "Joey" in *Mean Streets*) dropped out at the eleventh hour, Scorsese had to step into the role himself. And as Taubin writes, "When it's the director of the film talking about blowing a woman to bits with a .44 Magnum because she's having an affair with a 'nigger,' the words carry more weight than they would if said by a day-player. Scorsese articulates what Travis refers to as the bad thoughts in his head, the thoughts he can't bring himself to put into words—leaving him in the end no choice but to put them into action."

As Scorsese's passenger speaks, his words carrying the vilest images of racism, misogyny, and violence, Travis remains still, watching the man's reflection in his rearview mirror carefully. What the passenger sees—those eyes in that mirror—are our first impression of Travis, in the opening credits, his eyes isolated before we see him in full, an establishing shot and an establishing choice. The story is seen from his perspective, often literally (point-of-view shots are plentiful); we see the world as Travis sees it. And when we see what he sees, it's often out of sorts: through the wet and blurry windshield, in slow motion, or through a filter of smeary light—stylistic reminders that what Travis sees, he often sees askew. And the edits often duplicate the character's erratic perception, underscoring his anxiety and unease. Scorsese puts us in the character's shoes, whether we want to be there or not.

But because we're placed there, and spend such time in proximity to the character, some degree of empathy is all but impossible; we can't help but sympathize, if nothing else, with his loneliness and social discomfort. He seems to have learned all of his social cues from watching others and doesn't pick up on hints at his inappropriateness. Betsy is certainly wise to steer clear of Travis, especially in retrospect, but the way Scorsese shoots her ultimate rejection of him—by dollying away from Travis and settling his camera on an empty hallway—is telling. He will, over the course of the picture, show us violence, gore, misery, pain, and death. But not this. This is too much.

Travis Bickle's loneliness is ultimately at the root of the film's most quoted scene. It wasn't much of anything in Schrader's screenplay. "The script just said, 'Travis looks in the mirror. Plays like a cowboy. Takes out the gun. Talks to himself,'" the writer recalled. "So Bob said, 'What does he say?' I said, 'Well, you know, just like when you're a kid, and you got that little holster, the cap gun, and you're standing there, you're going, "Oh!"' I said, it's like that. He took it from there." The scene came late in the shoot, so Schrader was also aware of who the true authority was by then: "I told him, 'Bob, you know Travis Bickle much better than I do at this point.' The irony is that the most famous line is not mine."

De Niro looked at himself in the mirror and started riffing. He had conversations with himself, imagining the mirror as some no-account punk who made the mistake of messing with him; there was a fantasy/role-playing element to what he did, present not only in Travis Bickle or Paul Kersey, but in every would-be New York tough-guy who'd follow, from David Berkowitz to Bernhard Goetz to Curtis Sliwa. Finally, he landed on a variation of a line he'd seen a local comedian use in a bit: "Are you looking at me?" Travis looked at himself in the mirror, saw a potential victim, and asked, "Are you talkin' to me?"

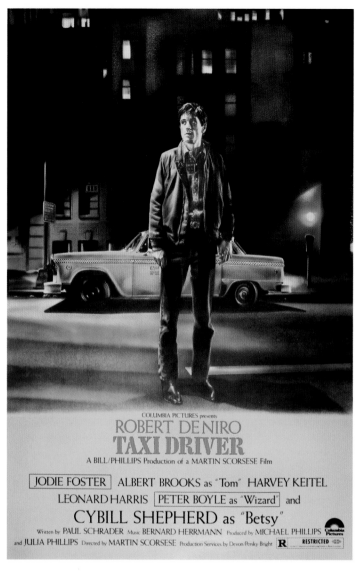

It was one of the last things they shot. They were in an apartment of a condemned building on 89th Street and Columbus Avenue, which the production was using as its home base (they shot the bloody climax elsewhere in the same structure). It was, according to Scorsese, "one of the roughest and noisiest areas of New York. . . . I remember I was sitting at his feet, and I had headphones on, and all I could hear were the city sounds. I kept asking him to repeat himself." The actor complied, each time loading the question and its follow-ups with more impotent rage and short-fuse menace, looking into the mirror as a man, but reflecting a ticking bomb. "When Travis looks in the mirror," Amy Taubin writes, "he sees himself and he sees the other on whom he's projected everything he despises in himself." Thus, Travis is "rehearsing a murder that is also a suicide."

"It is the last line, 'Well, I'm the only one here,' that never gets quoted," Roger Ebert wrote. "It is the truest line in the film."

▬

Standing on the street outside of the Belmore Cafeteria, Travis fumblingly attempts to reach out to another person: Wizard (Peter Boyle, "Joe" himself), the confident king of the late-night cabbies. Travis rambles about his fears and frustrations; he hints at the actions he's planning. "I got some bad ideas in my head," he says, before trailing off in his own discomfort. Wizard's response is unhelpful but honest: "You got no choice. I mean, we're all fucked! More or less."

Inelegant as Wizard might be, his philosophy wasn't exactly an outlier in New York in the summer of 1975. As the months wore on, protests grew rowdier and angrier, not only over budget cuts and layoffs, but also over a proposed increase in subway and bus fares. Mayor Beame was booed and heckled at the August dedication of the Federal Hall National Memorial downtown; a member of the angry crowd summed up the city's attitude toward the mayor succinctly for the *Times*: "Look, this guy was Controller [*sic*] for eight years. He must have known this was going to happen to the city."

Beame did his best to meet the benchmarks set by the MAC board, but it was a lose-lose situation; their aims were, fundamentally, at odds with those of most of his constituents. His administration revised their pleas for help from the federal government, to no avail; President Ford and his advisors firmly believed that New York's financial woes were the unavoidable result of its reckless spending, the financial toll of liberals and their Great Society, and if the lesson must be learned by bankruptcy, so be it. The president put it plainly in an appearance at the National Press Club on October 29, promising to veto any bill providing emergency aid to New York.

The *New York Daily News* headline the next day put an even finer point on it. FORD TO CITY: it screamed, in 144-point type. DROP DEAD.

The *Daily News* headline is perhaps the most famous of the decade; what few remember is that Ford held the line for barely six weeks. On December 9, Ford signed a bill granting federal aid to the city, though he claimed it was *not* a bailout: "New York City has bailed *itself* out," the president insisted. New York City—in this case, the Beame administration, its Emergency Financial Control Board, and the Municipal Assistance Corporation—had done so by promising and implementing even deeper cuts to the city's social services, public works, and capital improvements. The public workforce was slashed by nearly seventy thousand employees; transit fares were raised, while the aging busses and trains fell further into disrepair.

To attract private enterprise, the 1976 economic recovery plan proposed extensive steps in "the marketing of the city." A new program, bankrolled by the state, the city, and existing business interests, had three goals: to "convey New York's advantages as a place to do business and to stress the City's positive attitude toward business," to "encourage companies to locate in the City and to stay and expand here," and to "attract more tourists and conventions."

What the officials behind this plan didn't seem to realize was that their glittering marketing plan could not change the image of the city captured by movies and television. And the crippling cuts they had advocated would result in a picture of the city, in the coming decade and a half, that it would take all of their marketing muscle to offset.

▬

Paul Schrader had been out late the night before *Taxi Driver* opened in New York City ("It was one of those times") and overslept the next morning, blowing his plan to come early and watch it unspool, for the first time, with an audience. Unable to get a cab, he ran from the Sherry-Netherland to the Coronet, where it was playing. "I got there, and there was a huge line outside of the theaters," he said. "And I thought, 'Oh my God, something's gone wrong, they've closed the theater.' I went up to the woman and said, 'What happened? What happened?' She said, 'Well, they're about ready to start the movie.' I said, 'Well, why are all these people out here?' She said, 'They're for the next show!' And I walked up into the theater, it was the very first screening in New York, and the cab pulls out of the steam, and it says *Taxi Driver*, and the

Still images from *God Told Me To* (1976), directed by Larry Cohen, photographed by Paul Glickman.

**TOP**
Secretary of H.U.D. Patricia Harris, President Jimmy Carter, and Mayor Abraham Beame tour the South Bronx.

**CENTER**
Manhattan residents hit the streets during the July 1977 blackout.

**BOTTOM**
The morning after.

audience applauded. That had never been projected before. It was some kind of New York groundswell that just, you know, was there."

The reviews certainly helped. *Variety* deemed it "a powerful film, an excellent credit for Scorsese, and a terrific showcase for the versatility of star Robert De Niro." The *Daily News*'s Kathleen Carroll praised Scorsese's "scathing vision of New York as a fiery inferno of neon lights and relentlessly hostile populace." "It's a movie that insinuates its way into your consciousness," wrote the *New York Post*'s Frank Rich, "that crashes into your dreams." Roger Ebert deemed it both "a brilliant nightmare" and "a hell."

There were some dissents—John Simon deemed it "overdone" and "hammily shot," while Rex Reed felt it was "sloppily directed," deeming Scorsese "a promising upstart who believes his own press clippings"— and even some of the good notices, like Canby's in the *Times*, hedged their praise ("It seems less than the sum of its parts"). Yet the generally positive notices for this dark, upsetting picture—along with its shared win of the Palme d'Or at the Cannes Film Festival three months later—turned it into a surprise commercial success, with a total domestic gross of over $28 million.

But there was something else. As Schrader jogged up to the Coronet that first morning, he noticed most of the people in that long line for the next show were young men, and many of them looked not unlike the picture's protagonist. They were drawn by the poster, by its image of Travis walking down Eighth Avenue with a porn marquee behind him, head down, hands in pockets, an image complemented by a simple tagline: "On every street in every city in this country, there's a nobody who dreams of being a somebody."

Those "nobodies" came in droves, and perhaps identified with the film's antihero more than his creators intended. Schrader later surmised, "The sheer violence of it really brought out the Times Square crowd," while Scorsese, who was also at the Coronet that first day, recalled that while the daytime shows went as expected, "The last show, at ten p.m., was a little different. They seemed to be enjoying the shootout, and I didn't intend that. I intended what the first audience seemed to be feeling. I wanted a gasping, a sort of pulling back."

But he shouldn't have been shocked. The New Yorkers who turned out for *Taxi Driver* in the spring of 1976 saw, on the Coronet screen, the pressure cooker they'd been living in for months, a garbage-strewn no-man's-land of misery, neglect, and lawlessness, and at the end of the movie, Scorsese opened the release valve. It's not surprising they applauded. Frankly, it's surprising they didn't riot.

▬

The letter ran in the *Daily News* on June 5, 1977, as *Star Wars* and *Smokey and the Bandit* were filling New York movie houses—but it was like an excerpt from the *Taxi Driver* screenplay, a Travis Bickle journal entry that wound up on the cutting-room floor. "Hello from the gutters of N.Y.C. which are filled with dog manure, vomit, stale wine, urine and blood," it began. "Hello from the sewers of N.Y.C. which swallow up these delicacies when they are washed away by the sweeper trucks. Hello from the cracks in the sidewalks of N.Y.C. and from the ants that dwell in these cracks and feed on the dried blood of the dead that has settled into these cracks."

History has not recorded if the author of the letter, signed "Son of Sam" but known to those around him as David Richard Berkowitz, saw *Taxi*

*Driver* that spring of 1976. But he was working as a taxi driver on July 29 of that year when he murdered Donna Lauria and shot her friend Jody Valenti as they sat in a car outside a Bronx apartment building, the first of eight murders he would commit over the next twelve months. Unlike Travis Bickle, this taxi driver plucked off his victims in pairs, and they weren't pimps or johns; they were young couples, often young women, guilty only of parking in cars to neck.

Another film, released in October 1976, accidentally captured much of the hysteria prompted by Berkowitz, then called the ".44 Caliber Killer," and eerily predicted his motive. Larry Cohen's *God Told Me To* concerns a hard-boiled NYPD detective (Tony Lo Bianco) who is baffled by a series of murders committed by seemingly normal New Yorkers. When he asks the first one, a street sniper, why he killed fourteen people from atop a building's water tower, he offers a baffling explanation: "God told me to!"

"Somebody's tryin' to terrorize the people in this city," the cop fumes, "and they're gonna do it in a big way!" In Cohen's New York, the terrifyingly random killings cause riots in the streets and mass hysteria; it's a scene not much exaggerated from the fear that would grip the city in the months after its release, as police warned citizens to "be careful . . . especially the young women," prompting a massive drop in business at borough discotheques. The neighborhoods he'd hit were soon patrolled not only by police, but by their own vigilante patrols as well, would-be Paul Kerseys looking to oust any threatening-looking outsiders.

Berkowitz was finally captured in August 1977, following the largest manhunt in the city's history—an arrest prompted not by any particular investigative prowess, but by the suspect parking his car too close to a fire hydrant. After he was led in handcuffs from his dour, Bickle-style studio apartment, he told detectives that he had been "told to" not by God, but the devil.

But by then, the city had truly, finally exploded.

▬

The summer of 1977 was brutally hot. The stifling heat contributed to the general sense of chaos and disrepair—everything seemed to be broken, and thanks to the massive budget cuts, nothing was getting fixed. As a heat wave approached that July, citizens were concerned that summer power brownouts, which Con Edison had managed to keep at bay over the past two years, would return. Charles Luce, the electrical provider's chairman, appeared on a Sunday-morning talk show to assure New Yorkers that their lines were safe and sound. There would be no outages this summer.

It started at 8:37 p.m. on July 13. The circuit breakers in Westchester County were tripped by a lightning strike at the Buchanan South substation, prompting a domino effect of failing breakers and over-loaded transmission lines all the way down the grid, first in Westchester and then into the city. The power was out in all five boroughs by 9:34 p.m. Citizens were trapped in subway trains between stations and elevators between floors. Hospitals switched to generators. LaGuardia- and JFK-bound flights were diverted to Newark and Boston.

Mayor Beame was in the midst of a speech in the Bronx when the lights went out. He was hustled off, first to Gracie Mansion and then to City Hall, for emergency meetings with his key commissioners. "This is bad indeed," noted the Mayor.

He had no idea.

A postmortem police report pinpointed the first instances of looting at 9:40 p.m.—six minutes after the lights went out. It was widespread, and it was comprehensive. Stores in thirty-one neighborhoods, mostly in Brooklyn and the Bronx, were opened up, emptied out, and/or torched. Police officers, already down in numbers and morale after the previous summer's layoffs, were ill-equipped to handle a crime wave of this scale. Many didn't even bother; though all available officers were ordered to check in with their precincts, some 40 percent (roughly ten thousand cops) had not yet done so by midnight. And that was when things really started to get out of hand.

Many of the overnight fires were still burning when morning dawned. The outage, and the looting, continued well into the daylight hours. The morning editions of the papers hit the streets, carrying news of the violence and vandalism. (The *Daily News* staff was able to work with the help of generator-powered klieg lights, borrowed from the production of *Superman* that was shooting down in their lobby.)

By the time full power was restored at 10:40 p.m. on July 14, police had arrested 3,776 people. More than 1,600 stores were damaged or looted, and 1,037 fires had been set. Nearly 100 police officers had been injured on the job. The city hit bottom, in the full view of the nation. Mayor Beame dubbed it, simply, "a night of terror."

Commentators were quick to condemn the looters and, through them, the city. "The 1977 blackout looting in New York only seemed to confirm everyone's worst suspicions about the city," Jonathan Mahler writes in *Ladies and Gentlemen, the Bronx Is Burning*. "To go with the fictional portrayals of the dangerous, dystopian metropolis in recent movies such as *Taxi Driver*, there was now documentary footage." They were all animals, the common wisdom seemed to go, and given the opportunity, they acted like them.

Some of the most horrifying commentary came from New York's own citizenry. "The warning should have gone out that every looter would be shot on the spot," one wrote in a letter to the *Times*. "The Puerto Ricans can go back to P.R. They belong there anyway and if the blacks do not shape up they can go back to the South. It would probably be an educational lesson for them."

The question few bothered, or cared, to ask was what could have caused such a massive, immediate wave of thefts—after all, nothing like this had happened in the last citywide blackout, back in 1965. But New York City was a very different place, socially and economically, than it had been twelve years earlier. "Maybe a long time ago there weren't too

Still images from *Manhattan* (1979), directed by Woody Allen, photographed by Gordon Willis; *Husbands* (1970), directed by John Cassavetes, photographed by Victor J. Kemper; *Desperate Characters* (1971), directed by Frank D. Gilroy, photographed by Urs Furrer; *An Unmarried Woman* (1978), directed by Paul Mazursky, photographed by Arthur J. Ornitz; *Kramer vs. Kramer* (1979), directed by Robert Benton, photographed by Néstor Almendros.

many looters," shrugged a young mother in a later interview, "because people had jobs then and you know they didn't do too bad; the city wasn't low of money; but now it's like that."

"They couldn't understand why we were arresting them," a Harlem officer told the *Times*. "They were angry with us. They said, 'I'm on welfare. I'm taking what I need.'"

In the weeks following the blackout, a sense of outright nihilism penetrated the city. An August *Times* editorial, noting "a shared sense of outrage and impotence," asked, "Is New York City, after all, a failed ultraurban experiment in which people eventually crack, social order eventually collapses, and reason ultimately yields to despair?" President Jimmy Carter, barely half a year into the job and in town for events at the United Nations, took an unannounced trip to the South Bronx to survey damage. Though he looked concerned and called the visit "sobering," he would ultimately offer only $11.3 million in grants and loans to the city. A couple of weeks after his visit, as game two of the World Series unfolded at Yankee Stadium, sportscasters Howard Cosell and Keith Jackson casually noted—and ABC's cameras caught—a fire raging out of control in an abandoned building nearby. They checked in on it periodically through the game. There did not appear to be any effort to extinguish the blaze.

Barely a year later, Roger Corman's New World Pictures released *Blackout*, a Canadian production with some exteriors shot in New York. In it, a thunderstorm causes a Con Edison substation to go haywire, plunging the city into darkness. As looters invade stores and cabbies price-gouge customers ("The whole city's in an emergency!"), a trio of escaped convicts take over a fancy high-rise apartment building, robbing tenants, stabbing their walls, and even burning up their art. It's like a feature-length expansion of the *Death Wish* opening, with thugs invading the sanctity of the upscale high-rise, breaking down the gates that keep the riffraff out.

Thankfully, the blackout birthed other, better art than *Blackout*. The first heartbeats of hip-hop were rumbling in the Bronx, a music born out of resourcefulness; budget cuts had left inner-city schools with no funds

Fear City, Blackouts, and *Taxi Driver*

for music programs or instruments, but everyone's living room had a stack of records and a turntable. Soon, rap originators were throwing park parties, with their record players and speakers powered by electrical outlets on the bases of streetlamps—but there were only a handful of crews making the music. The blackout changed that; would-be DJs and MCs hit the electronics stores, and according to pioneer DJ Disco Wiz, thanks to that looted equipment, "the very next day sprung this whole revolution of DJs."

That kind of no-budget ingenuity, paired with the squalid aesthetic inherent in the era, resulted in the vibrant, scrappy, and often downright dangerous cultural scene in the late 1970s. Some of them dubbed the movement "no wave," positioning their art, music, theater, and films as anti-capitalist and anti-commercial, leaning into their minuscule budgets and minimal resources as a pathway to creating art that was rooted in purity and directness rather than mainstream appeal.

They took over abandoned lofts in former industrial districts like SoHo and Tribeca, or dumpy apartments on the Lower East Side. Young artists, similarly stifled by cuts to visual arts programs in schools, instead hit the streets with spray cans and turned graffiti writing into a form of expression and civic pride (and, at the same time, a never-ending irritant for authority figures). "Punk movies" like Vivienne Dick's *Beauty Becomes the Beast*, James Nares's *Rome '78*, and Amos Poe's *Unmade Beds* used all-but-abandoned LES environments to create their own scuzzy cinematic landscape, while porn-adjacent auteurs like Andy Milligan, Roberta Findlay, and Abel Ferrara crafted portraits of Midtown sleaze. And down on the Bowery, a dirty, sketchy club called CBGB showcased mind-blowing new sounds from punk and New Wave acts like the Ramones, Blondie, Patti Smith, and Richard Hell.

The beautiful people had also found a home away from home, farther uptown. Studio 54 opened in April 1977 and immediately became the late-night destination for the city's biggest celebrities, who would take their limousines over after dinner and drinks at Elaine's or McMullen's to participate in the coke-infused, sexually fluid dance-floor bacchanal. 54, like many of those who danced there, lived fast and died young—by early 1980, its doors were closed and its owners were headed to prison for tax evasion.

But it burned bright, quickly becoming the symbol of all that was joyful and decadent in this crumbling metropolis. *Saturday Night Fever* (1977), shot during that first summer of 54, is rooted firmly in the lives of a working-class family in Brooklyn; its hero, Tony Manero (John Travolta), has to contribute part of his meager hardware-store salary to the family grocery budget, since his old man, a construction worker, is currently out of a job after twenty-five years. He spends what's left on shiny shirts and tight pants to wear to the local Bay Ridge discotheque, 2001 Odyssey, where he's the king of the dance floor. But director John Badham includes countless shots of the Brooklyn Bridge, from far away and up close, his hero gazing at it and imagining life on the other side, emphasizing how that short piece of road can seem miles longer than it is. "Right over there, right across the river," insists the sophisticated girl of his dreams, "everything is different."

Yet even those who inhabit the island long to escape it. A running thread throughout New York movies of the 1970s is the endless promise baked into the notion of just leaving (if only there were a way)—that the boundaries of the city run inherently counter to living a "normal" American life. It became part of the template in *Midnight Cowboy*, with Rizzo selling Joe Buck on the promise of those Miami dames and

orange trees, but it goes all the way back to early pictures like *Golden Boy* ("I'll share your home, Joe. A home somewhere far away") and *The Lost Weekend*, whose hero thinks that if he can get away for a long weekend in the country, he can get away from his drinking.

In *Cops and Robbers*, a friend of our heroes invites him to his suburban spread, explaining, "The city distorts your mind!" *Born to Win*'s hero tells an associate, "If I could break out of this town, I'd kiss your feet." *Klute*'s Bree can imagine a life with the title character, but not in New York: "I just can't stay in the city." At the end of *The Warriors* (1979; see sidebar on page 214), Swan looks over the rooftops of Coney Island from the elevated platform and muses, "This is what we fought all night to get back to? Maybe I'll just take off." Peter offers Liz a suburban getaway in *Dressed to Kill* (1980); Sonny longs to escape not only the city but the law as well by taking off for "sunny climes" in *Dog Day Afternoon* (1975; see sidebar on page 210). The pressures and tensions of city life are put on hold in *Panic in Needle Park* and *Eyes of Laura Mars* (1978) for idyllic walks in the woods, surrounded by leafy greens and singing birds (their lives will go back into the toilet as soon as they return). And in *Taxi Driver*, Iris expresses her desire to move to "one of those little communes in Vermont," though Travis is skeptical: "I don't go to places like that."

Yet even escape isn't always cut-and-dried. *The Prisoner of Second Avenue*'s Mel and Edna attempt a country getaway and find it to be just as insipid and aggravating as the city: a swamp of bugs, poison ivy, manure, and self-satisfied siblings. Mel returns to their apartment with new resolve: "This is my city, and we're gonna stay in my city!" And the miserable marrieds at the center of *Desperate Characters* (1971) find momentary relief as they flee Gotham, joking and laughing for the first time since the story's commencement, only to find that their country home has been burglarized and vandalized. For that, they could've just stayed in the city.

That film's opening is symbolic of a particular kind of domestic drama of the era, starting with a well-populated street on the Upper West Side, then panning to the backs of the buildings and pushing in on a single window. Several adult-oriented comedy/dramas ran counter to the gritty, streetwise pictures of the era, a reminder that those wealthy and insular enough did not have to concern themselves with the filthy subways or gaudy Times Square marquees. "Any film you name that depicted that," Leonard Maltin notes, "was countered by something that showed a glossy, chic view of New York, the center of sophistication, the style-making, the trend-setting."

"The Woody Allen films," Scorsese says, "when I first saw them, particularly the films in the '70s—*Annie Hall*, *Manhattan*, and others—the world that they were in, they were foreign. I loved them, but to me, they were foreign films." In these witty, urbane comedies with dramatic undertones, well-heeled, well-educated, entirely white Upper East Siders would exchange bons mots at Elaine's and Bella Abzug fund-raisers, and romantic partners after. Allen's on-screen avatar admits, in the opening sequence of *Manhattan*, that he romanticizes the city "all out of proportion"; the director would do the same himself, excising a joke about muggings during a carriage ride through Central Park in that film, lest it spoil the mood.

Other filmmakers played in Allen's sandbox of upper-class therapy, confession, and recovery. Jerry Schatzberg's *Puzzle of a Downfall Child* (1970) details the breakdown of an aging fashion model (Faye Dunaway), with as keen an interest in her therapy sessions and country

Still images from *Hair* (1979), directed by Milos Forman, photographed by Miroslav Ondrícek; *Godspell* (1973), directed by David Greene, photographed by Richard G. Heimann; *Fame* (1980), directed by Alan Parker, photographed by Michael Serasin; *The Wiz* (1978), directed by Sidney Lumet, photographed by Oswald Morris.

Fear City, Blackouts, and *Taxi Driver*

Mayor Koch,
Congresswoman Bella
Abzug (one of his rivals for
the Democratic nomina-
tion), and President Jimmy
Carter, 1978.

home as her glamorous job. Dunaway goes to the other side of the camera in *Eyes of Laura Mars*, as a brand-name fashion photographer who slums it with a cop (Tommy Lee Jones); in a city like this, the well-off can always get a look at how the other half lives.

In Frank Perry's *Diary of a Mad Housewife* (1970), a depressed spouse finds momentary escape from her emotionally taxing marriage in the New York party scene, where a flirtation with a hotshot writer becomes a torrid affair. Paul Mazursky's rich, complicated *An Unmarried Woman* (1978) gets at the way lives can change in full view, as the marriage at the film's center dissolves right there on the sidewalk, the title character blowing through a range of emotions from shock to rage to hurt as strangers pass right by, just as they do when the long-separated mother and child reunite emotionally in Central Park, to the displeasure of the now-single father, in *Kramer vs. Kramer* (1979).

Some filmmakers punctured these figures. In Elaine May's *A New Leaf* (1971), Walter Matthau's Henry Graham comes across as a scathing portrait of the city's entitled class, proudly lazy and profoundly stupid, wandering the streets of the city in despair and whimpering "I'm poor!" when he has finally spent all of his inherited wealth; Otto Preminger's *Such Good Friends* focuses on Julie (Dyan Cannon), a rich twit who tosses off self-owning observations like "And those foolish people in the ghettos think they have problems," or, when frustrated by her black maid, "Why did they abolish slavery?"

These snapshots of upper-class life offered some kind of escape for those crushed under the city's thumb, not unlike the white-telephone pictures and backstage musicals of the Depression era. The musicals of the seventies, however, weren't always so upbeat. The film adaptation of the stage hit *Godspell* (1973) positions itself explicitly as escapism, opening with sights and sounds of chaotic city life: gridlock, flaring tempers, overcrowding, heat, jackhammers, and jackasses. But its characters flee those irritations for the pageantry at hand, and are able to treat the entire, now-vacated city as their stage, with numbers mounted in Central Park, in Lincoln Center, on the Times Square billboards, and on the top of the still-in-progress World Trade Center towers. And then, when it's over, the sidewalks are full again.

Milos Forman's adaptation of *Hair* (1979), already a period piece a dozen years after its off-Broadway bow, similarly uses the city as its stage—Central Park specifically, where characters sing, dance, and skinny-dip in the pond while mounted police horses ape their dance steps. Like few other films have, *Hair* hones in on the musicality of city sound, of the rhythms created by its constant movement. Sidney Lumet's *The Wiz* (1978), on the other hand, uses a few real locations (like the amped-up World Trade Center plaza), but mostly dwells in a stylized, theatrical version of the city, constructed at the Astoria studios.

Even backstagers, those sunny standbys of the early talkie era, would be bleak and gritty, populated by pill-popping directors, horny producers, and sleazy filmmakers. *Fame* (1980) is set at a Times Square–adjacent school for performing arts, so its musical numbers build out of the narrative, rather than stopping for it—and by the time the first one arrives, it's an explosion of pent-up energy, impatience, and hormones, spilling out into the streets around the school. *All That Jazz* (1979), on the other hand, is a razzle-dazzle musical as open-wound confessional, ending with our hero zipped into a body bag; the city itself is only glimpsed briefly, through theater doors and out cab windows, because our characters rarely leave their stages and rehearsal halls. Their whole lives are there.

———

The 1977 Democratic mayoral primary was among the most contentious in New York's history—and that didn't even count the ousting of the sitting mayor. Beame attempted to run as the grinder he'd always been ("Tough decisions were needed, and I made 'em," he growled), but the horrors of the previous summer, coupled with the less-than-glowing picture painted in an SEC report on the fiscal crisis and its causes, sunk the incumbent. Near the end of a primary debate on the night of August 30, a spectator rose to his feet and chucked an apple pie at His Honor. It was barely more humiliating than the outcome of the primary; he lost, badly, to Ed Koch and Mario Cuomo, who then battled it out in a particularly nasty runoff. Koch won by running as barely a Democrat, openly contemptuous of unions, voters of color, and the city's liberal past, and instead assembling a coalition of Republicans, centrists, social conservatives, and business interests.

That was enough to win; it remained to be seen if that was enough to govern. Filing from Bushwick, a community still steaming from the fires of the blackout, *Daily News* columnist Pete Hamill wrote, "This is the city that Ed Koch will have to cure, a city abandoned, a city unrepresented, a city cynical, the ruined and broken city."

Under Koch, to be fair, the city did recover. But it was a very different city, focused on the needs of a very specific New Yorker. As Kim

A poster from Ed Koch's 1977 mayoral campaign.

Jodie Foster, Robert De
Niro, and Martin Scorsese
during photography of
*Taxi Driver*.

Phillips-Fein writes in *Fear City*, "the scare of the near-bankruptcy brought together the elite groups within the city and enabled them to act in concert in ways that otherwise would have proved difficult to attain." Once the city's power had been redistributed and its priorities had been recast, the central goal of servicing business interests—in the form of tax cuts, tax credits, and other incentives—would extend past the crisis, into the Koch administration and the mayors who followed him. And it would extend past New York City, into the rhetoric of Ronald Reagan and the Republican Party that would oust Jimmy Carter at the beginning of the next decade.

And thanks to savvy investments in marketing and the cycles and styles of media, the public perception would change, slowly but surely, in the years to come. In June 1977, during the city's toughest summer, the State Commerce Department launched NYC's first official marketing campaign: "I ❤ New York." It targeted tourists and conventions, reframing gritty Gotham as a fun and vibrant place to visit; it reminded corporations that New York was the center of the world and assured them that the city would welcome them with open arms. As the message landed, and as visitor numbers went up and empty high-rises began to fill, suddenly the same media that had spent the past several years telling horror yarns about New York had a new narrative: a comeback story.

But in movies, comeback stories were best told on a small scale. The New York films of the 1980s would lean into what had worked in the decade before: savage dispatches from an urban hellscape.

The die had been cast, in many ways, by *Taxi Driver*. Locals may have been indifferent, or even hostile—an anonymous New York cabbie told the *Times*'s Vincent Canby, "The person who made that slanderous movie about cab drivers should be taken out and shot"—but the picture's impact around the world was undeniable and somewhat frightening. Just three months after *Taxi Driver*'s release, the *Daily News* reported an incident in Norfolk, Virginia, in which a twenty-one-year-old man killed four people and injured three more before turning his gun on himself; he reportedly spouted a Bickle-esque proclamation about cleaning out pimps, pushers, and prostitutes.

The film's most disturbed fan also aimed at the biggest target—not just a presidential candidate, but an elected commander-in-chief. On March 30, 1981, John W. Hinckley Jr. fired six shots at President Ronald Reagan and his entourage, wounding but not killing Reagan and three others. FBI agents discovered a shrine to Jodie Foster in Hinckley's hotel room, and a letter in which he explained that he had committed this "historic act" to prove his love for her, just like Travis had done at the end of *Taxi Driver*. Psychiatrist William T. Carpenter testified at Hinckley's trial the following year that the accused had seen the film fifteen times and believed it was speaking to him personally. As part of that trial, the defense presented the film to the jury in its entirety. Hinckley was found not guilty for reason of insanity.

Schrader was "chilled" by the reports of Hinckley's obsession, but not surprised: "I think that character was afloat in the culture and certainly very much afloat in me." In the passing years, the character's omnipresence has grown, if anything, stronger, with nightly news reports of Travis Bickle wannabes, young white god-fearing men, often rejected by women they felt they deserve, taking up arms to right the perceived wrongs of society.

Scorsese was so shaken by the trial that he contemplated walking away from directing entirely. Instead, he made *The King of Comedy*, a kind of anti–*Taxi Driver* about mental illness, delusion, and celebrity. He would not make a sequel to *Taxi Driver* (though Robert De Niro met with Scorsese and Schrader in 2001 to discuss ideas for an aborted follow-up), but in 1999, the director and screenwriter reteamed for *Bringing Out the Dead*, a kind of spiritual sequel, following the desperate journey of a nighttime ambulance driver in Hell's Kitchen and Times Square in the early 1990s. Schrader called it "a more adult version of those roiling emotions Marty and I felt twenty-five years ago."

By then, Times Square was a very different place. The year *Taxi Driver* was released, local business interests formed the 42nd Street Development Corporation, which aimed to clean up and shine up the Deuce. Young developer Donald Trump took advantage of loopholes and property-tax breaks to renovate the Commodore Hotel. The grindhouses of *Midnight Cowboy* and *Taxi Driver* were gut-renovated or razed and rebuilt altogether into ritzy Broadway houses. The mayors who followed Abe Beame would, put simply, do what Travis asked Senator Palantine to do: They cleaned up the scum and filth, and flushed it out.

Some viewers—especially those who didn't live in New York in the 1970s—bemoan the Disneyfication of Times Square, and look longingly on *Taxi Driver* as a time capsule of this lost era. Paul Schrader is not one of them. "My office is right in the heart of the new Times Square, the theme-park Times Square, but the old Times Square was pretty fucking scary," he said. "You wouldn't go down 42nd Street. It was all drug dealers and hookers—and I don't know how nostalgic you can be for that."

# THE LANDLORD
# THE PANIC IN NEEDLE PARK
# THE FRENCH CONNECTION
# ACROSS 110TH STREET
# THE TAKING OF PELHAM ONE TWO THREE
# DOG DAY AFTERNOON
# GIRLFRIENDS
# THE WARRIORS

# THE LANDLORD

## 1970
## Director: Hal Ashby

"Now, children. How do we *live*?" So go the opening lines of this 1970 comedy/drama, and in the film—one keenly interested in dual frameworks—it's both a philosophical and practical question. Elgar Enders (Beau Bridges), the privileged young white man at the story's center, has an idea of how he wants to live: "Everybody wants his own home, you know. And I've never had a place of my own!" So he buys an old building in Park Slope, with the intention of kicking out its renters and renovating the place for himself.

But his mother is horrified. "Good God, Elgar," she asks, "are you aware that that's a *colored* neighborhood?" And so he is, but his (black) real estate agent advises him to "start a trend in urban renewal," and she takes him to another white client around the block, who insists, "This neighborhood's gonna be very chic, very chic. Let's hope this influx of the beautiful people is the beginning of an inclination, huh?"

And thus, we have an early story of gentrification in Park Slope, an area that would indeed become the province of "the beautiful people"—or, at least, the rich and the white and the frequently clueless, just like Elgar. But *The Landlord* isn't merely noteworthy for its prescience; the filmmaking of editor turned director Ashby (making his directorial debut) is electrifyingly experimental, and the screenplay, by the great Bill Gunn (adapting Kristin Hunter's novel), is full of the kind of willful provocations one might expect from the co-writer of *The Angel Levine*, a film that similarly juggles the hand grenades of race, class, and privilege.

In the film's first act, Gunn and Ashby tread into the kind of culture-clash territory one expects. When Elgar first arrives at his new domicile, his convertible VW bug filled with potted plants, he's promptly chased down the street by the large group of (African American) neighbors on the stoop. But they're laughing all the way, reveling in playing their role, and exploiting his predictable fear. (Ashby and Gunn are crafting a similarly cynical portrait of the dopey moneyed class as Elaine May in *A New Leaf*.) And once the initial conflicts and confusion pass, Elgar predictably gets into the spirit of things, finding a few allies and a couple of lovers, letting his hair down at a funky "rent party," even donning a dashiki when his causally racist mother comes to visit.

These scenes are rooted in the still-radical realization, coming out of the turbulent 1960s, that people who *seem* different still share common dreams, and sadness, and humanity. And in that way, it's a quintessential New York movie, a high-intensity version of the melting pot, the shared space way of life all but the richest New Yorkers experience.

But Gunn—an African American playwright, actor, and filmmaker—makes it clear that the black struggle is not a costume this visitor can simply swoop in and adopt as his own. The easy laughs of the party scene are interrupted by snatches of confession, in which his neighbors lay out the difficulty of their lives and the battles they fight every day; much time is spent on the story of Lanie (Marki Bey), the half-black woman he falls for, and the code-switching and tricky assimilation that define her existence.

Elgar ultimately learns that nothing is as simple as he thinks—that a single rich tenant cannot just bulldoze into a community and bend it to his will. Or, at least, he couldn't do that as easily in 1970.

Still image from *The Landlord* (1970), directed by Hal Ashby, photographed by Gordon Willis.

# THE PANIC IN NEEDLE PARK

## 1971

### Director: Jerry Schatzberg

The white block text that fills the black screen, to a silent soundtrack, is terse and to the point. Junkies gather to score and soar at the corner of Broadway and 72nd street; "To addicts, it's known as Needle Park." The story of Needle Park, and two young lovers who descend into addiction there, was first told in a *Life* magazine article and photo essay; the text for that story was written by James Mills, who then expanded it into a novel, which was subsequently adapted into a screenplay by Joan Didion and John Gregory Dunne. Dunne's brother, Dominick, pitched the project to David Brown, then an executive VP at 20th Century Fox, and the story of junkie love found an unlikely studio home.

To shoot the film, Schatzberg, fashion and celebrity photographer (he shot some of the most iconic Bob Dylan images of the 1960s, including the *Blonde on Blonde* cover), reteamed with his *Puzzle of a Downfall Child* cinematographer, Adam Holender, who'd also lensed *Midnight Cowboy*.

"When I talked to Adam," Schatzberg explains, "I said, 'I want to look like we just took our camera, set it up here, open the lens, and when we're finished just close the lens.'

That's the way we did it! Long lenses, most of the time, so we were able to not have everybody look into the camera. We'd be a block away sometimes."

The director underscored that authenticity by shooting only on real locations—the walls of the grimy apartments have the caked layers of peeling paint specific to bad NYC rentals—though he moved the action from the real Needle Park to a tighter median area a block away ("I just felt that the subway there and everything was just too much, and a block away is a block away"). And Taylor augmented the cast of stage pros like Pacino, Kitty Wynn, Raul Julia, and Paul Sorvino with real addicts and street characters.

Studio executives weren't quite sure what to make of that authenticity. "The studio head—no names—watched dailies and sent us a request for a phone call," Holender recalls. "They said, 'I didn't see New York! I didn't see the Empire State Building!' We sat down with the producer for ten minutes at lunch and said we were after something different: 'We're not looking for landmarks, but the texture of life on the streets of New York.'"

Their effort shows. *Panic* is a harrowingly convincing portrait of heroin culture, with Bobby (Pacino) serving as a tour guide through the scene; Helen (Wynn) serves as the audience surrogate, her stunned expressions and reactions matching ours as she's exposed to more of the city's seamy underbelly. At first she's touched by Bobby's sweetness and experience, finding the romanticism in their street scrounging and apartment surfing. But soon enough, they're running around the Upper West Side looking for drops in phone booths and trash cans, and when those sources run dry ("It's an election year, man, that's why there's no shit"), he's sending her up to 119th Street. "You're not just asking me to score for you," she notes, accurately. "You're asking for something else." Their descent into emotional and physical abuse is rendered with such grim poignancy, it set the template for NYC addiction dramas; you can see Schatzberg's fingerprints all over such later efforts as *Bad Lieutenant* (1992), *Requiem for a Dream* (2000), and (especially) *Heaven Knows What* (2014).

Still images from *The Panic in Needle Park* (1971), directed by Jerry Schatzberg, photographed by Adam Holender.

# GOD HELP
# BOBBY AND HELEN

They're in love in Needle Park

20th Century-Fox presents

# the panic in
# needle park

starring AL PACINO and KITTY WINN produced by DOMINICK DUNNE directed by JERRY SCHATZBERG
screenplay by JOAN DIDION and JOHN GREGORY DUNNE a DUNNE-DIDION-DUNNE production COLOR BY DE LUXE®

# THE FRENCH CONNECTION

## 1971
## Director: William Friedkin

The dread-infused music by Don Ellis that opens Friedkin's cop classic—horn notes blasted rather than played, sounding less like trumpets than sirens—immediately creates a sense of chaos and terror that permeates all that follows. The movie is similarly impatient; the opening credits barely take time to list the key personnel before we're tossed into a sting in progress, with Popeye Doyle (Gene Hackman, in an Oscar-winning performance) incognito in a Santa suit, joining his partner Buddy Russo (Roy Scheider) in breathless pursuit of their subject.

"*The French Connection* marks one of the most ambitious movie projects ever to be filmed in New York City," boasted the press notes. "Eighty-six separate locations throughout the city were utilized, covering Gotham scenically as it has rarely been before in a feature film." Friedkin and producer Philip D'Antoni coordinated principal photography between December 1970 and February 1971, because, per D'Antoni, "the winter was when the actual events occurred." Scenes were shot in Grand Central Station, in Central Park, on Madison Avenue, and on the Lower East Side in Manhattan; in Maspeth and at LaGuardia in Queens; in Bedford-Stuyvesant and Coney Island in Brooklyn; and even at Ward's Island in the Upper East River.

The precedent set by D'Antoni's earlier *Bullitt* was part of the reason the *French Connection*'s iconic chase existed at all; it wasn't part of the original police case, or Moore's book. "I felt challenged to do another kind of chase," Friedkin wrote, "one which, while it might remind people of *Bullitt*, would not be essentially similar." The key difference was vehicular: *Bullitt* was a car chasing a car, but *The French Connection* was a car chasing an elevated subway train.

This meant the production had to not only coordinate, as usual, with the mayor's office, but with the NYC Metropolitan Transit Authority. After some wrangling over the accuracy of the details of the sequence, the MTA granted the production permission to shoot on the Stillwell Avenue line in Brooklyn. Friedkin and his team marked off an ideal stretch from Bay 50th Street to 60th Street, and worked through a plan to shoot the sequence in two chunks (one for the train and one for the car) in bits and pieces over a five-week period—and only between ten a.m. and three p.m., between the line's rush hours.

To shoot Hackman (and his stunt double, Bill Hickman) driving under the track, Friedkin and cinematographer Owen Roizman mounted three cameras on and inside the car, and used three simultaneous cameras when shooting from the street. "Because we were using real pedestrians and traffic at all times, it was impossible to undercrank, so everything was shot at normal speed," Friedkin wrote. "In most shots, the car was going at speeds between 70 and 90 miles an hour. . . . We prayed a lot, and kept our fingers crossed."

The danger of New York City, the noisiness and chaos and disorder that Friedkin so adroitly transformed into tension, could also be cranked by less-graceful talents, with less finesse, into a kind of urban exploitation. Friedkin called it "a crude poem to the city," but historian James Sanders puts a finer point on it. "Where the police once helped maintain a healthy civic order, now that very order is seen as diseased," he writes. "Ordinary urban life, according to *The French Connection*, is a nightmare."

Still images from *The French Connection* (1971), directed by William Friedkin, photographed by Owen Roizman.

204

# ACROSS 110TH STREET

## 1972

## Director: Barry Shear

*Across 110th Street* was produced and promoted like a typical New York urban crime picture, just another "blaxploitation" potboiler like *Shaft* or *Super Fly* (which preceded it) or *Black Caesar* (which was released six weeks after it), and as Greil Marcus writes in *Mystery Train*, it "looked enough like all the others to make it easy for nearly all critics to dismiss it. The film was almost unbelievably violent, which gave reviewers license to attack it. It began with the same clichés everyone else used, but intensified them mercilessly. It pumped so much pressure into the world of the new black movies that it blew that world apart."

The title—and the title song by Bobby Womack, reappropriated a quarter-century later by Quentin Tarantino for *Jackie Brown*—is taken from a boundary both geographic and sociological, that 110th is the clear demarcation line between white and black New York City, that (as one white gangster notes) Central Park is "the no man's land that separates us from the black Harlem." But organized crime makes for strange bedfellows; as Yaphet Kotto's up-and-coming Lt. Pope notes, "What else brings whites to Harlem but business?" In this use, "business" doesn't just refer to mobsters, or clientele—it also means the cops, like Captain Mattelli (Anthony Quinn), especially those who are also on the mob payroll.

Mattelli and Pope are paired up to find the crew that knocks off an uptown hideout in the opening sequence, leaving several bodies and fleeing with over $300,000 in mob money. (Right away, it's a story of the haves and have-nots—director Shear cuts from the bloody robbery to a ritzy children's birthday party, thrown by one of the men who just got hit.) This odd-couple pairing of the rule-bending old white cop and his forward-thinking young black colleague sounds, at first, like a Northern riff on *In the Heat of the Night*, but it more often plays like an answer record to the Harlem bar scene in *The French Connection*—a portrayal of how ineffective an old-fashioned "tough" white cop would actually be in the streets. "Look, I am sick and tired of your liberal bullshit!" Mattelli insists, when his partner reprimands him for roughing up a suspect. "Are you a cop, or one of them social workers?"

In its own, quiet way, *Across 110th Street* is as damning an indictment of police corruption as *Serpico*, because here, the graft and payoffs aren't even the focus of the story; they're an understood and acknowledged norm. It also offers no great comfort regarding the NYPD's skill as an investigative unit; Pope and Mattelli are perpetually one step behind the mob in tracking the culprits, who are plucked off one by one, as gruesomely as possible. It is not, as so many of its blaxploitation cohort were, a good-time escapist fantasy; even the momentary pleasure of spending one's hard-earned robbery money is disrupted by a brutal public beating (of not only the robber but also the woman he's with). Cynicism and despair seep into every frame.

Nowhere is this more evident than in a long, uncomfortable dialogue scene between one of the other culprits, Jamaica (Paul Benjamin, also of *Midnight Cowboy* and, later, *Do the Right Thing*), and his lady. "LOOK AT ME!" he demands of her—and of us. "YOU'RE LOOKING AT A 42-YEAR-OLD EX-CON NIGGER! Now who the hell would want me for anything but washing cars or swinging a pick?" He's keenly aware that, because of his reckless act, his days are numbered, but he's looked at the kind of life he'll have otherwise, and he's passing on it.

It's not a scene you'll find in most crime pictures, which do not typically let a criminal explain his motivations, and his hopelessness, in such grim, kitchen-sink detail. The presumption is that criminals commit crimes because they're criminals, and that's that. But this tough, angry sequence explicitly addresses the causality of a life of crime—and the frustrations of the time and place that feed into it. And in the case of 1970s New York (and even more so as the decade continued), the city's poor would find themselves driven to acts of desperation by nothing more complicated than a lack of other options.

Still image from *Across 110th Street* (1972), directed by Barry Shear, photographed by Jack Priestley.

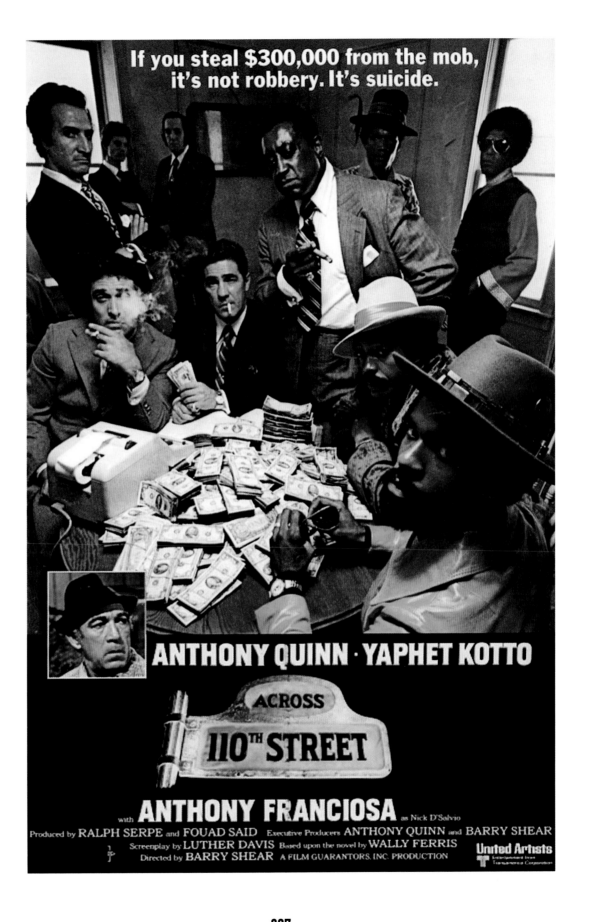

# THE TAKING OF PELHAM ONE TWO THREE

## 1972

### Director: Joseph Sargent

When producers Gabriel Katzka and Edgar J. Scherick first approached the MTA about their film adaptation of John Godey's novel, in which four armed men take over a New York subway car and hold its seventeen passengers hostage, the Transit Authority firmly refused to cooperate with the production. Why would it want to put ideas into people's heads? It took assurances from the filmmakers to go light on details, as well as the pleas of outgoing mayor Lindsay, to get the picture a go-ahead—that and a $20 million "kook insurance" policy, to cover costs in case the movie inspired any real-life hijackings.

United Artists also wrote the city a $250,000 check to cover the costs of renting the Court Street station, a stretch of adjoining track, and several spare subway cars. Since the title train is running on the IRT line, art director Gene Rudolf and his team took pains to re-dress the station to match that line's color schemes and lettering styles. They also built a dispatcher's room at the Filmways Studios in Harlem, replicating the layout of the real McCoy, and wiring it up for practical use, complete with working switches, lights, intercoms, and telephone lines.

But there was one area where the film's replication of detail fell short: The city insisted that the subway cars featured in the film be scrubbed free of graffiti. "New Yorkers are going to hoot when they see our spotless subway cars," Sargent told the *Los Angeles Times*. "But the TA was adamant on that score. They said to show graffiti would be to glorify it. We argued that it was artistically expressive. But we got nowhere. They said the graffiti fad would be dead by the time the movie got out. I really doubt that."

In the closing credits, the producers of *The Taking of Pelham 123* acknowledge and thank the city for its cooperation and assistance while carefully noting that no city officials offered official consulting or technical advice. But they took something away from it; to this day, superstitious dispatchers carefully avoid scheduling any Manhattan-bound 6 trains to leave Pelham Bay Park at 1:23.

Still image from *The Taking of Pelham One Two Three* (1974), directed by Joseph Sargent, photographed by Owen Roizman.

# DOG DAY AFTERNOON

## 1975

## Director: Sidney Lumet

GAY BANK ROBBER TO BE FILM HERO, read the January 17, 1973, headline in *Variety*, which reported, "Plans are in the works to lens a feature film based on the highly publicized robbery of a N.Y. bank last summer by a bi-sexual young man who was seeking money to finance a sex-change operation for his homosexual boyfriend."

The film reunited Al Pacino with his *Serpico* director, Sidney Lumet, who decided that the only way to play this stranger-than-fiction true story was as simply and naturalistically as possible. The production would dispense with the customary distancing devices. The bulk of the action took place inside the bank, which most productions would construct on a studio stage, where Lumet could move walls and light scenes freely. But that would mean filming the bank exteriors in an entirely separate location, restricting their ability to move freely between them in some scenes. Lumet's fix: "We found an excellent street that had a [street-level] warehouse floor we could rent. We built the bank inside the warehouse so I could have my 'wild walls' and still have constant access between the street and the interior of the bank."

His approach to the material was similarly immersive. The film opens with a to-the-point title card: WHAT YOU ARE ABOUT TO SEE IS TRUE. What follows is a montage of documentary-style images, shot with a hidden camera, of New York in the summer: the Circle Line off the pier, a dog digging in the trash, a rooftop pool party, construction workers, tollbooths, tennis courts, homeless people, beachgoers, moviegoers, commuters, trash collectors. These are snapshots of the city, taken with the immediacy and off-handedness of news footage—so when the actors enter the frame and the first proper scene begins, it first feels like just another stolen shot.

So what does all this effort at verisimilitude capture about New York in the summer (of both 1972, when it takes place, and 1974, when it was shot)? The overwhelming theme is *people under pressure*. Sonny is the quintessential 1970s New Yorker, who has been (per his lover, Leon) "crazy all summer," constantly railing about "the pressure's I've been havin'" and the "shit" everybody's giving him, how he's all alone, how he's trying his best. "I'm a fuckup, and I'm an outcast, and THAT'S IT!" he explodes, and perhaps it's that specific, relatable stress that makes him such a sympathetic character.

It certainly seems to endear him to the crowd out front, and one of the keener insights of Frank Pierson's perceptive screenplay is the degree to which the gathered crowd of Brooklyn looky-loos immediately takes to Sonny, greeting him as a folk hero (The City was always looking for one)—and how quickly they turn on him. His anti-authoritarian rabble-rousing earns him cheers, and those cheers turn into a high for Sonny, a respite from the pressure-cooker environment inside the bank; by the midpoint the crowd is booing his antagonists, be they cops or attackers, and he's downright strutting for them, like a stand-up having a particularly good set down at the Improv ("I got nothin' up my sleeves!"). But the love of New Yorkers is a fickle thing, and once Leon shows up, they shift; the same people who were calling his name are catcalling him and the one he loves. And then, because every action in New York prompts an equal reaction, he finds support again, when gay activists turn up to cheer him on.

Yet, for all of his devotion to realism, Lumet occasionally yields to stylization. When Sonny is on the phone with Leon, Lumet slowly takes away the sounds of the city that have been a constant throughout the picture. Suddenly, when he talks to Leon, Sonny is surrounded by quiet and stillness, a reminder of how someone you love can create an island of sanity in New York's sea of madness.

Still image from *Dog Day Afternoon* (1975), directed by Sidney Lumet, photographed by Victor J. Kemper.

The robbery should have taken

10 minutes.          4 hours later,

the bank was like a circus sideshow.

8 hours later,          it was the

hottest thing on live TV.

12 hours later,          it was history.

And it's all true.

**AL PACINO**

An Artists Entertainment Complex, Inc. Production

**DOG DAY AFTERNOON**

Also Starring
JOHN CAZALE · JAMES BRODERICK and CHARLES DURNING as Moretti · Screenplay by FRANK PIERSON · Produced by MARTIN BREGMAN and MARTIN ELFAND
Directed by SIDNEY LUMET · Film Editor DEDÉ ALLEN · TECHNICOLOR® From WARNER BROS. A WARNER COMMUNICATIONS COMPANY  **R** RESTRICTED Under 17 requires accompanying Parent or Adult Guardian

# GIRLFRIENDS

## 1978

## Director: Claudia Weill

Painter turned documentarian turned fiction filmmaker Claudia Weill had a simple idea: She wanted to make a movie about the kind of girl movies usually weren't about. "There was always the lead girl," Weill explained. "And then there was the sidekick, the best friend. And she was always a little bit more ethnic, maybe Jewish." She was funny, funnier than the lead girl, and maybe not quite so *conventionally* attractive. *Girlfriends* would be about her.

That character, in this case, is Susan Weinblatt (Melanie Mayron), a listless photographer who finds herself set adrift in a sea of bad dates, worse roommates, and unconsummated crushes when her best friend and roommate, Anne (Anita Skinner), gets married and moves out.

And if Weill's protagonist is less "glamorous" than the standard romantic-comedy lead, so then is her milieu off the beaten path as well: At a time when the New York City romantic comedy was being defined by Woody Allen and his well-heeled Upper East Siders, here was a portrait of Manhattanites barely getting by. They dwell in tiny, lived-in walk-ups on the Lower East Side. They struggle to pay the bills; one night, Susan's electricity just shuts off, out of nowhere. "I HATE IT!" she screams to the empty apartment. Two scenes later, Anne asks how living alone is going. "I like it!" she insists.

Soon that neighborhood would become too pricey as well, and Susan and Anne's spiritual successors, like the characters in Lena Dunham's *Girls*, would have to live in Brooklyn. Dunham has frequently pinpointed *Girlfriends* as a key influence on that show; the plot of the young woman who goes into a free fall when she loses her roommate and best friend in one fell swoop also found its way into *Frances Ha*. Like those films, *Girlfriends* feels like the work of a storyteller and a tour guide; Weill knows these spaces inside and out, and when Susan finds herself out of her element at Anne's fancy new apartment, or schlepping through Tribeca with her portfolio under her arm, you feel as though Weill has been there too.

Still image from *Girlfriends* (1978), directed by Claudia Weill, photographed by Fred Murphy.

"Melanie Mayron is romantic and offers evidence that some mysterious quality we call sex appeal is harder to define than it ever was and continues to be what movies are all about. —*Molly Haskell, New York Magazine*

"Melanie Mayron is warm and funny human and lovable," — *Richard Grenier, Cosmopolitan*

"Sensitive, engrossing and touching. An intelligent off-beat movie about real people who come alive." — *Jeffrey Lyons, CBS Radio*

"This is a movie to treasure. ★★★½" — *Kathleen Carroll, New York Daily News*

"A fine...film experience. A pleasant and welcome surprise."— *David Sterritt, Christian Science Monitor*

"*Girl Friends*...a movie so full of life and love and feeling, you're bound to take some of it home with you." — *David Sheehan, CBS-TV*

# girl friends

Cyclops films presents a film by Claudia Weill. "Girl Friends" *starring*. Melanie Mayron. *featuring*. Anita Skinner, Eli Wallach, Christopher Guest, Bob Balaban, Gina Rogak, Amy Wright, Viveca Lindfors, & Mike Kellin. *produced & directed by*. Claudia Weill. *co-producer*. Jan Saunders. *screenplay*. Vicki Polon. *story*. Claudia Weill & Vicki Polon. *music*. Michael Small.

780099

"Girl Friends"

# THE WARRIORS

## 1979

## Director: Walter Hill

When producer Lawrence Gordon sent director Hill a copy of Sol Yurick's 1965 novel *The Warriors* as a possibility for his next film, Hill was uninterested—for a number of reasons. "When you talk about gangs," the filmmaker explains, "that fits into the category of 'social problem' movies, and this is very far from that kind of idea, where everybody's gonna somehow end up a doctor or a lawyer or go to college." Plus, the film was set in New York, intimately immersed in the city's geography, and "I had visited New York a few times, but I was a very California guy, you know. Very American in my taste, but not a New Yorker."

But as Hill thought about the picture, he began to puzzle out solutions to the problems. "I thought it could be a pure chase movie with classical overtones," he recalls, and rather than try to learn the city, he'd lean into his outsider status. "I didn't do any research," he says, "because it's in a nameless, dystopian future. It's much more like a movie that came out a couple years later, John Carpenter's movie *Escape from New York*, in that it *feels* very New York, it *is* very New York, but at the same time, it's not a realistic film at all. Nor does it pretend to be. So I just tried to catch the vibe of New York then, and projected a few years ahead."

That cock-eyed, alienated view is present from the opening images—nighttime on Coney Island, where the neon lights of the Wonder Wheel make it look like a spaceship. Hill draws on the iconography and imagery of the American Western (a genre he'd play in several times in the years to come) to frame the city's various street gangs boarding subways like outlaws saddling up, as they gather all the way out in the Bronx for a big meet-up that culminates in an assassination, for which the Warriors are (wrongfully) accused. And thus, our "heroes" find themselves on the wrong end of the IRT line, trying to make their way back to their turf alive.

"When you look at the movie now," Hill says, "a kind of harsh realism is not the first thing that occurs to you about it. It looks very stylized, and it looks more like a musical than it does a hard, tough story of the streets. But in those days, it seemed more real.... Often the real gangs of the neighborhoods knew we were coming. So they would object, and say 'Get out of here,' and of course, we would say

no, but they would throw rocks or couple of times up on the elevated tracks, they'd stand up there and piss down on our guys when they were going by." But for most of the shoot, the peace was easy to keep. "They said, 'You're on our turf, you want to park your trucks and'—it was always the same thing—'we'll keep your trucks safe, but we'd like a certain amount of money for that.' And extortion usually works, at least in the short run."

*The Warriors* certainly seemed real to audiences; when it landed in February 1979, it was blamed for three gang-related deaths at or near theaters. Paramount briefly suspended and then altered the picture's ad campaign, which featured a central image of scores of gang members and the taglines "These are the Armies of the Night. They are 100,000 strong. They outnumber the cops five to one. They could run New York City. Tonight they're all out to get the Warriors."

"When the movie came out, there were a lot of people attacking the movie for what they perceived to be the movie's association with crime and gangs," says Hill. "But Mayor Koch and the people of New York really never attacked the movie; as a matter of fact, they said nice things about the film on the whole. I think it would have been a cheap shot—but it would have been an easy shot. And they never did that, and I'm forever in their debt that way. I mean, the rest of the country was steamed up, but *they* were terrific."

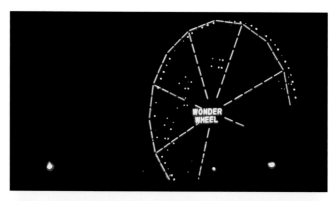

THESE ARE THE ARMIES OF THE NIGHT.
They are 100,000 strong. They outnumber the cops five to one.
They could run New York City. Tonight they're all out to get the Warriors.

Paramount Pictures Presents A Lawrence Gordon Production "THE WARRIORS" Executive Producer
Frank Marshall Based Upon the Novel by Sol Yurick Screenplay by David Shaber and Walter Hill
Produced by Lawrence Gordon Directed by Walter Hill

**R** RESTRICTED

© 1979 Paramount Pictures Corporation. All Rights Reserved.

**OPPOSITE**
Still images from *The Warriors* (1979), directed by Walter Hill, photographed by Andrew Laszlo.

# 1980

# Two Cities, Ed Koch, and *Wall Street*

# 1989

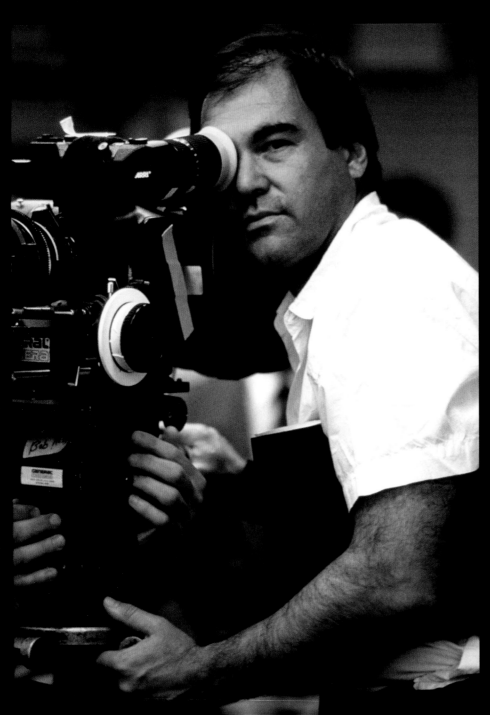

**PREVIOUS SPREAD**
Oliver Stone directs Charlie
Sheen in *Wall Street* (1987).

**LEFT**
Oliver Stone at work.

"I grew up in a New York that I thought of as tough," Oliver Stone says. "It was the '50s, the '60s. My parents were well-off at that time, until 1960. Everything changed when they got divorced in '62, but basically it was a city where it was always grimy and always realistic, in black and white." Even as a child, he saw The City like it was a movie.

Aerial view of the city.

Stone left that tough city for Yale, and then dropped out to go to Vietnam—first as a teacher, later as a soldier, returning to New York in 1969 with a Bronze Star and a Purple Heart in his knapsack. He attended NYU film school for two years, crafting his first short films and crewing on others, including *Street Scenes*, a documentary project for one of his professors, Martin Scorsese. Stone graduated in the summer of 1971.

"Well, it's a typical New York story," he says. "Starved, poverty, struggle, writing scripts, treatments, trying to get an agent, trying to see people in the business. Endless fucking rejection, piles of letters. It was tough to keep going." He worked on a few low-budget films and odd jobs, including driving a taxi at night ("I was a taxi driver in '72, '73, in that area. He [Scorsese] made the movie in '76. Maybe I was one of the models, who knows?"). He spent his days writing; a few of the scripts were optioned, but none of them sold, and none made much noise until he decided to write about his experience as an infantryman in Vietnam.

"My biggest break was writing *Platoon*, but no one bought it," Stone recalls. "They liked it, said it was a good writing sample. So then I went to LA because it was a place of opportunities in 1976." He used the *Platoon* script as a calling card to land increasingly higher-paying and higher-profile writing gigs, including *Midnight Express, Conan the Barbarian*, and *Scarface*. It took a decade for Stone to garner the cachet to make *Platoon*, both writing and directing. But it was worth the wait; the film won Best Picture at the 1987 Academy Awards, and he won the Oscar for Best Director.

Oliver Stone was forty years old and wasn't sure what to do next. *Platoon* was not only a professional high point, but also a potential artistic impasse; after the rough violence of his eighties screenplays, it felt like the end of an era. "There's no question that *Platoon* is the end of the blood cycle," he told the *New York Times*, shortly after his Oscar triumph. "I think I got everything I had to get out of me on that." Having mined the most significant moment of his past, he started thinking about his father, a frustrated writer who had made his living as a stockbroker.

"My father was on Wall Street all his life, and it was a very distant place to me," Stone says. "Tie and suit, he looked very professional. It was kind of a serious business. I had no interest in it, but it was the mood, the atmosphere that was interesting. Business. The concept." Maybe that, Stone thought, was worth exploring.

▬

The City entered the 1980s with a profound sense of weariness and exhaustion. In the December 31, 1979, issue of *New York*, the magazine's editors noted, sadly, "We have left the decade of the last free ride," and shouted out "the anonymous dancer at Studio 54 who said, 'This is as near to heaven as I'll ever get.' She may have been right. It doesn't look as though the eighties are going to be that much fun."

New York might have "recovered" from the depths of the near bankruptcy of 1975, but the economy was still slippery; a nationwide recession was on the horizon, unemployment was climbing, and the city was more interested in investing in tourism and marketing than its residents. More than one hundred thousand of the Bronx's housing units (over 20 percent of the borough's dwellings) were lost in the 1970s, and the fires were still commonplace—by the next decade, movies like Amos Poe's *Alphabet City* (1984) were incorporating shady arsons as plot points. Infrastructure was failing, and there was no money for

**ABOVE**
Mayor Ed Koch in 1981.

**BELOW**
Mayor Koch in a clip from
the documentary *Style Wars*
(1983), directed by Tony
Silver.

repairs; thanks to a crack on FDR Drive, even the mayor's official residence, Gracie Mansion, was on the verge of collapse.

It felt like even the momentary distractions, the fleeting pleasures that had made the preceding years bearable, were disappearing. Studio 54's owners, Steve Rubell and Ian Schrager, were indicted in the summer of 1979 for evading taxes due on funds skimmed from the club, which closed its doors for good in February 1980, after one last, big, blowout bash that was billed as "The End of Modern-Day Gomorrah."

Some New Yorkers looked at the coming decade with optimism. "I'm really talking to the people who grew up with me," John Lennon said, in a radio interview in December 1980. "I'm saying, 'Here I am now, how are you? How's your relationship going? Did you get through it all? Wasn't the '70s a drag? Here we are, let's try to make it through the '80s, you know?'" A few hours later, a crazed fan shot the forty-year-old former Beatle dead as he entered the Dakota apartment building on the Upper West Side.

"I was at Gracie Mansion when I heard," Mayor Ed Koch recalled. "He had captivated people, in some mystical way." But Koch also took the opportunity, as he always did, to defend his city; when a London newspaper chalked up the murder as typical to this violent nation and its urban center, the mayor fired back, "Are there no monsters in Britain? Ask the people of Ireland," and noted that the city was "very proud that Lennon had chosen to make New York his home."

It was the kind of response that came to define Ed Koch, who served twelve years as not only New York City's mayor, but also its chief cheerleader, enthusiast, and promoter. He became an avatar for the public perception of the "New Yorker": loud, boisterous, enthusiastic, thin-skinned, angling for a fight, maybe just a little corrupt, and always looking for affirmation, as evidenced by his catchphrase, "How am I doin'?" He was an unapologetic neoliberal, believing that the road to New York's fiscal prosperity was paved by private enterprise, and he was willing to offer whatever deals, rebates, incentives, and cuts would lure big business back to Gotham.

Koch's first real test came in April 1980, when he presided over an eleven-day transit strike that primarily succeeded in marshaling public sentiment against the union. The mayor felt he had learned the lessons of the disastrous 1967 strike, in which Lindsay famously coined the "fun city" shorthand and, more pointedly, asked New Yorkers to stay home if possible; Koch encouraged them to walk, bike, and ride to work, and stood on the Brooklyn Bridge cheering on the approaching commuters. "I thought: 'There are the municipal workers coming to save the city,'" he wrote in his 1984 autobiography.

His hard-line stance in the strike made him a vaunted voice in the 1980 presidential campaign, where he half-heartedly endorsed his fellow Democrat, incumbent President Jimmy Carter, while slyly back-slapping the Republican challenger, Ronald Reagan (who would do Koch one better in his approach to striking air traffic controllers in 1981). After Carter lost, Koch took it upon himself to explain the thinking of a typical Reagan voter: "'I've had enough. Government has got to take a step back. The pendulum has gone too far.' . . . They really believe in local government. Is that conservative? I happen to think that is liberal."

By the following year's mayoral election, Koch had become so popular, he was able to run in, and win, both the Republican and Democratic primaries, and took 79 percent of the vote in the general election against a handful of third-party candidates. "Hizzoner" was so proud of this win, which he dubbed a "superlandslide," he took *New York Post* publisher Rupert Murdoch up on his challenge for New Yorkers to DRAFT KOCH to run for governor the following year, against his old mayoral rival, Mario Cuomo.

It was a disaster. No sooner had Koch announced his candidacy than a recent *Playboy* interview surfaced, conducted before the "draft," in which the mayor insisted, "Anyone who suggests that I run for governor is no friend of mine. It's a terrible position, and besides it requires living in Albany, which is small-town life at its worst. I wouldn't even consider it." The candid conversation also included sentiments like "This rural America thing—I'm telling you, it's a joke," which, to put it mildly, did not play well with upstate voters. Cuomo trounced Koch in those counties come primary season—in fact, the mayor barely eked out a meager .5 percent victory over the governor in the city itself.

Koch went back to City Hall and licked his wounds. His bid for the governor's mansion wasn't the only failure of the second term. Though he'd restored the city's credit, balanced its budget, and successfully completed the implementation of austerity measures begun under Beame, the social effects of those measures were creating problems of their own—not just physical breakdowns in infrastructure, but cracks in the psyche of the city as well. With social services all but vanished, there was no safety net for the city's less fortunate, those who weren't benefiting from the pro-business policies and incentives of the Koch administration. With unemployment cut to the bone, the city's housed poor became its homeless. With drug rehabilitation programs long gone, the city was ill-equipped for the rise of cocaine—especially its low-budget variation, crack. And with welfare assistance disappearing, street crime rose exponentially.

Koch, unsurprisingly, was mostly concerned with the more visible of these epidemics. In August 1980, the *Times* reported that "after one of his infrequent subway rides," the mayor reiterated his distaste for the spray-painted graffiti that had become a floor-to-ceiling feature of most trains ("It's as vile as ever") and proposed fencing in subway storage yards and letting loose unescorted dogs to attack graffiti writers. "If I had my way," he continued, "I wouldn't put in dogs, but wolves."

Graffiti certainly wasn't the most pressing issue for New Yorkers, or even the biggest irritation for patrons of the MTA, whose trains were plagued by unexplained delays, sudden outages, and broken doors, tracks, and signals. But those capital improvements required money that Koch's slender budgets didn't allow, so he focused on the graffiti instead, launching an anti-"bombing" campaign with the cumbersome slogan "Make your mark *in* society, not *on* society." In a clip from the campaign's unveiling, seen in Tony Silver's documentary *Style Wars* (1983), even Koch himself can't get through the phrase without mangling it.

And once again, the mayor and his administration set their sights on Times Square—more specifically, Eighth Avenue and 42nd Street. In July 1981, the *Times* did another of its periodic check-ins on the "entrenched lawless subculture that threatens outsiders," populated by "a parade of shadowy figures, drug peddlers, con artists, vagrants, men wearing the clothes of women, and young hangers-on from New York City and its suburbs." But to their credit, the paper of record also noted that the block had become the only "regional, low-income

Still images from *Basket Case* (1982), directed by Frank Henenlotter, photographed by Bruce Torbet; *The Driller Killer* (1979), directed by Abel Ferrara, photographed by Ken Kelsch; *Fear City* (1984), directed by Abel Ferrara, photographed by Dick Halligan; *The Exterminator* (1980), directed by James Glickenhaus, photographed by Robert M. Baldwin.

Two Cities, Ed Koch, and *Wall Street*

The New York skyline at dusk.

entertainment center" in Midtown, thanks to "what is probably the densest collection of movie theaters in the world—14 across two 800-foot-long block-fronts," and "some of the cheapest ticket prices in the city—$2 to $4 for double and triple features with as many as eight consecutive previews thrown in."

But such simple, affordable pleasures were not worth preserving, at least in the eyes of the 42nd Street Development Corporation. Its first proposal for the redesign of the block saved some of the theaters but demolished others (along with such mainstays as the Times Tower) to make room for office towers, a two-story shopping mall, radio and television studios, an IMAX theater, and a theme park. Even Koch wasn't on board, dubbing it "Disneyland on 42nd Street." (He had no idea.)

While city planners, city government, and local vendors spent the next several years arguing over how to best remake 42nd Street, its all-night movie houses continued to grind through exploitation pictures for their spirited denizens. Increasingly, they were seeing their own environment on the big screens in front of them. The early 1980s saw a wave of "Deuce movies," genre flicks set (at least in part) amid the squalor of the Times Square district, which were met with chuckles of recognition by moviegoers—or, at least, the conscious ones.

*Basket Case* (1982) features not only a protagonist who takes up residence at a grimy Times Square flophouse, but also a scene in a proper 42nd Street grindhouse, wherein the picnic-style basket holding the picture's titular monster is swiped by an overenthusiastic pick-pocket. (It doesn't turn out well for the pickpocket.) A key sequence in *The Exterminator* (1980) features a scumbag picking up a Times Square streetwalker for a "date," then locking her in a red-walled sex dungeon that turns out to be a hot spot for "chicken hawks."

William Lustig's genuinely scary and unapologetically grizzly *Maniac* (1980) seems similarly at home in the squalor of the area's seediest hotels, where its "hero" (co-writer Joe Spinell) takes a streetwalker for a thrill-kill. He spends most of his time hunting young women on streets, in discos, and in parked cars (the film came out three years after the Summer of Sam), creating suspense sequences in urban environments like apartment buildings, discotheques, and subway stations—in stark contrast to the rural and suburban settings of more typical slasher fare in the vein of *Halloween* (1978), *Friday the 13th* (1980), and *A Nightmare on Elm Street* (1984).

Abel Ferrara similarly uses found objects of the city (like glass-partitioned bus stops) as kill props in the grimily authentic *The Driller Killer* (1979), whose protagonist is driven to murder by noisy neighbors and a shitty landlord (who can't relate?). This blood-splattered sleaze-fest, lit and framed like a snuff film, is a post–*Taxi Driver* exploration of the kind of murderous desperation that seemed to infest the city in this period. The director would explore the nuts and bolts of the Times Square sex trade in his 1984 film *Fear City*, which peaks behind the velvet curtain to focus on a talent agency that supplies girls for the area's copious strip clubs and peep shows, with, of course, plenty of documentation of said girls plying their trade. Yet this film also trafficks in real fears and urban terror; its slasher kills women while walking alone on the city's streets or waiting for its tardy subway trains on empty platforms.

In light of such abundant exploitation, some filmmakers pulled their punches. Allan Moyle's *Times Square* (1980) is a strange combination of gnarly portraiture and teen fun flick, in which the daughter of the commissioner trying to clean up Times Square escapes his clutches and joins up with a fellow runaway to become the area's young mascots/ folk heroes, The Sleez Sisters. The father fumes, mostly out of political embarrassment. After all, it reflects poorly on his organization, "The Times Square Renaissance" (its motto: RECLAIM—REBUILD—RESTORE). His message, at a big community meeting, is simple and pointed: "Do we want to live in an X-rated city?"

Another key film of this period imagined what seemed, at the time, a logical extension of The City's lawlessness. According to the opening crawl of John Carpenter's *Escape from New York* (1981), by the year 1997, "The once-great city of New York becomes the one maximum-security prison for the entire country." The island of Manhattan, bound by its water and a wall, houses "only prisoners and the world they have made," and inside, "the rules are simple: Once you go in, you don't come out." Prisoners en route to this godless hellscape can *choose to be cremated* rather than be sent to live in New York.

It's hard to blame them. The streets of Carpenter's future Manhattan— shot, of course, predominantly in California and St. Louis, Missouri—are strewn with garbage, abandoned cars, and burnt-out furniture, and the subways are patronized only by "the crazies" who live in them. "You don't walk around here at night!" explains Ernest Borgnine's seen-it-all taxi driver, before cheerfully tossing a Molotov cocktail.

———

"Ever since the 1980s," writes Kim Phillips-Fein in *Fear City*, "the embrace of private enterprise as the sole way to fuel social development has helped to justify and legitimize the economic inequality that seems to define our day." David Burke, secretary to Governor Hugh Carey, defined the city and state's appeal of the decade more definitively: "The people we've been appealing to throughout this crisis are not so much the voters as the investors." If the city came back to life, it was in a turbocharged version, where the extremes were wider and more pronounced; the poor got poorer, and the rich got richer. And richer. And richer.

"Not since the Gilded Age had New York seen such unbridled displays of wealth," writes William Grimes in *The Times of the Eighties*, "as a wave of freshly minted billionaires preened and strutted, fighting their way into the upper reaches of society by funneling their wealth into charity balls and clamoring to join the boards of august institutions like the Metropolitan Museum of Art and the New York Public Library."

Through those "boom years" of 1977–87, the city's class divide, already suffocating, became sharper. Scholars dubbed it the "dual city" phenomenon, and it showed no signs of shifting; even as tax revenues from real estate, tourism, and individual incomes ballooned, and the Koch administration found itself, for the first time in decades, with budget surpluses, the austerity cuts to public housing and social programs were not fully restored. Those funds were instead shifted to "quality of life" issues that affected tourists, corporations, and "yuppies": marketing, graffiti removal, and shining up the city center. The citizens left behind would, in great numbers, manage as best they

The New York Stock Exchange, as it looked in the 1980s.

could; good-paying, steady, unionized blue-collar jobs and public sector work had become increasingly scarce (thanks, in no small part, to the policies of the Koch and Beame administrations), leaving only low-paying and unstable work in service of the moneyed classes. "Money alone won't do," *Bonfire of the Vanities* author Tom Wolfe told the *Times.* "The ultimate certification of your status is seeing people jump, and New York is a city set up to see people jump."

Much of that money was flowing from Wall Street, and the city drowned in it, thanks to a years-long bull run that started in 1982. With that reservoir of cash came a new way of doing business. In Oliver Stone's father's day, "it was a gentleman's business"; not anymore. "You have to understand there was a shift," Stone explains. "It's another kind of aggressivity that's coming out. These guys are for real, they'll rip your guts out. They want to fuck you in the ass, that kind of thing. I'd never heard that kind of talk from Wall Street." These tough-guy, party-hard, cash-flashing types, these "Masters of the Universe," ruled over an era of leveraged buyouts, corporate takeovers, junk bonds, and insider trading.

The decade began on a much quieter note. The dollar was weak, foreign investments were surging, the bond market was in a state of turmoil, and inflation was on the rise. Weeks into his term, Reagan said the country was in "the worst economic mess since the Great Depression." He adopted an everything-but-the-kitchen-sink approach, attempting to strangle inflation while encouraging the fiction of "trickle down" spending via tax cuts for the wealthy. Finally, in 1981, the dollar began to rise, Reagan's tax cuts were passed, and the following summer, the market began to rally. (Its quiet deregulation through the decade was also key, if less frequently noted.)

High-end tech stocks were market leaders—these were the years when the "personal computer" began its shift from science fiction to everyday fact—but much of the fuel that lit the decade's fire was provided by the takeover boom. "The election of Ronald Reagan in 1980 sent a powerful 'anything goes' message to the financial markets," James B. Stewart writes in his history *Den of Thieves.* "One of the first official acts of the Reagan Justice Department was to drop the government's massive ten-year antitrust case against IBM. Bigness apparently wasn't going to be a problem in the new era of unbridled capitalism."

**CLOCKWISE FROM TOP**
Scenes from the city in the '80s: *The King of Comedy* (1982), directed by Martin Scorsese, photographed by Fred Schuler; *Broadway Danny Rose* (1984), directed by Woody Allen, photographed by Gordon Willis; *Perfect Strangers* (1984, directed by Larry Cohen, photographed by Paul Glickman); *The Muppets Take Manhattan* (1984), directed by Frank Oz, photographed by Robert Paynter; *Coming to America* (1988), directed by John Landis, photographed by Woody Omens.

**225**

**CLOCKWISE FROM TOP**

Still images from *Gloria* (1980), directed by John Cassavetes, photographed by Fred Schuler; *Crossing Delancey* (1988), directed by Joan Micklin Silver, photographed by Theo van de Sande; *Fatal Attraction* (1987), directed by Adrian Lyne, photographed by Howard Atherton; *Street Smart* (1987), directed by Jerry Schatzberg, photographed by Adam Holender.

Thus there were takeovers and mergers galore, at costs of multimillions, if not billions: Conoco, Gibson Greeting Cards, Beatrice Foods, Safeway Stores, and finally, at the end of the decade, RJR Nabisco. At $23 billion, it was the largest takeover in history. In many of those deals, the key to raising that much money was a redheaded stepchild of the industry, the high-yield bond, better known by the vulgar shorthand of "junk bond." The king of junk bonds was a trader named Michael Milken, a showy, greedy, master manipulator who ran his own shop out of Beverly Hills.

Much of what Milken did was illegal, but then again, much of what they were *all* doing was illegal. "Financial crime was commonplace on Wall Street in the eighties," Stewart writes. "A common refrain among nearly every defendant charged in the scandal was that it was unfair to single out one individual for prosecution when so many others were guilty of the same offenses, yet weren't charged." No one seemed to mind much through those boom years, because the money was flowing so freely; new securities were being issued, corporate profits were surging, bonds were selling. It was one of the longest periods of postwar growth in American history.

■

"Such is the ardor of the moviemakers' current love affair with New York," reported the *Times*'s Lawrence Van Gelder in April 1980, "that it seems well nigh impossible to go almost anywhere in the city—from the waters of the Hudson River (*Cruising*) to the streets of mid-Manhattan (*Times Square*, *Fame*, and *The Fan*) to the Bronx (*Fort Apache, The Bronx*) to the Verrazzano-Narrows Bridge between Brooklyn and Staten Island (*Saturday Night Fever*)—without stumbling upon the location of a movie in progress or a movie already seen." The uptick in local production of the 1970s would only increase in the decade to follow, thanks in no small part to a mayor who was, like Lindsay before him, an impenitent ham.

Going into the 1980s, the problem facing New York filmmakers—and the city attempting to accommodate them—was that the outreach effort was too effective, and productions were running into a shortage of space. There was plenty of room on the island and in the boroughs for outdoor shooting, of course. But there was a serious lack of studio space, forcing productions to fight and compromise over precious resources.

Relief finally came early in the decade. In 1982, the old Astoria studio, which had been used piecemeal for films like *All That Jazz*, *The Wiz*, and *Kramer vs. Kramer*, was handed over to the city by the federal government, which also provided part of the funding for a $14.1 million renovation and expansion project. (The first production in the refurbished facility would be *The Cotton Club*, reuniting Francis Ford Coppola with his *Godfather* producer, Robert Evans.) The next year, in adjoining Long Island City, the new Silvercup Studios opened and quickly booked up its first available stage, including a week of pickups for Woody Allen's *Broadway Danny Rose*.

It wasn't all good news, however. Budget-minded filmmakers were increasingly lured, by both tax incentives and ease of production, to use other cities (particularly Toronto and Montreal up north) as doubles for New York. When *Panic in Needle Park* director Jerry Schatzberg was hired by the notoriously cheap Menahem Golan to direct the Times Square- and Harlem-set *Street Smart*, Schatzberg recalls, "He sent me to Pittsburgh with an assistant of his. And I come to Pittsburgh, and I'm looking down the street and at the end of the street, there's a mountain. I turned the other way, and at the end of the street, there's a mountain. I

couldn't turn the camera to where there weren't mountains." The producer complained about Schatzberg's inflexibility (telling the filmmaker, "A big city's a big city!") before granting a few weeks of location shooting in New York if Schatzberg could fake the rest of the film in Montreal.

Other filmmakers pinched their pennies—and expanded the visual template of the New York movie—by seeking out less photographed areas. Favorite son John Cassavetes returned to Gotham to make the crime drama *Gloria* (1980), shooting mostly in the South Bronx and in Manhattan's uptown neighborhood of Washington Heights, with Yankee Stadium occasionally visible through apartment windows. Even the interiors are unmistakable; as the location managers for *Law & Order* would later discover, there's something inimitable about the lobbies, hallways, and staircases of pre-war uptown walk-ups. Writer/producer/director Buddy Giovinazzo would shoot his grimy, sweaty *Taxi Driver* riff *Combat Shock* (1986) out on Staten Island while staging its Vietnam flashbacks upstate. And J. Michael Muro made his stomach-churning "melt movie" *Street Trash* (1987) on the streets of the Brooklyn neighborhood of Greenpoint.

Some of the more knowing movies of the era employ scattered geography and offbeat locations to underscore narrative and thematic elements. In Joan Micklin Silver's *Crossing Delancey* (1988), Amy Irving's Izzy escapes the Lower East Side and lives uptown, where she moves in a world of authors and sophisticates, but her grandmother nonetheless tries to set her up with Sam (Peter Reigert), the neighborhood pickle vendor. "I don't live down here, I live *uptown*," she assures him, and spends much of the film fighting her genuine interest in this kindhearted downtown guy. Her attraction seems overpowered by her hesitation about the earthiness of his work (she's visibly turned off by the sight of him handling his pickles), which she clearly sees as a rejoinder to her successful assimilation, some kind of a shameful backward step into the neighborhood she's transcended. Sam, for his part, is unapologetic: "You think it's so small, my world? You think it's so provincial?"

A similar geographical dynamic is at play in the megahit *Fatal Attraction* (1987), in which philandering lawyer Dan Gallagher (Michael Douglas) lives with his family in the stable, somewhat ritzy Upper West Side (and, later in the film, in the even ritzier suburbs), while his mistress Alex (Glenn Close) lives way downtown, in Tribeca. That area was still in transition in the mid-1980s, from a meatpacking district—men are literally loading meat trucks in the background of one exterior scene—to an area of high-priced lofts and artfully distressed apartments. Director Adrian Lyne put Dan's temptress in a different world, and a more vibrant, happening, wild one at that. (Lest we forget, this area is also where many of the roughest leather bars were located.)

Such temptations also beckon Paul Hackett (Griffin Dunne) in Martin Scorsese's 1985 black comedy *After Hours* (see sidebar on page 254); the UES-dwelling word processor meets a pretty girl in a coffee shop, discovers she's staying in SoHo, and immediately replies, "Oh, nice! A loft?" Guys like Dan and Paul are just visiting when they come downtown, seeking out a few minutes of pleasure, a peek at the other side of New York life. But for years, that area was the home of an entire, vibrant scene of its own.

■

"It was a great time to be creative and poor, because life was cheap there," Susan Seidelman says, of living in New York in the late seventies

and early eighties. "And because of that, there was a lot going on—especially downtown." The film scene was a logical outgrowth of the entire downtown ethos, an incestuous cross-pollination of the worlds of outsider art, punk rock, dance, graffiti writing, and the earliest iterations of hip-hop.

"What is crucial," explains independent film legend John Pierson, "is the degree of comingling and intermingling there was, especially downtown, between all the different arts. You've read it, you've heard it a hundred times, and it's true. It's just completely true." "The biggest part was the conversation between artists," agrees filmmaker Bette Gordon. "Between music, art, film, writing, dance, and sculpture, people were using different mediums to speak to each other."

Harnessing the frenetic nihilism in the air, amateur filmmakers and actors formed a community in this abandoned area of the city, scraping together whatever money and equipment they could, pooling resources, crossing media, and making these strange, squalid little movies. "The Lower East Side looked like a war zone, like we dropped a bomb on ourselves," explains the narrator of Edo Bertoglio's *Downtown 81*, and most of these films worked within that aesthetic; we get the impression that an entire corner of the city is lawless and abandoned, and no one seems too worked up about it.

Many of the first wave of films were shot on Super 8 sound cameras that entered the scene's bloodstream via the mysterious "Freddy on Houston Street," who sold hot merchandise. Patient Zero for the movement was *The Blank Generation* (1976), a nonfiction chronicle of the scene from director/producers Ivan Král and Amos Poe, who used silent cameras to shoot performances by the likes of the Ramones, the Talking Heads, and the Patti Smith Group at downtown venues and synced them up with demo recordings; they edited the entire film in a twenty-four-hour speed-fueled burst in the Maysles brothers' editing suite.

Poe's subsequent films were at the forefront of the ensuing movement, dubbed "No Wave" cinema: proto-"mumblecore" movies, dialogue-driven, low-fidelity, sporting a hang-out vibe, and, more often than not, amateurish production values (the acting is frequently stilted, camerawork is clumsy, and sound is muddy, seemingly post-recorded in somebody's apartment). Yet these films are undeniably energetic and present, and often clever as well; Poe's first solo feature, *Unmade Beds* (1978), "a French film made in New York," includes such winking narration as "There are eight million stories in the naked city, but I can't even remember one of them."

Other key early films in the movement included Poe's *The Foreigner*, Eric Mitchell's *Kidnapped*, and James Nares's *Rome '78* (all 1978); Charlie Ahearn's *The Deadly Art of Survival* (1979); and Mitchell's *Underground USA*, Bette Gordon's *Empty Suitcases*, Ulli Lommel's *Blank Generation*, Anders Grafstrom's *The Long Island Four*, and Jim Jarmusch's *Permanent Vacation* (all 1980). As the movement settled into a style and found outlets for its product—including the video-capable New Cinema on St. Mark's Place, the Kitchen Center for Video and Music at the Mercer Street Arts Center, occasional screening nights at the Mudd Club, and public access shows like Glenn O'Brien's *TV Party*—more female filmmakers began to emerge, including Lizzie Borden, Vivienne Dick, Casandra Stark Mele, Kathryn Bigelow, and Seidelman.

"Honestly, we didn't know we couldn't make movies, you know?" Seidelman says now, and Borden concurs: "Nobody was stopping us.

**228**

**ABOVE**
Still images from *Cruising* (1980), directed by William Friedkin, photographed by James A. Contner.

**BELOW**
Still images from *Nighthawks* (1981), directed by Bruce Malmuth, photographed by James A. Contner; *Prince of the City* (1981), directed by Sidney Lumet, photographed by Andrzej Bartkowiak.

And very often, we thought we were just making them for ourselves." Gordon's *Variety* (1983) could have only been made (or at least, made well) by a woman; the story of a shy writer who takes a job as a ticket taker at a Times Square porn house, it sees past the easy winks of its setting to explore, in an almost dream-like fashion, its protagonist's sexual awakening. Borden's *Born in Flames* (1983) is an honest-to-God radical work of art, done in the style of a TV news special marking the tenth anniversary of "the war of liberation," documenting how "the very first true socialist democracy" goes awry; it concludes, disturbingly enough, with the bombing of the World Trade Center.

Other new voices helped expand the canvas of the movement. Slava Tsukerman's cuckoo-bananas downtown epic *Liquid Sky* (1982) stirs the soup of the scene—fashion, modeling, dancing, drugs—and determines the only way to make sense of it is as science fiction. Bill Sherwood's *Parting Glances* (1986) is in most aspects a typical, charming, low-budget NYC romantic comedy/drama, except that its subjects are all men, so it thus doubles as a snapshot of the mid-eighties gay social scene, with circles converging at dinner parties, casual get-togethers, discos, and out on Fire Island.

By the time *Parting Glances* hit theaters, the downtown film scene had shifted. An aggressive new movement, dubbed by its own manifesto as the "Cinema of Transgression," aimed to break taboos and push envelopes with extreme subject matter; it was a reaction to both the rise of eighties conservatism and capitalism, and the mainstreaming of the downtown scene via such crossover hits as Seidelman's *Smithereens* (1982; see sidebar on page 250) and Jarmusch's *Stranger Than Paradise* (1984).

"There were a bunch of these people that were doing things that were more experimental, that were coming more out of art cinema," Seidelman explains, "and they didn't attempt, or maybe even want, to penetrate into a more mainstream audience. I was coming from NYU, with a love of stories and characters, and Jim can speak for himself, but certainly *Stranger Than Paradise* has strong characters and a definite narrative; even if the characters don't go anywhere, they're on a *journey* of some sort. And I think that's what made those films a little bit more accessible and break out a little bit, because they weren't intended just to be shown at the collective." Those films, along with Spike Lee's *She's Gotta Have It* (1986), were laying the groundwork that would establish New York City as ground zero for the indie film explosion of the following decade.

Not everyone had an easy time shooting in the city in the eighties. In his July 16, 1979, *Village Voice* column, Arthur Bell wrote that William Friedkin's *Cruising* (1980) "promises to be the most oppressive, ugly, bigoted look at homosexuality ever presented on the screen, the worst possible nightmare of the most uptight straight and a validation of Anita Bryant's hate campaign." Bell predicted that the film would "send gays running back into the closet and precipitate heavy violence against homosexuals," and advised his readers "to give Friedkin and his production crew a terrible time if you spot them in your neighborhood (the film will be shooting for the next seven weeks at Badlands, the Eagle's Nest, the Underground, Police Plaza, and on Christopher and West Streets)."

Bell's readers were up to his challenge. The production was greeted not only with organized protests and marches; bottles and bricks were thrown at crew members, and since Friedkin was shooting in real Village apartments rather than studio sets, neighbors blasted stereos, whistles, and air horns to disrupt audio recording. (Most of that dialogue had to be looped in post-production.) When Friedkin attempted to shoot on the streets, passersby mugged at the camera, and gay bars withdrew previously granted permission for the company to shoot on their premises. Activists pleaded with Koch to withdraw the support of the Mayor's Office of Film, Theatre & Broadcasting; their request was refused. "It is the business of this city's administration to encourage the return of filmmaking to New York City by cooperating to whatever extent feasible with filmmakers," Koch said.

It's not hard to see what activists found so upsetting about *Cruising*, an overwhelmingly seedy brew of dread, violence, and graphic sexuality. But it's also not as though the film paints gay life only as grim and unpleasant; no one in *Cruising* comes off particularly well, no matter what their sexuality. The most reprehensible characters in the picture, in

fact, are a pair of uniformed policemen (Mike Starr and *Maniac*'s Joe Spinell), who are seen soliciting and then assaulting a pair of trans sex workers.

Such portraiture was not uncommon in the cop films of the era—even the most conventionally heroic cast a deeply cynical eye on the operations of the NYPD. Sean Boyd (James Brolin), the protagonist of *Night of the Juggler* (1980), is a former cop shunned for "ratting" on his fellow officers. "Little too smart for your own good," sneers one of his former colleagues, "so when the city went broke and they laid off all those cops, that gave 'em an excuse to get rid of you, right?" (The villain of the film, in another ripped-from-the-headlines touch, attempts to kidnap the daughter of a rich real estate developer who is buying up abandoned South Bronx properties on the cheap.) *Prince of the City* (1981) found director Sidney Lumet returning to his *Serpico* turf, albeit with a more morally compromised subject: Detective Daniel Ciello (Treat Williams), who actively participates in the corruption he eventually helps investigators prosecute, exposing a culture among the ranks of the NYPD of, as Ciello puts it, "We're gonna take his fucking money! Fuck him and fuck them and FUCK YOU!"

The most cartoonish of the eighties New York cop movies is William Lustig's *Maniac Cop* (1988), in which a wordless psychopath in a police uniform terrorizes the city, capitalizing on the inherent trust of that uniform by citizens who will, as one character puts it, "do anything a cop tells 'em." The film happily traffics in the urban exploitation tropes of the era, with copious set pieces of pretty young white girls getting mugged and assaulted, always by brown or black criminals—unless it's the main villain, a juicy role that inevitably goes to a white actor. But screenwriter Larry Cohen, the poet laureate of NYC sleaze cinema, slyly complicates matters, slipping an African American man-on-the-street into a TV news report to explain, "I've seen plenty of my friends murdered by cops. Shot in the back. Shot when they didn't have a gun or a knife, claiming the subject had a shiny object."

Pro-NYPD pictures, on the other hand, would often frame their protagonists as streetwise guys handcuffed by procedure and formalities. In Bruce Malmuth's *Nighthawks* (1982), street cops Sylvester Stallone and Billy Dee Williams are drafted for an interdepartmental task force to stop a dangerous terrorist; they giggle through the endless briefings like schoolkids, stopping only to note that all this prep and talk is a waste of time. "Isn't this overkill?" Stallone's Deke asks, and Malmuth intercuts the terrorist landing in Gotham and going to work to prove him right.

*Nighthawks*'s protagonists are Vietnam vets, and Deke's initial reluctance to pull the trigger on the job is a key character point (eventually to be overcome, of course). When he's asked why he has so much trouble, considering his fifty-two confirmed kills in the 'Nam, he replies, "That was war." But by the end of *Nighthawks*, he's wised up to the picture's implicit inference: New York City is also war, at least for a cop in the 1980s.

Deke's real-life counterparts were in short supply in this high-crime era. Active duty numbers kept falling (there were twenty-two thousand cops on the job in 1981, down from thirty-one thousand before the financial crisis), and Koch showed no intention of bolstering their numbers; he told reporters in 1980, "I am not prepared to lay off additional teachers to have more cops." Police commissioner Robert McGuire saw the job as "smoke and mirrors," merely creating the appearance of law and order, rather than actually reducing crime. By late in the decade, reported the *Times*'s Michael Wines, police began "to focus instead on keeping some neighborhoods from descending into outlaw rule by drug dealers or gangs." The murder rate in some of those areas increased by more than 50 percent between 1985 and 1986, when crack, the most powerfully addictive (and most affordable) form of cocaine, began to take root.

"The city is, in effect, conducting a vast social experiment," Commissioner McGuire told the *Times*. "The experiment is, 'How far can you cut back your police force before crime runs rampant?'" In light of that philosophy, and the limitations in policing that prompted it, it's unsurprising that the "New York vigilante" movie became such a popular subgenre of eighties exploitation. Riffing on a formula well established by *Death Wish* the decade before, films like *Defiance* (1980), *The Exterminator* (1980), *Ms .45* (1981), *Vigilante* (1982), and *Exterminator 2* (1984) showcase wronged protagonists giving audiences the justice they so longed for on the streets outside the grindhouses where these pictures frequently played. (Sadly, *Death Wish*'s third installment, which sent Paul Kersey back to New York for another round of "punk" target practice, was obviously and rather incompetently shot in London.)

These films were only vaguely connected to the realities of the city, of course, pumping up the lawlessness to lurid levels. In *Ms .45*, a garishly entertaining cross between an exploitation movie and the SCUM Manifesto, crime in the city is so bad that our heroine is brutally raped in an alley on her way home to an apartment *where a burglar is waiting to rape her again*. In *The Exterminator*, both the title character and the police detective investigating him are Vietnam vets; when a date asks the latter what Vietnam was like, he tells her it was "not as bad as New York City." *Vigilante*, from the *Maniac Cop* team of Lustig and Cohen,

**CLOCKWISE FROM OPPOSITEE**
Still images from *Wolfen* (1981), directed by Michael Wadleigh, photographed by Gerry Fisher; *C.H.U.D.* (1984), directed by Douglas Cheek, photographed by Peter Stein; *Ms. 45* (1981), directed by Abel Ferrara, photographed by James Lemmo; *Q: The Winged Serpent* (1982), directed by Larry Cohen, photographed by Fred Murphy.

**ABOVE LEFT**
Hal Holbrook and Charlie Sheen work with Stone. (20th Century-Fox Film Corp. /Everett Collection)

**ABOVE RIGHT**
Stone with producer Edward Pressman. He would also produce Stone's *Talk Radio* the following year. (Photofest)

**BELOW**
Stone and Michael Douglas on the set. (Photofest)

**OPPOSITE**
Stone reteamed with his *Platoon* leading man, Charlie Sheen. (Photofest)

stacks the deck most egregiously; when Robert Forster objects to a plea bargain that sets the man who killed his child and raped his wife free, the judge sends the *mourning father* to jail for thirty days for contempt of court. Okay, sure!

Some filmmakers found conditions in the city so terrifying, they could only be chalked up to supernatural forces. If *Fort Apache, The Bronx* (1981; see sidebar on page 248) imagined the borough as a figurative hell on earth, *Wolfen* (1980) made it literal, with the destruction of the South Bronx for urban redevelopment raising the spirits of Native American wolf monsters, who spend the film fighting off interlopers to protect their "hunting ground." Larry Cohen's *Q: The Winged Serpent* (1982) is an old-fashioned, *King Kong*–style monster movie in a very contemporary Manhattan, with the title creature nesting in the Chrysler Building and raining blood on pedestrians. The cult classic *C.H.U.D.* (1984) concerns underground creatures popping up from the sewers to chomp up "Bowery bums" and tourists, while John Schlesinger returned to Gotham to direct *The Believers* (1987), in which all of The City's powerful and privileged are part of a voodoo cult, complete with ritual sacrifices in Central Park.

Yet alongside these pervasive images of a lawless, dangerous, blood-stained city, Mayor Koch's popularity flourished. His 1984 book, *Mayor: An Autobiography*, was a bestseller (advisor Dan Wolf described it as "the best love story since Tristan and Isolde, only Ed Koch plays both parts"), and in the months that followed its publication, His Honor appeared in music videos, comic books, and as host of *Saturday Night Live*. Koch coupled his celebrity with an ambitious proposal for low-income housing and wound up with another landslide victory in the 1985 mayoral election, winning 63 percent of the Democratic primary vote, and 78 percent in the general.

"I am committed over the next four years," Koch said on election night, "to do what I can, to come as close as I can in that four-year term, to achieve those aspirations for all the people in this town, without regard to race, religion, national origin or sexual orientation." That would turn out to be easier said than done, and the next four years would prove bumpy for even the rich citizens so central to the Koch constituency.

■

"When I was working on *Scarface* and spending time in Miami and New York," Oliver Stone says, "there was a whole new breed of brokers. They were young, in their twenties and early thirties, making millions of dollars in a year. It was just astounding figures, and the brashness of these young people is what hit me. And of course, my friend was using coke. He was like a coke dealer, but he was making a fortune, much more money than fucking coke dealers in Miami. So here I have my father's generation, which is very staid, I know this group. I thought, this is *Scarface* comes to Wall Street."

Stone was itching to get right back to work after the triumph of *Platoon*. "I remember hearing that directors get fucked up if they get an Oscar, because they start thinking too much. I didn't want to get in that hole, I just wanted to move and keep doing. Here was an Oscar after so many years of rejection. It was a chance to go, so we went." Edward Pressman, who had produced Stone's *Conan* script and an earlier, unsuccessful stab at directing called *The Hand*, eagerly agreed to take on Stone's next picture; the pair hired Stanley Weiser, an old NYU classmate with "that New York style," to collaborate on the script.

After flirting with the idea of making a drama about the quiz-show scandals—which Robert Redford would eventually direct a few years later—Stone stopped himself. "I said, 'No. Let's go with what I know.

I want to go with New York and I want to get back to the mood of those buildings and those people.'" Weiser wrote a first draft, Stone a second, and they continued to kick the script back and forth—"I got more and more excited about it over that period," he recalls. "The pace came from Weiser and me because we were New Yorkers. He's funny, and I'm kind of weird in my way. Like he said somewhere, 'Oliver talking on the phone, you could get a lot of the Gekko dialogue,' because I sometimes get really passionate."

Pressman was enthusiastic about the subject matter; his stepfather was also a stockbroker. The influence of that older generation, those gentlemen of finance, is pronounced in Stone and Weiser's script, both in the character of Hal Holbrook's stately firm head ("The things he tells young brokers would be things my father would have said," Stone explains, "because if you play the market for thirty, forty years, you have to have a philosophy to survive") and in the father-son conflict at the center of the story.

Bud Fox (Charlie Sheen) is an up-and-comer, a hungry young stockbroker convinced that he can work his way into the big time, and the big money, if he can just get into a room with Gordon Gekko (Michael Douglas), one of the most powerful and ruthless figures on the Street. Bud's background is humble; his father (played by Sheen's own father, Martin) is a working-class guy, a longtime mechanic for a small, regional airline, and Bud uses a bit of inside information about that airline to make his first impression on Gekko, and to make him some money. Bud's star rises, but the die has been cast—he's clearly willing to bend or break the law to stay in Gekko's good graces, much to the consternation of his blue-collar father.

Stone's first choice for the role of Fox was Tom Cruise, who was ultimately unavailable (Stone would work with him two years later, directing the actor to his first Oscar nomination for *Born on the Fourth of July*). Sheen, Stone's surrogate in *Platoon*, was the next logical choice. "I cast Marty because I thought that would be a good contrast—that with me and my dad, it would be Marty and his son," Stone says. "I thought that would work because they're very close—there's something in the skin between them." Stone and Weiser set the film in 1985, at the height of the bull market. It was also the year Stone's father died. The film is dedicated to him.

To play the role of Gordon Gekko, Stone cast another Hollywood offspring: Michael Douglas, son of Kirk, who had spent the past few years unexpectedly transitioning from producer and supporting player into leading man. By the time cameras rolled on *Wall Street* in April 1987, Douglas already had another hit in the can: *Fatal Attraction*, which helped solidify his image as the quintessential eighties everyman, handsome and rich and sleazy. "Douglas was a secondary character, but he was a good character," Stone says. "He took over the picture, I guess, in the mythology of the thing; he became the Oscar winner. No one ever saw that coming."

That victory came, in no small part, thanks to the character's show-stopping monologue, which Stone based on a 1986 commencement speech by Ivan Boesky, the fabulously successful arbitrageur subsequently convicted of insider trading. "Greed is all right, by the way," Boesky told the graduates of the School of Business Administration at UC Berkeley. "I want you to know that. I think greed is healthy. You can be greedy and still feel good about yourself."

Stone's riff, the "Greed is good" speech, is delivered to the board and stockholders of a company Gekko is on the verge of taking over (and stripping for parts). "We don't really know what a stockholder is," Stone recalls. "We talk about it, but we don't know what it looks like. So we actually researched it, and we staged in the Roosevelt Hotel so we would get a feeling for what they're actually doing." But the genius of the speech—and part of the reason it's still quoted, unironically, by Gekko types today—is that it's not cut-and-dried. "I was not attacking Wall Street. People misunderstand that," Stone insists. "I was laying out the picture. My point of view? Yeah, Gekko did have some points. The company management was suspect, because it was bad. There is a hell of a lot of it in this country still. Greedy, corrupt corporations that feed from the top."

That corruption, Stone and Weiser's script argues, flows all the way down. "It's a zero-sum game," Gekko says. "Somebody wins, somebody loses." That philosophy of winner-take-all deal-making was pervasive on the Street in the mid-1980s, and in the city in general; the month before *Wall Street* hit theaters, Random House published *The Art of the Deal*, a bestselling volume of flagrant self-promotion by Donald Trump.

"He's Gekko; he would have had to have seen the movie," Stone says. "*The Art of the Deal* is his acceptance. It's okay to make money, to be on covers, it's okay. Well, it wasn't okay in my father's day. A businessman on the cover was not done. It was gauche to talk about money. You don't talk about money, you whisper about money." No more.

*Wall Street*'s production was announced in *Variety* on February 11, 1987, as well as its April start date. Stone had to work fast—he was attempting to outrun a looming Directors Guild strike—but he likes working fast. "There's an energy to it," he says, shrugging. (He extended that energy to post-production, with multiple teams of editors working to get the film ready for its looming December release date.) Throughout the film's writing and production, he employed a team of consultants and technical advisors, from raiders to bankers to prosecutors.

The company took over a vacant high-rise at 222 Broadway and used it as home base, constructing both Gekko's lair and the offices of Fox's company, Jackson-Steinem. The building's downtown location was a key component. "All I remember at that time was that I was into *location*," Stone recalls. "*Platoon* is on location, it's a jungle. It was like a Werner Herzog film. I mean, it was hard work. I was proud of it, and *Salvador* was extremely difficult, location-wise: no interiors, no studio work there, really. So both films were really tests. New York was nothing for us. What the hell? This is luxury, beautiful locations." Stone even got permission to shoot on the floor of the Stock Exchange during trading hours. "We were on it for an hour or two, shooting in full business mode," he says. "They loved me because of *Platoon*. 'Hey, Oliver Stone's on the floor!' It was exciting. Ed Pressman's stepfather had a seat on the Exchange, and a lot of people knew my father from the old days."

The location shooting wasn't just a question of alchemy or proximity. Throughout *Wall Street,* The City is always looming, its skyscrapers jutting into the frame through the windows, a reminder to every character that no matter how hard they're working, someone else is out there working harder. That sense of aspiration and competition fuels Bud Fox's adulation of Gordon Gekko, which begins like a courtship; Fox enters Gekko's den with a birthday gift and his hair styled in the manner of his idol. The relationship, once established, takes on a *Sweet Smell of Success*–style master/servant dynamic; Bud calls Gordon "Mr. Gekko,"

Still images from *Wall Street* (1987), directed by Oliver Stone, photographed by Robert Richardson.

**235**

but Gekko calls the younger man "Sport" (i.e., "Don't screw it up, Sport, you think you can handle that?").

Gekko smells Queens on Bud Fox and doesn't hesitate to shame the younger man for it (when they meet at 21, Gekko sneers, "Buy yourself a decent suit, you can't come in here lookin' like that"). But he also knows the ascension is possible, because he did it himself; a "City College boy," Gekko confesses to Bud, "I bought my way in, now all these Ivy League types are suckin' my kneecaps." Their contrasts are best underscored in Stone's staging of a key telephone conversation between the men: Bud is chained to the landline in his dumpy apartment, while Gekko strolls on the beach, talking on a cell phone (then the very picture of a luxury item).

Bud gets it from all sides—if the class divide between him and Gekko is wide, so is the friction between him and his old man, who doesn't understand why the kid doesn't just work with him at Blue Star Airlines, or why he won't even come live rent-free in Queens. "Look, I gotta live in Manhattan to be a player," Bud explains. "There's no nobility in poverty anymore, Dad." His dad's work may be honorable, but you can't get rich doing it; hell, even his $50K salary "does not get you to first base in the Big Apple." When Bud goes to visit his dad on the job, one of his

co-workers jokes, "C'mon, we'll teach ya how to do an honest day's work." It's a telling moment; manufacturing jobs like these have become (and will become more) scarce, but no one mistakes what Bud Fox and Gordon Gekko do for "honest work."

No one is more aware of this than Gordon Gekko himself. "Look at this," he notes, pointing out the window of his limousine at a businessman and a homeless man, the extremes of New York living. "You're gonna tell me the difference between this guy and that guy is *luck*?" When Bud confronts him with an act of deceit, Gekko makes no apologies for his pursuit of wealth; in fact, he predicts a talking point thirty years into America's economic future. "The richest 1 percent of this country own half our country's wealth," he explains. "It's the free market. And you're part of it."

Perhaps that's why Gekko's speech to the stockholders made such an impression on audiences then, and why it's lingered in the popular memory: because, through Gekko, Stone and Weiser were articulating the governing ethos of the 1980s. "Greed, for lack of a better word, is good," Gekko announces, with a twinkle in his eye. "Greed is right. Greed works. Greed clarifies, cuts through, and captures the essence of the evolutionary spirit. Greed, in all of its forms—greed for life, for money, for love, knowledge—has marked the upward surge of mankind. And greed, you mark my words, will not only save Teldar Paper, but that other malfunctioning corporation called the USA."

Gekko might have hoped this was true. Reagan certainly did, as did Koch. On October 19, 1987, the Street proved them wrong.

———

They called it "Black Monday." As on "Black Thursday," the flashpoint of the 1929 crash, the exact cause of the panic was difficult to pinpoint—to a great extent, it was a panic caused by panic, by too much "hot money" (high-velocity funds that moved from market to market) in play by increasingly nervous parties. "Ample supplies of hot money floating around at the time of the market break caused all the markets to dive together," writes Charles R. Geisst in *Wall Street: A History*, and by the end of the day, the Dow Jones was off more than five hundred points, the NASDAQ composite was off by fifty points, and the Standard & Poor's stock index had fallen by 30 percent. It was, according to New York Stock Exchange chairman John Phelan, "the worst market I've ever seen, as close to a financial meltdown as I'd ever want to see."

New York Stock Exchange trading floor on Wall Street.

Michael Douglas, whose *China Syndrome* was in theaters when a nuclear reactor melted down at Three Mile Island in 1979, again found himself in a major motion picture that seemed to predict a national news event. Stone didn't miss a beat. "We were not surprised at all, judging from everything we had heard during the six-month shooting of *Wall Street*," he told the *Times*'s Lawrence Van Gelder, four days after the meltdown. "Our film takes place in 1985, but I think it reflects a situation where not only are the stocks overinflated, but also the lifestyles of our characters. Our story is about a paper wealth that is extremely distorted and is, hopefully, being shaken out by this current drop."

For a moment, it looked as though a change in that culture was, in fact, in the offing. High-profile prosecutions had begun before "Black Monday" and *Wall Street*, with the May 1986 arrest of Drexel Burnham Lambert's managing director, Dennis Levine. Ivan Boesky was charged with insider trading later that year; he paid a $100 million fine but served only about half of his three-and-a-half-year sentence thanks to a plea bargain deal with the US attorney for the Southern District of

Every dream has a price.

AN OLIVER STONE FILM

# WALL STREET

TWENTIETH CENTURY FOX PRESENTS · AN EDWARD R. PRESSMAN PRODUCTION · AN OLIVER STONE FILM
MICHAEL DOUGLAS · CHARLIE SHEEN · DARYL HANNAH · MARTIN SHEEN · WALL STREET
HAL HOLBROOK AND TERENCE STAMP ORIGINAL MUSIC BY STEWART COPELAND DIRECTOR OF PHOTOGRAPHY ROBERT RICHARDSON
CO-PRODUCER A. KITMAN HO WRITTEN BY STANLEY WEISER & OLIVER STONE PRODUCED BY EDWARD R. PRESSMAN DIRECTED BY OLIVER STONE

Still images from *Big Business* (1988), directed by Jim Abrahams, photographed by Dean Cundey; *Working Girl* (1988), directed by Mike Nichols, photographed by Michael Ballhaus; *The Secret of My Success* (1987), directed by Herbert Ross, photographed by Carlo Di Palma; *Baby Boom* (1987), directed by Charles Shyer, photographed by William A. Fraker.

New York, Rudolph Giuliani. ("No one pretends now that that is anywhere near the total of his illegal gains over the years," writes James B. Stewart.)

It took longer to get to Michael Milken, who was indicted in 1990 on nearly one hundred counts of racketeering; he would serve three years and pay fines in excess of $1 billion. (By then, another financial scandal had rocked the country: the failure of the savings and loan industry.) But none of the banks failed, or had to take up the Fed on the offer of emergency reserves. The junk market declined, investors took huge losses, and New York real estate prices began to fall. But the disciplinary period was short, and mostly fell on a handful of egregiously bad actors.

It was an era of "national greed," Stone explains. "Reagan allowed the age of greed to expand to almost unheard levels." The "Greed is good" speech Stone wrote with Weiser struck a chord because it so crisply encapsulated the general thinking of both New York and America itself as conspicuous consumption ballooned without apology or pretense (the year before the film's release, Milken's total salary and bonus earnings topped $550 million). In the seventies, Stone says, "the corruption seemed to be under control." But in the eighties, "it just got horrible. And it's never stopped."

*Wall Street* landed in theaters on December 11, 1987, to robust box-office and mixed-positive reviews. *New York*'s David Denby compared it favorably to *Sweet Smell of Success*, writing, "the picture may not be a work of art, but it's a great potboiler and the most enjoyable movie of the year." In the *New York Times*, Vincent Canby was slightly dismissive, calling it "a tantalizing, Sidney Sheldon–like peek into the boardrooms and bedrooms of the rich and powerful," and raving over its second lead: "Mr. Douglas, in the funniest, canniest performance of his career, plays him with the wit and charm of Old Scratch wearing an Italian-designer wardrobe."

*Newsweek*'s Kathleen Carroll similarly described Gekko as "a devil in Versace pin stripes." But the *New Republic*'s Stanley Kauffmann was critical, writing, "The action in Stone's new picture, for all the dexterous direction and satiric reproduction of ultramod behavior, is 1930s Warner Brothers morality drama." *Variety* was similarly negative: "It lectures, which is great as a case study in business school but wearisome as a film." And the *Wall Street Journal* was unsurprisingly down on the picture, which critic Julie Salamon deemed "a silly, pretentious melodrama that panders to the current fascination with insider trading."

The *Journal* was perhaps prodded a bit—Salamon's review begins with a line of dialogue from the film, in which sex with a young woman is described as being "like reading the *Wall Street Journal*," and it's not intended as a compliment. But more than one New York periodical took the opportunity to offer Wall Streeters equal time, with "factchecking *Wall Street*" pieces in which corporate raiders like Irwin Jacobs insisted that "my love is not raiding, it's creating," and decried the smears of Stone: "The sad thing is, a lot of people are going to see this and believe this is the way Wall Street is run."

But, as was so often the case, Roger Ebert got to the heart of the matter. "What's intriguing about *Wall Street*," he wrote in the *Chicago Sun-Times*, "is that the movie's real target isn't Wall Street criminals who break the law. Stone's target is the value system that places profits and wealth and the Deal above any other consideration." The Gekko ethos, in other words, wasn't confined to Gekko's office.

*Wall Street* brought in a robust $43 million at the domestic box office, bolstered not only by its timeliness and the buzz gathering around Douglas's performance, but also by a general fascination, among American moviegoers, with the workings of the world of high finance. Universal's *The Secret of My Success*, from the same year, was rooted in the (perhaps apocryphal) legend of how Steven Spielberg began working for the studio: by sneaking into an empty office on the lot and faking like he belonged. *Success* finds an ambitious mailroom kid (Michael J. Fox) doubling as a fired executive in a financial firm where everyone is screwing everyone, literally and figuratively; by the picture's conclusion, he's bagged the girl and is running the company, rich beyond his wildest dreams.

Another 1987 release, *Baby Boom*, finds Diane Keaton booted from her corner office when she inherits a baby from a distant relative, though she makes a triumphant return when she launches a wildly successful artisanal baby-food company. The takeover comedy *Big Business* (1988) culminates, as these films so often do, with a big "stockholder's meeting," in which corporate intrigue is revealed and hostile takeovers are reversed; such gatherings usually aren't quite so dramatic. The year 1988 also brought *Working Girl*, a kind of gender-swapped *Wall Street* with Melanie Griffith as the wide-eyed would-be power player from the sticks and Sigourney Weaver as the mentor/exploiter; director Mike Nichols and writer Kevin Wade also lovingly capture the woes of working women of the era, struggling to apply makeup on the Staten Island Ferry and changing from sneakers to heels under their desks. *Brewster's Millions* (1985) refreshingly takes conspicuous consumption, the subtext of so many of the era's films, and makes it text: It concerns a busted-out nobody (Richard Pryor) who inherits a distant relative's $300 million fortune under the condition that he can first spend $30 million in 30 days and have no assets to show for it. Brewster and his entourage roar through Manhattan like a tornado, feeding strangers in fancy restaurants, throwing extravagent parties, and mounting a novelty mayoral campaign. It is a city, he discovers, where it's not that hard to spend a lot of money quickly.

*The Secret of My Success* and *Big Business* overlap with another pervasive New York movie of the mid- to late 1980s. If the black comedies that dominated the early years of the previous decade had given way to frightening visions of darkness and vigilantism, the pendulum swung back to laughs in this era—thanks to a spate of "fish out of water" comedies that mined their laughs from the incongruity of their naïve out-of-towners interacting with the craaaaaazy big city folk. Such wide-eyed culture shock is, in this period, usually seen in the form of an MTV-style "Welcome to New York" pop-song montage; *Big Business* gives us two, first for Bette Midler's city-lovin' country girl learning the Midtown ropes (she buys sneakers, learns how to hail a cab, visits FAO Schwarz, and yodels along with a sidewalk steel drum band), then for Fred Ward's cornpone country boy, who lands in Times Square and gets propositioned on Eighth Avenue.

A typical early scene in *The Secret of My Success* finds our straight-off-the-bus-from-Kansas hero calling his mom on a pay phone, assuring her he's safe as a robbery/shoot-out breaks out around him. Such scenes of cheerful resignation to constant crime are a cornerstone of these films; when the visiting African prince of *Coming to America* (1988) arrives in Queens, his luggage is immediately stolen from the sidewalk in front of his lodgings, where strung-out tenants fall down the stairs ("YOUR RENT IS DUE, MOTHERFUCKER!" shouts the landlord) and his apartment is a literal crime scene.

Crowd scene still images from *Big Business* (1988), directed by Jim Abrahams, photographed by Dean Cundey; *Tootsie* (1982), directed by Sydney Pollack, photographed by Owen Roizman; *Crocodile Dundee* (1986), directed by Peter Faiman, photographed by Russell Boyd; *Midnight Cowboy* (1969), directed by John Schlesinger, photographed by Adam Holender.

Mick Dundee, the Australian bushman hero of *Crocodile Dundee* (1986), ends up fighting back—taking out purse-snatchers, taming dogs, and beating up pimps. The picture's portraits of the "freaks" that give him pause have aged poorly (he seems most baffled by a trans woman and a jive-talking African American), but by its 1988 sequel, he's conquered the city, making friends with neighborhood kids, talking jumpers off ledges, and fishing in the Hudson, where he's chastised with a hearty chuckle by police officials. *Crocodile Dundee* also includes the quintessential image of the 1980s fish-out-of-water NYC movie (albeit dating back to *Midnight Cowboy*): a medium-to-wide sidewalk shot, with a long lens, of our hero sticking out like a sore thumb among an endless sea of faceless New Yorkers.

Ron Howard's *Splash* (1984) was the most literal of fish-out-of-water stories, concerning as it does a mermaid who washes up at (where else?) the Statue of Liberty to find her dream man (Tom Hanks). "Cut her some slack, she's from outta town, will ya?" he begs of his fellow Gothamites, after she commits such faux pas as taking over the televisions at Bloomingdale's or swiping a blind beggar's mug of pencils. The hero of John Sayles's *Brother from Another Planet* (1984) comes from even further, but is nevertheless fascinated, as such tourists often were, by the peep shows and dirty bookstores of the Deuce. But great distances weren't even necessary: Scorsese's *After Hours*, Susan Seidelman's *Desperately Seeking Susan* (1985; see sidebar on page 250), and Jonathan Demme's *Something Wild* (1986) found yuppies from the 'burbs or even just uptown pulled into the depths of the city and taken for a ride. These comic swings shouldn't be surprising; living in the city has "always been funny and it's always grand opera, just to get something done," Scorsese says. "It's always been funny, ironic, brutal. At times ugly, but beautiful and funny."

The most poignant of the fish-out-water pictures is Paul Mazursky's *Moscow on the Hudson* (also 1984), in which a Russian circus musician (Robin Williams), visiting with his troupe, decides to defect during a shopping expedition to Bloomingdale's. "This is New York City," a beat cop on the scene says with a shrug. "The man can do what he wants." Mazursky makes it clear, as his hero spends more time in the city, that everyone is a fish: "Everybody I meet is from somewhere else," notes the Russian immigrant, who intersects with an Italian girlfriend, a Cuban lawyer, an Indian doctor, and an Asian cabdriver. Even his African American best friend jokes, "I understand how the brother feels—I'm a refugee myself, from Alabama."

The tone of these films was markedly different from the New York comedies of the 1970s and reflective of the "open arms" approach of the city, and the people in charge of it, in this era. In the comedies of the seventies, the horrors of the city are played for laughs, but of the grim,

stick-in-the-throat variety; most of their protagonists are tough locals who've lived in the city long enough to know it's not going to get any better than this, so the best they can hope is that if they keep their heads down, they won't get mugged *this time*. In the eighties comedies our heroes are outsiders, and if they initially find the place off-putting, scary, or strange, they soon learn to settle in and fall in love with this crazy city, warts (and freaks and graffiti) and all.

As in the previous decade, there were a fair number of filmmakers whose subjects lived well above the fray anyway. Much of Woody Allen's eighties output was period and/or pastoral, and elsewhere, in films like *Hannah and Her Sisters* (1985), *Another Woman* (1988), and *Crimes and Misdemeanors* (1989), he rarely strayed from the comfortable confines of his Upper East Side neighborhood (*Hannah* was even shot, in part, in the apartment of his star and then partner, Mia Farrow). But Allen worked outside his bubble in *Broadway Danny Rose* (1984), or at least his current one; this broadly comic tale of a low-rent Times Square talent agent was based on stories the filmmaker heard during his early days as a struggling stand-up comedian and presents a rare Allen-lensed view of the city's seedy underbelly.

Sydney Pollack's *Tootsie* (1982) tracked its protagonist's rise from a barely surviving actor/waiter to a nationwide television sensation—by adopting the identity of a spunky, no-nonsense actress. (It also spotlighted the New York–based world of television soap opera production, which, unlike feature filmmaking and prime-time broadcasting, mostly resisted migration to California.) Films like *They All Laughed* (1981), *Moonstruck* (1987), and *When Harry Met Sally* (1989) carefully steered their characters away from the crime and grime to emphasize the endless coupling options of this city of eight million.

Even a sleazy thriller like Brian De Palma's *Dressed to Kill* (1980) dwells in a world normally untouched by crime: Its heroine has a home in the suburbs, visits her shrink in a fancy brownstone, picks up a lover at the Metropolitan Museum of Art, and screws him in his sleek apartment; even her pristine white gloves are a plot point. De Palma's world of swanky hotels and high-priced call girls is one that Koch made possible, even though no more than a select few New Yorkers could afford to live in it.

Director Walter Hill, returning to Gotham six years after *The Warriors* for *Brewster's Millions*, noticed a shift in metropolitan energy. "The street vibe of city was much less . . . Wild West, shall we say?" he laughs. "Things had kind of come back under some reasonable civil authority. And maybe it was the nature of my locations, I don't know. But I really felt, when we were out there making *The Warriors*, it was a wild experience every night, and you never quite knew what was going to

Two Cities, Ed Koch, and *Wall Street*

happen. *Brewster's*, everything was very civilized, and everything was very kind of constrained. The city had come to grips with its financial problems, and suddenly everything was very positive again. The dystopian overlay had vanished, I think—or at least had been set aside."

—

It wasn't all smooth sailing. The trades chattered with reports of a "commotion in Gotham" in June 1988, when the coordinator of film permits in the Mayor's Office of Film, Theatre & Broadcasting was suspended for "misconduct," an absence that "riled a number of producers and production managers working hereabouts," according to *Variety*. But this trouble in the film office barely registered amid the many scandals that plagued Ed Koch's third term.

Charges of corruption ran rampant, with credible accusations of favoritism, kickbacks, racketeering, bribery, and fraud in the administration—most notably in the parking bureau. A scheme to extort millions in kickbacks for data-entry contracts led to the convictions of Bronx Democratic chair Stanley Friedman and three others, as well as the suicide of Queens borough president Donald Manes, also under investigation in the scandal.

Koch's third term was not without its successes—his low-income housing program was "as responsible as any other factor for the decline in crime" in the 1990s, according to the *Village Voice*'s Wayne Barrett, one of the mayor's fiercest critics—but its failures were overwhelming. The continuing erosion of social services, along with the ongoing depletion of the city's manufacturing base, made homelessness one of New York's most prevailing and seemingly hopeless issues of the decade; thousands of destitute men, women, and children (an estimated 7,500 a night, according to the *Times*) slept in shelters, churches, and synagogues, while countless more spent their nights in parks, on sidewalks, and in doorways.

Charles Lane's *Sidewalk Stories* (1989) gave the problem the silent treatment; set in contemporary Manhattan but rendered in black and white and without dialogue, this story of street performers and homeless people lifts its basic story from Chaplin's *The Kid* but casts a grimmer pall over the narrative, with moments of genuine violence and vivid portraiture of the problem. The filmmaker finally breaks his silence at the film's conclusion, ending with a devastating sequence of its homeless subjects ranting, despairing, and begging for spare change, a chorus of misery and desperation.

The next great shame of Koch's third administration first appeared in the *Times* during his second. "The persistence of a serious disease whose victims are primarily homosexual men has touched off anxiety among homosexuals in New York City, where nearly half of the nation's cases have been reported," wrote Robin Herman in the August 8, 1982, edition. "The disease—called acquired immune deficiency syndrome, or A.I.D.S.—produces a suppression of the body's natural defenses and sets the stage for the intrusion of several deadly afflictions, including a rare form of cancer called Kaposi's sarcoma and a rare pneumonia."

By 1985 the paper was reporting more than fifteen thousand cases of the virus, and that an AIDS patient occupied one in four beds at Bellevue. But Koch was slow to fund AIDS awareness and prevention programs; in Arthur J. Bressan Jr.'s *Buddies* (1985), the first feature film to tackle the crisis, patient Robert (Geoff Edholm) fumes, "Here in the Big Apple, there's not even an AIDS clinic! Here in New York City, it's an *epidemic*, and I was lost until that gay crisis group took me in. No money from the city, the state. No bucks from Washington." Some activists surmised that Koch's own sexuality, an object of widespread conjecture and whispers since the 1977 campaign, was fueling his reluctance; if he showed too much sympathy to the cause, this theory went, his own preferences would become a hot topic again.

The last of the Koch years were dominated by another issue that also reared its head during that first campaign: race. His comments about the blackout looters and blasting of "poverty pimps" made headlines in 1977, and during his first term, an old interview appeared in which he insisted that African Americans were "basically anti-Semitic" and "whites are basically anti-black." Few Democratic mayors had seen such unfavorable approval numbers among people of color, and Koch did himself no favors by closing Harlem's Sydenham Hospital, losing the trust of prominent black politicians, to whom he'd promised to keep the facility open. (He further upset the African American community by voicing his opposition to making Dr. Martin Luther King Jr.'s birthday a city holiday, citing fiscal concerns.)

As the decade wore on, the city's already searing racial tensions were further inflamed by a series of hate crimes and violent incidents in which the mayor was, too often, on the wrong side of the issue. When Bernhard Goetz went on his subway rampage, Koch insisted that "vigilantism will not be tolerated in this city." But after the NYPD tip line was flooded with calls of support for the subway shooter, the mayor (up for election later that year) reversed course, approving of a city grand jury's initial decision to charge Goetz merely on a weapons infraction rather than for homicide. More charges were added, but Koch again inserted himself into the issue by publicly supporting the vigilante's later acquittal for attempted murder.

He also supported another grand jury's refusal to indict the police officer who killed Eleanor Bumpurs, a mentally ill sixty-six-year-old African American woman, when she wielded a kitchen knife at officers dispatched to evict her from her apartment in a Bronx housing project over eighty-eight dollars in past-due rent. More controversies dogged the department: Reverend Lee Johnson, an African American seminary student, said he was insulted, arrested, and beaten after a traffic stop in Harlem in 1983; later that year, an African American artist named Michael Stewart was arrested (for scrawling graffiti in a subway station, police would claim) and died in police custody amid reports of choking and beating. Two years later, an all-white jury acquitted the six police officers charged with negligent homicide.

Koch attempted to quell the perception of racial bias in the NYPD by appointing Benjamin Ward as the city's first black police commissioner, telling reporters, "He's black. There is no question about that. If that is helpful, isn't that nice?" But his hostility toward the city's black community was a lit fuse, waiting to explode. The first such conflagration came in 1982, when three black men were attacked by a mob of fifteen to twenty white youths in Gravesend, Brooklyn, where their car had stalled. William Turks, a thirty-four-year-old transit worker, was beaten to death; his two co-workers escaped with minor injuries. One of them, thirty-year-old Dennis Dixon, told the *Times*, "They came at us, yelling, 'Nigger, get out of here.'"

An uncomfortably similar incident occurred in December 1986, when twenty-three-year-old Michael Griffith was killed after he and two friends were stranded by a failing car in Howard Beach, Queens. They

were chased through the neighborhood by roughly a dozen white residents (all three men were black) and onto the Shore Parkway, where Stewart was struck by a car. "All crimes are terrible, but crimes involving racial bigotry are the absolute worst," Mayor Koch insisted at an afternoon news conference, but it was hard not to connect such crimes to the atmosphere he'd created, in his earlier words and actions, to court the "working class" white vote.

Such incidents of racially fueled violence were at the top of Brooklyn-born filmmaker Spike Lee's mind when he announced his next project in the summer of 1988. "The film takes place on the hottest day of the summer," he told the *New York Times* during a visit to the film's Bed-Stuy set. "And it's about how heat affects already tense racial relations in the city. To me, it's an examination of race relations between different ethnic groups in the city, how in the last eight years the whole black-white thing has been polarized by His Honor, Mayor Ed Koch. . . . There are a lot of things New Yorkers have to come to terms with if we don't want to keep heading the way we're heading. Something has to happen."

Something certainly happened when *Do the Right Thing* (1989; see sidebar on page 256) debuted at the Cannes Film Festival the following spring. The film culminates with a brutal sequence in which, following an altercation at Sal's Famous Pizza—owned and operated by an Italian American family in a predominantly African American and Latinx neighborhood—NYPD officers murder a black youth with a choke hold. Onlookers explode, rioting in protest and burning the pizzeria to the ground; reinforcements are called in, including firefighters who turn their hoses on the angry crowd.

"There was this thought that when this film comes out in the summer of 1989," Lee recalled, "black people are gonna run amuck." *Newsweek*'s Jack Kroll said the film was "dynamite under every seat." *New York*'s David Denby predicted, "*Do the Right Thing* is going to create an uproar," and warned, "if some audiences go wild, he's partly responsible."

It was not, in fact, "some audiences" that went wild that summer; the film provoked no riots, no violence, and no trouble. But on August 23, a black teen named Yusuf K. Hawkins was murdered by a group of white teens in Bensonhurst—the Brooklyn neighborhood where Sal and his sons live. "We should stay in Bensonhurst, and the niggers should stay in their neighborhood," opines son Pino. Hawkins's murderers apparently felt the same way.

Koch called the killing "an enormous tragedy," but the more perceptive comment came from Manhattan borough president David Dinkins: "The tone and climate of this city does get set at City Hall." Koch had further alienated black voters with a bizarre, ill-advised public campaign against 1988 presidential candidate Jesse Jackson, which rendered him even more vulnerable to a primary challenge for his fourth term. He got it from Dinkins, who won with an astounding 97 percent of the black vote, making him the city's first African American mayoral nominee for the Democratic Party. After a tough, close race against Rudolph Giuliani, Dinkins would become the city's first black mayor.

The ousting of Koch made the conclusion of the decade feel, in one more way, like the end of an era. In a December 31 report, the *Times*'s Georgia Dullea relayed a consensus, among the Wall Street rich, that "it was time to tone down, at least in public." Milken was sentenced; so was Leona Helmsley, the Manhattan hotelier who became one of the city's

poster children for unchecked greed. At her trial, a housekeeper testified that Helmsley bragged, "We don't pay taxes. Only the little people pay taxes." Helmsley was sentenced to four years in prison and $7.1 million in fines for tax evasion.

"The world was more corrupt than I thought," Oliver Stone says. "We went back in 2010 to revisit this issue, and Wall Street hasn't fucking changed." The sequel Stone made that year, *Wall Street: Money Never Sleeps*, came on the heels of yet another financial meltdown; the issues, divisions, and greed he'd explored twenty-plus years earlier were not only still present, but exacerbated, turbocharged by the vulture capitalism of the ensuing years. "It's now a billion dollars," he says. "A million dollars is nothing. Understand the fucking difference? It's enormous. When I left the film in '87, I thought, because of Black Monday, I thought it would all come down again. It never did. It kept going."

NOW SHOWING

FORT APACHE, THE BRONX

SMITHEREENS

DESPERATELY SEEKING SUSAN

GHOSTBUSTERS

AFTER HOURS

DO THE RIGHT THING

# FORT APACHE, THE BRONX

## 1981
## Director: Daniel Petrie

A 1976 *New York* magazine article by the South Bronx's 41st Precinct captain Tom Walker titled "The Siege of Fort Apache" was one of the sources for Heywood Gould's screenplay; the other was the experience of Thomas Mulhearn and Peter Tessitore, two former officers assigned to the 41st Precinct in the mid-1960s. By the time director Daniel Petrie brought Paul Newman and Ken Wahl to the South Bronx to star in *Fort Apache, The Bronx*, crime in the precinct had dropped 65 percent, and when filming began in the neighborhood in the spring of 1980, a leaked script set off a fury among community activists.

Ten of those groups, under the collective name of the Committee Against Fort Apache, filed suit against the film's producers. The suit was not intended to halt production of the film (already hovering around the midpoint), though according to the *New York Times*, "action by the community would be directed to that end." The group demanded changes to the script, objecting to its violence, the lack of "positive" characters of color, and the lack of contextualization for the area's ills.

It's not hard to understand their concerns. *Fort Apache* attempts to merge the scary urban exploitation messaging of *Death Wish* with a good cops/bad cops narrative of the *Serpico* school, so while it gives us two sympathetic central cops that ultimately inform on a pair of out-of-control colleagues who throw an innocent Puerto Rican teen from a rooftop, it also opens with a grisly scene in which two cops are murdered in their patrol car, after which neighborhood thugs crawl out of the abandoned buildings nearby to strip their car and pick their pockets. The film's outgoing captain warns his successor, "There's enough dirt in this precinct to bury every smartass cop in this city," but also tells him, "You'd do better walkin' a beat in Beirut than here."

Petrie refused to modify his picture, telling the *Times*, "It is a kind of idiocy to take the metaphors of some of the violent people or prostitutes in the film and say these characters represent all Puerto Ricans or all women." That perspective is mirrored in the script, in which the new captain (Ed Asner) tells Newman's long-timer, "I can see, Murphy. I can see the people out there. Not just the hookers, the pimps, and the junkies—those people who are trying to build something up here. And I want them to know who's running this precinct." And the producers added an opening disclaimer ("Because the story involves police work it does not deal with the law abiding members of the community nor does it dramatize the efforts of the individuals and groups who are struggling to turn the Bronx around"), though it seemed an empty gesture to the film's critics. "It runs twenty seconds, and then there are two hours of violence, sex and gore," said the Reverand Neil A. Connolly, vicar of the Roman Catholic Church in the South Bronx. "Who's going to remember the disclaimer?"

Still image from *Fort Apache, The Bronx* (1981), directed by Daniel Petrie, photographed by John Alcott.

# 15 Minutes From Manhattan There's A Place Where Even The Cops Fear To Tread.

# PAUL NEWMAN in FORT APACHE, THE BRONX
## The Cops Last Stand.

TIME-LIFE FILMS PRESENTS A DAVID SUSSKIND PRODUCTION
PAUL NEWMAN in
FORT APACHE, THE BRONX
Starring EDWARD ASNER  KEN WAHL  RACHEL TICOTIN
DANNY AIELLO  PAM GRIER and KATHLEEN BELLER  Music by JONATHAN TUNICK
Produced by MARTIN RICHARDS and GILL CHAMPION  Written by HEYWOOD GOULD
Directed by DANIEL PETRIE  Executive Producer DAVID SUSSKIND

TIME-LIFE FILMS

FORT APACHE, THE BRONX

# SMITHEREENS

## 1981

# DESPERATELY SEEKING SUSAN

## 1985

### Director: Susan Seidelman

*Smithereens* announces itself with a roar of loud music and fierce, rattling energy, sustained throughout its duration. It's a noisy, jittery movie, with a sense of everyday danger and an edge that's almost anarchic; it lives in a world of dirty clubs and dumpy walk-ups, all of them inhabited by heroine Wren, who embodies a specific, angry, take-no-shit type, all sneers and dry wit. We first see her putting up flyers of her face on the subway—not advertising a show or a skill, but merely herself. She's a hustler, an opportunist, and a liar, a young punk female Ratso Rizzo, yet not unsympathetic—perhaps because the film's writer/director saw so much of herself in her creation.

"She's an extension of parts of me," Susan Seidelman admits. "A bored suburban girl who left the Philadelphia suburbs looking for adventure, looking to be a part of some more exciting, artistic thing." That drive to get out of the 'burbs was more of her motivation to enter NYU film school than any notion that she could make it as a filmmaker, but Seidelman found herself inspired—not only by the curriculum of the school, but also by the possibilities all around her in the city, at that moment.

*Smithereens* is, in many ways, a fairly traditional romantic entanglement story, in which everybody wants somebody who wants somebody else. What makes the picture special is its gnarly authenticity, its sense that Seidelman is at home on these streets and in these lofts. "That inspired the kinds of characters and the look of the film," she says. "It was dirty and grungy and there was something about that, the textured feeling of the city, that made it very cinematic and interesting to me."

The critical and commercial success of *Smithereens* (it went on to play at the Cannes Film Festival) brought

Seidelman another iconic 1980s New York movie. *Desperately Seeking Susan* takes a screwball premise (a bored housewife, living vicariously through a wild child she follows in the personal ads, gets amnesia and is mistaken for said wild child) and shines it through an eighties action/comedy prism, but it also offered Seidelman the opportunity to ground the movie in a downtown reality.

"It changed, once I got involved," she recalls. "It was set in the East Village, and the character of Susan wasn't this downtown punk kind of person. At that time she was a little bit more like a hippie traveler—it was more like Diane Keaton, *Annie Hall*–ish, that kind of a character. And what I thought would be interesting—again, because I was familiar with the current of that time, downtown culture—was to kind of morph it a little bit into the characters I knew, and that I thought could be interesting in that role. So the character of Susan changed a little bit, and then *certainly* when we cast Madonna."

Seidelman has worked steadily in the years since that whammo one-two punch—most notably, she directed the pilot episode of *Sex and the City*—while resisting the urge to move to Los Angeles. She's watched the city change rapidly in those years, often in bemusement. "Who would have thought that the Lower East Side, which was so vibrant in the '90s, or welcomed new immigrants at the turn of the century, would now be where the rich stockbrokers all want to live and pay a fortune to get a corned beef sandwich at Katz's Deli, you know?"

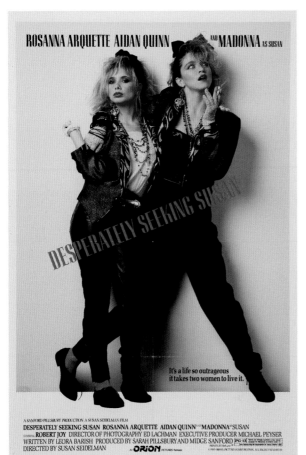

# GHOSTBUSTERS

## 1984

## Director: Ivan Reitman

The wisecracking comedy/horror mash-ups that co-writer/co-stars Dan Akroyd and Harold Ramis were aping with *Ghostbusters*, like Bob Hope's *The Ghost Breakers* and *Abbott and Costello Meet Frankenstein*, were typically set in isolated haunted-house environs. But the screenwriters imagined that the urban setting was appropriate not only to the comic riffs of their characters (and the unflappable locals), but also to the mythology they were creating for their demons and ghouls.

The buildings in New York are old and rich with history, full of ghosts and their legends; when the titular trio arrives at the swanky "Sedgewick Hotel," the manager assures them that the hauntings on the twelfth floor are an open secret among the staff: "The owners don't even like to talk about it." The skyscrapers that jut sharply into the cloudy Manhattan horizon aren't just ornate relics of earlier architecture eras—their intricate designs and harsh angles are better camouflage for entries into other dimensions. "As so often happens in the movie city," James Sanders writes in *Celluloid City*, "the imaginative visions of filmmakers serve to activate the latent possibilities of the skyline, encouraging us to look twice at that which we usually take for granted."

*Ghostbusters* is also worth contextualizing into the particular time and place of mid-1980s NYC for the character of Mayor Lenny Clotch (David Margulies); if the homophonous surname weren't a giveaway, the image of a thin-haired Jewish mayor who stops raising his voice only long enough to suck up to the city's cardinal would have been. Koch was a nationwide celebrity by the time *Ghostbusters* took over popular culture in the summer of 1984, with his (first) memoir, *Mayor: An Autobiography*, charting on the *New York Times* bestseller list for much of the previous spring. (One other, darker echo: Mayor Clotch ends up calling in the National Guard for the ghost crisis, just as mayoral candidate Koch had advocated calling in the Guard to handle looters during the 1977 blackout.) As with a similar gag in *The Taking of Pelham One Two Three* a decade earlier, one of the picture's biggest laugh lines garnered even bigger guffaws in Gotham: Bill Murray's Peter Venkman assuring the voters that, if these freelance spectral cops are allowed to save the day, "you will have saved the lives . . . of *millions* of registered voters."

Still image from
*Ghostbusters* (1984),
directed by Ivan Reitman,
photographed by László
Kovács.

# AFTER HOURS

## 1985
## Director: Martin Scorsese

Considering his previous filmography, it's perhaps appropriate that much of what transpires in Martin Scorsese's 1985 comedy, *After Hours*, can be blamed on a taxi driver. Paul (Griffin Dunne) is merely trying to get downtown, from his very small, very beige apartment on the Upper East Side to SoHo, where the nice girl (Rosanna Arquette) he just met in a coffee shop is staying. But the driver is going *so fast*, for *no good reason*, and though he puts the $20 bill (all the cash he's got) in the tray, the taxi is moving so fast that the money flies right out the window, and that's that. ("Based on a real cab ride that happened to me," Scorsese says, "with flamenco and everything.")

It's the first in a series of injustices and unfortunate events that befall poor Paul, the very definition of a mid-eighties New York yuppie, who works as a word processor in Midtown. But this girl is exciting, and when she suggests he come over (even though it's already 11:32 at night, and she lives all the way downtown), he decides to take the plunge. What could go wrong? Well, he finds out.

Looking for a quick, commercial project in a rocky professional period, Scorsese made what looks, on its surface, like a typical eighties "one long night" farce—he even goes to the trouble of casting such mainstays of the era's studio comedies as Cheech and Chong, Teri Garr, and Bronson Pinchot. But that's just its exterior. The picture is suffused with a sense of creeping, existential dread; Paul lands in SoHo like an alien dropped from the distant planet of the UES, and everyone in this land acts strange, says peculiar things, and seems to be laughing at a joke he's not in on.

As Paul drifts (or, later, races) through this world of lofts, all-night diners, dive bars, and punk clubs, he's never allowed to forget that he's a visitor, and that sense of alienation and paranoia becomes the picture's defining traits. There's just something *off* about this world, which seems downright vacant even after the rain lifts. "I was living there too," Scorsese says of the shoot. "The strangeness of the place, as you see it in the film, it was something that was quite real to me. There was a world there, but I couldn't find it. I wasn't part of that, and I didn't want to [be] quite honestly. I just wanted a place where I could live." But that solitude was an asset to the production: "At night in that area, which was isolated at that time, it was total freedom. It was total freedom. We had just an extraordinary experience."

**OPPOSITE**
Still image from *After Hours* (1985), directed by Martin Scorsese, photographed by Michael Ballhaus.

# DO THE RIGHT THING

## 1989

## Director: Spike Lee

The opening sequence of *Do the Right Thing* comes on like a Category 5 hurricane of light, color, music, dance, and aggression—much like the film itself did, that summer of 1989. Rosie Perez, in her film debut, takes over set decorations of a Brooklyn block, and dances, sneers, punches, and stares down the camera in time to Public Enemy's disobedience anthem "Fight the Power"; Lee lays a horn track by the score's featured soloist, Branford Marsalis, over the PE song, somehow making it even noisier and more chaotic. It's one of the brashest openings in all of cinema, and one of the most appropriate.

Lee's story takes place on one block in Bed-Stuy, Brooklyn, over roughly twenty-four hours—the hottest day of the summer, we're told, with 100+ temperatures and short showers due to a concurrent water shortage. It begins like a regular Saturday; friends hang out, tell jokes, bust balls, and try to stay cool.

But there's troubling foreshadowing, from the beginning. "I'm gonna kill somebody today," announces Sal (Danny Aiello), the owner of the corner pizzeria, and he says it in jest, as an exclamation of frustration, but he's not wrong. And it's early in the day when he asks Buggin' Out (Giancarlo Esposito), "You lookin for trouble? Are you a troublemaker?"

Buggin' Out just might be; he's the neighborhood activist, and when he notes (seemingly for the first time) that the "Wall of Fame" at Sal's Famous is decorated only with photos of Sal's fellow Italian Americans, he wonders why there aren't any "brothers on the wall," since African Americans are Sal's primary source of income. Sal responds that when Buggin' Out has his own place, "You can do what you wanna do.... But this is my pizzeria. American Italians on the wall only." That tiny spark lights the fuse for the conflict that will explode at the end of the day, and of Lee's film. One of the masterstrokes of his smart screenplay is how he refuses to stack the deck; in the Sal/Buggin' Out conflict there are, as Lee himself points out in the film's audio commentary, "two valid points."

Lee also manages to avoid the didacticism of a lazier filmmaker via his clever narrative sleight of hand. The neighborhood setting, and its built-in cast of characters, allows much of the picture to function as something akin to a situation comedy; he revels in the dynamics of the pizzeria staff, the back-and-forth love/hate relationship between Da Mayor and Mother Sister, and the Greek-Chorus-meets-Def-Comedy-Jam razzing and kibitzing of the Corner Men. With so many easy, earthy laughs to enjoy, Lee can elegantly sprinkle in all the little flare-ups and microaggressions through the day that culminate in the riot at the story's end, without calling particular attention to any of them.

The climax also feels inevitable because the neighborhood and its inhabitants seem bonded; it feels like a real block, and these feel like people who really live there. "When you do a movie like *Do the Right Thing*," explained production designer Wynn Thomas, "so much of that intangible atmosphere you get from the location; you wouldn't get those same air molecules in a studio." So the crew took over a block of Stuyvesant Avenue between Quincy and Lexington for six weeks in the summer of 1988, battling high temperatures the entire time.

Amy Taubin of the *Village Voice* noted, "There are no stand-ins and no air-conditioned trailers to hide out in. Spike likes to hire actors for the entire shoot (not just for the days they appear), so 22 people are constantly on call." This unorthodox strategy also gives the block its own life; characters can wander through scenes that aren't about them, coming to and from other scenes that merely happen off-screen.

James Sanders connects *Do the Right Thing* to "the classic 1930s New York street movies, especially *Street Scene* and *Dead End*." But Lee didn't have to shoot his movie on a "New York block" set on a California backlot; he went to the real thing, and the film is richer for it.

1990

City in
Transition,
the Indie
Movie
Boom,
and *Kids*

2000

"It's a different world," Larry Clark says, of New York City—and, particularly, 42nd Street—today. "Now, it's like Disneyland. But back then, it was prostitution and drugs, out in the wide open. And the police would leave after like ten o'clock! It was just this wild, wild street, with a lot of shit going on." The Tulsa, Oklahoma, native arrived in New York in 1964, fresh out of art school, taking photographs of the city as he saw it for about year before he was drafted into the US Army, serving in Vietnam from 1964 to 1966. He returned to his hometown afterward, photographing his burnout friends and the world they inhabited, assembling those images into a striking yet unnerving portrait of misspent youth, which he called *Tulsa*.

That book, published in 1971, was both influential and well received; Clark leveraged its success into an NEA grant to fund the creation of a follow-up photography/book project, which would take him twelve years to complete. While crisscrossing the country to shoot pictures for this project, he further descended into what he called "the outlaw life," indulging his fondness for drugs, booze, sex, and violence. In 1976, he shot a man in the arm during a card game and was convicted of "assault and battery with a deadly weapon with intent to kill," serving nineteen months in prison.

After his release, Clark went back to New York. It was 1978. "My probation officer was on 40th Street," he recalls, "so I used to go up there. And I was amazed by 42nd Street, so I started documenting that." Clark's "42nd Street photos" became an integral piece of his next book, which he gave a title that could also apply to much of his subsequent work: *Teenage Lust*.

Recurring themes began to emerge in those initial volumes; chief among them was an interest in outsiders: people living (and living hard) on the fringes of civilized society. "As I look back on everything," Clark explains, "I'm showing a small group of people that you wouldn't know about otherwise. Every film, every bit of work, you would not know about these people if I didn't make the film." And he harbored an unapologetic (some would say disturbing) fascination with sexuality, teenage and otherwise. "Kids have sex!" he says with a shrug. "I don't usually respond to it, I don't have to respond to it—this is the work, take it or leave it. Pretty simple!"

But photography and publishing were never his endgame. "I always wanted to make films," he says. "The first book, *Tulsa*, is like a film. In fact, I wanted to make *Tulsa* as a film, but it wasn't possible to do that. So I made the book, which is like a film." His biggest influence was another New York maverick: "The first film that really did it for me was John Cassavetes's *Shadows*, which I saw when I went to art school in Milwaukee in the early sixties," he said. "The style, the look, the acting—there's an honesty to all his films."

That was the approach Clark wanted to take. "So I decided to make a film," he says. "I had to clean up, because no one's gonna give money to a junkie, so I cleaned up for the purpose of getting money to make a film. And I had done so much autobiography, I wanted to do something that wasn't about me at all. I wanted to find out what was going on with kids then."

▬

The 1989 mayoral election had been one of the closest in New York City's history. "Mr. Dinkins was the candidate of moderation," wrote the *New York Times*'s Celestine Bohlen, "a middle-of-the-road choice for a city that seemed eager to lower its own decibel level." His Republican opponent, Rudolph "Rudy" Giuliani, took the opposite approach, running a divisive and negative campaign that almost worked, capturing the votes of wavering white Democrats by exploiting the populace's racial divisions.

The city Dinkins took over was already on a precipice of disaster. In November 1990, *New York* magazine ran a cover story titled "Hard Times," illustrated with a Depression-era image of a street urchin selling apples for a nickel. Inside, restaurateur Patrick Clark (no relation) summed up the city's fiscal outlook thus: "It was like the nineties came in and everyone said, 'We have no more money to spend.'" State comptroller Edward Regan put it in far bleaker terms. "By any relevant

City in Transition, the Indie Movie Boom, and *Kids*

Mayor David Dinkins on
*Late Night with Conan
O'Brien*, 1993.

measure, the New York City economy is in recession," he said. "There is every reason to assume the economic situation will get worse before it gets better."

In those circumstances, Dinkins was all but set up to fail. "The battle for survival is being fought on the sidewalks of New York, not in the ledger books," wrote *Time* magazine's Joelle Attinger. "And so far, Dinkins' lackluster performance has strengthened the unsettling sense that he is simply not up to his job." This was written in September 1990—nine months after the mayor's inauguration. It appeared in a splashy cover story titled "The Decline of New York," which noted, in all fairness, that Dinkins had "inherited the whirlwind sown by decades of benign neglect, misplaced priorities, and outright incompetence at every level of government." That whirlwind included roughly ninety thousand homeless citizens, twenty-seven thousand AIDS victims (19 percent of all confirmed cases in the country), and streets that had "become public rest rooms for both people and animals."

"What was once the bustle of a hyperkinetic city," Attinger wrote, "has become a demented frenzy."

At the heart of the city's struggle was fear—more specifically, fear of crime. People were fleeing the city in record numbers, with "crime" the most oft-cited cause, and for good reason: The city's total crime index had risen steadily for the past two decades. In a 1990 report and strategy paper, Police commissioner Lee P. Brown suggested a focus on community policing, announcing, "the beat cop is coming back to New York City." But Dinkins's 1989 opponent was waiting eagerly in the wings, watching his every misfortune, calling out his every mistake, and formulating a far splashier policing strategy for his next run.

The city itself might have been looking over an economic cliff, but the film business was booming. The Mayor's Office of Film, Theatre & Broadcasting issued 119 film permits in 1990, plus another 314 for TV movies, specials, and series; in the first ten months of the following year alone, it had issued 127 permits to filmmakers and 532 to television producers. Film production, the Mayor's Office announced, was pumping half a million dollars per day into the local economy—a figured cited both as a boast and as an attempt to quiet the increasingly strident complaints of disrupted residents ("Having a film crew in your

neighborhood is like being occupied by a foreign army," sneered one Village resident). Kaufman Astoria and Silvercup Studios were operating at capacity; there was talk of building a new studio, in the developing Chelsea Piers, to accommodate the considerable overflow.

And then it all ground to a halt. The higher cost of New York production had long been a burr in the side of Hollywood number-crunchers, since the primary cost differential was due to strict East Coast union overtime rules, enforced for the kind of night and weekend work typical of shooting in Manhattan (for easier crowd and traffic control). In 1990, the studios banded together in an attempt to force those unions to agree to the same terms recently negotiated with their West Coast counterparts. When they didn't, the studios boycotted all New York production for nine months, beginning in November of that year. Shoots were shifted to Toronto, Atlanta, Chicago, or the backlots. Millions were lost during the stalemate, which lasted until mid-May 1991.

Not all Gotham production ceased, however, in this period. The isolated pockets of New York filmmakers (John Cassavetes, Shirley Clarke, Paul Morrissey, Jonas Mekas) of the 1960s had given way to full-on scenes, first in the form of the No Wave and downtown filmmakers of the late 1970s and early 1980s. Those films were something of an acquired taste. "Nothing they did . . . seemed very good," chuckles programmer, producer, and historian John Pierson. But by the back half of the decade, that scene had blossomed into a burgeoning, indigenous indie film culture. As mainstream moviemaking segued from the idiosyncratic, auteur-driven seventies into the corporatized, homogenous eighties, filmmakers like Jim Jarmusch, Susan Seidelman, and Spike Lee helped position New York as the epicenter of the alternative. "It seemed easy to just be like, 'Hey, let's put on a show,'" says Pierson. "Which I think is both because of the cheap, cheap venues and real estate that you could get, and the low cost of living. So people could just take a shot trying *anything*."

That adventurous spirit, and the freedom within it, was a marked departure from the increasingly safe confines of studio product. "In shaping their films around the existing landscapes of the city," writes film historian James Sanders, "they were mapping out an alternative approach to the making of American features, laying the groundwork for the emergence of a new, homegrown industry that would look to New York not only as a base of production, but as a major source of inspiration."

On September 16, 1992, the New York Police Department rioted. Its union, the Patrolmen's Benevolent Association of the City of New York, called a rally in front of City Hall to protest Mayor Dinkins's proposal to create a Civilian Complaint Review Board—the same kind of outside disciplinary agency that caused Mayor Lindsay so much friction with the NYPD during *his* first term. Thousands of off-duty cops swarmed police barricades and blocked traffic on the Brooklyn Bridge; they held up racist signs and lobbed that vilest of epithets at a WCBS cameraman and a passing Brooklyn city councilwoman, among others. "The 300 uniformed officers who were supposed to control the crowd did little or nothing to stop the protesters," reported the *Times*'s James C. McKinley Jr. "In some cases, the on-duty officers encouraged the protesters."

And standing in the middle of it all was Rudy Giuliani. The event's featured speaker whipped the crowd into a frenzied fury, bellowing the union's grievances against Dinkins into a microphone and dismissing the mayor's actions, twice, as "bullshit." Pressed for an apology two days

**ABOVE**
Still images from *She's Gotta Have It* (1986), directed by Spike Lee, photographed by Ernest R. Dickerson; *Stranger Than Paradise* (1984), directed by Jim Jarmusch, photographed by Tom DiCillo.

**RIGHT**
Still images from *Smithereens* (1982), directed by Susan Seidelman, photographed by Chirine El Khadem; *Night on Earth* (1991), directed by Jim Jarmusch, photographed by Frederick Elmes.

City in Transition, the Indie Movie Boom, and *Kids*

later, Giuliani insisted, "One of the reasons those police officers might have lost control is that we have a mayor who invites riots."

Giuliani had not yet announced his candidacy, but the rally was a rough preview of his 1993 campaign, as well as the voters he would target. Some of his policy ideas in 1989, particularly with regard to the city's still-growing homeless population, were as progressive as his Democratic opponent's; no such centrism would infect Rudy 2.0. He spent a considerable amount of his downtime before the 1993 contest soaking up the ideology of the Manhattan Institute, a right-wing think tank. He also met with William Bratton, then a higher-up in the Boston Police Department after a stint as chief of the New York City Transit Police, to discuss strategies for the NYPD's future. They also met with criminologist George L. Kelling, one of the authors of the *Atlantic* article that Ed Koch had read back in 1982, as a key to Bratton's success with the transit police, he told Giuliani, was embracing the Broken Windows theory.

"If the first broken window in a building is not repaired," wrote Kelling and co-author James Q. Wilson, "then people who like breaking windows will assume that no one cares about the building and more windows will be broken. Soon the building will have no windows. Fixing what is wrong with the city sends a message that the authorities are in control and that increases the power of authority to maintain order." In Boston, Bratton had determined that applying the theory to urban policing—placing an emphasis on "quality of life" crimes like graffiti writing, turnstile jumping, and panhandling—had caused a drop in overall crime rates. Dinkins dismissed the theory, insisting that "killers and rapists are a city's real public enemies, not squeegee pests and homeless mothers."

Giuliani would get to test Bratton's strategy soon enough. In their November 1993 rematch, Giuliani bested Dinkins by roughly the same margin (fifty thousand votes) that he had lost by in 1989. It was a history-making defeat, the first (and last) time in the twentieth century that a New York mayor who served a full term lost an election for the next. The Giuliani campaign leaned hard on racial coding, and the candidate even claimed that he would "win by 15 or 20 points" if "you take the issue of race out of this," like "a normal American election." His strategy of racial grievance paid off big when a referendum on the possible secession of Staten Island (the city's whitest borough) appeared on the same ballot, driving his target voters to the polls in even larger numbers.

**TOP**
Mayor Rudolph "Rudy" Giuliani.

**ABOVE**
Giuliani with Republican Senator Bob Dole.

The fight against crime was the top priority of Giuliani's first term. He named Bratton as police commissioner and hired 2,400 new recruits for the NYPD. In his inauguration speech, he promised to give the city back to "conventional members of society." Part of that strategy meant again slashing public assistance (all of a piece with the Republican wave that would take over Congress the following year), refusing welfare and shelter to thousands of families, and forcing those who received aid into "workfare"—mandatory jobs in city agencies, which could be snatched away for minor infractions. Giuliani advised citizens living in poverty to "start a small business. Start a little candy store. Start a little newspaper stand. Start a lemonade stand."

Predictably enough, the cutting of services caused the already-astronomical homeless numbers to rise further. To keep up the appearance of "quality of life" in the city, the administration began sweeping homeless people off the streets of Manhattan "from Battery Park to 110th Street, river to river," according to a Department of

Giuliani with President
Bill Clinton, who shared his
"tough on crime" stance,
in 1993.

Homeless Services monthly outreach report. NYPD brass put out a "reference guide," helpfully suggesting a dozen quality-of-life infractions useful for arresting homeless citizens. Many of those the city swept up were placed in barracks-style shelters; when those filled, they bussed homeless singles to Camp LaGuardia, a former prison upstate.

Early on, Giuliani's primary target for quality-of-life arrest was "squeegee guys," who would descend on cars at stoplights for an unprompted cleaning of motorists' windshields with dirty water, rags, and squeegees, then demand payment. But it was a comparatively minor issue; an NYPD report could find only seventy-five of them in the city as of 1993, and Dinkins's police commissioner, Ray Kelly, got them all off the streets before Giuliani was even inaugurated. "Ironically," Bratton would write in his 1998 memoir, "Giuliani and I got the credit for the initiative."

What mattered, of course, were appearances, the truth at the center of the Broken Windows theory—and other aspects of the city's image. "For years," writes James Sanders, "films had employed exactly the kinds of physical disorder Kelling identified (vandalism, graffiti, smashed phone booths, trash-filled streets, broken windows) to establish the plausible setting for acts of urban violence, knowing full well that in the minds of their audience—the general public, in other words—disorder was *intimately* connected to serious crime."

The decade began with the kind of scuzzy, crime-ridden portraiture that had defined New York cinema for the past two decades. There was *Q&A* (1990), another Sidney Lumet–directed exposé of dirty cops; Abel Ferrara's *King of New York* (1990) and Mario Van Peebles's *New Jack City* (1991), warring stories of big-city crime kingpins; Larry Cohen's *The Ambulance* (1990), whose title vehicle shuttles innocent citizens off for demented medical experiments, extending the theme, from Cohen's *Maniac Cop* scripts, that those in the uniform of the city cannot be trusted; and *Night and the City* (1992), with Robert De Niro as a fast-talking, forever-scheming, sleazy New York bullshit artist.

But even genre pictures like these found the changing shape of The City impossible to ignore. Phil Joanou's *State of Grace* (1990) concerns a turf war between Irish and Italian gangsters, but the former seem just as concerned about what's become of their Midtown environs. "Where'd our fuckin' neighborhood go?" asks prodigal son Terry (Sean Penn). "I don't even recognize the place. Bunch a yuppie condos or somethin'. They coulda left at least ten blocks for the Irish."

"They don't even call it Hell's Kitchen no more," replies his buddy Jacky (Gary Oldman). "Renamed it 'Clinton'! Sounds like a fuckin' steamboat."

The first major indication of a shift in the winds arrived on-screen in November 1992. The sequel to the surprise smash of two previous Christmases, *Home Alone 2: Lost in New York*, transferred that film's suburban quaintness to the Big Apple and gave its cartoonish slapstick an urban edge. This time, little Kevin McCallister lures thieves Joe Pesci and Daniel Stern to his aunt and uncle's Upper West Side town house—currently undergoing gut-renovation, naturally—for comic torture. "The sadism he metes out there," Mark Asch notes in his book *New York Movies*, "would satisfy Bernhard Goetz, who opened fire on four black teenage would-be muggers on a 2 train in 1984; or Curtis Sliwa, whose satin-jacketed 'Guardian Angels' patrolled subway cars looking for lowlifes to rough up throughout the late 70s and 80s; or indeed Travis Bickle."

In retrospect, the film plays like a preview of Broken Windows policing—in fact, Kevin literally breaks a store window to alert police of the thieves' activities. (He later pays for the window, without even being asked.) Watching *Home Alone 2* is like watching a 120-minute tourism ad, assuring you that the setting of all those urban thrillers and slasher movies—the city where you wouldn't even walk the streets a few short years back—is now so safe that a ten-year-old can travel there safely, all by himself. He might encounter a few semi-spooky hookers and homeless people at nighttime near Central Park, but if he simply talks to one, she'll dispense pearls of wisdom like "Follow the star in your own heart" before sneaking him into Carnegie Hall to hear orchestral music. In fact, the scariest person Kevin encounters in Gotham is Donald Trump, then the owner of the Plaza Hotel, who made his cameo appearances a requirement of any film shooting on the property. (Most filmmakers were wise enough to humor him with the shoot but leave the scene on the cutting-room floor.)

Some New York filmmakers felt the changes coming and adjusted. "I just don't feel New York is menacing now," said Sidney Lumet. "The movies and TV created a stereotype of the city—but that was then, and this is now. You have to portray New York accurately, and I'm portraying it as a beautiful city now." Nora Ephron approached the shift more cheerfully: "I've probably always had a very romanticized view of New York, and now, finally, the reality of New York has caught up with it."

If the rest of the city had become "beautiful" (i.e., gentrified), St. Mark's Place—a stretch of the East Village running from the doorstep of NYU down to Alphabet City—was one of the last remaining splashes of color. Gutter punks and prep school kids comingled with junkies and freaks at record stores, clubs, barbershops, and the affordable sit-down restaurant Dojo. They took out movies from Kim's Video, the storied cinephile haven, stocked with bootleg tapes, international titles, and famously rude clerks (many of whom became indie filmmakers themselves). "Uptown kids, drag queens, punk rockers, skaters, book nerds, and ravers loitered side by side on stoops, drinking forties," writes Ada Calhoun in her definitive history, *St. Marks Is Dead.* "There was still crime, but not too much; danger, but not too much."

The skater kids congregated at the Astor Place Cube or up at Washington Square Park. This was where Larry Clark found himself scoping out ideas for his movie about teenagers. "I decided the most interesting idea, cinematically, was skateboarders," he says. "So I started hanging out with skateboarders—I hung out with them for like three years. It was hard for me, skating, but the kids saw that I was okay. After a while, they treated me just like each other. And I got the idea for *Kids.*"

Before he got that idea, he met a strange, memorable teenage boy in the park. "He came up to me, and I had a Leica, and he said something to me about my Leica, and something about Robert Frank, and I said, 'Wow. Really knows his shit.'" The kid proceeded to tell Clark about his aspirations for screenwriting and filmmaking, and about the short film script he'd written. "So about a year later, when I got ready to do *Kids*, I said, 'I can't write this film. It would be great if it could be a kid who could write . . .' and I remembered, 'Oh, I met this kid a year ago, Harmony.'"

Harmony Korine brought Clark his short screenplay, and on the basis of that sample, Clark hired him to write *Kids.* "I told him the story, just the basic story, that simple," Clark says. Korine, the legend goes, banged out the script in three weeks, and that was pretty much the movie Clark shot. "He was a kid and he knew kid-speak, and wrote this brilliant screenplay, all the dialogue, which was incredible. And if you look at *Kids*, you may think that it's a lot of improv, but I made them speak the lines."

The story Clark handed Korine focused on Telly (Leo Fitzpatrick), a would-be Lothario who specializes in "de-virginizing" young girls, whom he considers safe for condom-free sex. The problem is, Telly himself is HIV-positive and is passing the virus to all of his partners— including Jennie (Chloë Sevigny), who receives her shocking diagnosis early in the film. Over the course of one long, unsupervised summer day, Telly and his best buddy Casper (Justin Pierce), hang out, smoke weed, talk shit, and scope out Telly's next victim as Jennie desperately tries to track Telly down.

Beyond its alarmist messaging and sleazy authenticity, Korine's script captured the flavor of an old, dirty East Village that was already disappearing. Giuliani's gentrification efforts included tightening zoning restrictions, leaning on ancient cabaret laws to prohibit dancing in clubs on the LES and elsewhere. The city began a new crackdown on graffiti in the subway, this time in the form of scratched-up scrawlings ("scratchiti"), which are much more difficult to remove than spray paint.

But for some citizens, the proof was in the pudding: Crime was on the decline. It began under Dinkins; according to FBI crime statistics, crime in the city had dropped 16 percent over thirty-six consecutive months, the last three years of his single term. But local media barely covered the shift (and credited the mayor even less), and candidate Giuliani insisted, in the run-up to the '93 vote, "If you believe crime has been reduced, you are living in a never-never land." Of course, he would not doubt the credibility of those stats when they reflected crime drops in his own administration.

There is no doubt that crime continued to fall, and rapidly, throughout the 1990s. But was that steep decline a result of this particular mayor

and his aggressive policing policies? Or was he merely lucky enough to take office during a major economic boom, which dovetailed with a drop in serious crimes that affected virtually every major city in the nation? Were declining crime rates actually accelerating at a faster rate in New York City, or were the mayor and his police chiefs fudging numbers and altering data to make it appear so?

Most importantly, were the aggressive tactics of Giuliani's NYPD, from the willy-nilly "stop and frisk" searches (found, in a later report by state attorney general Eliot Spitzer, to disproportionately target black and Latinx citizens) to the hands-off approach of the rough-and-tumble Street Crime Unit, genuinely effective? Perhaps not. "A look at other cities around the nation suggests that large reductions in crime can be achieved in places that rely less on the confrontational law enforcement measures New York has used," wrote the *New York Times*'s Fox Butterfield, at the conclusion of the decade. "In fact, some cities, notably San Diego and Boston, have recorded as big or even larger drops in violence while employing strategies that rely on close cooperation between the police and the community and have ended up improving race relations."

Even the areas where the NYPD focused much of its energy—like Times Square—saw crime levels decline in numbers roughly commensurate to areas like Canal Street, which saw no major physical or demographic changes, as well as no increased police presence. But Times Square was a tourist hot spot and media center, perhaps the most outward-facing district of the city, so extra effort was exerted. Police cracked down on panhandling, public drinking, and three-card monte games. Uniformed security officers from the Times Square Business Improvement District (BID) augmented the NYPD presence. The BID also joined Giuliani in targeting porno theaters and sex shops on the Deuce and Eighth Avenue, producing a 1994 report insisting that "adult use establishments" had negative "secondary effects" on the district.

And so it came to pass that in March 1995, the City Council passed harsh zoning restrictions on any stores in the area with "a substantial portion of their stock in trade or materials characterized by an emphasis on specific anatomical areas or sexual activities." It came to be known as the "60/40 rule," because sex shops had to augment 40 percent of their porn stock with 60 percent of something (anything) else. Some did, indeed, close up shop; others simply pushed their porn tapes to the back of the store and filled the shelves in the front with violent action, kung fu, and horror flicks. But the shops that adjusted and stuck around were on Eighth Avenue and a few side streets, like 40th; 42nd Street, the dirty ol' Deuce that had once offered up door-to-door porn, was rid of adult entertainment entirely—and ready for new, corporate tenants.

So *Kids*, which filmed in the summer of 1994, became one last Polaroid picture of a vanishing city. "I think that if it had been later," Clark says, "I don't think it would have been made—in terms of what the movie was *and* what the city was."

And even then, making the movie was a stretch. It took Clark more than a year to raise the funds to produce it; certainly no studio was going to be interested, so for producer Cary Woods, it was a matter of finding the right kind of hands-off backer. "We were able to get a couple of venture capitalists' kids," Clark recalls, "with millionaire fathers who gave them like eight million dollars to keep them happy or something. They gave us the money. And we just did it, it was that simple—and that difficult, too."

**TOP**
Still image from *New Jack City* (1991), directed by Mario van Peebles, photographed by Francis Kenny.

**CENTER LEFT TO RIGHT**
Still images from *King of New York* (1990), directed by Abel Ferrara, photographed by Bojan Bazelli; *Home Alone 2: Lost in New York* (1992), directed by John Hughes, photographed by Julio Macat.

**BOTTOM**
Still image from *State of Grace* (1990), directed by Phil Joanou, photographed by Jordan Cronenweth.

Still images from *Kids* (1995), directed by Larry Clark, photographed by Eric Alan Edwards.

**BELOW**
Still image from *Pi* (1998),
directed by Darren
Aronofsky, photographed
by Matthew Libateque.

**BOTTOM**
Times Square in the
Giuliani years.

Part of financiers' reluctance may have been Clark's fierce determination in regard to casting. He didn't want to fill it with twenty-somethings pretending to be teenagers, and he didn't want to use precocious "movie kids" who'd been directed their entire lives. "Nobody had acted before," he says. "They were all in Washington Square. They were skateboarding kids. Justin Pierce, Leo Fitzpatrick, Harold Hunter, Chloë, all the girls, they were just around." Harold Hunter, nineteen years old at the time, was something of a rock star in the St. Mark's scene, described by fellow skater Billy Rohan as "the Bruce Lee of skateboarding." Chloe Sevigny was also nineteen years old; Leo Fitzpatrick was seventeen. Rosario Dawson, making her film debut as Jennie's best friend Ruby, was all of fifteen years old.

The financing came through with only six weeks left of summer, leaving Clark and Woods an unusually short window to lock in the cast, prepare the production, and get the picture in the can while the weather was cooperating. And in the midst of this chaos was a first-time director, albeit one with very clear ideas about how he wanted this film to feel and look.

"Some of the production team just thought I was crazy, that I didn't know what I was doing," Clark says now. "But I knew *exactly* what I was doing. Because I knew exactly what I wanted the film to look like—I wanted it to look like you were eavesdropping on this world, and you wouldn't have a chance to know about it otherwise. And I wanted it shot like that. So it's in kind of a documentary style: We just put them out there and shot 'em, with a long lens, and followed them. We just shot on the street."

As Rudy Giuliani led local and national media in proclaiming the city's Broken Windows–led policy an unqualified success, New York–set mainstream moviemaking increasingly reflected an upper-class, homogenous, gentrified vision of the city—portraits of the people inhabiting those luxury condos that the movies of earlier eras (or, at least, those not directed by Woody Allen) were sneering at. Fred Schepisi's adaptation of John Guare's Broadway smash *Six Degrees of Separation* (1993) at least attempted to grapple with the spiky dynamics of race and class that were so prevalent in the city at the time, specifically via how the young black hustler at the story's center uses the liberal guilt of his Central Park West marks to gain their confidence. But as the decade continued, films like *The First Wives Club*, *One Fine Day*, and *The Mirror Has Two Faces* (all 1996); *As Good As It Gets* (1997); and *Living Out Loud* and *You've Got Mail* (both 1998)—many of them sparkling entertainments—were nonetheless willing to gaze often uncritically at these insular lives, led from behind the safety of zealous doormen.

And it was perhaps in response to this, as James Sanders writes, that "the city now became associated with a kind of readily identifiable American film: small in scale, idiosyncratic in theme and mood, the product not of studio story conferences but of the personal—or downright quirky—vision of its writer and director (who often enough were one and the same)." Many were genre exercises, though often dealing subtextually with the struggles of the city and its residents; *State of Grace* (1990), *Light Sleeper* (1992), and *Little Odessa* (1994), for example, were all stories of criminals trying (in various ways and with varying degrees of success) to change—stories of bad guys who can perhaps, like New York itself, find redemption.

Other indies, like Darnell Martin's vibrant, energetic *I Like It Like That* (1994), Leslie Harris's uncommonly intimate *Just Another Girl on the*

*I.R.T.* (1992), and Jim Fall's high-spirited *Trick* (1999) brought diversity into a scene that was, like the mainstream industry around it, dominated by straight white men. And as technology advanced, allowing feature films on rapidly decreasing budgets, more New York indies began to wear their tiny costs as a badge of honor, using their scrappy handheld camerawork, gnarly 16mm photography, stolen locations, and unpolished performances as markers of street cred. Stories of street hustlers, like Nick Gomez's *Laws of Gravity* (1992; budget $38,000) and Matthew Harrison's *Rhythm Thief* (1995, $36,000) went into neighborhoods big movies now ignored, hanging out on ugly street corners and in shabby apartment buildings. Films like *Rhythm Thief* and Darren Aronofsky's *Pi* (1998, $60,000) further separated themselves from slick studio pictures by shooting on high-contrast black-and-white film, an aesthetic choice also embraced by directors Jeffrey Arsenault, Michael Almereyda, and Abel Ferrara for, respectively, *Night Owl* (1993), *Nadja* (1994), and *The Addiction* (1995).

Those three films, all vampire stories, were often grouped with Larry Fessenden's contemporaneous *Habit* (1995) as metaphors for sexual anxieties in the era of AIDS. True enough, but they also seem, at least subconsciously, products of gentrification. All three work from a common assurance that the freaks are still present in The City—they're just hiding during the day, driven underground by the yuppies and trust fund kids whom they pick up at designer watering holes at night and take home to devour.

Yet none of those movies made as much noise as *Kids*. "Wait until they see the movie," Clark confidently told *New York*'s Lynn Hirschberg, a few hours before its midnight premiere at the 1995 Sundance Film Festival. "Then we'll have something to talk about." It exploded out of Park City like a hand grenade. "The screening was, I dunno, three hundred and fifty people, maybe?" Clark says now. "Probably ten thousand people have told me they were there. It's one of those. Incredible."

It debuted with distribution already in place, via Bob and Harvey Weinstein's Miramax Films, the New York–based center of the indie universe. The Weinsteins originally contemplated investing in the film but pulled out at the last minute due to their pending acquisition by the Walt Disney Company, "and they were afraid of Disney," Clark laughs. "But then they came back after I made the film and bought the film—for much more money than it would've cost them to *make* the film."

The Disney connection still presented a problem for the distributors, however, as their distribution agreement with the family entertainment company prohibited the release of NC-17–rated or unrated pictures. And no one who saw *Kids* thought it was going to get an R rating. Harvey Weinstein appealed the MPAA's NC-17 designation anyway— a tried-and-true generator of free publicity—but to no avail, so the brothers personally acquired *Kids* from Miramax, effectively buying it back from themselves, and created a one-off company solely for the purpose of releasing it unrated.

"They created a company called Shining Excalibur, as a goof on Disney, a *Sword in the Stone* kinda thing," Clark says. "But it was really Miramax doing it all."

*Kids* hit theaters in July 1995, to mostly ecstatic reviews. *Variety* called it "an exemplary work of naturalistic cinema," while the *Daily News*'s Jami Bernard put it simpler terms: "*Kids* looks so real that it makes the viewer feel unhinged and skeevy." The *Times*'s Janet Maslin wrote,

"THE REAL MOVIE EVENT OF THE SUMMER."
PETER TRAVERS, *ROLLING STONE*

THE DEBUT FILM FROM LARRY CLARK

AN EXCALIBUR FILMS RELEASE INDEPENDENT PICTURES AND THE GUYS UPSTAIRS PRESENT A FILM BY LARRY CLARK "KIDS"
LEO FITZPATRICK JUSTIN PIERCE CHLOE SEVIGNY CASTING BY ALYSA WISHINGRAD MUSIC SUPERVISOR RANDALL POSTER
PRODUCTION DESIGNER KEVIN THOMPSON COSTUME DESIGNER KIM DRUCE MUSIC COMPOSED BY LOU BARLOW AND JOHN DAVIS
CO-PRODUCER CATHY KONRAD EXECUTIVE PRODUCER GUS VAN SANT EXECUTIVE PRODUCERS MICHAEL CHAMBERS
AND PATRICK PANZARELLA EDITED BY CHRISTOPHER TELLEFSEN DIRECTOR OF PHOTOGRAPHY ERIC EDWARDS
WRITTEN BY HARMONY KORINE CO-PRODUCERS CHRISTINE VACHON AND LAUREN ZALAZNICK
PRODUCED BY CARY WOODS DIRECTED BY LARRY CLARK

READ THE GROVE PRESS BOOK

iNdePendent PictUres

NEW MUSIC BY LOU BARLOW/JOHN DAVIS & DANIEL JOHNSTON·SOUNDTRACK ON

Original theatrical poster
for *Kids* (1995), designed by
Farhan Creative.

"Think of this not as *cinéma vérité* but as a new strain of post-apocalyptic science fiction, using hyperbole to magnify a kernel of terrible, undeniable truth."

Other critics were skeptical. "*Kids* sticks to the visual surface," noted the *Wall Street Journal*. "It's a frightening surface, as rendered by cinematographer Eric Alan Edwards, but it tells us nothing we might like to know about who these kids are in their heart of pitiless hearts." *Film Comment* criticized Clark's "unbearable and disturbingly erotic vision of predatory boys and naïve girls." Other viewers, including those situated in the scene it was ostensibly capturing, accused the film of exaggeration, calling it a *Reefer Madness* for teen sexuality (the *Times* augmented Maslin's rave with four more garment-rending think pieces). According to Ada Calhoun's *St. Marks Is Dead*, "Plenty of locals considered the film absurd—a melodramatic, alarmist representation of what was in fact a more or less harmless community." And perhaps there *was* something worrisomely conservative about a film that garnered the applause of noted scold Brent Bozell, who wrote in the *New York Post*, "*Kids* asserts the paramount importance of traditional family life by depicting, in all its sordidness, what usually happens when children are deprived of it."

Though its rating greatly restricted its spread (at its widest, it played on only 187 screens) and commercial prospects, *Kids* grossed a respectable $7.4 million and found more eyeballs on the less-policed format of VHS. In the aftermath, Clark was offered "all *Kids* rip-offs. I turned down a lot of money." Instead, he proceeded down his own path, with more stories of fringe figures and trailer-park ennui, and reteamed with Leo Fitzpatrick for the 2001 feature *Bully*. Chloë Sevigny and Rosario Dawson used *Kids* to launch lucrative acting careers, moving gracefully from similarly small-scale indies to studio pictures, and back again at will.

Others weren't so lucky. Justin Pierce moved to Los Angeles to pursue an acting career, but he had difficulty harnessing his raw energy and charisma; "Justin would go into auditions drunk and get into fights," Korine said. "Casting directors loved him but they were also scared of him." Five years after *Kids*, he hung himself, though his motivations are foggy—his old co-star Leo Fitzpatrick surmised, "I think Justin was just drunk and made a mistake. And I think we've all been there. Some of us are smart enough to sleep it off and others aren't." Harold Hunter, the skateboard king of Washington Square Park, died of a heart attack following a night of drug use in 2006; he was only thirty-one years old.

Today, *Kids* has become increasingly hard to see, its exhibition and streaming rights mired in the legal complications of the Weinstein empire's destruction in the late 2010s, following revelations of Harvey Weinstein's years of sexual harassment and abuse. But in some ways that's perfect. It *should* be hard to see; it should be a taboo artifact of another era, even if it has, as Sevigny told the *Times* upon its twentieth anniversary, a timeless quality. "It endures because kids love coming-of-age movies," she said. "There's something captivating about rebels, and it's shocking, appalling, titillating."

——

By the end of the 1990s, the long-promised and long-delayed Times Square cleanup was finally complete. It had taken most of the eighties to work through the resistance of (and litigation from) the local landlords; as the nineties dawned, developers had to wait out a recession. When the work was finally done, Giuliani predictably claimed credit, and most observers cheerfully assigned it to him. Detractors

Still images from *The Addiction* (1995), directed by Abel Ferrara, photographed by Ken Kelsch; *I Like It Like That* (1994), directed by Darnell Martin, photographed by Alexander Gruzynski; *Just Another Girl on the I.R.T.* (1992), directed by Leslie Harris, photographed by Eric Sadler; *Night Owl* (1993), directed by Jeffrey Arsenault, photographed by Pierre Clavel, Howard Krupa, and Neil Shapiro.

**ABOVE**
Still image from *Die Hard with a Vengeance* (1995), directed by John McTiernan, photographed by Peter Menzies Jr.

**RIGHT**
Still image from *Men in Black* (1997), directed by Barry Sonnenfeld, photographed by Donald Peterman.

**BELOW**
Still image from *The Paper* (1994), directed by Ron Howard, photographed by John Seale.

**OPPOSITE**
Still image from *The Devil's Advocate* (1997), directed by Taylor Hackford, photographed by Andrzej Bartkowiak.

similarly blamed the mayor for the "Disneyfication" of the district, for its transformation from a bustling, vibrant entertainment center to what historian James Traub dubbed "a corporate-theme-park version of urban life," replacing local arcades and grindhouses with overpriced multiplexes, chain restaurants, and, yes, a Disney Store. It became exactly the sort of tourist midway that Ed Koch had rejected back in the eighties.

Yet "Disneyfication," and its close cousin gentrification, is also oversimplification. "The argument over social control," Traub writes, "was really a debate about who it was that urban spaces like Times Square belonged to—who deserved to be considered its 'authentic' dwellers and users." What's undeniable is that Giuliani and his ilk determined that the only way to make spaces like Times Square, Union Square, Tompkins Square Park, and others "desirable" was to target, via enforcement, those on the margins—though, as Traub also notes, "it is the teenagers who hang out on 42nd Street today who benefit from the new doctrines of social control as much as the tourists from Ohio."

Whatever the logic or methodology, the outcome of the concentrated efforts to commercialize and clean up the district was a kind of amassed identity: Times Square was invaded by a new, twenty-first-century branding and, in effect, became a brand itself, as much as Disneyland, Rodeo Drive, or the Las Vegas Strip. In many ways, the city around the district followed suit.

The successful cleanup and commercialization of Times Square was one of the few noteworthy achievements of Giuliani's second term. It was primarily defined by what biographer Wayne Barrett deemed "pointless wars—with jaywalkers, street vendors, community gardeners, and taxi drivers," as well as his travels around the country, "sporting transparently premature presidential or vice presidential ambitions." Giuliani was haunted by patronage scandals and administrative failures (including a costly attempt to build a new Yankee Stadium on the West Side of Manhattan). He deepened the city's racial fault lines with his fumbling of horrifying cases of police brutality, and of murders of unarmed men of color: the 1994 death of Anthony Baez, choked to

death by an officer for accidentally kicking a football into two patrol cars; the 1997 police attack on Abner Louima, who was sodomized with a stick in a police bathroom; the 1999 killing of Amadou Diallo, who was shot nineteen times by police for the crime of reaching for his wallet. The severity of Giuliani's responses varied, based on how close he was to an election, but he inevitably sided with the police and meted out far harsher criticisms to the citizenry who protested them.

By the middle of Giuliani's second term, tensions in the city were fraught enough to make national news. In an April 1999 feature titled "A Mayor Under Siege," *Newsweek* writers Matt Bai and Gregory Beals reported that the "hard-nosed mayor" had "barricaded himself" inside City Hall, while a thousand people were arrested across the street for protesting Diallo's death. As the crisis raged, police commissioner Howard Safir and his wife jetted off to the Academy Awards as guests of Revlon president George Fellows. "They're personal friends," a spokesperson told the *Times*'s Andrew Jacobs, who noted, "Mr. Giuliani knew about Mr. Safir's visit to Los Angeles, although he did not know the trip included a night at the Oscars."

Around that same time, Giuliani began positioning himself for a run at Daniel Patrick Moynihan's open Senate seat the following year. It was a disaster, falling apart in rather spectacular fashion over two weeks in the spring before the primary, in which Giuliani disclosed that he was fighting prostate cancer and announced that he was separating from his wife (she found out, with the rest of the city, in a press conference) to continue an extramarital relationship. He dropped out of the race in May 2000.

His presumed Democratic opponent, Hillary Clinton, easily won the senatorial election that November. Prohibited by term limits from running for mayor again, Giuliani was left merely to ride out the rest of his term. It seemed unlikely that he would do so with much distinction.

NOW SHOWING

# QUICK CHANGE
# BAD LIEUTENANT
# WALKING AND TALKING

# QUICK CHANGE

## 1990
## Directors: Bill Murray and Howard Franklin

*Quick Change*, co-directed by Bill Murray and screenwriter Howard Franklin (adapting Jay Cronley's novel), subtly captures the end of an era, a hinge from on-screen portrayals of the city as a dirty, scuzzy hellscape into a gentrified urban space. It opens with what seems like a wink to the previous summer's *When Harry Met Sally*, with a picturesque skyline shot accompanied by Nat King Cole crooning "L-O-V-E." But the camera pulls back, revealing that image is merely a subway advertisement; we pan down a long line of miserable commuters, landing on our hero, Grimm (Murray), in clown makeup.

The ensuing sequence seems to set the film up as a comic riff on *Dog Day Afternoon*: On a hot summer day, a bank robber stuffs everyone into a vault and waits for the police negotiator to arrive as a crowd assembles to boo the police and cheer the criminal. His plan is ingenious; the first three hostages released are his accomplices and himself (out of his clown makeup), all with cash strapped to their bodies. The daring bank heist turns out to be the easy part. The hard part is just getting to the goddamn airport.

Along the way, they encounter a mugger, gun-toting yuppies, a cabbie that doesn't speak English, street jousters, a spooky street vendor, an anal-retentive bus driver, clueless city workers, and a wide variety of miserable New Yorkers. That's all fairly typical of how Hollywood saw the city in the era, but Murray and Franklin also captured the first hints of a transition just around the corner. When the gang tries to hide out temporarily in the apartment that Phyllis (Geena Davis) has just left, they discover that her landlord raised the rent from $1,260 per month to $2,600. ("Excuse me, I don't know you very well," says one of the new tenants, "but you must be crazy if you gave this place up!")

More pointedly, in the midst of sorting out the aftermath of the heist, the chief of police (Jason Robards) notices an old building across the way slated for destruction, making way for a gaudy new office complex, and grouses, "Oh my God, now this one's going. Tear 'em down no matter how great they were." In the very next scene, Grimm spies a similar tear-down and rebuild situation, and articulates the same frustration: "Look at this. Why do they have to do this?" These two men may be on opposite sides of the law, and in the midst of perhaps the most stressful situation of their lives. And yet they're bound by two things: They hate the city, and they can't believe anyone is trying to change it.

Still image from *Quick Change* (1990), directed by Bill Murray and Howard Franklin, photographed by Michael Chapman.

The bank robbery was easy.
But getting out of New York was a nightmare.

# BILL MURRAY
# GEENA DAVIS
# RANDY QUAID
# JASON ROBARDS

*Quick* **CHANGE**

A major metropolitan comedy

WARNER BROS. PRESENTS A DEVOTED PRODUCTION  BILL MURRAY · GEENA DAVIS · RANDY QUAID · JASON ROBARDS  QUICK CHANGE
EDITED BY ALAN HEIM, A.C.E.   DIRECTOR OF PHOTOGRAPHY MICHAEL CHAPMAN   MUSIC BY RANDY EDELMAN   EXECUTIVE PRODUCER FREDERIC GOLCHAN   BASED ON THE BOOK BY JAY CRONLEY
SCREENPLAY BY HOWARD FRANKLIN   PRODUCED BY ROBERT GREENHUT AND BILL MURRAY   DIRECTED BY HOWARD FRANKLIN AND BILL MURRAY

# BAD LIEUTENANT

## 1992
## Director: Abel Ferrara

Every addict knows you sometimes have to hit bottom to see how far you've fallen. If the New York story of the 1990s was one of cleanup and recovery, that's the story being told in that era's movies, and if one movie represents hitting bottom, it's Abel Ferrara's grimy 1992 story of sin (and sin, and sin) and redemption.

The titular NYPD detective—played by Harvey Keitel, and never referred to by anything other than his title—seems to lead a life of suburban domesticity typical of a mid-grade NYC cop, running his kids to school and dismissing their excuses for their lateness. But there's an edge to his impatience, its source quickly revealed; he can barely wait for them to get out of his car before stealing a couple of toots of cocaine in front of their school.

Over the scenes that follow, Ferrara and co-writer Zoë Lund dramatize a catalogue of bad behavior that forms into something like a reign of terror: booze, drugs, prostitutes, racism, harassment, brutality, theft, gambling. Ferrara's camera tends to keep him at a distance—even *he* seems afraid of getting too close to this scumbag. We've seen bad behavior from burnt-out New York cops before, but nothing like this; this is a guy who wakes up in a church pew after sleeping one off and pulls out a bottle for a little hair of the dog. He thinks himself destructible ("I been dodgin' fuckin' bullets since I was 14," he brags to his bookie), and acts accordingly.

But then something shakes him. A nun is gang-raped in her church (this element is drawn from a real crime in Spanish Harlem in 1982; Bo Dietl, the detective who apprehended the suspects, appears briefly in the film), and the Lieutenant is assigned to the case. But the victim won't tell him who did it, because she's already forgiven them. A lapsed Catholic, our protagonist is reminded that anyone can be forgiven. Even those guys. Even him.

Keitel, one of the quintessential New York actors, delivers his most searing performance, reveling in the character's bad behavior, pursuing his compulsions with single-minded abandon. His bellowing plea for forgiveness, a primal scream at the altar of the crime, is as raw and unguarded a moment as an actor could hope for.

It is, against all odds, a moment of redemption—and catharsis, much needed in a film that starts bleak and somehow gets bleaker, from the beginning of the picture to its bitter end, when the Lieutenant's massive gambling debt finally catches up to him. He's gunned down in his car near Port Authority, in front of a giant banner advertising Donald Trump's Trump Plaza Hotel and Casino. A headshot of Bill Cosby looks on. IT ALL HAPPENS HERE, the banner promises.

Still image from *Bad Lieutenant* (1992), directed by Abel Ferrara, photographed by Ken Kelsh.

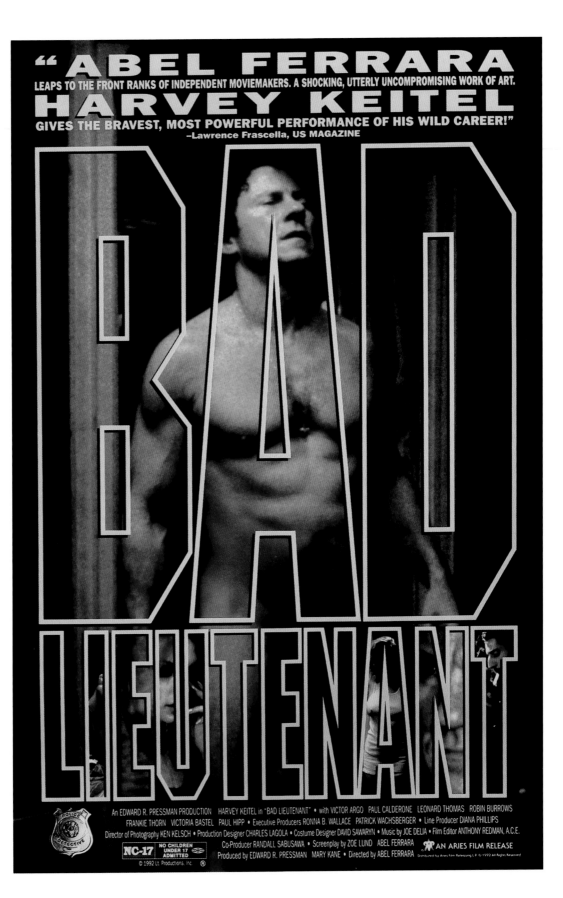

# WALKING AND TALKING

## 1996

## Director: Nicole Holofcener

When we look back at the history of New York independent moviemaking, Claudia Weill's *Girlfriends* starts to look like the Velvet Underground of the movement—the NYC indie corollary to Brian Eno's comment that the band might not have sold many records, but everyone who bought one started a band. One of the most direct successors to Weill's film was this 1996 comedy/drama from first-time writer/director Nicole Holofcener; it, too, tells the story of two long-time friends whose relationship (temporarily) hits the skids when one gets married and the other gets abandoned.

Alongside *Girlfriends*, the other key influence on the film, which tells the story of two longtime friends whose relationship hits the skids when one gets married, was Woody Allen, and not by accident; first-time writer/director Nicole Holofcener's stepfather, Charles H. Joffe, was one of Allen's longtime producers, and she would eventually work

on his films as an extra, production assistant, and apprentice editor. (In turn, *Walking and Talking*'s editor, Alisa Lepselter, would become Allen's, cutting all of his films from 1999's *Sweet and Lowdown* onward.)

"When I wrote the movie I was single and related to the Catherine Keener character," Holofcener said. "But by the time we shot it I was married, so I kind of became the Anne Heche character. I think it inevitably helped the film that I got to be in both characters' shoes."

Holofcener spent years making the script sharper and richer, and imbuing it with uniquely NYC experiences: picnics in the park, weekend road trips to "the country," Laura's little almost-fling with a handsome young waiter/actor (including the unfortunate experience of sitting through one of his terrible plays), and Amelia's awkward courtship with the neighborhood video store guy and would-be screenwriter, who takes her to gross-out horror movies ("Can I talk you into *Freak Show 7*? There's a late show") and fan conventions—but is himself writing a script based on the life of nineteenth-century French writer Colette.

Though *Walking and Talking* was not initially a commercial success ("Miramax opened the film at the same time the company was releasing *Emma*. Let's just put it this way: There was not a lot of focus on *Walking and Talking*"), but it would find its audience on home video, and allow her to continue making sharp-witted, funny comedy/dramas centered on women. She would return to New York for 2010's *Please Give*, with her frequent collaborator Keener as an upper-class Upper West Sider trying to be a good, giving person in an economically polarized city.

**OPPOSITEE**
Still image from
*Walking and Talking*
(1996), directed by Nicole
Holofcener, photographed
by Michael Spiller.

# 2001

# 9/11, Recovery, and *25th Hour*

# 2010

**At 5:45 a.m. on the morning of Tuesday, September 11, 2001, two men checked in at Portland International Jetport in Portland, Maine, for a brief commuter flight to Logan International Airport in Boston. An hour later, they arrived at their destination, where three other men joined them before boarding American Airlines Flight 11, bound for Los Angeles, California. Elsewhere in the airport, five more men cleared security with tickets for United Airlines Flight 175, also bound for Los Angeles.**

At 7:24 a.m., another team of men boarded United Airlines Flight 93, departing Newark International Airport for San Francisco. Five minutes later, at Dulles International Airport near Washington D.C., a fourth team boarded American Airlines Flight 77, bound for Los Angeles.

At 7:59 a.m., American Flight 11 lifted off in Boston. Fifteen minutes later, as United 175 departed Boston, Flight 11 was hijacked. The plane veered from its flight plan and headed toward New York. Approximately thirty minutes later, as that plane approached lower Manhattan, United Flight 175 was also hijacked and re-routed toward New York City.

At 8:46 a.m., Flight 11 struck the north tower of the World Trade Center, crashing into the 93rd through 99th floors, igniting over twenty thousand gallons of jet fuel, and rendering stairwells above the impact zone impassable. CNN interrupted its broadcast with "a very disturbing live shot . . . we have unconfirmed reports this morning that a plane has crashed into one of the towers of the World Trade Center." A few minutes later, as firemen began ascending stairwell C of the north tower, hijackers overtook American Flight 77, diverting its route back east, toward Washington D.C.

At 9:03 a.m., Flight 175 crashed into the south tower of the World Trade Center, eliminating any hope that the crash seventeen minutes earlier had been an accident. Firefighters escorted workers down the stairs of both towers before climbing back up to help more survivors. Debris rained into the streets of lower Manhattan. Phone lines were jammed. The 911 system was overwhelmed. Men and women trapped on upper floors frantically called their loved ones. Some, unable to bear the heat and smoke, leapt through the windows to their deaths.

At 9:37 a.m., American Flight 77 crashed into the Pentagon.

At 9:50 a.m., the south tower of the World Trade Center collapsed.

At 10:03 a.m., United Flight 93 crashed into a field in Somerset County, Pennsylvania.

At 10:28 a.m., the north tower of the World Trade Center collapsed.

Nearly three thousand people were killed in the 9/11 attacks, most of them in New York City: civilians working in the World Trade Center; passengers and flight crew in the airplanes; firefighters, police officers, and EMTs in the towers and on the ground. It was the most devastating act of terrorism in the country's history, and most people watched as it happened, live on television. The images they saw, of urban destruction and buildings afire, were familiar from disaster and action cinema, echoing scenes from *The Towering Inferno* and *Die Hard* and *Armageddon*.

Everyone kept saying it was like something out of a movie.

———

Spike Lee was not in New York City on September 11—a rarity, for a filmmaker who lived and worked in the city and had for his entire life. "I was in Los Angeles," he recalled, "and I was up early because it was my son Jackson's first day at school. I called to wish him luck because he was going to be away from Mommy and Daddy. Tonya [Lee's wife] told me to turn on the TV."

When Lee burst onto the scene with his 1986 independent smash, *She's Gotta Have It*, most of the writing around him homed in on his

9/11, Recovery, and *25th Hour*

Still images from *Summer of Sam* (1999), directed by Spike Lee, photographed by Ellen Kuras; *Clockers* (1996), directed by Spike Lee, photographed by Malik Hassan Sayeed; *Mo' Better Blues* (1990), directed by Spike Lee, photographed by Ernest R. Dickerson; *Jungle Fever* (1991), directed by Spike Lee, photographed by Ernest R. Dickerson.

importance as an African American filmmaker—and for good reason. "Everybody talks about it now, but it was much easier and clearer to point out then that identity politics was a huge thing in movies," explains John Pierson, an investor and producer's rep for Lee's debut feature, which "really found a black audience that was not being served—even blaxploitation films were pretty much over by then. So there was nothing."

Perhaps, however, because of his outsized influence among African American filmmakers—and the controversies that would eventually engender—Lee's importance as a New York filmmaker was often undervalued. Yet he stands alongside Scorsese, Lumet, and Allen as one of the key chroniclers of contemporary Gotham; when the towers fell, he had already directed ten feature films set in The City, from contemporaneous snapshots (*Do the Right Thing*, *Jungle Fever*, *Clockers*) to portraits of the past (*Crooklyn* and *Summer of Sam*, the latter of which opens and closes with columnist Jimmy Breslin announcing, "There are eight million stories in the Naked City—this was one of them").

Some of *She's Gotta Have It*'s admirers compared Lee to Allen, but in a shallow, surface way: Both were bespectacled New Yorkers making New York movies in which they frequently appeared (also, both were die-hard Knicks fans). Lee resisted the comparison, Pierson says, but "on the other hand, *yeah, I want to make films every year, like Woody Allen*. So he had a decade's worth of stories that were pretty much coming out straight from his gut. Straight from his heart."

And his heart was moved by what he saw happening in his city, both from afar and when he returned (after a three-day train ride—all air travel had been shut down). "New York City is so amazing, and sometimes you think the rest of the United States is like it, but it's not," Lee said. "People outside NYC view it as not even part of America, that it's Babylon. . . . This gap was definitely shortened after September 11. There was a lot of love for New York City that was not felt before: At that time everybody was a New Yorker."

At first, the city—and the country—ground to a halt. All major league baseball games were cancelled, for the first time since D-Day. Broadway shows were paused; tourist attractions were locked up. The Staten Island Ferry was out of service for several days. There were rumors of more threats: of bombs in schools, of more planes in the air. But quickly, and without any particular direction to do so, New Yorkers came to each other's aid. It began during the evacuation, in which an estimated twenty-five thousand people helped each other out of the towers in an orderly, safe fashion. When the clouds of debris from the fallen buildings filled lower Manhattan, survivors picked each other up and moved through the ashes together. A makeshift armada of tugboats, yachts, and water taxis began evacuating people from the edge of the island. Several blocks away, volunteers took up hammers to build wooden stretchers. Around the city, and the country, people went to donate blood, the lines stretching and winding for blocks.

Down at the former site of the towers—an area quickly dubbed "Ground Zero" by those watching it, and "The Pile" by those working it—volunteers assembled and did what they could. Some began the dirty business of cleanup, removing debris and human remains. Some came to provide food for those workers, some to provide physical support, or moral support, or prayers. "The desire to help was overwhelming for a great many people," Rebecca Solnit writes in *A Paradise Built in Hell*, "and because the attacks were perceived as an attack on the nation, not

**288**

**ABOVE**
Two men help an injured
woman evacuate the area of
the World Trade Center.

**RIGHT**
Three nuns visit a wall of
makeshift missing person
notices after 9/11

**BELOW**
Rescue workers amid
the debris.

on the city, and because the media covered everything about them exhaustively, the convergence and contributions were on an unprecedented scale."

There was a feeling of calm and camaraderie after the chaos—a sense of solidarity and spirit, articulated by Mayor Giuliani in an address to the city (and the world) that night, that New York City would not only survive but thrive, greater than ever. Television news hunkered down into commercial-free, nonstop coverage mode, framing the day's events as "America Under Attack," and filling their frames with flapping-flag motifs. Flag sales swiftly spiked around the country; Walmart sold 116,000 American flags on 9/11 and 250,000 on 9/12.

But around New York, the response was more complex than this kind of unfettered patriotism would allow. On walls around the city, those stars and stripes were adornments for makeshift bulletin boards filled with flyers seeking loved ones who hadn't made it home who presumably hadn't made it out of the towers. Union Square became a public forum, where the citizenry met to share information, sing, argue, comfort, pray. "Overnight," philosopher Marshall Berman wrote, it "became the kind of thriving agora it was said to have been a hundred years ago."

"One of the hoariest clichés," Clyde Haberman wrote in the *Times* on September 16, "is that hard times bring out the best in New Yorkers, whose hometown did not achieve international greatness by being witless and docile in adversity. The thing about clichés is that they are usually rooted in essential truth." The theaters and museums reopened; the trains and planes and ferries began running again. Slowly, life in New York City returned to something resembling normal.

---

The history and symbolism of the twin towers was complicated. The headline- and TV news banner-friendly "Attack on America" framing was perhaps damagingly simplistic: The terrorists had not attacked "America," but its symbols of financial and military power. (Some might say those ideas are one and the same, but that's another discussion.) The World Trade Center had barely existed for more than a quarter of a century; before that, other buildings in lower Manhattan had fallen, mostly shops and markets, to make way for it.

The complex opened on April 4, 1973, something like a billion dollars over budget and five years over schedule. It was the brainchild of the banker (and brother of the governor) David Rockefeller, an attempt to transform this retail and warehouse district into a business center— and, in doing so, to save the economy of lower Manhattan, which had been dying with the closing of the ports and the migration of companies to Midtown (or out of the city altogether). Much as the Empire State Building had inexplicably risen just after the crash of the stock market, the twin towers, this symbol of luxury and capitalism, was erected just as the city was tumbling into a recession. City leaders tried to use the striking, tall pillars at the tip of the island as an oversized logo for the city's recovery, but its managers had trouble filling the offices inside (a problem they couldn't lick until the financial boom of the 1980s).

And the towers were not particularly loved by the city beneath them. Architecture critic Lewis Mumford described them as "a characteristic example of the purposeless giantism and technological exhibitionism that are now eviscerating the living tissue of every great city." Filmmakers didn't really know what to make of them. They were as ubiquitous in city establishing shots as they were in the skyline itself, but aside from a handful of memorable appearances—in the climax of the 1976 *King Kong* remake, as part of the Emerald City in *The Wiz*; as Snake Plissken's landing strip in *Escape from New York*—the simple, block-like design of the buildings didn't do much for the visual medium. (*Times* critic Vincent Canby objected to the *Kong* remake moving its action downtown, because "the World Trade Center is a very boring piece of architecture. The Empire State Building is not.") And thus the towers rarely played a pivotal role in New York cinema, aside from simply being present. They're most striking in early-seventies films like *Klute, Godspell*, and *The Hot Rock*—when they're still under construction.

Or when they're being destroyed. As the seventies disaster movie came back into vogue in the 1990s, effects-heavy blockbusters like *Independence Day* and *Armageddon* rained fire and death down on the urban skyline. These were the images rattling around the collective consciousness when people talked about how September 11 was like a movie—that those nineteen men had hijacked those visual ideas of terror as surely as they'd hijacked the four airplanes. And, as writer Jenny Kijowski notes, "they did so in a way that would be most appealing for visual consumption by a culture that understands and respects spectacle above all else."

In the immediate aftermath of 9/11, filmmakers did their best to erase such clear visual connections. *Kissing Jessica Stein* had premiered, to great acclaim, at the Toronto International Film Festival on September 10; co-writer and co-star Jennifer Westfeldt was at a screening of another film when the towers were hit. "They didn't stop the movie," she recalls, "and we got out, and everything felt really weird. I had something like forty-three messages on my cell phone, no service, and I couldn't hear the messages." Their triumphant Toronto tour became "just a big sob festival in the hotel room," and once they'd processed what had happened in their hometown, another concern arose.

"Of course, we had gloriously beautiful shots of the skyline and the towers all over the movie," she says. "I didn't go to see the second screening, but everyone said there were just, like, audible gasps every time there was a shot of the skyline." This visceral response led the team—after "a very, very long, in-depth conversation" among themselves and with other filmmakers—to remove and replace those images.

**ABOVE**
Still images from *The Hot Rock* (1972), directed by Peter Yates, photographed by Edward R. Brown; *King Kong* (1976), directed by John Guillermin, photographed by Richard H. Kline; *Escape from New York* (1981), directed by John Carpenter, photographed by Dean Cundey.

**BELOW**
Still image from *Klute* (1971), directed by Alan J. Pakula, photographed by Gordon Willis.

9/11, Recovery, and *25th Hour*

**CLOCKWISE FROM ABOVE**
Still images from *When Harry Met Sally* (1989), directed by Rob Reiner, photographed by Barry Sonnenfeld; *Superman* (1978), directed by Richard Donner, photographed by Geoffrey Unsworth; *Die Hard with a Vengeance* (1995), directed by John McTiernan, photographed by Peter Menzies Jr.; *Saturday Night Fever* (1977), directed by John Badham, photographed by Ralf D. Bode.

"Our movie was coming out in March," Westfeldt says. "We just determined that it was too raw and too painful, especially in this genre where we were trying to spread some joy."

They weren't the only ones to arrive at that conclusion. The makers of *Zoolander, Serendipity, Stuart Little 2,* and *People I Know,* among others, chose to digitally remove the towers from the New York skyline, or edit out shots in which they appeared. The climax of 2002's *Men in Black II,* originally set in the World Trade Center complex, was reshot. A teaser trailer for the following summer's *Spider-Man,* in which the hero captures a helicopter in a web spun between the towers, was hastily pulled from theaters, as were posters in which they were seen in a reflection of the city skyline. A similar Photoshop job was performed on the art for Edward Burns's rom-com *Sidewalks of New York,* though the film's low budget made alterations or reshoots impossible; the twin towers loom large in the background of several direct-to-camera "interview" scenes.

Some filmmakers went the other way. *Entertainment Weekly* reported that when the towers flashed across a background of the Michael Douglas thriller *Don't Say a Word,* out later in September, the audience at a Times Square preview screening cheered. Cameron Crowe elected to leave the towers intact in the fantasy version of New York seen in the background of the climax of his *Vanilla Sky,* out that December. And when Martin Scorsese ended his *Gangs of New York* (released in December 2002) with a series of images of the New York skyline sprouting through the ages, he ended with the World Trade Center intact.

Still images from *The Siege* (1998), directed by Edward Zwick, photographed by Roger Deakins.

But the general consensus was that audiences were seeking to escape the horrors of the moment, not to be reminded of them. Similarly, in the days after the attacks, some video stores placed warning stickers on recent releases with unfortunate connotations and connections. One of the most frequently mentioned of these potentially triggering titles was Edward Zwick's *The Siege*, released three years earlier, yet eerily prescient of not only the attacks of September 11, but also the reactions to them. Denzel Washington stars as an FBI agent, Anthony Hubbard, investigating a radical terror cell in Brooklyn with the help of Elise Kraft (Annette Bening), a mysterious CIA operative. Called to a hostage situation on a New York City bus, Kraft notes the news helicopters overhead and observes, "They're not here to negotiate. They were waiting for the cameras. They want everybody watching." And with that, the bus explodes, showering the street with glass, paper, ash, and debris. There is another bombing, at a Broadway theater, and then a third, in which a van full of explosives drives through Manhattan and into the lobby of One Federal Plaza, reducing that building to a giant pile uncanny and uncomfortable in its resemblance to Ground Zero.

"We're not the first city to have to deal with terrorism," Hubbard insists. "This is New York City. We can take it." He acknowledges the cooperation of Muslim leaders, who "love this country as much as we do," but nevertheless instructs his agents to "turn the heat up" at community centers and among student organizations, just as surveillance activities would spike at mosques and among New York's Muslim communities in the months and years after 9/11. In the aftermath of these acts of terror, according to a TV news report, "Retail sales are down 27%. Hate crimes have skyrocketed. . . . Once busy streets are eerily silent as many people have fled."

*The Siege* eventually progresses into a worst-case scenario as martial law is declared in Brooklyn; tanks roll down the streets, soldiers conduct house-to-house searches, and a Muslim internment camp is set up in Downing Stadium. "We intend to seal off this borough," announces General William Deveraux (Bruce Willis) as the twin towers loom behind him, "and we intend to squeeze it." But when that squeeze escalates to torture of a suspect, Hubbard raises his voice. "What if what they really want is for us to herd our children into stadiums, like we're doing?" he asks. "And put soldiers on the streets and have Americans looking over their shoulders? Bend the law? Shred the Constitution just a little bit? Because if we torture him, General, we do that, and everything we have fought and bled and died for is *over*." It's a powerful speech, potently delivered by one of our most passionate actors. In the years that followed, as the Bush administration went to "the Dark Side" to mount its War on Terror, similar sentiments were either not articulated in the intelligence community or not heeded.

Lawrence Wright, one of the film's screenwriters, would later pen the Pulitzer Prize–winning book *The Looming Tower: Al-Qaeda and the Road to 9/11*; while promoting that book, he would claim that in the days after the attacks, *The Siege* was the most rented movie in America. Other films would attempt to address those events more directly, including rapid-response documentaries like *9/11*, *WTC: The First 24 Hours*, *Seven Days in September*, and *Underground Zero*. (In the following years, these films would be supplemented by low-budget, tinfoil-hat conspiracy theory documentaries contesting the official account of events, like *9/11: In Plane Site*, *Painful Deceptions*, and the *Godfather* of the subgrenre, *Loose Change*.) Producer Alain Brigand assembled an omnibus film titled *11'09"01: September 11*, in which eleven directors from eleven countries each crafted a short film within

**ABOVE**
Mayor Giuliani at Ground
Zero with Secretary of
Defense Donald Rumseld,
November 2001.

**RIGHT**
Edward Norton, Rosario
Dawson, and director
Spike Lee in rehearsal for
*25th Hour*.

two parameters: that it run 11 minutes, 9 seconds, and one frame, and that it in some way speak to the events of that day. The film's admirable inclusion of a diversity of voices and perspectives brought some welcome complexity to the conversation around the attacks. Or, as *Variety* put it, "Several of the segments are stridently anti-American."

Such sentiments would be carefully avoided in studio productions. A month after the attacks, a group of roughly forty entertainment executives met with representatives of the Bush administration. The *New York Times*'s Jim Rutenberg reported discussions of "incorporating antiterrorism themes into television shows and movies, making documentaries about newly urgent matters like the threat of anthrax and producing pro-American television and radio programs for foreign audiences." Just as studios (and marquee filmmakers) offered up their services as the country entered World War II, Rutenberg quoted Leslie Moonves, then president of CBS Television, as telling the administration's reps, "Tell us what to do. We don't fly jet planes, but there are skill sets that can be put to use here."

A month later, more of the "Hollywood power elite" met with Karl Rove, Bush's top advisor and strategist, at the Beverly Peninsula Hotel "to explore how the entertainment industry can assist the Administration's war on terrorism," according to the *Nation*'s Marc Cooper. The meeting was co-hosted by Paramount's Sherry Lansing and Viacom's Jonathan Dolgen, "two stalwarts of Liberal Hollywood." Rove insisted he was not there to give marching orders, but merely to brief execs on the messages that the White House wished to stress, including "This is a global war that needs a global response," "Americans should support the troops," and "This is a war against evil." Luckily for Rove, several war movies were already in the can and slated for release in the coming months, and as Guy Westwell notes in his book, *Parallel Lines*, the films *Behind Enemy Lines* (November), *Black Hawk Down* (December), and *We Were Soldiers* (March 2002) "aligned neatly with Rove's directive and served to discursively amplify the dominant ideological response to 9/11: a nationalist call to arms."

Spike Lee's response, thankfully, would be more nuanced. His next film was already in the works before the attacks: a film adaptation of David Benioff's New York–set novel *The 25th Hour*, published in 2000. According to Benioff, actor Tobey Maguire had optioned the book with the intention of playing the leading role. Benioff—who would later co-create and co-run HBO's smash adaptation of the *Game of Thrones* books—penned the script himself. "I was really scared that some guy who had never been to Brooklyn before was going to write the screenplay," he explained. "Then I was scared that they would get a director who had only been to New York once and stayed at the Four Seasons."

By the time the script made its way to Lee, Maguire had been cast in Sam Raimi's big-budget *Spider-Man* movie, so he demurred from starring (but remained on board as a producer). The project was acquired by Disney subsidiary Touchstone, where Lee had made his last two features, so he was sent the script at the same time as actor Edward Norton. "We had expressed an interest in working together over the years," Lee said, "and Disney said, 'If you want to do it, we'll do it too.'" Lee's production company, 40 Acres and Mule, began working toward shooting in the city in early 2002. And then 9/11 happened.

Lee didn't hesitate. "In shooting a film like this in New York City," he explained, "so close to what happened on 9/11, in being responsible filmmakers we *had* to reflect that in the film. Ed Norton and I both felt that we could comment on post-9/11 New York City." It was not a motivation, but it was a bonus, he stressed: "9/11 was not the reason that I decided to make *25th Hour*. I didn't make it to show the pain of New York City, because you have to tell the story. The backdrop of 9/11 was something that we felt could help tell the story."

Norton was excited by Lee's approach, which he described as "We're not gonna ignore this, we're gonna weave it into the fabric. . . . Lots of movies get made and lots of movies float past, but I feel like the ones that stick, stick because they have a time stamp on them. They have an imprint of the moment that people were living in." Touchstone was willing to

approve the experiment—as long as Lee kept the budget to a low $15 million.

The low budget meant a "down and dirty" thirty-seven-day shoot, so Lee scheduled two weeks of all-day rehearsals at the 40 Acres office in Fort Greene. After work was done for the day, Lee would screen key New York movies as reference points, including *On the Waterfront* ("for the morality element"), *Dead End* (hence a reference in the film to its ensemble, the "Dead End Kids"), and *Midnight Cowboy* for, according to Norton, "that sense of floating through New York in the night, the textures of it." When *Midnight Cowboy* finished unspooling, the cast and crew sat for a moment in silence before Lee leapt from his seat, proclaiming, "Still a motherfucker!"

Before other events intervened, the biggest story of September 11, 2001, in New York was the mayoral primary. As the morning unfolded, the primaries were rescheduled for two weeks later. (In light of the tragedy, the term-limited Giuliani had proposed extending his administration by three months, but lawmakers at the state level blocked the idea, and Giuliani backed off of his threat to run for another term as a third-party candidate.)

After the second primary and a runoff, the Democrats nominated NYC public advocate Mark J. Green. His Republican opponent was Michael Bloomberg, a Massachusetts-born investment banker who made his fortune developing the "Bloomberg Terminal," a computer software system providing real-time financial data. He used that wealth to become a media mogul and philanthropist. The pendulum of city politics being what they were, it seemed safe to bet that voters would embrace a more traditional Democratic candidate. Even Bloomberg, who had never held a political office, didn't think he would win—and he barely did, by only thirty thousand votes.

Bloomberg resolved to run the city less like a government and more like a business and filled his administration with other businessmen. One of them, Deputy Mayor Daniel Doctoroff, explained their philosophy thus: "Government has a critical role to play in creating markets where they don't otherwise function, but the role of government should be limited to the minimum amount necessary to enable the markets to function effectively." Or, as the *New York Observer*'s Greg Sargent put it, "he would subject the city government to the same sort of treatment that chainsaw-wielding CEOs bring to bloated corporations," vowing to cut his staff by 20 percent and asking other government offices to do the same.

A month later, Bloomberg gave a major speech in lower Manhattan, outlining his agenda for economic development and recovery. "We will change our orientation toward business," he announced, as though the Koch and Giuliani administrations hadn't been aggressively business-friendly. "The city will think of its job-creating, tax-paying employers, big and small, as valued clients."

His administration's first priority was downtown flight; vacancy rates in lower Manhattan had reached an astonishing 45 percent in the months after 9/11. Luckily, Bloomberg had a promise of $20 billion in financial assistance from the federal government, some of which would be used to incentivize businesses and residents to remain or return to the area. The Lower Manhattan Development Corporation was set up to distribute those funds.

Some New Yorkers—real and fictional—hadn't gone anywhere. "Tell ya what," says Frank Slaughtery (Barry Pepper) in *25th Hour*, "Bin Laden can drop another one next door, I ain't movin'." That scene, in which he and schoolteacher Jacob Elinsky (Philip Seymour Hoffman) discuss the state of lower Manhattan from Frank's apartment overlooking "The Pile," was one of three major adjustments Lee and Benioff made to the film in the fall of 2001.

The primary narrative remained the same, telling the story of white-collar drug dealer Monty Brogan (Norton) and his last twenty-four hours of freedom before traveling upstate to begin a lengthy prison sentence. He attempts to make amends with his father (Brian Cox), a former firefighter, now a Brooklyn bar proprietor; he struggles with the unfortunate suspicion that his girlfriend Naturelle (*Kids* discovery Rosario Dawson) may have dropped the dime on him; and he goes out for a night on the town with Naturelle and his childhood pals Frank and Jacob, the latter of whom bumps into a student (Anna Paquin) for whom he harbors a decidedly unprofessional attraction.

For Jacob and Frank's window scene, Lee told his production designer to "find me a location that overlooks Ground Zero." They wound up in an office dressed as an apartment; Hoffman and Pepper performed their scene in a long two-shot as real workers raked through the rubble below, still searching for human remains. In one of the scene's more chilling moments, Jacob warns his friend, "The *New York Times* says the air is bad down there," to which Frank responds, "Oh yeah? Well, fuck the *Times*. I read the *Post*. The EPA says it's fine." The Bush administration had edited those EPA reports, and Giuliani helped disseminate the propaganda. In the years that followed, tens of thousands of rescue workers and civilians would seek medical help for "Trade Center cough," lung disease, and worse.

Another adjustment was made, more extemporaneously, during production. From March 11 through April 14, 2002, an installation of eighty-eight searchlights, replicating and extending the fallen towers, was placed at Ground Zero as a "Tribute of Light" to those lost on the day. Lee called the powers that be and asked for permission to photograph the lights for the film's opening credit sequence and was enthusiastically welcomed. It's a haunting, magnificent sequence, beginning with obliquely photographed, almost-abstract shafts of light,

the true nature of their presence and placement slowly revealed as the frames and compositions grow wider and wider, finally revealing the iconic New York City skyline, but with light in absence of those structures. The nature of the tribute is never explained in dialogue—it doesn't need to be—but these beautiful tableaus, and their ethereal musical accompaniment, are a powerful substitute for the now-familiar images of towers falling, New Yorkers fleeing, and smoke filling the streets.

The final, key addition came in the middle of Monty's Last Supper with his father, in which he excuses himself to the bathroom, catches a look at himself in the mirror (and a "FUCK YOU" scrawled upon it), and embarks on a long, angry, racist diatribe against his city and everyone in it. It's a key moment in the novel, and much of it is translated verbatim (though a line encouraging "the Arabs" to "bomb it all to rubble" was understandably softened), though Benioff's original screenplay didn't include the scene. Lee discovered it when he read the book after the script and asked the writer why it was gone. "I said I just couldn't figure out how anyone could shoot it and make it dramatic," Benioff recalled, to which Lee replied, "That's *my* job!"

Lee certainly had practice—the scene explicitly recalls the sequence of racially charged, direct-to-camera insults in *Do the Right Thing*. Monty turns the "FUCK YOU" on the mirror into a chance to insult the squeegee men, Pakistani and Sikh cabbies, gays, Korean grocers, Russian mobsters, Hassids, Wall Street brokers ("Michael Douglas, Gordon Gekko wannabee motherfuckers"), Puerto Ricans, Dominicans, Bensonhurst Italians, Upper East Side wives, "uptown brothers" on courts, corrupt cops (complete with side mentions of Diallo and Louima), Catholic priests, Bin Laden, and Al-Qaeda ("You towel-headed camel jockeys can kiss my royal Irish ass"). But then it gets more personal as he calls out his friends, then his girlfriend, then his dad, then his city ("Let the earthquakes crumble it"), and then, finally, himself. "No, no, fuck you, Montgomery Brogan," he seethes. "You had it all, and you threw it all away, you *dumb fuck*."

But Lee doesn't just stare at Monty as he stares at himself; he takes his camera out into the streets of the city, with stylized images of those faces, some bellowing, some suspicious, some scheming. And yet the faces he's pummeled with hate return at the end of the film as Monty's

Still images from *25th Hour* (2002), directed by Spike Lee, photographed by Rodriego Prieto.

father drives out of town, and this time they're smiling, warm, wishing him well, saying goodbye not with vindictiveness, but forgiveness. "When you get to the end of the film," Norton says, "you see that all of these same things, all of this tapestry of the things that he hates, are the things that he loves about the city." They are no longer the images of a people split apart; they are the faces of a city trying, not without difficulty, to come together.

Those faces appear as Monty's father, approaching the George Washington Bridge on the West Side Highway, offers up an escape, an off-ramp to an alternate future to the one at the end of this road. He can drive him west, away from the city, away from his punishment, away from his obligation, to a tiny town in the middle of nowhere, the opposite of New York City, where he can disappear. He can live and work anonymously, and never come back—though maybe Naturelle will come out some day so that they can watch the ball drop in Times Square in their tiny apartment, where they'll start their family and live their new lives. And one day, maybe they'll tell their children and grandchildren the real story, once it's all in the past; maybe they'll tell them, his father proposes, how "it all came so close to never happening. This life came so close to never happening."

It's a classic Hollywood ending—and a New York ending, because it proposes, all evidence to the contrary, that the future is not predetermined and that the possibilities are endless. Monty considers those possibilities, but his dad does not take the turn, because to do so would be a betrayal of what came before. Lee and Benioff are telling a story of contemplation, reflection, and guilt; throughout the film, in both his flashbacks to the past and his reckonings with his present, Monty Brogan is trying to take stock of his life and atone for his sins. And many Americans took 9/11 and the days after to measure what it truly means to be an American and a New Yorker. "9/11 is the twenty-fourth hour implied by the title," writes Guy Westwell. "The twenty-fifth hour is what comes after, which Lee's film tells us looks a lot like prison."

▬

In addition to restoring the city's economy and physical presence, Bloomberg's administration had a much tougher, less tangible goal:

Still images from *25th Hour* (2002), directed by Spike Lee, photographed by Rodriego Prieto.

repair the damage done to the city's image. "We are all New Yorkers" platitudes were easy; it was another thing to actually visit the city, which now seemed, to the outside world, not only broken but also a target. Tourism dropped by 25 percent.

Producers and directors were among those fleeing. When the Mayor's Office of Film, Theatre & Broadcasting crunched the data for 2001, it discovered the number of feature films shot in the city had declined by 14 percent, and the total number of shooting days were the lowest they'd been since 1994. "Quite frankly, we're afraid to shoot in New York these days," an anonymous Los Angeles producer told the *Hollywood Reporter* in December, while Sony Pictures Classics executive Tom Bernard told the *New York Post*, "It's down with movies going to Canada and to Europe. If they do come to New York, they only come for a week or two, just enough to do coverage and move on." That sounded familiar.

It was also a matter of economics. Shooting in the city had always been more expensive; now penny-pinching producers had even more reasons to go north with the 1998 enactment of a production services tax credit in Canada, along with additional subsidies in individual provinces. In the wake of the attacks, New York papers ran multiple features reminding their readers (and the filmmakers among them) of the great New York movies, and the Museum of Modern Art mounted an elaborate series of them, called "Wonderful Town." But production remained sluggish. When Katherine Oliver, the commissioner of the Mayor's Office, traveled to Los Angeles in the summer of 2002 to meet with studio heads, "many of them told me that when they got a script with New York in it, they would send it back and say, 'Change the city.'"

──

"We were very careful how we were going to portray Sept. 11 because we know it's still very painful and that it will always be very painful for those who lost people," Lee told the *New York Times*, as *25th Hour* neared its release date. "But at the same time, we couldn't stick our heads in the sand and pretend like it never happened." Some contemporaneous reviewers seemed to wish he had; A. O. Scott's otherwise positive *New York Times* review, for example, deemed the film's 9/11 evocations "a little jarring" and "at times . . . obtrusive."

But in the *Nation*, Stuart Klawans seemed to get what Lee was going for. "These images contribute nothing to the story, and in the best way possible," he wrote. "They don't raise Monty's situation to the world-historical level; they don't teach him that his problems are really very small; and they sure as hell don't turn into metaphors. These are facts, as arbitrary as they are painful, which Monty lives with just because they're present, and which Lee put into the movie for the same reason."

Even the positive notices—and there were plenty—couldn't get the picture in front of audiences. Disney fumbled the release, hurrying it into five theaters just before Christmas in hopes of making it an awards contender, somehow not realizing that those favorites had already been selected at the fall festivals they'd missed. "You can't take a little movie like this and slip it out in the last week of December and expect it to punch into that equation," Norton said. When the buzz and nominations didn't materialize, neither did the marketing push the filmmakers were expecting in the spring. *25th Hour* never played more than five hundred screens, and its domestic gross didn't even cover its budget. "They weren't trying to bury it," Lee insisted, but at a certain point, Disney simply cut its losses. Or maybe, Lee said, shrugging, people "were still kinda iffy about New York and 9/11."

It's also instructive to compare the release and grosses of *25th Hour* with the movie Tobey Maguire left it to make. Sam Raimi's *Spider-Man* opened on more than 3,500 screens in May 2002, and pulled in $114 million that weekend *alone*; it would go on to gross more than $400 million domestically and another $400 million–plus worldwide. Much of that was thanks to the character's familiarity and a savvy marketing campaign. But it's also impossible to separate the success of *Spider-Man*, and the tsunami of superhero mega-movies that followed, from the trauma the country had just suffered. In the wake of 9/11, moviegoers weren't interested in morally complicated protagonists, like a sympathetic drug dealer. They were looking for good guys beating bad guys, and the simpler each of those roles was played, the better.

But *Spider-Man* (like many of the superhero films that followed) wasn't just filling a vague, general psychological need; there are scenes that not only speak to the aftermath of 9/11, but also seem to be a response to the event itself. The "World Unity Festival" sequence, with the Green Goblin buzzing the buildings of Times Square, was shot before September. But it's hard to overstate the impact for audiences—especially New York audiences—looking for a summer popcorn movie and finding a set piece centered on a terror attack on a New York landmark. *This* time, however, there is a hero there to foil it, and even to save a falling victim before she lands on the sidewalk. (Five years later, Bryan Singer's *Superman Returns* would also implicitly quote 9/11, in a sequence where our hero prevents a commercial airliner from crashing into a packed baseball stadium.)

Other scenes, shot and inserted after the attacks (and you can tell), crassly and rather nakedly exploited the sentiments of the city, of which Spider-Man/Peter Parker had always been a stated resident (as opposed to Batman's NYC-styled Gotham or Superman's Metropolis). In one, a carefully curated cross-section of "typical" New Yorkers saves Spidey from the Goblin, and taunts him afterward with such on-the-nose

proclamations as "This is New York!" and "You mess with one of us, you mess with all of us!" In the film's final shot, after Spidey flies through downtown New York on a series of slung webs, he lands and perches atop a flagpole flying Old Glory.

As the decade continued, many a spectacle-minded filmmaker would mine the residue of 9/11 to build their own apocalyptic visions—some more thoughtfully than others. When Steven Spielberg's contemporary, New Jersey–set take on *War of the Worlds* landed in theaters in the summer of 2005, the filmmaker acknowledged that its renderings of clouds of dust, fleeing crowds, and missing-person posters were drawn from the images of 9/11 "that I haven't been able to get out of my head." Drew Goddard's *Cloverfield* (2008) told its story of alien invasion in Manhattan solely through the lens of a consumer camcorder—much as 9/11 had been so strikingly captured on the fly by amateur videographers, and then repurposed in post-2001 documentaries. And Francis Lawrence's *I Am Legend* (2007) imagined (at great expense and inconvenience to residents) an abandoned, post-apocalyptic island of Manhattan. But such visions often failed to elicit a response in New York; the *New York Observer*'s Dale Peck reported titters at urban destruction at the New York premiere of *The Day After Tomorrow* (2004), "a reminder that New Yorkers, living under the continually implied threat of actual destruction, no longer seem to invest much in mocked-up cinematographic fantasies of that end."

Some films would deal more directly with the attacks and their aftermath. Aside from Paul Greengrass's *United 93* and Oliver Stone's *World Trade Center* (both 2006)—after-the-fact dramatizations of September 11 that focused narrowly on acts of heroism and survival— a small cycle of "therapy films" like *The Guys* (2003), *Reign Over Me* (2007), and *Extremely Loud and Incredibly Close* (2011) dealt specifically with the psychological fallout of the event on those left behind, forgoing the political and social implications to focus on personal

EDWARD NORTON

A Spike Lee
Joint
25th hour

Can you change your whole life in a day?

Original theatrical poster,
*25th Hour.*

healing. (*The Guys*, first written and performed as a play mere weeks after the attacks, is a two-hander about a writer helping a fire captain pen several eulogies for his fallen men; it is, in a sense, an instant reaction about instant reactions.) Even Nora Ephron's *Julie & Julia* (2009) falls into this grouping; its contemporary heroine works for the Lower Manhattan Development Corporation, and embarks on her ambitious cooking project as a coping mechanism for days spent on the phone with crying and/or angry survivors and families.

Other New York–set films of the following years, while dealing with unrelated tragedies and traumas, could not help but take on the weight of the attacks. Jane Campion's *In the Cut* (2003)—like *25th Hour*, a film based on a book published before 9/11 but shot in the city after—opens with images of New York accompanied by a jarring, almost atonal rendition of "Que Sera, Sera"; at its conclusion, a substance uncomfortably similar to ash rains down from the sky. (It is, we discover, a "petal storm.") The narrative concerns a serial killer, but the gory grisliness of his murders takes on a darker edge; *In the Cut* seems a film made with an awareness of the unstoppable onset of darkness, infected by the horrors of daily life, the sheer *weight* required simply to move through this city.

The heroine of Kenneth Lonergan's *Margaret* (shot in 2006, though not released until 2011) walks with a similarly heavy foot and soul, particularly after she too is confronted by death in the streets. A pedestrian is killed in a bus accident; curious passersby stumble upon a gory scene, her blood spewing on Good Samaritans like a fountain. Lisa (Anna Paquin, in a role not far removed from *25th Hour*) finds herself turned inside out by the death and her proximity to it.

The most conflicted—at times, baffling—of these films is Neil Jordan's *The Brave One* (2007). On its surface, it plays as a modernized, gender-swapped *Death Wish* riff, with Jodie Foster as a thoughtful public radio host who documents "stories of a city that is disappearing before our eyes." But when her lover is murdered (and she is badly beaten) in a mugging, and she finds the cops ineffective and unfeeling, she heads to the gun shop and starts popping scum in the streets.

Aside from the callbacks to Foster's other films (she gets her first taste for blood in a bodega shooting, just as Travis Bickle did) and troubling politics (she's mostly terrorized by people of color), *The Brave One* is noteworthy for how explicitly it references real, racially charged crimes in the city's history. The inciting crime occurs in Central Park, perpetrated by a group of young men uncomfortably similar to the (innocent but wrongly convicted) Central Park Five; her second and third victims are a pair of young African American men on a subway car whom she shoots point-blank, Bernie Goetz–style.

But beyond those unsettling echoes, *The Brave One* captures a seemingly quintessential New Yorker living in fear, traumatized by the very sounds she used to find such a comfort. "New York is the safest big city in the world. But it is horrible to fear the place you once loved," she tells her audience. "I always believed that fear belonged to other people. Weaker people. It never touched me. And then it did."

The low-budget *Keane* (2004) treads similar territory. It opens with a visibly shaken man at the ticket window of Port Authority, asking for help: "I bought some tickets from you last September. The twelfth." On that day, he says, while waiting for a bus, his six-year-old daughter was

Still images from *Spider-Man* (2002), directed by Sam Raimi, photographed by Don Burgess.

9/11, Recovery, and *25th Hour*

**CLOCKWISE FROM TOP LEFT**
9/11 restaged in *Extremely Loud and Incredibly Close* (2011, directed by Stephen Daldry, photographed by Chris Menges); a post-apocalyptic Manhattan envisioned by *I Am Legend* (2007, directed by Francis Lawrence, photographed by Andrew Lesnie); 9/11 invocations in *War of the Worlds* (2005, directed by Steven Spielberg, photographed by Janusz Kaminski) and *Cloverfield* (2008, directed by Matt Reeves, photographed by Michael Bonvillain).

abducted—though the more time we spend with him, the more plausible it seems that this incident (or the daughter herself) was imagined. Nonetheless, director Lodge Kerrigan follows the man as he wanders through the Port Authority and the surrounding streets, calling for his daughter in desperation and begging strangers for help.

He walks some of the same streets as the unnamed suicide bomber at the center of Julia Loktev's *Day Night Day Night* (2006), who walks through Times Square with a backpack full of explosives and orders to detonate them. Loktev, like Kerrigan, shot her film guerilla-style, on consumer video cameras, placing her character among real tourists and New Yorkers in this urban center. The film is deeply unnerving because it's so present—we're at least subconsciously aware that she's in the midst of all of these real people, and that she really could have anything in that bag, and they have no idea. These characters' proximity to the "real" New York is a quiet reminder that while the days after 9/11 saw New Yorkers looking at each other with renewed empathy, that feeling was also often coupled with fresh suspicion.

There was plenty of that to go around in the summer of 2004, when President Bush and his party took over Madison Square Garden for the Republican National Convention. It was not a smooth fit; the streets were swarmed with protests against the wars the president had launched, with the attacks in New York and Washington D.C. as justification, in Afghanistan and Iraq. Aside from those organized demonstrations, the *Times* reported harassment of delegates returning to their Times Square hotels or heading out for a night at the theater.

Former mayor Koch implored New Yorkers to "be nice" to their visitors, while Mayor Bloomberg—still a member of the Republican Party, though that would shift with the winds in the years to come—offered buttons and shopping discounts to peaceful protestors. The following year, he would cruise easily into a second term; as Ben Smith noted in the *Observer*, "Not since Ed Koch's victory on both Democratic and Republican lines in 1981 has a mayor emerged from an election with no coherent opposition." (Earlier that year, fiery young Democratic congressman Anthony Weiner was weighing a run at the office, but he elected to wait.)

Bloomberg was a rich mayor, governing an increasingly rich city. Taxi fares increased, for the first time in eight years, while rents and real estate continued to skyrocket. Average annual income for the island of Manhattan reached $92,000—the highest in the country. "As a city, New York is no longer upper-middle-class," wrote Choire Sicha. "It's über-middle-class, and the shifting of the ground under our feet is just beginning to register."

From the beginning of his first administration, Bloomberg had encouraged companies to look to the boroughs for more space. Middle-class residents were doing the same, flocking to areas like Astoria or Jamaica in Queens, Williamsburg in Brooklyn, and Riverdale in the Bronx, where their dollars could stretch across more square footage. Artists and hipsters were gentrifying Brooklyn neighborhoods like Flatbush, Bushwick, and Greenpoint, while the areas that had done the same the previous decade—like Fort Greene and Park Slope— became the comparatively stolid status quo.

Out of that economic environment came a burgeoning Brooklyn indie film scene, most prominently seen in so-called mumblecore movies like Andrew Bujalski's *Funny Ha Ha* (2002) and *Mutual Appreciation* (2005), and Aaron Katz's *Quiet City* (2007). Those films, and other outliers like

Eric Eason's Washington Heights–set *Manito* (2002), were in many ways reminiscent of the No Wave films of the late seventies and early eighties: low-budget and unpolished, often amateurishly produced and acted, yet undeniably authentic. They feel lived-in and overheard, their intimacy heightened by their handheld photography and off-the-cuff style. And if the minimal production value gives them a home-movie feel, they also showcase filmmakers admirably grasping and using whatever tools they could find to tell their stories. Peter Sollett's Lower East Side coming-of-age drama *Raising Victor Vargas* (2002) was a bit more polished, but similarly insular; its specific landscape, of housing projects and public pools, becomes so self-contained that the occasional exterior shots, of the distant skyline or a passing train, are almost jarring.

Increasingly, these outlying areas were where "New York stories" were being told. A 2005 *New York Sun* headline asked why "they don't make movies about Midtown anymore," but the short answer was that Midtown was boring. The movies set in those neighborhoods were, increasingly, fluffy wish-fulfillment romantic comedies like *Maid in Manhattan* and *Two Weeks Notice*; Manhattan-set movies became just as gentrified as the land itself. James Gray, a Flushing-born filmmaker with a Lumet-ian sensibility, had to set his New York stories in Queens (*The Yards*, 2000) or Brooklyn (*Two Lovers,* 2008). Years later, in *The Immigrant*, he would finally tell a story set in Manhattan—but he had to place it in the 1920s.

That said, location shooting was finally back on the upswing. The Mayor's Office had initiated a series of short-term initiatives to further simplify production in the city post-9/11, and to make big asks happen (like an extended shutdown of the Brooklyn Bridge for *Stay*, or a shoot in the United Nations building—a first—for *The Interpreter*). But Mayor Bloomberg knew it was going to take money to get filming back up to speed, and in January 2005, he offered it. His ambitious "Made in NY" incentive program supplemented the state's 10 percent tax credit with an additional 5 percent credit on qualified expenses. On some projects, that meant it was cheaper to shoot in Manhattan than in Canada.

The program was wildly successful—so much so that within a year and a half of the credit's introduction, the Mayor's Office ran out of money and had to boost the program's budget. By that point, in mid-2006, shooting days in the city were more than double their 2002 levels. Films that weren't even set in New York City were produced there; the most notable was native son Martin Scorsese, who dressed New York as Boston for his 2006 Oscar winner, *The Departed*.

The robust financial health of the city and its citizens would shift in 2008. The financial meltdown, like those of 1929 and 1987, was long in coming, the result of a failure in the housing market and (once again) shady manipulations on Wall Street. The mayor of New York publicly entertained speculation that he might join the next presidential administration as an expert administrator, or even secretary of the treasury. But he would ultimately decide to thwart the will of voters—who had twice, post-Koch, approved term-limit referendums—and push a reversal of term limits through the City Council. The mayor felt he, and only he, had the financial expertise necessary to lead the city through the crisis.

Voters agreed, begrudgingly. His victory, over city comptroller William J. Thompson, was far slimmer than in 2005, considering the $100 million of his own fortune he spent on the campaign (Thompson spent roughly one-tenth of that). He quickly went to work on the $4.1 billion deficit in

the next city budget, promising to reduce spending via the usual methods: cuts to school budgets, child care, parks and playgrounds, and personnel.

Other stories would capture New Yorkers' interest in the years after 9/11: the pyramid scheme of self-proclaimed financial wizard Bernard Madoff, who lost billions for his clients; the fall of crusading attorney general turned governor Eliot Spitzer, caught in a prostitution sting; the Hudson River landing of US Airways flight 1549 with Captain Chesley B. Sullenberger III at the controls, with not one life lost; the galvanizing election of Barack Obama.

In other words, the city was back to normal. In an October 2001 *Times* article, Michelle O'Donnell wondered what exactly that would mean. "I think there's a distinction between the city psychologically mourning and the people mourning who lost someone close to them," Kenneth T. Jackson, the historian and president of the New-York Historical Society, told her. "Their mourning may take forever, but the city will eventually recover."

In the summer of 2005, the Manhattan community board approved the proposal for Park51, a 92nd Street Y–style Muslim community center two blocks north of the WTC site. Its opponents, including campaigning politicians and families of those killed in the attacks, dubbed it the "Ground Zero Mosque" or the "Victory Mosque." The project's developer ultimately bowed to pressure and cancelled plans for the center. He instead used the land to build a luxury condominium building.

The brutal, politicized public discourse surrounding the site was perhaps the strongest indication that the post-9/11 version of the city had vanished. To be fair, those days and weeks had been somewhat romanticized—there were plenty of examples of hate speech and hate crimes against Muslims and people of Middle Eastern descent, in the city and elsewhere—and in the Obama era, conservative figures like Glenn Beck would attempt to appropriate that vision of "9/12" for their own utopian ideals.

In light of all that murkiness, *25th Hour*—which has since claimed its rightful place among Lee's finest works—stands as an even more valuable simulacrum of the city. "This film is not a documentary, but it really documents the feelings of New Yorkers, the city, and how New York City was post-9/11," he said. "The city took a big blow, we were down, but we bounced back—because New Yorkers are like that. We have our differences, but when certain things happen, we're all gonna get together and say, 'Fuck that. We're coming together, and we're gonna do what we're gonna do.' And 9/11 was a great demonstration of the beauty and the heart of New Yorkers." That it was—but it also demonstrated the ability of New York filmmakers to capture a fleeting moment. That skill would prove even more essential, in this ever-shifting city, in the years to come.

**CLOCKWISE FROM TOP**
Still images from *Margaret* (2011), directed by Kenneth Lonergan, photographed by Ryszard Lenczewski; *In the Cut* (2003), directed by Jane Campion, photographed by Dion Beebe; *Keane* (2004), directed by Lodge Kerrigan, photographed by John Foster; *Day Night Day Night* (2006), directed by Julia Loktev, photographed by Benoît Debie.

NOW SHOWING

# VANILLA SKY

# ETERNAL SUNSHINE
# OF THE SPOTLESS MIND

# MAN PUSH CART

# VANILLA SKY

## 2001

### Director: Cameron Crowe

Cameron Crowe is a West Coast director—his first two films, *Say Anything* and *Singles*, were set and shot in Seattle, while his *Jerry Maguire* and *Almost Famous* were set primarily in California. So *Vanilla Sky* falls into the rich tradition of outsiders taking it all in—clearly enjoying the city, its look, and its very specific energy, and crafting their film under its spell.

For Crowe, that also meant creating one of the most memorably haunting New York City sequences of the era. *Vanilla Sky* (based on Alejandro Amenábar's 1997 Spanish film *Abre los ojos*) opens with an eerie dream sequence, in which a wealthy publisher (Tom Cruise) wakes and drives down Central Park West to his office—but is first confused and then baffled by the emptiness of the streets. It's 9:15 in the morning, but there isn't a car or another person in sight, near the park or on any of the side streets. So he goes to the one place where there are always people: Times Square. And it, too, is completely, creepily empty.

That scene—in which Cruise pulls into the abandoned area, parks his car, looks around, and runs down Seventh Avenue in a panic—was done entirely practically, without the assistance of digital effects. As Lieutenant John Battista, the former commanding officer of the NYPD's Movie-TV unit, explained to *Scenes from the City* author James Sanders, when the filmmakers asked to shoot in an emptied-out Times Square for six daylight hours, they were all but laughed out of the room. But one of the film's producers was Cruise himself, who has a way of getting people to do the impossible.

So Battista staked out Times Square on a Saturday night, and discovered that from the time the bars emptied at four a.m. until about six a.m., "it was pretty much a ghost town." So he told Cruise, "You'll come in on Saturday night at one o'clock in the morning and you'll prep cameras and the roadway, and then once first light hits on Sunday you'll have to be ready to go." He estimated they'd have an hour to an hour and a half to get the scene—and sure enough, one Saturday in November 2000, Tom Cruise was running through an empty Times Square at five o'clock in the morning, traffic and pedestrians held at bay by fifty cops. They got the scene in less than two hours.

"Well, I suppose the empty street meant loneliness," shrugs Kurt Russell, as Cruise's court-appointed psychiatrist. The psychological thriller that follows probably could have been set in any number of cities (as evidenced by its origin), and another setting might have even saved some discomfort for its original audiences—there was something a little unnerving about a December 2001 release that ends with a man swan-diving off of a New York skyscraper. But in setting his remake where he did, and opening it in such a spectacular way, Crowe made the most memorable cinematic use of Times Square since its dirty old days.

Still image from *Vanilla Sky* (2001), directed by Cameron Crowe, photographed by John Toll.

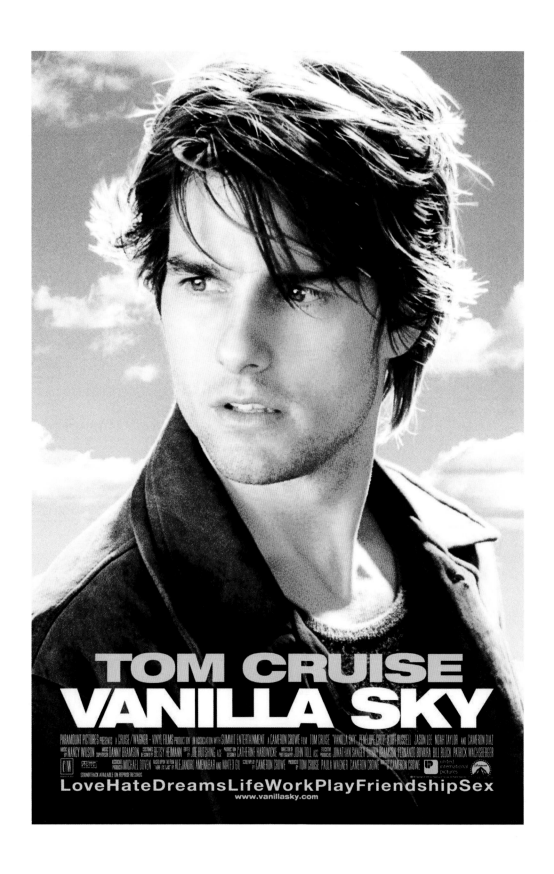

# ETERNAL SUNSHINE OF THE SPOTLESS MIND

## 2004

### Director: Michel Gondry

Joel (Jim Carrey) and Clementine (Kate Winslet), the protagonists of director Michel Gondry and screenwriter Charlie Kaufman's mind-bending sci-fi romance, live in Rockville Centre, located about 30 miles east of New York City in Nassau County. But scenes from the film were also shot in Yonkers and Brooklyn, and mixed in with more recognizable spots in Manhattan, including Chinatown, Grand Central Station, and 34th Street near Madison Square Garden (where they watch the arrival of the Ringling Brothers elephants, an unplanned scene grabbed on the fly). As a result, this story seems set in a peculiarly, purposely vague near New York.

This kind of topographical indecision is often distracting in other films; in this one, it seems all of a piece with the narrative. *Eternal Sunshine*'s inciting actions take place at Lacuna, Inc., a NYC-based company that specializes in memory erasure—usually of the romantic kind, allowing former partners to entirely eradicate their memories of relationships gone bad. Joel discovers Clementine has had him erased, so he goes to Lacuna to do the same; much of the film's running time is concerned with "the procedure," as Joel wanders through his memories of Clementine, from their most recent meeting to their first, as those remembrances fall out of his consciousness.

So, in a way, spatial disorientation is part of the process. Early on, in fact, Gondry stages a sequence in which Joel attempts to follow a fleeing, angry Clementine, and the geography quite literally scrambles around him—every time he turns around, the street has shifted, replacing the block as he saw it with a new corner or strange building.

*Eternal Sunshine* was conceived before September 11th but written and shot after, and its effect on the film is subtle yet undeniable. Disorientation in a familiar place was certainly rampant after 9/11. But more importantly, the idea of literally erasing bad memories—forgetting the bad thing entirely, and thus removing a crippling, daily trauma—must have seemed like an appealing fantasy to some viewers.

Still image from *Eternal Sunshine of the Spotless Mind* (2004), directed by Michel Gondry, photographed by Ellen Kuras.

# MAN PUSH CART

## 2005

### Director: Ramin Bahrani

Some of the best New York movies, for New Yorkers, are those that take a fact of daily urban life and explain how it works. (It's part, for example, of what makes the opening scenes of *The Taking of Pelham One Two Three* so fascinating; many of the protocols of those old trains are still in use today.) Iranian American director Ramin Bahrani, a native of North Carolina, attended Columbia University in New York City, and was interested enough in the stainless-steel push carts, where the city's business and working class buy coffee and pastries on their morning commutes, to make a film about one of the men inside them.

A fair amount of *Man Push Cart*'s slender running time is spent merely observing the logistics of how this work is done. Each morning, long before dawn, Pakistani immigrant Ahmad (Ahmad Razvi) picks up his cart from the garage where the carts are stored and walks it down the busy streets of Manhattan. (The name of these carts, and thus the title of the movie, is a misnomer; they are never pushed, but pulled.) He sets up in his designated sidewalk spot, brewing the coffee, carefully arranging the donuts and bagels for display. When the morning rush has passed, he walks it back from where he came, and spends the rest of the day hustling bootleg DVDs and picking up whatever

work he can. Eventually he makes his way back to his tiny apartment in Brooklyn; sometimes he catches a nap on the train. As night turns into day, he does the whole thing again.

Bahrani drew inspiration from Albert Camus's *The Myth of Sisyphus*, and just as that man spends every day pushing a rock up a hill that he will have to push up again the next day, Ahmad spends every day pulling his cart through the streets, back and forth and back again. Bahrani underscores this slog with recurring urban motifs—the cart weaving through traffic, bags going into the back of trash trucks, workers hosing down sidewalks. (As so many New York filmmakers had before him, Bahrani often shot with a concealed camera, to better capture the rhythms of these streets—and since his tiny budget wouldn't allow staging scenes with extras.) Ahmad's routine is observed with an almost Bressonian passiveness; Roger Ebert, one of the film's champions, compared Bahrani's style to Italian neorealism.

But there's something equally pressing and timely about his film. It is, above all, an immigrant story, capturing the loneliness of this existence, and the feeling, when one finds another immigrant, that merely coming from the same place is an immediate and important connection. Ahmad befriends an affluent Pakistani businessman, who hires him to do some handyman work around his sleek apartment before recognizing Ahmad as a successful musician back home. "What are you *doing*, man?" he asks. "My friend and I used to listen to your CD all the time!"

Everyone comes from somewhere, the film gently reminds us, and everyone has a story. The tragedies of 2001 don't make their way into *Man Push Cart*, not explicitly. But at one point, a secondary character tells a story of being stabbed and nearly killed by three strangers who called him a terrorist, and it's a quiet, potent reminder that it was both important and bold to make a movie this humanistic, and this empathetic, to Middle Eastern immigrants at that particular historical moment.

Still image from *Man Push Cart* (2005), directed by Ramin Bahrani, photographed by Michael Simmonds.

# 2011

# Wealth, Bohemia, and *Frances Ha*

# 2020

**PREVIOUS SPREAD**
Greta Gerwig and Mickey
Sumner in a publicity shot
for *Frances Ha* (2012).

**ABOVE**
Greta Gerwig in a publicity
shot for *Frances Ha* (2012).

**OPPOSITE**
Noah Baumbach, in produc-

"I know the city so well, and I've spent most of my life here," Noah Baumbach explained, while promoting the release of *Frances Ha* (2012). "So I'm drawn to it, and I think I get a lot of ideas from the city. If I'm shooting on a street that I have memories of, there's always something extra about just showing up to work every day, even if there's no literal connection to the scene I'm shooting."

Baumbach was raised in a Brooklyn intellectual family; his parents were film critics and novelists. He worked as a messenger for the *New Yorker* before writing for its "Shouts and Murmurs" section; he studied English at Vassar, and his time there (and immediately after) inspired his debut feature, *Kicking and Screaming* (1995). That film, though set at an unnamed East Coast university, was shot in Los Angeles; his sophomore effort, *Mr. Jealousy* (1997), was his first New York production. He spent the next eight years writing screenplays with Wes Anderson and going to therapy, and his next directorial effort, *The Squid and the Whale* (a semi-autobiographical reflection of his parents' divorce), was the result of both. It was nominated for an Oscar for Best Original Screenplay.

His next feature, *Margot at the Wedding*, wasn't as well received; critics complained that it was too sour and cynical. His next screenplay was of a similar spirit, the story of a cranky New Yorker on an extended visit to Los Angeles, where he does not feel at home. Ben Stiller was cast in the title role in *Greenberg*, and Baumbach set about auditioning actors for the role of Florence, the romantic interest. And that was how he met Greta Gerwig.

Gerwig, a native of Sacramento, California, came to New York to attend Barnard, where she studied acting and playwriting. Her cinema education came from Kim's Video on St. Mark's, where she rented armloads of foreign and independent movies; after her mind was thoroughly blown by Claire Denis's *Beau Travail*, she realized that directing was something she could, and should, do. But after failing to land in any MFA programs for playwriting, she focused on acting, becoming the go-to ingénue of the "mumblecore" movement, acting for Joe Swanberg (*Hannah Takes the Stairs,* 2007) and the Duplass Brothers (*Baghead,* 2008), among others.

Most of those films were improvised, which Gerwig assumed was why Baumbach put her through so many auditions: "There was a little bit of 'Do you *know* what you're doing? Can you do this in a controlled way, or are you just some weird person who has no shame?'" But she stole the movie and captivated its director. "Greta has old studio-system chops," he said. "Carole Lombard, Katharine Hepburn, they could be in something totally dramatic, or totally funny; they could sing, they could dance."

Nearly every reviewer singled out Gerwig as the highlight of *Greenberg*, but the film itself never found an audience. Baumbach next attempted to adapt Jonathan Franzen's *The Corrections* into an HBO series; the network passed, and the costly endeavor left the filmmaker feeling unsatisfied. He wanted to bounce back with something simple and enjoyable.

So he sent Greta Gerwig an email. There was something "authorial" about her acting, he wrote. He wanted to make another movie with her, and thought maybe they could write it together.

---

"Not since NYC was the movie capital of the world—that'd be between 1894 and 1917—has so much filming been done here," wrote the *New York Post*'s Reed Tucker in the fall of 2011. "Last year, some 200 films were made in Gotham and this television season, a whopping 23 primetime series are being filmed here. That's a record, and a change from previous decades when even the exterior shot used for Seinfeld's 'Upper West Side' apartment was a building in LA."

Much of this activity was thanks to the ongoing production tax credits—$420 million a year by the early 2010s, according to the

Still images from *Frances Ha* (2012), directed by Noah Baumbach, photographed by Sam Levy.

Scenes from the city in the 2010s, from *2 Days in New York* (2012), directed by Julie Delpy, photographed by Lubomir Bakchev; *How to Be Single* (2016), directed by Christian Ditter, photographed by Christian Rein; *Skate Kitchen* (2018), directed by Crystal Moselle, photographed by Shabier Kirchner; *Birdman or (The Unexplained Virtue of Ignorance)* (2014), directed by Alejandro G. Iñárritu, photographed by Emmanuel Lubezki.

*New York Daily News*—but in the post-9/11 years, attitudes across the country had shifted. The East Coast freak show was now, strangely, seen as part of the nebulous, mostly rhetorical "real America." Tourism continued to boom, boosted by Mayor Bloomberg and his tax-exempt corporation NYC & Company, which invested considerable financial resources toward a goal of luring fifty million tourists per year to Gotham by 2015, and hit it four years early.

But by the 2010s, what exactly were they visiting? "Present-day New York has been made to attract people who didn't like New York," noted essayist Fran Lebowitz. "That's how we get a zillion tourists here, especially American tourists, who never liked New York. Now they like New York. What does that mean? Does that mean they've suddenly become much more sophisticated? No. It means that New York has become more like the places they come from." A reverse white flight was in full swing (urbanist Richey Piiparinen dubbed it "white infill"), in which the children and grandchildren of those who had fled to the suburbs in the seventies and eighties moved to the city for the adventure their elders had abandoned, but demanded the comforts of their suburbs when they got there.

And thus, as the twenty-first century continued, New York City's discount stores, coffee shops, pizzerias, diners, and restaurants were replaced by Target, Starbucks, Papa John's, IHOP, and Chick-fil-A. (When the evangelical chicken chain opened in 2015, customers lined up in the rain overnight. One of them, a twenty-four-year-old Georgia transplant, told the *New York Post*, "I have been waiting for this for a year and a half now, since I came to New York.") Union Square boasts The Strand and its "18 miles of books," but those intimidated by its high shelves and surly clerks can retreat to the Barnes & Noble across the way. In Times Square, steps from the authentic Italian food of restaurant row, tourists and transplants fill the tables of a three-story Olive Garden. "America has gotten its revenge on New York," Lebowitz said, "because it's moved right in. Now it is a mall."

And not many great movies are set in malls. But in the Bloomberg era, the city (and its stories) had been all but devoured by the ultra-wealthy—so The City reflected on-screen, in contemporary cinema, didn't just feel like a different era from the New York of earlier decades. It felt like another continent. A drab, flavorless one.

▬

Baumbach had very clear ideas about *how* he wanted to make his next movie: low-budget, shooting on digital video, with a small crew, guerilla-style. But he wasn't sure what it was *about*. "I just had more general ideas that it would be something in New York and something in black and white and something with Greta," he says. "But I suppose I had an instinct, to kind of involve her in the process of coming up with what it was going to be."

Gerwig was flattered by the offer, but only to a point; when he told her it was going to be "very stripped down, bare-bones," she says, "I think part of it was, he was like, 'You're cheap, right?'" She was also intimidated, sitting on the list she composed of ideas for characters and scenes ("three pages of stuff") for days before sending it back to Baumbach. "He said, 'This looks pretty great,' and he started adding ideas, and then this document just started growing and that became the script."

That script told the story of Frances (Gerwig), a young dancer who finds herself set adrift when Sophie (Mickey Sumner), her roommate and

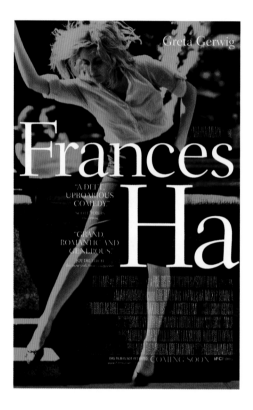

black and white," Baumbach says. "He was sort of bringing a grand, cinematic gesture to a thing that was kind of intimate, story-wise. It was intimate and interpersonal, and he was sort of telling it in a big way." The combination of returning to the city after the LA-set *Greenberg* and shooting, for the first time, in black and white "allowed me to see the city in a fresh way."

The visual romanticism was also baked into the experience of the writers. "I'm from Brooklyn, she's from Sacramento, and we both saw the city as a place that we might one day come to if we were able," he told the *A.V. Club.* "I always saw Manhattan as a place that maybe one day I'd be able to live. The joke on me is that now that I live in Manhattan, everyone's moving to Brooklyn."

Moving weighs heavily on *Frances Ha*, as it does for New Yorkers in general, and its impact is articulated by the picture's ingenious structure: The chapters of Frances's adventure are organized not by numbers or titles, but by the various addresses where she finds herself residing. "It was anthropologically right," Baumbach explains, "but it was also thematically right because it was about movement—sort of perpetual movement where you're not really going anywhere, or maybe lateral movement."

Finding affordable housing was, to put it mildly, not a problem unique to their protagonist. Throughout the decade, the already pressing housing crisis in the city worsened; after a brief dip following the recession, rents continued to soar, the vacancy rate remained low, and landlords found new ways to deregulate rent-regulated apartments. Supply simply couldn't keep up with demand, at least for those who couldn't afford the luxury apartments the Bloomberg administration was incentivizing; even buildings that provided the token number of (arguably) affordable units required by those tax exemptions and bonuses forced those residents to use a separate entrance, soon dubbed the "poor door."

"Now, to make films about New York, you basically make films about Wall Street," said film critic Amy Taubin. "You make films about bankers. It has become a city, especially in Manhattan and Brooklyn, of extremely wealthy people." Those economic woes, particularly for young artists, make for some of the most relatable moments in Baumbach and Gerwig's *Frances Ha* script: Frances awkwardly asking her boss for more classes to teach; treating a pal to a celebratory dinner when her tax return arrives (only to find herself running to an ATM after the check is delivered at the cash-only restaurant); asking her trust-fund roommates, with some urgency, "Do you know that I'm *actually* poor?"

"I think anyone who's an artist or an actor or a writer or doing anything that's at all difficult or precarious or unlikely that they'll ever be successful at *always* feels very close to the person who's not doing it and who's falling apart," Gerwig says. "It's not that in my *life* I'm so successful and together and then in *movies* I play these crazy people who are falling apart and unsuccessful. It's that the outside narrative of success is not how it feels internally."

But there was also something specific to the time and place, Baumbach said, that made this theme so present. "It's something that I related to in the Frances character, which was this idea of having a fantasy of the city and wanting to have that experience, with the city pushing back," he said. "It goes with the photography of the movie. It was a chance to shoot the city in the most beautiful way possible, while shooting a character who's dealing with the economic realities of living in New York

Wealth, Bohemia, and *Frances Ha*

**BELOW**
Still images from *They Came Together* (2014), directed by David Wain, photographed by Tom Houghton; *Premium Rush* (2012), directed by David Koepp, photographed by Mitchell Amudsen; *The Adjustment Bureau* (2011), directed by George Nolfi, photographed by John Toll; *Time Out of Mind* (2014), directed by Oren Moverman, photographed by Bobby Bukowski.

**OPPOSITE TOP**
Occupy Wall Street takes over Zuccotti Park, September 2011.

**OPPOSITE BOTTOM**
Mayor Bloomberg marches in the 2012 Veteran's Day Parade.

bestie, moves out of their apartment to cohabit with, and eventually marry, her longtime boyfriend. The void left by Sophie's exodus deepens; Frances tries on new friends and new apartments but none of them seem right, and her career isn't going anywhere, and should she even *be* here?

"It felt like a really natural collaboration," Gerwig says. "I didn't ever feel like either one of our voices was compromised in it. Though he's clearly the more accomplished of the two writers, he was never like 'Which one of us has an Academy Award nomination and which one of us doesn't?' Although he could have said that!"

From the beginning, they focused on a few key ideas. *Frances Ha* opens with what looks like a conventional NYC rom-com montage—frolicking in the city, eating al fresca, snuggling on the subway, etc.—but the subjects, Frances and Sophie, aren't romantically intertwined. "When we figured out that the Sophie/Frances relationship was going to be the through-line," Gerwig says, "then we actually went through the script and tried to beat it out like a romantic comedy: She has the girl, that's perfect, she loses the girl, she gets angry, she tries to get the girl back, she tries to make the girl jealous, and she rejects—like, we were trying to actually do that arc within the friendship."

The *New York Times*'s Zach Baron noted the picture's contradictions: "It is a deeply romantic film with no real romance at its center, a love letter to a city that is depicted, at times, as anything but lovable." That contrast was rooted in the film's biggest stylistic influences. "I was thinking of Woody Allen's movies with Gordon Willis, that they did in black and white," Baumbach says. "He was sort of bringing a grand, cinematic gesture to a thing that was kind of intimate, story-wise. It was intimate and interpersonal, and he was sort of telling it in a big way." The combination of returning to the city after the LA-set *Greenberg* and shooting, for the first time, in black and white "allowed me to see the city in a fresh way."

The visual romanticism was also baked into the experience of the writers. "I'm from Brooklyn, she's from Sacramento, and we both saw the city as a place that we might one day come to if we were able," he told the *A.V. Club.* "I always saw Manhattan as a place that maybe one day I'd be able to live. The joke on me is that now that I live in Manhattan, everyone's moving to Brooklyn."

Moving weighs heavily on *Frances Ha*, as it does for New Yorkers in general, and its impact is articulated by the picture's ingenious structure: The chapters of Frances's adventure are organized not by numbers or titles, but by the various addresses where she finds herself residing. "It was anthropologically right," Baumbach explains, "but it was also thematically right because it was about movement—sort of perpetual movement where you're not really going anywhere, or maybe lateral movement."

Finding affordable housing was, to put it mildly, not a problem unique to their protagonist. Throughout the decade, the already pressing housing crisis in the city worsened; after a brief dip following the recession, rents continued to soar, the vacancy rate remained low, and landlords found new ways to deregulate rent-regulated apartments. Supply simply couldn't keep up with demand, at least for those who couldn't afford the luxury apartments the Bloomberg administration was incentivizing; even buildings that provided the token number of (arguably) affordable units required by those tax exemptions and bonuses forced those residents to use a separate entrance, soon dubbed the "poor door."

shooting a character who's dealing with the economic realities of living in New York right now, which are not romantic. You can't live a bohemian life there anymore without money." (Or, as Sophie puts it, "The only people who can afford to be artists in New York are rich.")

New York had seen wealth gaps before. But it was more extreme in this era of widening income inequality and systemic "hyper-gentrification," a term used by Jeremiah Moss in his essential history/protest *Vanishing New York* ("gentrification on speed, shot up with free-market capitalism"). A staggering 21 percent of Manhattan residents were living below the federal threshold for poverty by the time *Frances Ha* hit theaters in 2013. The top 5 percent of households there were earning eighty-eight times as much as the bottom 20 percent. It was, according to Census Bureau data, the greatest dollar income gap of any county in America.

There were protests—most notably, the group that dubbed itself Occupy Wall Street and took over Zuccotti Park in the heart of the financial district in the fall of 2011. They generated headlines and captured conversation for two months, until Mayor Bloomberg sent the NYPD to clear the park in a middle-of-the-night raid, executed like a paramilitary strike (complete with advance, counterterrorism-style "disorder training" and a media blackout). His office claimed "the occupation was coming to pose a health and fire safety hazard to the protestors and to the surrounding community." And the "surrounding community," New Yorkers knew, was always Bloomberg's chief concern.

Baumbach made a unique deal with RT Productions, his financier on *Frances Ha*. "The only thing I guaranteed them was that I wasn't making an experimental movie," he told the *Times*. He didn't show them a script, and he told them that it would be in black and white. That was a key point. "It was such a contemporary subject," he says "and I think the black-and-white kind of brings a sort of nostalgic undercurrent to it. I think it feels both present and past, and old and new. That felt right for it."

They settled on a $3 million budget—much lower than the $25 million *Greenberg*—and he got to work. The project was not announced in the trades; most of the actors didn't see the entire script. (Co-star Michael Zegen recalled approaching the director and star on the set and inquiring, "I don't know if I'm allowed to ask this, but what's this movie about?") Baumbach and Gerwig cast friends and family—Gerwig's mother and father play her character's parents—and shot in real locations—including Gerwig's apartment, which doubles for the Chinatown flat she shares with Benji (Zegen) and Lev (Adam Driver). When he filed his permits with the Mayor's Office, Baumbach used the deliberately misleading title *Untitled Digital Workshop*.

"Baumbach has discovered that elective frugality gives him power," wrote the *New Yorker*'s Ian Parker. "By working with a tiny crew, and by asking people to accept a percentage of the film's earnings rather than up-front fees, he can impersonate Stanley Kubrick: He can afford to keep a production going week after week, revisit material that turned out badly, and fly to Paris to film a six-minute sequence."

He shot a fair amount of the film in Manhattan—albeit in tucked-away areas like Chinatown and Washington Heights—keeping in spirit with the rom-com conventions they were slyly subverting. By that time, the sparkling New York romantic comedy had become a parody of itself; 2014 saw the release of a feature-length, *Airplane!*-style spoof, *They Came Together*, featuring long riffs on the dusty idea that "New York

"Now, to make films about New York, you basically make films about Wall Street," said film critic Amy Taubin. "You make films about bankers. It has become a city, especially in Manhattan and Brooklyn, of extremely wealthy people." Those economic woes, particularly for young artists, make for some of the most relatable moments in Baumbach and Gerwig's *Frances Ha* script: Frances awkwardly asking her boss for more classes to teach; treating a pal to a celebratory dinner when her tax return arrives (only to find herself running to an ATM after the check is delivered at the cash-only restaurant); asking her trust-fund roommates, with some urgency, "Do you know that I'm *actually* poor?"

"I think anyone who's an artist or an actor or a writer or doing anything that's at all difficult or precarious or unlikely that they'll ever be successful at *always* feels very close to the person who's not doing it and who's falling apart," Gerwig says. "It's not that in my *life* I'm so successful and together and then in *movies* I play these crazy people who are falling apart and unsuccessful. It's that the outside narrative of success is not how it feels internally."

But there was also something specific to the time and place, Baumbach said, that made this theme so present. "It's something that I related to in the Frances character, which was this idea of having a fantasy of the city and wanting to have that experience, with the city pushing back," he said. "It goes with the photography of the movie. It was a chance to shoot the city in the most beautiful way possible, while

LEFT
Still image from *Heaven Knows What* (2014), directed by Josh and Benny Safdie, photographed by Sean Price Williams.

BELOW
Still image from *Gimme the Loot* (2012), directed by Adam Leon, photographed by Jonathan Miller.

BOTTOM
Still image from *John Wick – Chapter 3: Parabellum* (2019), directed by Chad Stahelski, photographed by Dan Laustsen.

OPPOSITE
Still image from *You Were Never Really Here* (2017), directed by Lynne Ramsay, photographed by Thomas Townend.

City is like another character" in those films. ("So if there was a movie about your story, it would probably start with aerial shots of the city," notes one character, before director David Wain does exactly that.)

Other filmmakers made movies that embraced the sleekness of the city's current iteration. David Koepp's bike messenger action movie *Premium Rush* (2012) treats Manhattan traffic like a *Mad Max*–style thrill ride, full of hazards like cab doors, careless pedestrians, and the occasional, inescapable need to use one's brakes. In *The Adjustment Bureau* (2011), director George Nolfi imagines a New York City filled with guardian angels who can shortcut through the city by manipulating a complex series of doorways.

But in general, the indie filmmaking landscape continued its migration toward Brooklyn. Alex Ross Perry's *Listen Up Philip* (2014) and *Golden Exits* (2017), meanwhile, dwell in the world of Brooklyn writers and artists, many of them sour, verbose, direct, and miserable. Dustin Guy Defa's *Person to Person* (2017) is most at home with the borough's (increasingly vanishing) oddballs: record collectors, watch repairmen, and the like.

"Why would we go to the city when there are plenty of good places around here?" asks the protagonist of Eliza Hittman's *Beach Rats* (2017), before the filmmaker cuts to a close-up of his date eating a Coney Island hot dog. That film never leaves the borough, nor does Hittman's Gravesend–set previous picture, *It Felt Like Love* (2013). She saw that first film in particular as "a conversation with the kinds of movies about young people that were being made in New York. I was thinking about *Tiny Furniture* [2010; see sidebar on page 338], and how there were so many micro-budget narratives that focused on people with . . . certain backgrounds." So, for Hittman, "it was interesting to focus on more underrepresented areas, in a way that harkened back to films of the '70s, where there was more specificity in terms of the neighborhoods and the backgrounds and the struggle of the people. . . . I was just thinking of the lives of people pushed to the margins as the city continues to get more and more expensive." (When she finally went to

Manhattan, for 2020's *Never Rarely Sometimes Always*, it was through the eyes of an out-of-towner.)

Not all indies fled Manhattan, of course. Oren Moverman shot *Time Out of Mind* (2014) using many of the oldest tricks for city photography: hiding his cameras to avoid drawing a crowd, using long lenses to shoot his protagonist (Richard Gere) living his life on the island, or his friend (Ben Vereen) riffing on various passersby. There was a good reason Moverman could set his story on the island: Gere and Vereen were playing homeless men.

Unsurprisingly, homelessness increased dramatically under Bloomberg's watch. By 2013, the Coalition for Homelessness was reporting that "more children and adults are homeless now in New York City than at any time since the Great Depression." On the same day that report was released, Gothamist reported, the Dow Jones hit 14,200 points—a new record for the index. It was hard to imagine a more poignant illustration of the wealth gap that had consumed the city.

By the midpoint of Bloomberg's third term, public sentiment had finally turned. In March 2011, a Quinnipiac University poll revealed a 51 percent disapproval rate; he had once enjoyed 70 percent approval. But he made the most of his remaining two years, pushing through major developments at Hudson Yards, Essex Crossing, Williamsburg, Greenpoint, and Long Island City, tripling the number of "supertall" (984 feet or taller) high-rises in the city. Even the devastating landfall of Hurricane Sandy in 2012—which killed forty-four people and caused damage into the billions—couldn't stop the building of high-rises on the shorelines. Architects and engineers' big work-around was moving mechanicals in the middles of buildings, rather than their ground floors. Developers, ever the opportunists, would claim they needed more floors than necessary for mechanicals, creating a "void" in the middle that allowed more high floors—and more pricey, high-floor apartments.

Although it's certainly a secondary concern, the aesthetics of the "supertalls" are also impacting the films that are made in the city, jutting into the comforting, familiar skyline like knives in the clouds. "These

**ABOVE**
Still images from *Mistress America* (2015), directed by Noah Baumbah, photographed by Sam Levy; *While We're Young* (2014), directed by Noah Baumbah, photographed by Sam Levy.

**OPPOSITE**
Still images from *The Meyerowitz Stories (New and Selected)* (2017), directed by Noah Baumbach, photographed by Robbie Ryan; *Marriage Story* (2019), directed by Noah Baumbach, photographed by Robbie Ryan.

horrific, high buildings just destroy character and destroy your shot," says writer, director, and actor Jennifer Westfeldt. "It's painful for someone who loves New York desperately like I do, and loves the pictures that it creates—the backdrops and the history, the vibe and the authenticity. It's like we're losing a lot of that. And I find that really heartbreaking."

Baumbach spent months editing *Frances Ha*, fine-tuning it into a fleet-footed eighty-six minutes. He also devoted considerable energy to the look of the film, working with re-toucher Pascal Dangin ("the photo whisperer," according to the *New Yorker*) to give cinematographer Sam Levy's digital images the richness and texture of black-and-white film. He showed the results to his friend and mentor, director Peter Bogdanovich—whose *They All Laughed* is a clear influence—and the elder director emailed him, "Son of mine, I'm extremely proud of your accomplishment."

In September 2012, the film—still unannounced, still not even listed on IMDb—debuted at the Telluride Film Festival as a surprise premiere. It received a standing ovation. "We lived the Telluride fantasy," Gerwig said, "which is that your movie is loved and people stop you in the street." Critics were just as receptive when it landed in theaters the following spring. A. O. Scott of the *New York Times* called it "delightful," praising its "swift, jaunty rhythms and sharp, off-kilter jokes." The *Toronto Star*'s Peter Howell raved, "Few films top Woody Allen's *Manhattan* for capturing New York City's blend of rapture and appre-hension. Noah Baumbach's *Frances Ha* comes close." And in *Time*, Mary Pols wrote, "I'm not sure I've seen anything that illustrates the loneliness hidden inside young friendships quite as truthfully as the very sincere *Frances Ha* does; it's a small and special movie."

Most critics noted that it was a softer, gentler, less bitter picture than Baumbach's norm. "*Margot at the Wedding* and *The Squid and the Whale* vibrated with neuroses and hurt feelings, while *Frances Ha* shows a new lightness of touch," wrote Stephanie Zacharek in the *Village Voice*. In the *New Yorker*, Richard Brody deftly pinpointed what remained—and what was new. "In cutting himself off from his acerbic anger, Baumbach has risked cutting himself off from his greatest source of inspiration," Brody wrote. "Fortunately, in Gerwig's collaboration, he has found another source; he puts aside his own dialectical exceptionalism—alternately that of the insider fighting to get out and the outsider struggling to get in—for her secular state of grace." The collaboration continued, on-screen and off-; roughly a month into the production (after, both would insist, Baumbach had separated from his wife, Jennifer Jason Leigh), Baumbach and Gerwig became a couple.

By the time *Frances Ha* was playing New York cinemas, New York's mayor was winding down his term, and contemplating his legacy. In the *New Yorker*, Andy Borowitz praised "his greatest accomplishment, creating unaffordable housing throughout New York. When Mike took office, this city was teeming with regular working people. Today, it's a magnificent tapestry of investment bankers, real-estate developers, and Russian oligarchs."

Borowitz was joking, but not by much. A 2013 *Times* survey asked residents, "Do you think New York City is becoming too expensive for people like you to live in?" Eight-five percent of respondents answered yes—including people making up to $100,000 a year. By the conclusion of his three terms, Bloomberg had rezoned 40 percent of the city, from Harlem to Queens to Tribeca to Hell's Kitchen to Coney Island, for luxury

high-rises and upscale development. In 2012, Planning Commissioner Amanda Burden told the *Times*, "What I have tried to do, and think I have done, is create value for these developers, every single day of my term." At least Robert Moses *pretended* like his work was for the public good.

The campaign to fill Bloomberg's shoes was, to put it mildly, a colorful one. Initially, the Democratic front-runner was Anthony Weiner, whose comeback narrative—the fiery congressman had resigned his seat after a sexting scandal—crumbled when he was caught in *another* sexting scandal. Bloomberg's endorsement, and that of the newspapers, went to council speaker Christine Quinn, but the voters selected Brooklyn councilman Bill de Blasio, whose populist appeal (and loud objection, back in 2008 to allowing Bloomberg a third term) seemed like the pendulum swing voters were looking for.

De Blasio leaned into that pitch, promising an end to such signature Bloomberg issues as corporate subsidies, lower taxes for the rich, and the NYPD's controversial "stop and frisk" technique (in effect, sanctioned racial profiling). The candidate ran ads with his mixed-race son confessing his fear of police profiling; he emphasized his days as a student activist at NYU. He beat the Republican candidate, Giuliani deputy Joe Lhota, in a landslide.

In his inaugural address, de Blasio committed to "a new progressive direction in New York," calling for an end to the "tale of two cities" and to "economic and social inequalities that threaten to unravel the city we love." Other speeches called out the state of the city more explicitly. Bloomberg looked on from the stage's front row, stone-faced, arms folded, "as speaker after speaker tore apart his legacy," according to the *Daily News*. The *Times* editorial board objected to the ceremony as well: "Mr. Bloomberg had his mistakes and failures, but he was not a cartoon Gilded Age villain." They were right—no cartoon Gilded Age villain had the power to change the face of the city like Mayor Bloomberg had.

Bloomberg's Made in NY program, however, continued to prove a success. The city's 2015 report on the media and entertainment industry in NYC reported that filmed production in the city had increased 6.4 percent per year since 2011, and had increased nearly 90 percent since the lows of 2004. But those productions were increasingly based in television (including *The Americans*, *Gotham*, and the indestructible *Law & Order* franchise), which saw an explosion in demand for content as streaming services took off. Film studios, on the other hand, were making fewer films—but bigger ones, tent poles and adaptations, in the hopes of bigger rewards.

Even the studio pictures and mainstream indies that were shot in the city rarely felt like "New York movies" anymore. *Frances Ha*, in a way, is a film as adrift and idiosyncratic as its heroine: Manhattan is no longer the kind of place where great New York stories can believably happen, because so few great New York characters can actually afford to *live* there. In the 1980s, someone like Frances could've occupied a cheap walk-up on the LES or a loft in Tribeca. As of this writing, less than a decade after the film's release, she couldn't even afford her apartment in Washington Heights or room in Chinatown anymore.

Yet a few honest-to-goodness traditional New York filmmakers have thrived, and managed to capture the spirit of The City. Writer/director Adam Leon grinded it out as a production assistant and editorial intern for Woody Allen before making a splash with *Gimme the Loot* (2012), the story of two graffiti-writing teens on a mission to "bomb" the Mets'

celebratory "Apple" at Shea Stadium; that challenge provides a ticking clock, but the film has the loose, hang-out vibe of *Mean Streets* or of *Do the Right Thing*'s first hour as its protagonists joke and hustle their way through the West Village. That same mixture of off-the-cuff energy and low-key time killing is present in Leon's follow-up, *Tramps* (2016), a scrappy mixture of crime picture and romance under pressure, culminating in the ultimate gesture of Gotham affection: "I wanna give you my Metrocard."

The clearest inheritors of the "New York movie" tradition are Josh and Benny Safdie, and that seems by design; their films, particularly early on, explicitly echo iconic pictures of the past. Their 2010 debut, *Daddy Longlegs*—the story of two young brothers and the two weeks they spend in the care of their wildly irresponsible father—is clearly influenced by the early style and subjects of John Cassavetes, while its 2014 follow-up, *Heaven Knows What*, plays like an update of *The Panic in Needle Park*, right down to its Upper West Side sidewalk and park locations. (There's also more than a dab of *Midnight Cowboy* present, particularly a sequence in which its protagonists try and fail to escape the city on a bus bound for Florida.)

The Safdies' next picture, the cranked-up *Good Time* (2017), begins with a *Dog Day Afternoon*–style amateur bank robbery, and follows its perpetrator (Robert Pattinson) through a dizzying series of improvisations and bad ideas. But the Safdies also give the film a postmodern self-awareness, subtly noting the character's sly exploitation of white privilege to get out of sticky situations. Their most recent effort, *Uncut Gems* (2019), is the culmination of their efforts, a *Fingers*-style exploration of a compulsive gambler and risk-taker, set in Manhattan's Diamond District (and its protagonist's suburban home in Long Island.)

Though the director herself was a native of Glasgow, Scotland, Lynne Ramsay's *You Were Never Really Here* (2018) captured the seedy underbelly of the contemporary city as few other films did—an underbelly, it should be noted, where the most dangerously depraved citizens are the ultra-rich and powerful. And Chad Stahelski's *John Wick* series (2014, 2017, 2019) further imagined an entire elite criminal class operating just below the shiny, cleaned-up surface of the city, making their own rules, frequenting their own establishments, even trading their own money.

Baumbach plugged away, his sometimes biting, sometimes gentle explorations of upper-class ennui filling a void left by the fall (from both public grace and artistic vitality) of Woody Allen. He continued to mine the fertile soil of generational friction and artistic struggle with his 2014 release *While We're Young*—written without Gerwig, and noticeably more cynical about its youthful hipsters. Baumbach's most "New York" movie, post-*Frances*, is probably *The Meyerowitz Stories (New and Selected)* (2017), whose portraiture of frustrated artists keenly captures how living in the city can put one in heartbreakingly close proximity with people who are succeeding when you're not. (It also opens with an extended sequence of a uniquely New York stress-inducer: trying to find a parking spot, and then parallel park in it.)

But his most poignant film, at least in the context of the changing city, is his second screenwriting collaboration with Gerwig, *Mistress America* (2015). Brooke (Gerwig) is the soon-to-be-stepsister of naïve undergrad Tracy (Lola Kirke); she lives, hilariously, in Times Square ("I thought this was the cool place to live!") and shows her new protégée the cool bars and bands. "Being around [her] was like being in New York City," Tracy, a budding author, writes. "It made you want to find it, not hide from it." But

Tracy begins to see through Brooke's delusions, particularly as she longs to own and operate the kind of New York neighborhood restaurant that is doomed to failure in the suburbanized city. The problem becomes clear when they visit one of Brooke's ex-boyfriends, a rich finance type who has relocated to Connecticut and now waxes rhapsodic about his days slumming it. "I lived in the city for many years," he recalls. "I lived in an East Village walk-up. I was the people people make television shows about." Brooke's vision of her future is as idealized as that man's past; she is desperately reaching for the kind of New York life that just doesn't exist anymore, because that version of The City doesn't exist anymore, either.

———

There were high hopes for de Blasio, and early in his administration, he scored a victory for working-class families with the successful implementation of universal pre-K—a giant, difficult initiative, and an unalloyed good. And as every progressive mayor had before him, he weathered tensions with the NYPD. Former commissioner Ray Kelly spoke for many on the force when he characterized de Blasio's criticism of stop-and-frisk as indicative of "an anti-police campaign." When two NYPD officers were targeted and killed while on duty in December 2014, police and union leaders blamed it on de Blasio, accusing the mayor of stoking anti-police rhetoric after a Staten Island grand jury chose not to indict Daniel Pantaleo, the officer responsible for the choking death of Eric Garner (captured in a viral video that bore an eerie resemblance to Radio Raheem's murder in *Do the Right Thing*).

The mayor stumbled through a Housing Authority scandal and, over public objections, used a police motorcade for daily trips to his old gym in Park Slope for workouts. But most depressingly, de Blasio failed to take back the city from the developers—"either because he's in their pocket, as many news sources and New Yorkers believe," writes Jeremiah Moss, "or because he's no match for the power they've long taken from a City Hall that's been happy to give." In 2015, he announced

The iconic New York City
skyline, circa 2018.

his affordable housing plan, which relied heavily on the private sector. Henry Grabar, writing about the proposal for *Next City*, joked, "Entrusting affordable housing to real estate developers is a bit like going to McDonald's to lose weight."

By 2017, low- and middle-income New Yorkers were giving up; the *Post* reported that more people were leaving the area than any other large population center in the country, with more than a million people migrating away since 2010. The median rent on a New York City apartment had topped $3,100; commercial rents increased 34 percent in the decade between 2004 and 2014. In January 2019, the *Times* trumpeted the most expensive residential sale in the city's—and country's—history: Kenneth C. Griffin's $238 million purchase of a single Central Park South penthouse. The seventy-story building it sat atop was still being built; the land underneath it had previously housed a twenty-floor building full of rent-stabilized apartments. Those tenants had been evicted to make way for the skyscraper.

By the time Griffin bought his property, the nation was focused on another rich New Yorker who loved his penthouses. When Donald Trump began his bid for the presidency by riding down the escalator in the lobby of his Fifth Avenue Trump Tower, his candidacy was perceived by many as a bad joke or, at best, a publicity stunt. New Yorkers, who had cheered and jeered at "The Donald" for decades, were particularly cynical; since his first profile in the *Times* in 1976 ("Mr. Trump . . . says he is publicity shy"), he had been best known in the city as a tabloid fixture and shady businessman. He had been satirized for years, most memorably in Joe Dante's 1990 *Gremlins* sequel, which features John Clover as builder and brander "Daniel Clamp."

But in spite of his boorishness and reverse-Midas touch, and thanks to the incentives and subsidies of Koch and his successors (at least $885 million worth, according to a 2016 *Times* report), Trump established himself as a quintessential New Yorker. He evolved "from rough-edged rich kid with Brooklyn and Queens political-clubhouse connections to an international name-brand commodity," wrote the *New Yorker*'s Mark Singer in 1997, in a profile filled with such warnings to the future as Alair Townsend's memorable quip, "I wouldn't believe Donald Trump if his tongue were notarized." It also tips at Trump's eventual political ambitions: "What if, say, a troublemaker like Muammar Qaddafi got his hands on a nuclear arsenal? Well, Trump declared, he stood ready to work with the leaders of the then Soviet Union to coordinate a formula for coping with Armageddon-minded lunatics."

After flirting for decades with running for either party's nomination, or as an independent, Trump entered the Republican race to succeed his nemesis, President Barack Obama; the unlikely candidate marshaled a base of reality show viewers, Fox News junkies, and "economically anxious" white working-class voters to clinch the office in a shocking 2016 upset. One of the most striking qualities of Trump's presidency was its peculiar discombobulating of time; the president seemed perpetually a product of his original era, the go-go New York of the 1980s, even though all remnants of that time and place were gone. CBGB closed its doors in 2006; in 2015, it reopened as a theme restaurant in Terminal C of the Newark Airport. "A sanitized facsimile of the real," wrote Jeremiah Moss, "here is dirty New York without the dirt, without chaos or punk surprise. Just the empty shell."

Such simulations and simulacra abound in the 2000s and 2010s: The Waverly Inn, the Beatrice Inn, the Minetta Tavern, and other remnants of old New York were gobbled up by rich restaurateurs and turned into what the *Times*'s Diane Cardwell called "a theme park of the past," exploiting their original names and nostalgia while throwing out the authenticity and cranking up the prices, "papering over its real history with an imagined one."

All over the city, iconic neighborhoods and seemingly indestructible institutions were renovated beyond recognition or disappeared altogether. The Chelsea Hotel was sold to a "lifestyle hotel brand defined by modern luxury with eclectic influence." The McBurney Y (subject of the Village People's "YMCA") was sold and converted into luxury condos and a high-priced gym. Cooper Union discontinued its free tuition and slapped up a hulking, 400,000-square-foot office space that locals dubbed "The Death Star." The notoriously seedy Mars Bar, home of the famed "East Village Is Dead" mural, would dramatize that sentiment; its space is now occupied by a TD Bank. Harlem's Lennox Lounge, where Billie Holiday crooned and Miles Davis played, was bought by Nobu's Richie Notar but never re-opened; it was demolished in 2017, its space now filled by a Wells Fargo branch.

Development and gentrification continued to spread, to the edges of the island (including the long-promised and extravagantly pricey Hudson Yards) and farther into the boroughs, with families and businesses displaced for the Atlantic Yards/Pacific Park development and the Barclays Center arena. Sunset Park, *Do the Right Thing*'s Bed-Stuy, *Saturday Night Fever*'s Bay Ridge, and even the South Bronx, once the go-to area for urban blight and white fear, have been marked for "revitalization."

And by now, we know what that means. Jeremiah Moss writes, "It's the displacement of the working class and the poor, people of color, artists and oddballs. And it's the changed psychic climate. A city once famously neurotic is becoming malignantly narcissistic."

Meanwhile, in January 2020, the Bloomberg news website (ironically enough) shared a report by Halstead Development Marketing, exposing a glut of unsold, newly built luxury condos, most of them not formally listed for sale. "It would take 74 months—more than 6 years—to clear all of Manhattan's unsold units at the pace of contracts in 2019," wrote Bloomberg's Oshrat Carmiel. "The glut is a product of a post-recession construction boom aimed at globe-trotting investors, who now show little interest in collecting lavish Manhattan homes. And most newly built apartments are out of reach for the majority of New Yorkers."

When that report was published, Noah Baumbach was receiving the best reviews of his career for *Marriage Story*, the story of a divorcing couple fighting for custody of their son; the father (Adam Driver) wants to maintain New York as their home base, while the mother (Scarlett Johansson) relocates the boy to Los Angeles. The film's best running joke is the selling point of the West Coast that's chirpily shared by all the natives: "The space!" New York audiences chuckle loudly at those lines; that *is* what we hear, from friends and relatives who live, well, basically anywhere but New York. And as the space here is increasingly left empty for moneyed absentee tenants, those laughs stick in the throat.

That feeling, of melancholy for the current state of a once-great city, is also nicely summarized by the final voice-over in Baumbach and Gerwig's *Mistress America*. "She was the last cowboy, all romance and failure," writes Tracy, of Brooke. "The world was changing, and her kind didn't have anywhere to go. Being a beacon of hope for lesser people is a lonely business." As the city moved into a new decade, it would only get lonelier.

NOW SHOWING

TINY FURNITURE

SHAME

PARIAH

UNCUT GEMS

# TINY FURNITURE

## 2010

### Director: Lena Dunham

Lena Dunham may have made her name (and notoriety) as the co-creator and star of HBO's thinkpiece-spawning *Girls*, but her 2010 breakthrough feature, *Tiny Furniture*, hewed much closer to her real life and experience—so much so that *New York Movies* author Mark Asch calls it "a Manhattan home movie," and it seems not a dig but a statement of fact. Dunham plays Aura, a recent college graduate (Dunham graduated from Oberlin in 2008) and would-be filmmaker (she uses her own short films as her character's) who returns to her parents' loft in Tribeca (shot in the Dunham loft in Tribeca), where she tries to get her life together while irritating her visual artist mother (played by Dunham's visual artist mother, Laurie Simmons) and her teen poet sister (played by Dunham's teen poet sister, Grace).

However, that one-degree-removed authenticity, when coupled with Dunham's witty dialogue and incisive characterizations, makes *Tiny Furniture* a particularly keen snapshot of a very specific moment for a very specific subset of New York: comfortable downtown Millennials, post-meltdown, Extremely Online, trying to figure out their lives in The City (if they'll be in the city at all). It's full of lived-in New York touches (Aura scooping out the cat box into a plastic Murray's bag) and knowing references (the way her sister sneers "Where, in *Fort Greene* or *Bed-Stuy*?"), and it knows this version of downtown, in all its splendor and occasional shade.

Still image from *Tiny Furniture* (2010), directed by Lena Dunham, photographed by Jody Lee Lipes.

# SHAME

## 2011

## Director: Steve McQueen

In one of the most memorable scenes in *Shame*, the protagonist's sister (Carey Mulligan) sings a slow, semi-tragic torch rendition of "New York, New York" in long, lingering close-ups. The instrumentation is stark, a piano that's barely there at all; she is, to some extent, all alone on that stage. In another sequence, her brother Brandon (Michael Fassbender) escapes his apartment—where she's having sex with his boss—by going for a late-night jog through his Chelsea neighborhood. Cinematographer Sean Bobbitt comes along for the run, zipping alongside Brandon in a long tracking shot; yet what's most striking is how few people he passes on that sprint from the mid-20s to Madison Square Garden.

On its face, *Shame* is a story of addiction—Brandon is a sex addict, careening wildly from one anonymous sexual encounter to another, wallowing in pornography and prostitutes, slowly becoming aware that his focus on the physical release of sex has destroyed his ability to create and sustain true intimacy. (On that front, it reminds us that in light of everything else that's changed, it is still a city where random sexual encounters are possible.) But throughout the film, director Steve McQueen's staging, Bobbitt's moody photography, and Harry Escott's mournful score poignantly capture the strange phenomenon of somehow feeling, in a city of eight million, a sense of loneliness. It's a huge, densely populated city, but it can feel so, so empty.

And few films have better captured the specificity of subway interactions, that phenomenon unique only to New York City and a few other mass transit–heavy metropolises, where the minutes or even hours of a daily commute are spent in the immediate proximity of strangers—and with the potential for meeting more. *Shame* is bookended by two such encounters between Brandon and a married, redheaded woman, with whom he exchanges loaded glances and wordless promises. But the subway isn't entirely for pick-ups; the film's grim climax begins with the emptying of a train due to a "police investigation," which every New Yorker knows is code for a death, most likely a track suicide.

It's worth noting that the key players in *Shame* are not New Yorkers, or even American by birth—McQueen and Mulligan both hail from London, Fassbender is Irish German, and McQueen's co-writer Abi Morgan is Welsh. Perhaps it took these foreigners to most accurately capture the city as it was at the close of the Bloomberg era: sleek and soulless, with human interactions amounting to little more than physical transactions.

Still image from *Shame* (2011), directed by Steve McQueen, photographed by Sean Bobbitt.

# PARIAH

## 2011
## Director: Dee Rees

"New York City's got me down," croons the singer, "runnin' around / chasin' the wrong crowd," and the lyrics fill the soundtrack of Dee Rees's *Pariah* as its protagonist, Alike (Adepero Uduye), in effect, puts on her drag. She's riding the bus home, to her family's brownstone in Fort Greene, and the teenager changes clothes; she takes off her big, baggy polo shirt and jeans, revealing tighter garments underneath, and she takes off her baseball cap and puts on her earrings. She can walk in only when she looks the way her mother wants her to look. But that's not who she is.

And that's an "AG," short for "aggressive" and the street name for (per the authority, Urban Dictionary) "a thug gay girl that looks and dresses like a guy. A tomboy." Alike is growing more comfortable with who she is, and with the friends she's made in that world. But her mother is a conservative Christian and her father is an NYPD detective, and they keep pushing her, in ways both subtle and obvious, to be someone else.

Characters like Alike don't make their way onto screen that often, even in independent films—which *Pariah* certainly was. Writer/director Rees hailed from Nashville, and attended graduate film school at NYU, where she studied under Spike Lee and worked as one of his interns on *Inside Man* and *When the Levees Broke* (both 2006). She wrote *Pariah* at NYU and shot the first act of it as her graduate thesis film; Lee served as executive producer of the feature expansion, a role he's filled on several of his former students' films.

Warm and sensitive, potent and powerful, Rees's film displays a keen eye and ear for the complexities of the contemporary African American family, a tricky intersection of race, class, sexuality, and spirituality. It also captures the Fort Greene neighborhood as it careens into gentrification, and even gives Alike some identifiably Brooklyn-hipster dialogue. When her new friend asks her what kind of music she listens to, Alike replies, "Just some underground stuff, none of that crap they play on the radio . . . you know, people you probably haven't heard of."

Still image from *Pariah* (2011), directed by Dee Rees, photographed by Bradford Young.

# UNCUT GEMS

## 2019
## Directors:
## Josh and Benny Safdie

When Adam Sandler met the Safdie brothers, he described them thus: "Josh looks like a yeshiva student who might shoot you, and Benny looks like a friendly dentist . . . who might shoot you." Their collaboration on the Safdies' 2019 hit, *Uncut Gems*, was the culmination of a decade-long effort by the brothers to nail down the comedian and actor, whose people spent years politely declining the script by these young New York filmmakers they'd never heard of.

So they kept fine-tuning the script (eventually cranking out over 150 drafts), delving deeper into their diamond district research, and making other films in the meantime—films which, bonus, sharpened them as filmmakers and craftsmen, and made each subsequent version of the script they kept sending to Sandler harder to resist.

The Safdies cast Sandler's character, Howard Ratner, on "a guy our dad worked with in the diamond district," and he's a classic New York grinder—a dealer of sketchily sourced diamonds and watches, and an inveterate gambler. Unlike the typical fall-from-grace narratives, *Uncut Gems* introduces us to Howard when he's *already* at rock bottom ("I'M EXHAUSTED," he howls, about five minutes in); we then watch him somehow dig deeper.

The Safdies' films strive to capture the din, the bustle, the increasing volume and intensity of life in The City, layering overlapping dialogue, pulsing music, and general controlled chaos. It's easy to peg the Safdies as throwbacks, in terms of both style and narrative, to the seamy New York movies of earlier eras. But it's not quite that simple. They've taken those pictures as their starting point, and one-upped their creators with a jittery, hyper-caffeinated, twenty-first-century sensibility. It's not just a question of style. "This is a fuckin' *feeling*," Howard tells Kevin Garnett—and, simultaneously, the Safdies tell their audience. "We both have it. They don't know. You and I know!

Still images from *Uncut Gems* (2019), directed by Josh and Benny Safdie, photographed by Darius Khondji.

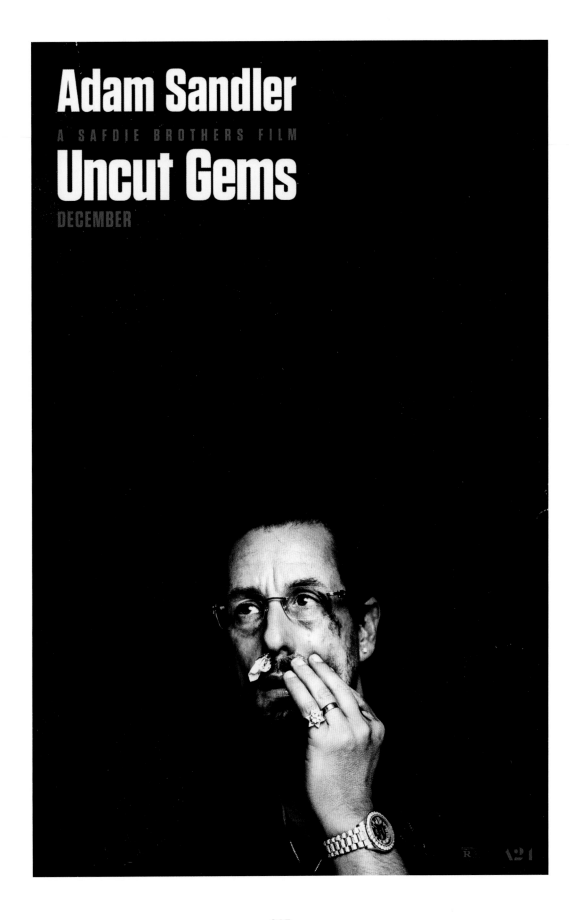

# EPILOGUE

"New York City is a living organism. It evolves, it devolves, it fluctuates . . . it changes every millisecond."

—Timothy "Speed" Levitch, *The Cruise*

"Cities that are haunted . . . seem to straddle past and present, as though two versions of the same city are overlaid on top of each other."

—Colin Dickey, *Ghostland*

In the spring of 2020, nature did to Manhattan what it had taken a team of special effects wizards to do for *I Am Legend*, and the clout of Tom Cruise to do for *Vanilla Sky*: it emptied the streets. The quarantine lockdown of the city—a hot-spot for the COVID-19 pandemic—filled TV news and social media channels with haunting images of empty New York streets and an empty Times Square. A few weeks later, another key Gotham movie seemed to merge with the city's increasingly surreal reality as the brutal murder of a black man at the hands of police led to a *Do the Right Thing*–style uprising, not only in New York, but across the nation. Protestors marched like it was 1968; newscasters shared images of the aftermath like it was the 1977 blackout.

But such historical allusions are ultimately a fool's errand; we're in new territory now, as a country and a city. But New Yorkers are used to it, because few notions are as constant as the malleability of New York City. "Why should it be loved as a city?" asked *Harper's*, back in 1856. "It is never the same city or a dozen years together. A man born in New York forty years ago finds nothing, absolutely nothing, of the New York he knew."

"One of the things that makes New York New York is that it's ever-changing," says director Susan Seidelman. "Unlike other major capitals of the world, whether it's Paris or Rome, they don't change that much. It may be part of their tourism allure, that Paris is Paris. But part of the myth of New York, and the reality is that it's always been an ever-changing city. It cycles around. It doesn't repeat; it kind of spirals."

"I don't necessarily like all the changes," Martin Scorsese says, "but that's the city. The city will constantly change. It was like ancient Rome, they said ancient Rome would be wonderful when it's completed being built. And it's constantly being built."

But the changes to New York City, particularly over the past two decades, are different. The escalation of the wealth gap, the scourge of suburbanization, and the onset of "hyper-gentrification" have rendered the city all but unrecognizable from its former essence. "New York is safer and richer but less like itself, an old lover who has gone for a face-lift and come out looking like no one in particular," Adam Gopnik wrote in 2007. "The wrinkles are gone, but so is the face. This transformation is one you see on every street corner in Manhattan, and now in Brooklyn, too, where another local toy store or smoked-fish emporium disappears and another bank branch or mall store opens. . . . These are small things, but they are the small things that the city's soul clings to."

The rapid (and incentivized) eradication of those "small things" isn't just a matter of concern for a shifting commercial landscape, or the disrupted skyline. It's a legitimate fear of losing what E. B. White called "the unexpungeable odor of the long past, so that no matter where you sit in New York you feel the vibrations of great times and tall deeds, of queer people and events and undertakings." That odor—sometimes, admittedly, a literal one—grows fainter by the day. Soon it may be gone altogether.

Many of its exemplars are, including the previously mentioned CBGB, Lenox Lounge, Mars Bar, and McBurney Y. The Village has bid adieu to Love Saves the Day, St. Mark's Bookshop, St. Mark's Comics, Lucky Cheng's, Dojo, and Kim's Video. Bleecker Bob's Golden Oldies Record Shop was shuttered in 2013. The Carnegie Deli closed its doors at the end of 2016. Tender Buttons on the Upper East Side went out of business after more than fifty years in 2019. In January 2020, Neir's Tavern in Queens (the neighborhood watering hole in *Goodfellas*) shut down over a rent increase. It was the borough's oldest surviving bar, operating since 1829.

To be sure, those places will still exist, in the memories and imaginations of those who ate and drank and shopped in them. "This place multiplies when you're not looking," wrote Colson Whitehead in *The Colossus of New York*. "We move over here, we move over there. Over a lifetime, that adds up to a lot of neighborhoods, the motley construction material of your jerry-built metropolis. Your favorite newsstands, restaurants, movie theaters, subway stations and barber-shops are replaced by your next neighborhood's favorites. It gets to be quite a sum. Before you know it, you have your own personal skyline."

And maybe that's enough. Or maybe that's why all those movies, the thousands of motion pictures shot in the streets and the parks, in the apartments and on the rooftops, of New York City are more than just movies. Men like Robert Moses, Ed Koch, and Michael Bloomberg spent their years in power remaking the city in their images—or, more precisely, remaking the city to better serve people like themselves. Doing that often meant hacking through New York with (as Moses so memorably put it) a "meat-ax." It meant destruction.

So, in retrospect, the production of those films—and all the additional expense, political maneuvering, and physical difficulty their production entailed—wasn't just an act of storytelling, or commercial ambition, or any of the other reasons people typically make movies. It was an act of preservation. Historical societies might not have been able to defend those buildings, businesses, and neighborhoods, to save them from Moses and his meat-ax, or Bloomberg and his abatements. But moviemakers did, and still do.

The Lower East Side of the 1920s is gone, replaced by expensive restaurants, trendy bars, and Target, but it lives on in *The Jazz Singer*. The Bowery of the 1950s is gone, replaced by John Varvatos and Nudie Jeans and Whole Foods, but it lives on in *On the Bowery*. The Times Square of the sixties and seventies is gone, replaced by Hard Rock and Bubba Gump and Madame Tussauds, but it lives on in *Midnight Cowboy* and *Taxi Driver*. The St. Mark's Place of the nineties is gone, replaced by Starbucks and Kmart and the Gap, but it lives on in *Kids*. And so on. And so on.

The myopic but seemingly inexorable march of "progress" may have eradicated the New York City of old—the bustling, vibrant metropolis of immigrants, hustlers, working-class families, freaks, drag queens, theater kids, and starving artists. That storied, playful, exuberant New York had a good run, and hung in for as long as it could. But it's gone, and probably for good.

Yet it lives on in the movies. In the movies, that New York City will live forever.

# SELECTED BIBLIOGRAPHY

Anbinder, Tyler. *City of Dreams: The 400-Year Epic History of Immigrant New York*. New York: Mariner Books, 2016.

Asch, Mark. *New York Movies*. New York: William Collins, 2018.

Barrett, Wayne (assisted by Adam Finfield). *Rudy! An Investigative Biography of Rudolph Giuliani*. New York: Basic Books, 2000.

Bascomb, Neal. *Higher: A Historic Race to the Sky and the Making of a City*. New York: Broadway Books, 2003.

Bishop, Jim. *The Mark Hellinger Story: A Biography of Broadway and Hollywood*. New York: Appleton-Century-Crofts, 1952.

Biskind, Peter. "*Midnight* Revolution." *Vanity Fair*, April 2000.

Bliven, Bruce. *New York: A History*. New York: W. W. Norton & Company, 1981.

Bragard, Véronique, Christophe Dony, and Warren Rosenberg (eds.). *Portraying 9/11: Essays on Representations in Comics, Literature, Film and Theatre*. Jefferson, NC: McFarland & Company, 2011.

Brin, David, with Leah Wilson (eds.). *King Kong Is Back!* Dallas: Benbella Books, 2005.

Buruma, Ian. *Conversations with John Schlesinger*. New York: Random House, 2006.

Calhoun, Ada. *St. Marks Is Dead*. New York: W. W. Norton & Company, 2015.

Cannato, Vincent J. *The Ungovernable City: John Lindsay and His Struggle to Save New York*. New York: Basic Books, 2001.

Caro, Robert. *The Power Broker: Robert Moses and the Fall of New York*. New York: Random House, 1974.

Carringer, Robert L. (introduction). *The Jazz Singer* (Wisconsin/Warner Bros. Screenplay Series). Madison: University of Wisconsin Press, 1979.

Corkin, Stanley. *Starring New York: Filming the Grime and Glamour of the Long 1970s*. New York: Oxford University Press, 2011.

Deveney, Sean. *Fun City: John Lindsay, Joe Namath, and How Sports Saved New York in the 1960s*. New York: Sports Publishing, 2015.

Diehl, Lorraine B. *Over Here!: New York City During World War II*. New York: HarperCollins, 2010.

Doctoroff, Daniel. *Greater Than Ever: New York's Big Comeback*. New York: PublicAffairs, 2017.

Douglas, Ann. *Terrible Honesty: Mongrel Manhattan in the 1920s*. New York: Noonday Press, 1995.

Ehrenstein, David. *The Scorsese Picture*. New York: Birch Lane Press, 1992.

Ellis, Edward Robb. *The Epic of New York City*. New York: Basic Books, 1966.

Erb, Cynthia. *Tracking King Kong*. Detroit: Wayne State University Press, 2009.

Eyman, Scott. *The Speed of Sound*. New York: Simon & Schuster, 1997.

Freeland, Michael. *Jolson: The Story of Al Jolson*. London: Cox & Wyman, 1972, 1985, 1995.

Geisst, Charles R. *Wall Street: A History*. New York: Oxford University Press, 1997.

Goldner, Orville, and George E. Turner (eds.). *The Making of King Kong*. Cranbury, NJ: A. S. Barnes and Co., 1975.

Greenberg, Miriam. *Branding New York: How a City in Crisis Was Sold to the World*. New York: Routledge, 2008.

Grimes, William (ed.). *New York Times: The Times of the Eighties: The Culture, Politics, and Personalities That Shaped the Decade*. New York: Black Dog & Leventhal, 2013.

Haber, Karen (ed.). *Kong Unbound: The Cultural Impact, Pop Mythos, and Scientific Plausibility of a Cinematic Legend*. New York: Pocket Books, 2005.

Hofler, Robert. *Sexplosion: From Andy Warhol to* A Clockwork Orange—*How a Generation of Pop Rebels Broke All the Taboos*. New York: HarperCollins, 2014.

Kashner, Sam. "A Movie Marked Danger." *Vanity Fair*, April 2010.

Kelly, Mary Pat. *Martin Scorsese: A Journey*. New York: Thunder's Mouth Press, 1991.

Kemp, Philip. *Lethal Innocence: The Cinema of Alexander Mackendrick*. London: Methuen, 1991.

Koszarski, Richard. *Hollywood on the Hudson: Film and Television in New York from Griffith to Sarnoff*. New Brunswick, NJ: Rutgers University Press, 2008.

Lawrence, Tim. *Life and Death on the New York Dance Floor, 1980–1983*. Durham, NC: Duke University Press, 2016.

Lee, Spike (as told to Kaleem Aftab). *That's My Story and I'm Sticking to It*. New York: W. W. Norton & Company, 2006.

Lewis, Jon, and Eric Smoodin (eds.). *Looking Past the Screen: Case Studies in American Film History and Method*. Durham, NC: Duke University Press, 2007.

Mackendrick, Alexander (edited by Paul Cronin). *On Film-making: An Introduction to the Craft of the Director*. London: Faber and Faber, 2004.

Macnab, Geoffrey. *The Making of "Taxi Driver."* London: Unanimous Ltd., 2005.

Mahler, Jonathan. *Ladies and Gentlemen, the Bronx Is Burning: 1977, Baseball, Politics, and the Battle for the Soul of a City*. New York: Picador, 2005.

Miller, Donald L. *Supreme City: How Jazz Age Manhattan Gave Birth to Modern America*. New York: Simon & Schuster, 2014.

Morton, Ray. *King Kong: The History of a Movie Icon from Fay Wray to Peter Jackson*. New York: Applause Theater and Cinema Books, 2005.

Mosedale, John. *The Men Who Invented Broadway*. New York: Richard Marek Publishers, 1981.

Moss, Jeremiah. *Vanishing New York: How a Great City Lost Its Soul*. New York: Dey Street Books, 2017.

Naremore, James. *BFI Film Classics: Sweet Smell of Success*. London: Palgrave Macmillan, 2010.

New York Observer (staff). *The Kingdom of New York: Knights, Knaves, Billionaires, and Beauties in the City of Big Shots*. New York: Harper, 2009.

Opotow, Susan, and Zachary Baron Shemtob (eds.) *New York After 9/11*. New York: Empire State Editions, 2018.

Parker, Ian. "Happiness: Noah Baumbach's New Wave." *The New Yorker*, April 22, 2013.

Petrovic, Paul (ed.). *Representing 9/11: Trauma, Ideology, and Nationalism in Literature, Film and Television*. Lanham, MD: Rowman & Littlefield, 2015.

Phillips, Julia. *You'll Never Eat Lunch in This Town Again*. New York: Random House, 1985.

Phillips-Fein, Kim. *Fear City: New York's Fiscal Crisis and the Rise of Austerity Politics*. New York: Metropolitan Books, 2017.

Raphaelson, Sampson. *The Day of Atonement*. New York: Brentano's, 1925 (reissued by PlanetMonk Books, 2014).

Remnick, David (ed.). *The New Gilded Age:* The New Yorker *Looks at the Culture of Affluence*. New York: Random House, 2000.

Roberts, Sam (ed.). *America's Mayor: John V. Lindsay and the Reinvention of New York*. New York: Columbia University Press, 2010.

Sanders, James. *Celluloid Skyline: New York and the Movies*. New York: Knopf, 2001.

Sanders, James. *Scenes from the City: Filmmaking in New York*. New York: Rizzoli International Publications, 2006.

Shelley, Peter. *Jules Dassin: The Life and Films*. Jefferson, NC: McFarland & Company, 2011.

Soffer, Jonathan. *Ed Koch and the Rebuilding of New York City*. Irvington, NY: Columbia University Press, 2010.

Solnit, Rebecca. *A Paradise Built in Hell: The Extraordinary Communities That Arise in Disaster*. New York: Viking, 2009.

Stewart, James B. *Den of Thieves*. New York: Simon & Schuster, 1991.

Stewart, Jules. *Gotham Rising: New York in the 1930s.* London: I. B.Tauris & Co., 2016.

Strausbaugh, John. *The Village*: 400 Years of Beats and Bohemians, Radicals and Rogues—A History of Greenwich Village. New York: HarperCollins, 2013.

Taubin, Amy. *BFI Film Classics: Taxi Driver.* London: British Film Institute, 2000.

Thompson, David, and Ian Christie (eds.). *Scorsese on Scorsese.* London: Faber and Faber, 1986.

Traub, James. *The Devil's Playground: A Century of Pleasure and Profit in Times Square.* New York: Random House, 2004.

Vaz, Mark Cotta. *Living Dangerously: The Adventures of Merian C. Cooper, Creator of "King Kong."* New York: Villard, 2005.

Wakefield, Dan. *New York in the Fifties.* Boston: Houghton Mifflin, 1992 (reissued by Open Road Media, 2016).

Wasson, Sam. *Fifth Avenue, 5 A.M.: Audrey Hepburn,* Breakfast at Tiffany's, *and the Dawn of the Modern Woman.* New York: HarperCollins, 2010.

Weegee (Arthur Fellig). *Naked City.* New York: Zebra Picture Books, 1945 (reissued by Hachette Book Group, 2002).

Westwell, Guy. *Parallel Lines: Post-9/11 Cinema.* New York: Wallflower Press, 2014.

White, E. B. *Here Is New York.* New York: Harper & Brothers, 1949 (reissued by The Little Bookroom, 2011).

Whitehead, Colson. *The Colossus of New York.* New York: Anchor Books, 2003.

Wilhite, Keith (ed.). *The City Since 9/11: Literature, Film, Television.* Madison, WI: Fairleigh Dickinson University Press, 2016.

Williams, Mason B. *City of Ambition: FDR, La Guardia, and the Making of Modern New York.* New York: W. W. Norton & Company, 2013.

Zimring, Franklin E. *The City That Became Safe: New York's Lessons for Urban Crime and Its Control.* Oxford: Oxford University Press, 2012.

## AUTHOR INTERVIEWS

Noah Baumbach, 5/9/13
Lizzie Borden, 10/20/20
Larry Clark, 8/19/18
Greta Gerwig, 5/9/13
Bette Gordon, 10/19/20
Walter Hill, 7/22/19
Eliza Hittman, 3/13/20
Adam Holender, 6/24/19
Leonard Maltin, 6/27/19
John Pierson, 10/3/19
Jerry Schatzberg, 4/17/19
Martin Scorsese, 3/6/20
Susan Seidelman, 6/26/18, 7/19/19
Oliver Stone, 11/26/18
Jennifer Westfeldt, 1/12/20

## AUDIO COMMENTARIES

Lee, Spike, and Edward Norton. *25th Hour.* Buena Vista Home Video, 2014.

Schlesinger, John, and Jerome Hellman. *Midnight Cowboy.* Criterion Collection, 2018.

Scorsese, Martin, and Paul Schrader. *Taxi Driver.* Sony Pictures Home Entertainment, 2016.

Wald, Malvin. *The Naked City.* Criterion Collection, 2007.

## DOCUMENTARY FILMS

*9/11: The Days After*. New Animal Productions, 2011.

*Blackout*. American Experience, 2015.

*Blank City*. Insurgent Media, 2010.

*Decade of Fire*. Independent Lens, 2019.

*Giuliani Time*. Cinema Libre, 2006.

*Inside 9/11*. National Geographic, 2005.

*Koch*. Zeitgeist Films, 2013.

*New York: A Documentary Film*. New-York Historical Society/Steeplechase Films/WGBH, 1999.

*NY77: The Coolest Year in Hell*. Firehouse Films/VH1 Rock Docs, 2007.

*Style Wars*. Public Art Films, 1983.

*Tighten Your Belts, Bite the Bullet*. Icarus Films, 1980.

## ACKNOWLEDGMENTS

The three years I spent researching and writing *Fun City Cinema* were far and away the most I've ever spent on a book, so first off, I want to thank (and apologize to) everyone who heard all about it, all the way through. Chief among those poor souls is my wife Rebekah, who was (as ever) an endless source of support, advice, and affection. Thank you, for everything, my sweet. I could not have written the book without the help of my longtime friend and collaborator Mike Hull, who watched the movies, read the chapters, gave edits and feedback, and then, on top of all of that, started a spin-off podcast with me when the book was done. Mike, you always go above and beyond, but you topped yourself this time.

Eric Klopfer is everything you could ask for from an editor—supportive, thorough, and enthusiastic. He saw the book here even when I couldn't, pinpointed the problems in early drafts that saved my hide, and, along with the invaluable contributions of Eli Mock, Mike Richards, Connor Leonard, and Alison Gervais at Abrams, helped pull it all together into something more than I could've imagined. Eric, my friend, I hope this is the first of many. And I must also thank my agent, Daniel Greenberg, who was so helpful in turning "I want to write a book about New York movies" into an actual, marketable structure and pitch.

When I started working on the book, I reached out to Mark Harris and said, quite simply, "I'm trying to write a Mark Harris book, can you help me?" To his credit, he took that as a compliment, and over coffee, gave me research and organizational advice that I could not have written the book without. And one of the keys to that research was the clippings archive at the New York Public Library for the Performing Arts, Dorothy and Lewis B. Cullman Center; thank you to the librarians there, who were so patient and helpful with my requests. And also I have to thank Melanie Locay and everyone at the Stephen A. Schwarzman Building of the NYPL, who gave me a desk in the legendary Allen Room and all the resources I needed to finish the book up.

And finally, a big thank-you to all the wonderful editors who've gently guided me over the years, and kept income coming in during this project, including (but not only) Caroline Stanley, Judy Berman, Tom Hawking, Gilbert Cruz, Austin Considine, Stephanie Goodman, Mekado Murphy, Rachel Handler, Katherine Brooks, and Rodrigo Perez.

Editor: Eric Klopfer
Managing Editor: Mike Richards
Designer: Eli Mock
Production Manager: Alison Gervais

Library of Congress Control Number: 2021932498
ISBN: 978-1-4197-4781-6
eISBN: 978-1-64700-469-9

Printed and bound in China
10 9 8 7 6 5 4 3 2 1

Abrams books are available at special discounts when purchased in quantity for premiums and promotions as well as fundraising or educational use. Special editions can also be created to specification. For details, contact specialsales@abramsbooks.com or the address below.

Abrams® is a registered trademark of Harry N. Abrams, Inc.

 ABRAMS
The Art of Books

195 Broadway
New York, NY 10007
abramsbooks.com

**ENDPAPERS**
(front) Still images from *The Producers* (1967), directed by Mel Brooks, photographed by Joseph Coffey; *Night Owl* (1993), directed by Jeffrey Arsenault, photographed by Pierre Clavel, Howard Krupa, and Neil Shapiro; (back) Still images from *No Way to Treat a Lady* (1968), directed by Jack Smight, photographed by Jack Priestley; *New Jack City* (1991), directed by Mario van Peebles, photographed by Francis Kenny

**PHOTO CREDITS**
20th Century-Fox Film Corp./Everett Collection: p. 232 (above left)
20th Century-Fox Film Corp./Photofest: p. 103
Alamy: p. 178
Bain News Service photograph collection, Library of Congress: p. 25 (above left)
Barry Wetcher/20th Century-Fox: p. 245
Bill Golladay, via Wikimedia Commons: p. 220 (above)
Billy Rose Theatre Division, The New York Public Library: pp. 24, 25 (above right), 75, 107 (below)
Carol M. Highsmith Archive, Library of Congress: pp. 219, 224, 236, 269 (bottom), 333, 334
Chad J. McNeeley/Department of Defense: p. 327 (bottom)
David Finn/Library of Congress Prints and Photographs Division: p. 289 (right)
David Shankbone/Wikimedia Commons: p. 327 (top)
Department of Labor/Wikimedia Commons: p. 332 (bottom)
Dick DeMarsico, New York World-Telegram & Sun Newspaper Photograph Collection, Library of Congress: p. 77
Don Halasy/Library of Congress Prints and Photographs Division: pp. 286, 289 (above)
Everett Collection: pp. 46, 57, 82 (above), 84 (below), 133 (below), 179 (right), 319
Farm Security Administration, Office of War Information Photograph Collection, Library of Congress: pp. 53, 69, 70–71
Gran Fury Collection, New York Public Library Digital Collections: p. 243 (below)
Harris & Ewing photograph collection, Library of Congress: pp. 23, 58 (left)
IFC Films: pp. 318, 322–23
John Matthew Smith/Wikimedia Commons: p. 264 (top)
Library of Congress: p. 52 (left)
Library of Congress Prints and Photographs Division: pp. 287, 289 (below)
Michael Vadon/Wikimedia Commons: p. 332 (below)
National Archives and Records Administration: pp. 30, 194
NBC/courtesy Everett Collection: p. 262
New York Public Library: p. 35
New York World-Telegram & Sun Newspaper Photograph Collection, Library of Congress: pp. 26–27, 48–49, 50, 124, 128 (top), 131 (left)
Orlando Fernandez, New York World-Telegram & Sun Newspaper Photograph Collection, Library of Congress: pp. 131 (right), 133 (above)
PBS: p. 188 (center and bottom)
Photofest: pp. 20, 28, 44, 56, 58 (below), 66, 72, 78–79, 82 (below), 83, 84 (above), 98, 102, 122, 135, 136 (left), 137, 141, 148, 160, 167 (right), 173, 174, 175, 177, 179 (below and bottom), 186 (below), 196, 218, 232 (above right and below), 233, 237 (below), 316

Photofest/ABC: p. 100
Photofest/Buena Vista Pictures: p. 284
Photographs of the White House Photograph Office, Clinton Administration/Wikimedia Commons: p. 265
Rachael L. Leslie/United States Navy: p. 306 (above)
Rob C. Cross/National Archief, the Dutch National Archives: p. 243 (left)
Robert and Elizabeth Dole Archive and Special Collections/Wikimedia Commons: p. 264 (top)
Robert D. Ward/U.S. Department of Defense: p. 295 (above)
Rodgers and Hammerstein Archives of Recorded Sound, The New York Public Library: p. 14
Schomburg Center for Research in Black Culture, Photographs and Prints Division, The New York Public Library: p. 31
Simon & Schuster: p. 130
Starstock/Photoshot/Everett Collection: p. 172
The Miriam and Ira D. Wallach Division of Art, Prints and Photographs: Art & Architecture Collection, The New York Public Library: pp. 51, 52 (below and far left), 105 (above)
The Miriam and Ira D. Wallach Division of Art, Prints and Photographs: Print Collection, The New York Public Library: p. 74
The New York Public Library Digital Collections: p. 105 (below)
Thomas J. O'Halloran/U.S. News & World Report Magazine Photograph Collection, Library of Congress: p. 290
United Archives GmbH/Alamy Stock Photo: p. 260
Universal City/Photofest: p. 244
U.S. National Archives and Records Administration: p. 188 (top)
U.S. News & World Report Magazine Photograph Collection, Library of Congress: pp. 128 (above), 222
Vergara Photograph Collection, Library of Congress: p. 144
© Walt Disney/courtesy Everett Collection: pp. 295 (right), 297
Walter Albertin, New York World-Telegram & Sun Newspaper Photograph Collection, Library of Congress: p. 106
Warner Bros., Village Roadshow Pictures: p. 306 (below)
Wikimedia Commons: pp. 22, 29, 129 (right)
Yanker Poster Collection, Library of Congress: p. 195